Cost Accountin

Cost Accounting

W M Harper ACMA

Third edition

THE M & E HANDBOOK SERIES

Pitman Publishing
128 Long Acre, London WC2E 9AN

A Division of Longman Group UK Limited

First published as *Cost and Management Accounting Vol I Cost Accounting* 1982
Second edition published as *Cost Accounting* 1987
Third edition 1993

©Macdonald & Evans Ltd 1982
©Longman Group UK Ltd 1987, 1993

British Library Cataloguing in Publication Data
A catalogue entry for this title is available from the British Library.

ISBN 0 7121 1043 7

Founding Editor: P.W.D. Redmond

Typeset by FDS Ltd, Penarth
Printed and bound in Singapore

Contents

Preface

This new edition of *Cost Accounting* is essentially an update of the previous edition which takes cognizance of the more recent trends in the relevant examinations. The long-term, on-going swing away from shop-floor matters to those of the boardroom continues its apparently inexorable progress — albeit I have doubts as to the wisdom of this, since no boardroom report can be better than the information on which it is based and much of that information is of shop-floor level origin — and this 'progress' is reflected in the text. Consequently, the previous three chapters on cost data have been reduced to one, while more questions and answers on the higher-level theory have been introduced. Also the chapter on estimation, previously in *Management Accounting*, has been moved into this book, since questions on regression lines and learning curves are increasingly arising in papers on cost accounting. As in the previous edition, the Progress tests are divided, where appropriate, into *Principles* (testing ideas, definitions, etc.) and *Practice* (testing the application of the principles). Suggested answers to the practice questions are contained in Appendix 3. Students should note that I have sometimes used the answers to illustrate points which are not illustrated in the chapter.

Acknowledgements

I gratefully acknowledge permission to quote from the past examination papers of the following bodies:

Association of Accounting Technicians (AAT)
Chartered Association of Certified Accountants (ACCA)
Chartered Institute of Management Accountants (CIMA)
Institute of Chartered Accountants in England and Wales (ICA)

W M Harper
1993

1
Introduction

Accountancy work can be divided into two categories. The first involves handling monetary figures in order to comply with legal requirements — this is the world of tax computations, published accounts, liquidations, executorships and the like. The second involves handling monetary figures in order to quantify business activities and plans.

This book is concerned solely with the second of these two categories.

Background

1. Dual role of money

Fundamental to a clear understanding of the whole field of management accounting is the appreciation that *money* in business plays a dual role — firstly as a physical economic factor of production and secondly as an abstract economic measure of performance.

(a) *Money as an economic factor of production.* Money in its physical form of currency is as necessary to an enterprise as any other economic factor such as materials or labour. In this form it is usually referred to as *cash* and consists, of course, of coins, bank notes and cheques. Without cash (or credit, which is essentially a form of cash to a businessman) an enterprise would quickly grind to a halt.

(b) *Money as a measure of economic performance.* Basically, the object of an enterprise is to combine a variety of economic factors (materials, labour, land, machines, etc.), so that from the combination some utility emerges which can be exchanged for cash. Since the combination can be varied (e.g. machines can be used in lieu of labour) it is necessary to be able to measure the economic value involved in any combination together with the value of the utility. Unfortunately, tonnes of material cannot be added to hours of labour nor compared with units of production. To make measurements in such circumstances, therefore, calls for the use of a common denominator, and money is the chosen measure.

> NOTE: In some ways the use of money as such a measure is unfortunate. People may confuse *money* used in this way with *cash*, and learning that on average it costs thirty pence a mile to run a particular type of vehicle, wrongly assume that by running the vehicle ten miles less they will have £3 more cash in their pockets. Moreover, money is an unstable unit, continuously affected by inflation, so the same economic performance one year has a different monetary value from an identical performance another year. Despite these serious disadvantages, however, it is the most practical measure we have.

In cost accounting it is important that the two roles are kept separate. In the main this is not difficult but in certain circumstances (and particularly where inflation arises, for then one must undertake the conceptually complex task of valuing cash in monetary terms) a clear-headed approach is essential.

2.   History of cost and management accounting
It is probably fair to say that, historically speaking, in the beginning there was costing, not cost accounting. Book-keeping at that time was concerned solely with money as an economic resource and no real attempt was made by accountants to use it to measure economic performance. When, ultimately, measurement in the form of ascertaining profit was called for, one gains the impression that the accountants of the day complied with little enthusiasm for either accuracy or consistency.

However, although the enterprise owners (usually owner-managers in those days, of course) were understandably more interested in cash than profit, the reverse was true for the enterprise engineers. Needing to quote a price for their work, much of which was done then on a job basis, they required accurate measurements of the value of the resources entering into each project. To this end they engaged cost clerks whose places were firmly alongside the engineer within the production function. There was no link between the cost clerk and the accountant, the clerk being left to dig around on his own initiative for the monetary figures which would enable him to prepare his cost statements.

As the deficiencies in this approach became more obvious, and as overheads which had previously been only a small percentage of the total costs grew in significance, the cost clerk moved more and more towards a full accounting approach to his tasks, and eventually the increasing complexity of his work led him and other similarly engaged clerks to claim professional status. Out of this came the founding of the Institute of Cost and Works Accountants. Cost accounting, however, still concentrated in the main on tracing costs, and this state of affairs continued until the Second World War, the literature of the 1930s debating such matters as how to define capacity and whether interest was a cost.

After the Second World War the emphasis began to change. Now the *managerial* significance of the figures began to be more appreciated and the preparation of statements that were useful to managers became emphasized. The term, 'management accountant' was eventually coined and the Institute of Cost and Works Accountants became the Institute of Cost and Management Accountants and then the Chartered Institute of Management Accountants. With the change of emphasis came a change in the approach to the accounting — no longer was it a matter of tracing past figures to jobs and departments but rather of predicting future costs and analysing these in terms of enterprise profitability. Moreover, the whole area of the accountant's influence widened. No longer was he merely reporting costs but instead he was considerably influencing top management decisions. From his corner in the works engineer's office he had risen to a seat at the boardroom table.

3. Financial, management and cost accounting

With this brief history of management accounting before us it will be clear that the distinctions between financial, management and cost accounting are more historical than logical. In reality there is only one function — that of the economic management of the enterprise. This function can be divided into managing cash (which includes accounting for its use and planning its economic manipulation) and measuring performance (which includes both past and planned performance). Because of its historical development the modern division of this basic function is slightly different in practice. The following is an attempt to make some logical distinctions between the actual divisions that have evolved.

(a) *Financial accounting.* This is concerned with *money as a physical economic resource*, i.e. cash. Consequently cheques, coins and notes, bank balances and overdrafts, debtors and creditors feature largely in this type of accounting. Just as managers of any other physical resource must know the sources, varieties and economic value of their resources, so financial accountants must know the sources of their finances, the varieties of finance available and the economic value (in interest terms) of that finance. Financial accounting is, then, primarily concerned with resource management and as such it is rather a specialist function.

(b) *Management accounting.* This is concerned with *measuring the economic consequences and implications of management decisions*. It concerns itself particularly with money as a measure of economic performance, and with using that measure to help managers manage. In truth, its 'accounting for' function is only one of its minor aspects and the management accountant has far more in common with the economist than with the traditional accountant.

(c) *Cost accounting.* This is really that aspect of management accounting which is concerned with *measuring the economic performance of departments, methods and equipment and of measuring the value of the resources consumed in producing goods and services.*

Clearly, in places the accounting categories overlap, but as broad definitions of the work of the modern accounting department these divisions suffice.

In this book financial accounting will be discussed as little as possible. It is a specialist field and only that part of it which impinges on the enterprise's need for cash will be considered. And only that aspect of management accounting that is important to cost accounting will be included here (discussion of the further and wider aspects being found in *Management Accounting*, Harper, M&E Handbook series), although, first, the place of management accounting in an enterprise will be outlined so as to orientate the student before looking specifically at cost accounting.

4. Management accounting and management

Management accounting is concerned with *management*. Students should imagine themselves as equal members of a top management team which has been set the collective task of managing an enterprise. Members of the team will naturally undertake specialist activities — one may manage the factory, another handle research. The management accountant's particular task will be to provide information to colleagues relating to the economic aspects of the operation of the enterprise. While he will take from the field of accountancy such techniques as will be useful, he will always look at the enterprise with the eyes of a manager, conscious of management's problems, responsibilities, opportunities, limitations, hopes and fears.

5. Management in the ultimate — decision-making

Managing involves an extensive and complex range of skills but at the end of the day all these culminate in a management decision. Management accounting, then, is concerned with assisting managers to make decisions.

6. The role of the future

At all times managers must, in effect, live in the future. They must always be looking ahead, for the instructions they issue in the present must be based on what they envisage the future will bring. This continual involvement with the future affects everything management accountants do. They are constantly concerned with what *will be* and every aspect of their work is structured so as ultimately to enable them to predict the future. Past and present figures only have value in so far as they foreshadow the future — although their potential to do just that should never be underestimated, for in the absence of definite information to the contrary the best predictor as to what will happen next time is what happened last time. It is, incidentally, for this reason that cost accounting is a part of management accounting and not merely a disassociated technique ploughing its own separate furrow.

NOTE: The student may wonder how the presentation of a priced past job cost (an obviously important if lowly task in the management accounting department) can have anything to do with future figures. The fact is, however, that there are a number of ways of pricing jobbing work and past jobs enable any existing pricing strategy to be tested for effectiveness — the result clearly affecting *future* pricing strategy.

Cost accounting

Although cost accounting is a part of management accounting it can perhaps be distinguished from the other parts of that subject by its considerable attention to actual past cost figures. Despite the fact that management accounting concentrates on future figures there is no doubt that much of the insight into what the figures will be in future circumstances is obtained by a careful consideration of what they actually were in the present or immediate past circumstances. In looking to actual figures, cost accounting is much more an 'accounting for' function than management accounting. As a result, it concerns itself with far more detail than the latter and so tends to need more space for its exposition than the other aspects of management accountancy. This allocation of space (virtually this whole book) is not, however, to be regarded as indicative of its importance. As has already been pointed out, past and present figures are only of value in predicting future figures, which are the real raw data for the management accountant.

7. Costing
Strictly speaking, cost accounting involves accounting for costs, i.e. explaining how they arose and detailing where they went. *Costing*, on the other hand, involves indicating to managers the *economic consequences of carrying out, or having carried out, any specified activity*. If a manager is, for example, considering the acceptance of a contract, he or she needs to know whether or not an adequate profit will arise from it — and if the contract is accepted, he or she will need to know how much profit was actually made (or lost) so that future actions can benefit from past experience.

From a management accounting point of view, then, our main interest in this field is in costing rather than cost accounting.

8. Cost
A *cost* is *the value of economic resources used as a result of producing*

or doing the thing costed. Note the word 'value'. In a majority of cases the value of the economic resources used is the amount of money spent in acquiring or producing them, but this is not always so. For instance, if the market price of an article were £5 at the time of purchase and rose to £7 by the time it was actually used in production, then one could well say that the cost is £7, since this is the *value* of the article used.

Some people would probably disagree with this view of cost, and would regard cost as simply what was paid for an economic resource. Yet clearly in the foregoing example, if the article were sold in its unmanufactured state for £6, then £5 as the cost means there would be £1 profit. But this is not a valid measure of management's *manufacturing* performance (though it may be a good measure of their speculative performance). This simpler concept of cost relates really to measuring excess of receipts over payments, that is, we are back to the financial accounting concept of money as cash. In cost accounting one should, however, always bear in mind the ultimate need to consider economic values for measuring economic performance rather than cash expenditure. (A word of warning: costing evolved as a practical business technique. As a result the practice is not always consistent with the theory. For example, a number of methods of costing stores issues aim only to recover the amount spent on purchasing the stores and not to show the value of the issues (*see* 2:**14–16**).)

9. Cost = usage x price

Cost has been defined as 'the value of economic resources used'. Note that for each resource the 'value' is always made up of two components: the units of the resource used and the resource price per unit. Cost, therefore, can be mathematically stated as:

$$\text{Cost} = \text{usage} \times \text{price}.$$

This means that costing involves ascertaining both a usage figure and a price figure. Students will find this double-component value arises throughout costing theory, and it is particularly significant in standard costing and variance analysis.

It should, incidentally, be appreciated that in costing it is the economic resources used that are really important — multiplying by price to give cost is only the conversion to the common denominator of money. Improvement by management of economic performance hinges on the more economical use of resources or the substitution of cheaper resources for more expensive resources. A management accountant should never forget, then, that it is the *resources* underlying the £ figures that are really significant.

10. Cost units

We cannot have 'costs' unless there are things being costed (such as cars, theatre performances, forests or herds of cows) and when these are the things that the enterprise or department is set up to provide, then such 'things' are termed 'cost units'. A cost unit, then, can be defined as *a unit of product or service in relation to which costs are ascertained*. Examples of cost units are:

(a) units of production: cars, tonnes of material, litres of liquid, books, pairs of shoes, construction contracts;

(b) units of service: kilowatt-hours, cinema seats, passenger-miles, consultancy hours.

> NOTE: Students should learn and understand this definition as the term is frequently used in costing. In most cases cost units are simply the individual items of production and, provided the wider meaning (e.g. service units) is appreciated, students may regard them as such for study purposes.

11. Cost centres

Costs can relate to things other than cost units. They can refer to individual parts of the enterprise. Such parts can range from an entire factory (in the case of a company with a group of factories) down to a single machine or salesperson. *Any part of an enterprise to which costs can be charged* is called a *cost centre*. A cost centre can be:

(a) *geographical*, i.e. an area such as a department, store-yard or sales area;

(b) *an item of equipment*, e.g. a lathe, fork-lift truck or delivery vehicle;

(c) *a person*, e.g. a salesperson.

Charging costs to a cost centre simply involves charging to that centre those costs which relate to it. Thus, a lathe can be charged with the cost of its depreciation, maintenance, power and cleaning and also with a share of the rent, rates and heat and light costs of the enterprise.

12. Current, past and sunk costs

Costs are sometimes quite subtle concepts. At this point it is necessary to distinguish between three kinds of 'costs', namely:

(a) *Current cost.* A current cost is one you incur as you carry out an activity. Thus, if you are paying someone £4 an hour to carry out an activity, your current cost is £4 per hour.

(b) *Past cost.* A past cost is one you incurred in the past but which still has benefit or value to you. Thus, if last month you paid a man £40 on the understanding he would supply you this month with 10 hours work, then the work he does this month carries a past cost of £4 per hour.

(c) *Sunk cost.* A sunk cost is one you incurred in the past and which now has no realizable benefit or value to you. So, if the man to whom you paid £40 last month fulfils his contract by digging a hole so that you can put down the foundations for a heavy machine, then (since a hole in the ground has no realizable benefit or value) the cost is a sunk cost (no pun intended).

Note that a cost can be both a past and a sunk cost, depending on the circumstances. Fixed assets almost always fall into this category for if you paid £10,000 for a machine that would last ten years, then each year you use the machine you incur a past cost of (have benefit worth) £1,000, but if the day you bought it you find you have no work for it and can only re-sell it for £3,000, you are faced with a sunk cost of £7,000. Generally speaking, resources involving past costs enter performance measurement and resources involving sunk costs enter decision making (or, to put it in its more usual form, only the re-sale value of a past cost is used to make decisions — sunk costs being ignored). This distinction, of course, is paralleled in accountancy by the distinction between the going-concern historical cost value of an asset and its realizable value.

13. Notional cost

Sometimes an enterprise is able to avoid incurring a particular cost (e.g. if its premises are owned by itself, then the enterprise will pay no rent). If in these sorts of circumstance the cost accountant wishes his costs to reflect the true economic value of the factor employed, he can make a notional charge for the factor — such as a charge being referred to as a *notional cost*.

14. Decision-driven costs

Most costs are incurred as a result of engaging in an activity and are quite inescapable. Thus, if you wished to process 5,000 kg of material, you would be obliged to pay for the 5,000 kg required (such a cost sometimes being referred to as an *engineered variable cost*). However, some costs are not obligatory. You do not *have* to incur advertising costs or research costs or public relations costs, though it may be unwise not to spend money on these activities. In other words, the amount of such costs depends solely upon your *policy decision* and not upon your product. Such a cost is called, therefore, a *decision-driven cost* (alternatively, a *policy cost* or a *discretionary fixed cost*) and is a *cost incurred as a matter of a policy decision*.

There is no sharp division between decision-driven costs and other costs, one shading gradually into the other. Sick pay is, by definition, a decision-driven cost, yet such a cost is to some extent like any other variable cost, since the greater the activity the greater the work-force and, therefore, the greater the payments made. Where such a cost can be analysed it should be; otherwise, since policy costs are not the direct consequence of the activity of the enterprise, they should, strictly speaking, be excluded from most cost analyses.

Finally, note that since a decision-driven cost is, by definition, an escapable cost its converse, an inescapable cost, is referred to as a *committed cost*.

15. Conversion cost and added value

These two terms can relate to any aspect of costing and need to be carefully distinguished.

(a) *Conversion cost* is the cost of converting raw materials to the finished state, or to the next stage of production. It includes direct wages, direct expenses and production overheads.
(b) *Added value* is the market value of a product less the costs of bought-out materials and services.

The main difference between conversion cost and added value

is that added value includes profit. The importance of this concept can be seen if one appreciates that the function of an enterprise is to take economic resources in the form of raw materials and services and create utilities having as great a value as possible. Added value measures the increase in value of the resources used as a result of the creation of such utilities.

16. Historical cost

The student should note in passing that the adjective 'historical' when applied to a cost (or any other term in the field of cost accounting) merely indicates that past *actual* amounts are being referred to.

17. Basic costing principles

During the preparation of any costing analysis there are a number of basic principles that must be observed. These are as follows:

(a) *A cost should be related as closely as possible to its cause.* A foreman's salary, for instance, cannot usually be pinned down to a single cost unit, but it should be recorded in such a way that the cost can be shared only among the cost units passing through that foreman's department and not among any units outside his department. This relating of cost to cause, pinning the cost down so that it covers neither more nor less than the cost units or cost centres which caused it, is an important aspect of good costing — and, indeed, is the principle on which activity based costing (*see* 3:**24**) is based. Grouping overheads into one single 'general expenses' category is to be avoided.

(b) *A cost is not to be charged until it is incurred.* This appears obvious, but is often forgotten. For instance, care should be taken that a cost unit is not charged with any selling costs while it is still in the factory, since units cannot incur selling costs until they are sold. Similarly, when the cost of lost units must be carried by good units such a charge cannot be imposed on units which have not passed the point of loss.

(c) *The 'prudence' convention should be ignored.* One of the historical functions of accounting is to value assets conservatively in order to avoid the risk of paying dividends out of capital. This results in the 'prudence' convention of accounting. This convention must be ignored in cost accounting, otherwise there is a danger that management appraisal of the profitability of projects may be vitiated. For instance, to fail to take advantage of a project which would in the event net £20,000 means that in effect the enterprise loses £20,000. Cost statements should as far as possible give the facts with no known bias. If a contingency sum needs to be taken into consideration it should be shown separately and distinctly.

(d) *Abnormal costs are excluded from costs.* Costing aims to provide information on economic performance to assist managers to manage. Abnormal costs, however, do not promote this object, since they do not relate to normal economic performance that management can influence but instead to infrequent accidents that cannot be controlled. Their presence in the costs, therefore, would tend to distort cost figures and mislead management as to their economic performance as managers under normal conditions. For instance, to charge Production with any gale damage costs may result in a doubling of normal costs per unit, but such a figure gives production managers no real information as to their production efficiency. Abnormal costs are therefore excluded from costs.

(e) *Sunk costs are never charged to future periods.* There is often a temptation to charge sunk costs, or unrecovered costs, to a later period on the grounds that these costs have to be recovered somewhere, and since the past has gone they can only be recovered in future periods. This is quite wrong. Inclusion of sunk costs in future periods results in the distortion of the performance figures for those periods and gives rise to a risk of misleading management. This, of course, does not mean that an earlier cost cannot be charged to a future period. If the object of a costing exercise is to *measure performance*, then the benefit of any earlier cost should be brought in to the analysis. For instance, you cannot accurately measure this month's performance of a sales manager if you ignore the fact that he or she has the benefit of a £1m advertising campaign incurred the previous month — even though for *decision-making* the whole of the £1m is sunk.

(f) *Profit appropriations are excluded from costs.* In costing, profit appropriations are always excluded from the costs. Thus, dividends and taxes arising from profits are never included in costing statements. This is because such appropriations are not deemed economic resources which are consumed by an activity.

But, again, in the case of *decision-making* it sometimes happens that different alternatives do not have the same tax incidence (e.g. different types of capital outlays may result in different capital allowances) and since management accounting is concerned with economic consequences, the consequential taxes must be shown on the comparative statements that detail the alternatives. (It should, incidentally, be noted that traditionally *interest* is also treated as a profit appropriation even though it can be argued that the money needed to finance an activity is an economic resource (*see* 1(a)) and interest its price.)

18. Classification of costs
There are numerous ways of classifying costs, the way chosen being determined by the purpose for which they are required. In a well-organized system of cost accounting it should always be easy to re-classify costs when desired, since it is rare (and inefficient) to prepare costs for one purpose only. The following are the main forms of classification:

(a) *Direct and indirect costs.* All costs fall into one of the two categories of direct and indirect costs.
    (*i*) A *direct cost* may be defined as a cost that arises *solely* from the existence of whatever is being costed. With a direct cost there can be no suggestion of sharing the cost between the things being costed. If the individual 'thing' — cost unit, cost centre or whatever — being costed had not existed the cost would not have arisen at all.
    (*ii*) An *indirect cost* does not depend solely on what is being costed. It therefore implies some element of sharing a cost that is common to, or jointly incurred by, two or more things being costed. When the things being costed are cost units, indirect costs can also be referred to as *overheads*.

This distinction between direct and indirect costs will be taken up again later (*see* 2:**30–35**), but it should be noted in passing that the definitions refer to 'whatever is being costed'. If departments, sales areas or even customer classifications are being costed, then the definitions should be applied with these in mind. For example, a departmental manager's salary is a direct cost if the department is being costed, though indirect if costing the cost units in the department. However, the terms direct and indirect costs are used far more often in relation to the costing of cost units, and so, unless the context clearly indicates differently, they should normally be regarded as relating to cost units.

(b) *Nature.* A further classification relates to the nature of the costs (i.e. what they are), the basic categories here being material, labour and expenses. These three categories can be further broken down as required, e.g. material can be subdivided into raw materials, components and maintenance materials, etc.; labour into supervision, cleaning and clerical work, etc.; and expenses into rent, power, depreciation, postage, etc.

(c) *Function.* Costs may also be classified according to the function to which they relate, typical categories being production, selling, distribution, administration, finance, and research and development. The category into which a given cost should be placed under this system of classification is sometimes uncertain. This is not particularly important: classification of costs by function is a traditional classification and is becoming less and less significant in modern costing, as the entire business process is rapidly becoming a single, integrated function. (For instance, if the sales manager insists on the factory placing an elaborate name plate on the product which acts mainly as a form of advertisement, is the cost of affixing this plate a production cost or a selling cost? The distinction is neither possible nor important.)

19. Elements of costs
Traditionally the cost of a cost unit can be regarded as being built up of a number of elements of cost. Such a build-up can be shown diagrammatically as follows:

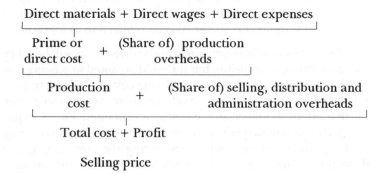

Direct materials + Direct wages + Direct expenses

Prime or direct cost + (Share of) production overheads

Production cost + (Share of) selling, distribution and administration overheads

Total cost + Profit

Selling price

The definitions of these terms are as follows.

(a) *Direct materials.* Materials that actually become part of the cost unit.

(b) *Direct wages.* Wages paid to employees for the time they are engaged in working on the direct materials.

(c) *Direct expenses.* Expenses incurred specifically on behalf of the cost unit.

> NOTE: The traditional term given to the sum of these three direct costs is *prime cost*.

(d) *Production overheads.* Overheads incurred in production, i.e. generally speaking, overheads incurred within the four walls of the factory proper.

(e) *Selling overheads.* Overheads incurred in inducing customers to place orders.

(f) *Distribution overheads.* Overheads incurred in getting finished production from the factory to the customer. It includes warehouse, packing and transport costs.

(g) *Administration overheads.* Overheads incurred in managing the enterprise. It includes top management costs, accounts, legal and (usually) personnel department costs, audit fees and other such general enterprise costs.

(h) *Profit.* The difference between the selling price and the total cost.

> NOTE: This profit is not quite the same as the accountant's profit (which means the amount available for appropriation), since the total cost does *not* include an allowance for abnormal costs (*see* **17(d)**), unrecovered sunk costs (*see* **17(e)**), unabsorbed overheads (*see* **3:21(c)**), discounts and bank charges (*see* **2:36**) and interest (*see* **17(f)**).

These definitions represent the traditional concept of costs, and differ slightly from the more modern concept. For instance, a salesperson's commission for selling a cost unit would be regarded as a selling overhead in the above definitions, but in modern costing it would be classed as a direct cost.

It should be appreciated that the above scheme relates only to costing cost units and that cost accounting extends far beyond this traditional task.

20. Coding of costs

Cost accounting is very much facilitated if the costs are coded — a *code* in this connection having been defined as 'A system of symbols designed to be applied to a classified set of items, to give a brief accurate reference facilitating entry, collation and analysis' (CIMA terminology). The actual form the code takes is, of course, a matter of individual choice, although there are certain basic principles that require the code to be:

(a) *Exclusive*. Each code number should relate to one type of item, and one only. There must be no duplication (e.g. if code 6666 relates to a certain size of steel rod it must not also relate to a similar size of brass rod).

(b) *Certain*. The code number must identify the item without any ambiguity or uncertainty whatsoever.

(c) *Elastic*. The code should be such that new items can be added easily and logically.

(d) *Brief*. Large code numbers take longer to write and are more subject to error. Numbers, therefore, should be as brief as possible without violating other principles.

(e) *Mnemonic*, if possible (i.e. assisting the memory, such as FVO for 'foundry variable overheads'). Mnemonic codes are both easier to remember and less subject to error.

(f) *Computer friendly*. Because computers are extensively used in cost accounting it is necessary to ensure that the coding is in the form that facilitates computer data-processing. On the whole, most typical codes meet this requirement, although sometimes a computer does need each section of the code to be of a fixed length. Also, one should remember that computers cannot see conceptual relationships between codes or descriptions, e.g. if it were looking at 'nuts, almond' it would consider 'nuts, brass' to be more closely related than 'nuts, brazil' since alphabetically 'brass' falls between 'almonds' and 'brazil'.

21. Book-keeping in cost and management accounting

Neither cost accounting nor management accounting are essentially recording techniques (although in cost accounting a certain degree of recording is a prerequisite of an effective costing system). Both aim to make economic assessments of the past and future activities of the enterprise in which they are practised, and these assessments rarely call for any formal accounting procedure. However, some such formal procedure, even if it is kept to a minimum, is usually necessary because:

(a) certain valuations form part of the final accounts of the enterprise (e.g. stock and work-in-progress) and it is desirable that these should be linked with the enterprise accounts;
(b) it is desirable on occasions to ensure that all the costs incurred by the enterprise have been incorporated into the cost and management analyses (e.g. in cost and profit control).

The book-keeping associated with the two subjects will, therefore, be discussed occasionally in this book. The technique adopted will be that of conventional double entry, partly because this form will be most familiar to the student but more importantly because this is the form needed for the examinations. It should, perhaps, be observed that the system of database accounting should soon become widespread, although it is suspected that examiners will continue to require a knowledge of double-entry methods for some time yet.

22. The basic principle of data selection and arrangement
It must be emphasized at this point that management accounting statements should always be prepared with the following question in mind: *for what purpose is the information required?* In management accounting you are continually faced with the problem of selecting which pieces of data you should use and if you always consider whether or not use of the data will help achieve the purpose, then it becomes easier to pass through the labyrinth of alternative treatments of data that are a feature of management accounting. Remember, too, that there are no definitive rules or statute laws that make the choice for you; books may point the way but always the final decision must be left to the judgement of the individual accountant.

23. Cost data as building bricks
Unlike most financial accounting data, cost data is not destined for a single accounting statement. In financial accounting an expenditure of £4 on a tin of paint would, for instance, normally simply form part of the 'purchases' figure in the Profit and Loss account and nothing else. In a costing system, however, the £4

could appear as a charge to the stores, to the cost centre using the paint, to the cost unit or activity on which it was used, and perhaps also to the persons who authorized its purchase and use respectively. In costing, then, each element of cost data — and the elements should be kept as small as is reasonably possible — is to be regarded as a building brick which is available to construct statement 'buildings' of whatever design is required. These bricks, moreover, are re-usable for as many occasions as is required.

24. Data presentation
Finally, in this connection it must be appreciated that whatever invaluable data accountants may collect, whatever inspired ideas they may have, unless they can present the data and their conclusions in a lucid and meaningful manner they will have wasted their time. And it should be also appreciated that the onus of effective reporting is wholly on the person reporting — not the person reported to.

> NOTE: Examination questions frequently call for a report and to assist the student to deal with this form of question, Appendix I includes an outline on how to write such a report.

25. Reliability of cost data
Cost accountants should never forget that cost data may not always be reliable. Much of it comes from the shop-floor — time-sheets, material requisitions, material returned notes, transfer notes, piecework tickets and scrap returns — and it should be appreciated that many shop-floor employees:

(a) are not clerks, nor are they really paid for their clerical ability;
(b) rarely have good clerical facilities (either office desks or even proper pencils);
(c) often regard paperwork as an unnecessary obstacle to 'getting the job out' (it should be noted, however, that the accountant who thinks the paperwork should have priority makes an even graver error);
(d) often have to record information from memory, because no written reference exists or because it is not at hand;
(e) may deliberately falsify the data.

This last possibility may be common where time-sheets are

involved, particularly if an incentive scheme is in operation. Two points should be noted here. First, if management uses a single record for both computing bonuses and preparing costs, it cannot really complain if the employees use them as instruments to maximise their bonuses in preference to recording accurate cost information. Second, attempts to enforce accurate time-recording usually prove abortive; loopholes are almost invariably found unless the scheme is so elaborate that it is uneconomic.

In view of such possible unreliability in much of their basic data, accountants must be cautious about jumping to conclusions. For instance, when booking time to a mixture of small and large jobs employees may easily forget they worked on some small jobs. Moreover, they are conscious that their excessive time is much more noticeable on a small job than a large job involving a number of other employees. As result, small jobs are almost always underbooked and large jobs overbooked and the accountant should allow for this.

26. Profitability and productivity

Profitability and productivity are two terms used in the measurement of economic performance which are frequently misunderstood, but which it is vital for the cost accountant to understand thoroughly. The important point to note is that they are *relative* measures and so must not be confused with profit and production which are *absolute* measures.

(a) *Profitability*. When we use the concept of profitability we are concerned only with which of two or more alternatives is the *more* profitable. Note that we do *not* need to find the profit from each alternative to do this. For example, if an article can be sold to A for £40 or to B for £50, then, other things being equal, it is clearly more profitable to sell to B. This is true whatever the costs are (provided they are the same in either case), and so we know which alternative is the more profitable without knowing the profit to be earned from either. Indeed, even if the costs exceed £50 (so that we make a loss either way) it is still more 'profitable' to sell to B since this results in a smaller loss than to A. Profitability, then, is a relative measure — it indicates the *most profitable alternative*. Profit, on the other hand, is an absolute measure — it indicates the overall amount of profit earned by a transaction or enterprise.

(b) *Productivity.* Productivity is a ratio of economic output to economic input, i.e.:

$$\text{Productivity} = \frac{\text{Economic output}}{\text{Economic input}}$$

Thus, if the same goods can be produced (i.e. output unchanged) for less labour hours (i.e. input reduced) then productivity has increased. Note that in this example the *production* has remained unchanged although the productivity has altered, and indeed it is obviously possible for production to fall while productivity increases (e.g. if output drops by 20 per cent but labour hours drop by 30 per cent).

Although discussions on productivity usually revolve round labour hours, the input can be any economic resource. For example, when considering those resources the consumption of which remains unaltered for small changes of output (e.g. land), then an increase in output clearly leads to increased productivity (since the input remains constant in this respect). Actually, of course, a number of input factors usually change from one situation to another so a common denominator is again required to enable the different forms of consumption to be added together. Hence more sophisticated productivity measurements tend to use the formula: productivity = output/cost (i.e. output per £ cost), while situations where the forms of output themselves differ and change require a sales/cost type of formula.

27. Just-in-Time (JIT)

'Just-in-time' is the name for an essentially production planning and control technique — although like many other management packages it tends to claim for itself attitudes and techniques that really relate to already recognized (if not adopted) good management practice. JIT's distinguishing feature is its emphasis on acquiring materials and producing goods and services, both internally and externally, just in time — i.e. at the very moment they are required rather than as and when convenient to management. So, ideally, materials from suppliers are received just in time to be incorporated into the initial production, components and other work-in-progress items are completed just in time to be incorporated into the main product, and finished goods are completed just in time to be sent to the customer. The main advantages and disadvantages of JIT can be summarized as follows:

(a) *Advantages.*

  (*i*) Stocks (raw material, work-in-progress and finished goods) are kept to the absolute minimum. This results in large savings in stock-holding costs (*see* 2:6)

 (*ii*) Considerable space in the working areas previously occupied by work-in-progress is often released so that these areas can be made smaller and less 'cluttered', and hence production becomes more streamlined.

(*iii*) A change in product specification can be made suddenly without affecting such a large volume of production already committed to the existing specification as would otherwise be the case — and, indeed, may result in far less obsolete finished goods and work-in-progress.

(*iv*) Lower management is kept more on its toes as a result of having to ensure work proceeds as planned.

 (*v*) Less obvious inefficiencies will show up more readily (e.g. components produced months ahead of requirements will stand out more like a sore thumb amid other work which is very much smaller in volume and much faster moving).

(b) *Disadvantages.*

  (*i*) There is always the risk that just in time becomes just too late. As is well-known, 'For the sake of a nail a kingdom was lost' — or, more appropriately here, a contract. So a £100 stock-holding cost saving can result in a £10,000 penalty-clause cost.

 (*ii*) JIT calls for a more frequent handling of smaller individual batches — with associated extra costs. A supplier who has to deliver half a truck-load of material twice a week will charge more for delivery than he would if he could deliver one full load once a week. Similarly, setting-up a machine twice a week costs more for the same total production as setting it up once a week.

(*iii*) The closer monitoring and control work necessary to operate JIT results in a higher cost for these functions.

(*iv*) The finer limits of timing error increases management stress — with its well-known health hazards.

 (*v*) Ensuring that production runs smoothly, management

tend to live more from moment to moment. As a consequence of losing the habit of sitting back now and then to take a longer view, potentially long-term improvements may not be noticed.

As can be seen, there are both cost advantages and cost disadvantages to JIT — and where the point of balance lies in any specific context depends very much on all the unique circumstances relating to that context.

Use of computers in cost accounting

Computers are obviously a great aid to accounting for costs. The following points should, therefore, be noted in this connection.

28. Strengths of a computer
A computer is:

(a) *very fast.* With a computer all calculations, even the most complex, can be carried out with great rapidity.
(b) *untiring.* A computer can be run day and night without any loss of effectiveness. This enables it to process considerable amounts of work.
(c) *very accurate.* Only a computer that is malfunctioning generates errors — and these are almost always so bizarre that the malfunction is immediately observable.
(d) *discerning.* Providing it has been programmed properly, a computer can make comparisons between elements in the data it is given and, on the basis of such comparisons, direct itself into whichever procedure is appropriate in the circumstances of the moment.

29. Weaknesses of a computer
On the other hand a computer has the following weaknesses:

(a) *Data invisibility.* Computer data is invisible — except on a specific order to print it on paper or display it on a VDU. This means that any search for data outside the established procedure is rather like looking, blindfolded, for a randomly placed needle in a monstrous haystack of near-infinite dimensions.

(b) *Liability to breakdown.* Because of their considerable power, computers are often given immense workloads. As a result a computer breakdown can create major problems — particularly if a deadline is involved (e.g. a payroll). Moreover, arising from weakness (a) it can mean that with a breakdown not only the means to process data is lost but also, to all intents and purposes, the data may be lost, too, since it cannot be retrieved from the system.

(c) *Program incomprehensibility.* It is astonishing how incomprehensible a program can look — even to its creator. Should it prove necessary to amend the program then in the absence of very comprehensive program documentation the task will be found to be on a par with correctly positioning all the available pieces of a jigsaw in which half the pieces are missing.

(d) *Training requirements.* Since computers have to be precisely instructed — either in terms of programming or in terms of keyboard operations — poor training can lead to a malfunctioning computer system.

(e) *Information swamping.* In the past, management has tended to suffer from too little information. Now it may find that the useful information computers can provide may be swamped by masses of trivia. More does not mean better when it comes to information and, since a computer has no innate ability to decide what is useful and what is not, it must be intelligently programmed to supply only useful information.

30. Computer packages

For the majority of standard computer applications there exist *packages* which are no more than pre-written programs that can be bought. With a package and its documentation it should be possible for relatively inexperienced personnel to run very complex programs. Such packages in the majority of cases involve either spreadsheets or databases.

(a) *Spreadsheets.* These are programs which in effect create a table out of the user's data. Each column and row can carry such titles as the user gives them and each entry is either an entered value or is computed from already entered data according to such a formula as the user designates. Column and row totalling is automatically carried out and the totals entered on the spreadsheet. A feature of these programs is that a change of any entry by the user results in a recomputation of the whole table. The table, incidentally, is not limited to the dimension of the computer's VDU — indeed, the table really exists in the computer's memory and the VDU merely displays that section of the overall table that the user directs it to. **(b)** *Databases.* A database program is one that holds units of data in its memory, each unit carrying pieces of information. Once a database has been created the user can extract required information relating to all units which hold a specified piece of information (e.g. the names of all debtors owing over £1,000) or can combine the information relating to each unit in a prescribed way (e.g. draw a graph showing how the total stock value of any specified class of stores has changed over the months).

31. Packages *v.* own programming

Whereas a package probably exists for any computer for any common application (e.g. payroll, debtors ledger, job costing), they can never, despite the ingenious adaptability built into them by their designers, do anything which they are not programmed to do. And so cost accountants who want something a little different will find that they are left to their own skills. It is at that time that it is necessary for accountants to be able to design their own programs — and, if they do not write them themselves, to have them written by one of their staff. There is no doubt that the need to design one's own programs brings a fresh approach to the solution of old problems. Indeed, methods which would never be viable manually become absurdly simple with a computer. For example, the convention in budgeting that for interest computations cash is deemed received or paid at the month end can be dispensed with and the daily budgeted amounts can be incorporated instead in a simple program. So, if interest is 12 per cent per annum nominal, i.e. effectively 0.0310537 per cent per day, £3,225 is banked for the first four days of any week in the year with £4,500 on the fifth day — when simultaneously £13,500 is withdrawn — then the program $x=1.000310537$: FOR $w=1$ TO 52: FOR $d=1$ TO 4: $s=s*x+3225$: NEXT d: $s=s*x+4500-13500$: $s=s*x\uparrow2$: NEXT w: PRINT s will display the year-end cash balance on the basis that interest is calculated on the daily balance. (In this program for each of 52 weeks and for each of 4 days in each week, the computer updates the current balance, s, by one day's interest and then adds the usual day's receipts — and then, after updating the balance again, it adds the fifth day's receipts less the weekly payments before updating the balance by the two remaining days of the week.)

Currently, computer development is at the railway train stage of transport. Just as catching a train is both the simplest, most comfortable, and, over distances of 100–200 miles, usually the quickest method of travel, so packages are the simplest, most comfortable and, within limits, quickest methods of solution. However, like trains, they lack flexibility and just as motor transport has far greater flexibility at the cost of greater effort, so writing one's own programs gives greater flexibility but again only as the result of greater effort. And just as one looks at train timetables to see where trains go to, so accountants look up package lists to see what packages do (and, like railway timetables, after but a few months these lists may become very out of date). However, computers will really come of age in cost accounting only when cost accountants design the majority of their own programs.

32. Conclusion

Unfortunately, this is about as much space as can be given to the topic of computers in a book on the principles of cost accounting. As you continue reading, however, you should reflect on how a computer could be of assistance for the topic being studied. And to help you see the role of the computer in such circumstances, here and there short programs that incorporate the procedures under discussion will be given.

Progress test 1

Principles

1. How does money take on a dual role? **(1)**

2. How do financial, management and cost accounting divide up in practice? **(3)**

3. What two components are always found in a cost? **(9)**

4. Distinguish between: (*a*) cost unit and cost centre; **(10, 11)** (*b*) current cost, past cost and sunk cost; **(12)** (*c*) direct and indirect cost; **(18(a))** (*d*) profit and profitability; **(26(a))** (*e*) production and productivity. **(26(b))**

5. Define: (*a*) costing **(7)**; (*b*) cost **(8)**; (*c*) notional cost **(13)**; (*d*) decision driven cost **(14)**; (*e*) conversion cost **(15(a))**; (*f*) added value **(15 (b))**; (*g*) direct materials and direct wages **(19)**; (*h*) prime cost **(19)**.

6. What costing principles do the terms 'prudence', 'abnormal', 'appropriation' and 'sunk' call to your mind? **(17)**

7. What are the principles of cost coding? **(20)**

8. What is the basic principle of data selection and arrangement? **(22)**

9. Why is cost data often unreliable? **(25)**

10. What is JIT, and what are its advantages and disadvantages? **(27)**

11. What are the strengths and weaknesses of computers when used in cost accounting? **(28, 29)**

12. Distinguish between spreadsheets and databases. **(30)**

Part one

Cost ascertainment

2
Cost data

Before any cost methods or techniques can be examined it is necessary to be fully conversant with the different types of cost data. It must always be remembered that a cost statement can never be more accurate or reliable than the cost data upon which it is based. Appreciation of the sources of such data and the background from which they originate is a vital part of the cost accountant's know-how.

Materials cost data — Stores procedures

Stores procedures relate to the recording of material location, levels and control.

1. Materials requisition

One of the key sources of materials data is the *materials requisition*. This is a form that details the materials wanted for production and that is used by the storekeeper both as:

(a) an authorization to issue the stated materials; and
(b) a source document to record material usage and withdrawal of material from the store.

2. Stores record cards and bin cards

The most important records in a stores are the Stores Record Cards and the Bin Cards.

(a) *Stores record cards.* These are cards prepared for *each item of material* and they normally show:

> (*i*) full identification of the material and its location in the stores;

(*ii*) quantities on order, received, and issued (and also, where appropriate, reserved and free stock) together with a running balance of the quantity in stock;

(*iii*) prices and values of all receipts and issues;

(*iv*) all materials control quantities (*see* 5).

(**b**) *Bin cards.* These are cards prepared for *each bin* or other storage location so that the material held there can be identified and the quantity quickly ascertained. The data recorded is, therefore, usually limited to:

(*i*) the location code of the bin;

(*ii*) full identification of the material;

(*iii*) the receipts, issues and remaining balance of the material held in that location.

It should be appreciated that, since there may be two or more bins for the same material (one at the front of the stores for ease of issue and others at the back to hold the bulk supplies), the same material may appear on more than one bin card, though never on more than one stores record card.

3.   Perpetual inventory and continuous stocktaking

A system of stores recording under which the up-to-date stock balances are always known is called a *perpetual inventory* system. Where a perpetual inventory exists it is possible to carry out *continuous stocktaking*, which is the continuous taking of stock, quantities counted being checked against the perpetual inventory balances. In the operation of the system a few items are checked each day so that all items are checked two or three times a year. Continuous stocktaking can often render the usual annual stocktaking unnecessary since if it confirms the accuracy of the perpetual inventory balances then at the year end those balances can be taken as the actual stock figures.

Continuous stocktaking has a number of important advantages over annual stocktaking. These include the fact that, since there is less time pressure, counting and identification is more accurate and also that any failure in the stores system is disclosed much sooner.

4.   Stores control

It is very important that both the costs of overstocking (e.g.

interest on the capital unnecessarily tied up) and the costs of understocking (e.g. profit on orders lost because of failure to deliver) are avoided. To this end control quantities are predetermined for each item of material and recorded on the stores record cards. By basing all purchasing action on these quantities the stock levels of all items can be held between acceptable limits.

5. Stores control quantities

The four most important control quantities are as follows.

(a) *Maximum level.* The maximum level of a given material is the maximum quantity that may be held in store. It is essentially an uppermost limit that the buyer must ensure is not exceeded (unless an excess is specifically authorized by higher management; for example, when unusually favourable purchasing conditions arise). It is set after consideration of:

    (*i*) rate of consumption;

    (*ii*) risks of obsolescence;

    (*iii*) risks of deterioration;

    (*iv*) costs of storing above-normal stocks;

    (*v*) storage space available.

(b) *Minimum level.* The minimum level is the lowest level to which stocks should fall. It is essentially a *buffer stock* which will not normally be touched. In the event of any item falling to its minimum level management must be immediately alerted and the acquisition of new supplies given top priority. It is set after consideration of:

    (*i*) rate of consumption;

    (*ii*) the time required in a top priority situation to acquire enough supplies to avoid a production stoppage.

(c) *Reorder level.* The reorder level is the level at which a new purchase is initiated. The level selected is such that, in the normal course of events, by reordering when the stock falls to the reorder level, *new supplies will be received just before the minimum level is reached*. It is set after consideration of:

    (*i*) rate of consumption;

    (*ii*) minimum level;

    (*iii*) delivery time (also known as *lead time*);

    (*iv*) variations in delivery time.

(d) *Reorder quantity.* The reorder quantity is the quantity to be reordered in normal circumstances. By setting this quantity in advance the buyer is saved the task of recalculating how much he should buy each time he orders. He may, of course, disregard this order quantity if he deems circumstances warrant it. It is set after consideration of:

    (*i*) rate of consumption;

   (*ii*) cost of holding stock as against cost of purchasing (*see economic order quantity* in **8** *et seq.* below);

  (*iii*) bulk discounts;

  (*iv*) transport costs (half a load involves virtually the same transport costs as a whole load);

   (*v*) obsolescence and deterioration risks.

6.   Costs of storage

In setting any control figure the costs of storage should be borne in mind. These costs include the following:

(a) *Capital costs.* The loss of return which could be obtained if the capital tied up in stock were employed elsewhere. (This cost is almost always the highest cost of all.)

(b) *Space costs* (rent, heating, lighting, etc.).

(c) *Equipment costs* (bins, racks, material handling equipment, etc.).

(d) *Personnel costs* (storing, stocktaking, security, etc.).

(e) *Insurance.*

(f) *Deterioration.*

(g) *Obsolescence.*

7.   Pareto (80/20) phenomenon

In a stores one will very often observe that a minority of materials comprise the bulk of the stores value — indeed, frequently to the extent that some 80 per cent of the stores value can be attributed to around a mere 20 per cent of the materials (e.g. in a store of 20 different materials worth £50,000, just four materials could have a value of £40,000). This imbalance is referred to as the Pareto (or, for obvious reasons, the 80/20) phenomenon. This being so, a storekeeper should not carry out his work on the basis that all types of material are equal for, clearly, a material which comprises a significantly high proportion of the total stores value must be given more attention than another the value of which is relatively insignificant.

Materials cost data — Economic order quantity

A problem that frequently faces managers responsible for the control of materials relates to the quantity of any item which should be ordered at the time of purchase.

8. The costs of purchasing and holding stock
The following two kinds of costs are involved in any purchase order decision.

(a) *Costs of purchasing*. Making a purchase always results in costs, which include the cost of the time involved in negotiating the order and completing the paperwork, together with the costs of telephone calls, stationery, postage, etc. There are also the costs of receiving the goods on delivery. Although these costs are rarely the same each time there is a purchase, it is nevertheless often possible to compute the average cost of making a purchase.

(b) *Costs of holding stock*. Holding stock also results in costs (*see* **6**), particularly the interest cost on the money tied up in the stock held, e.g. a £1,000 item held for six months when the interest rate is 14 per cent will have an interest cost of £70. These stock-holding costs can often be added together and expressed collectively as an annual percentage rate of the value of the goods in stock.

9. The economic order quantity (EOQ)
Clearly, these two kinds of costs vary inversely with each other over a given period of time; the smaller the quantities ordered the greater the costs of purchasing (for more purchases will need to be made during the period), but the less the costs of holding stock (as on average fewer units will be in stock) and vice versa. Equally clearly, it would be prohibitively expensive to order an item twice a day on the one hand, or only once in ten years on the other. Somewhere in between there is a point at which the total cost of purchasing and holding stock is at a minimum. The order quantity at this point is called the *economic order quantity*.

10. Illustrative figures
   To illustrate the computation of an economic order quantity the following figures and symbols will be used.

   Costs of placing a purchasing order (P): £5 per order.
   Costs of holding stock (H): 20 per cent per annum of the value held.
   Annual usage (N): 1,000 units.
   Purchase price per unit (U): £20.
   Order quantities will be symbolized as Q and the economic order quantity as EOQ.

11. Finding the EOQ by graphical methods
   To find the EOQ by graphical methods the following steps should be taken (*see* Fig. 2.1).

(a) Prepare a graph showing:
   (*i*) on the vertical axis, the *total annual cost of purchasing and holding stock;*
   (*ii*) on the horizontal axis, the *range of possible order quantities.*
(b) Select a number of order quantities and compute for each the following.
   (*i*) *The annual cost of purchasing.* This is found by multiplying the cost per purchase order (P) by the number of orders that would be placed in a year (which is the annual usage divided by the quantity ordered at each purchase, i.e. N/Q). So the purchasing cost is $P \times N/Q = PN/Q$.
   (*ii*) *The annual cost of holding stock.* This is found by multiplying the annual cost of holding one unit in stock (HU) by the average number of units held in stock. Since it is usual for units to be withdrawn from stock at an even rate, the average stock held between the receipt of one ordered quantity and the receipt of the next is half that quantity (and so this will be the stock held on average over the year). In other words, the average stock is $\frac{1}{2}Q$, and the annual cost of holding stock is, therefore, $\frac{1}{2}Q \times HU = QHU/2$. (Note that the cost of holding any buffer stock is the same whatever order quantity figure is selected, and can, therefore, be excluded from the calculations.)

(*iii*) *The total annual cost of purchasing and holding stock.* This is found by adding the costs in (*i*) and (*ii*).

(c) Plot on the graph the total annual cost of purchasing and holding stock against each selected order quantity and draw a smooth curve through the points.

(d) Find the minimum point of this curve. This point identifies the economic order quantity (in our illustration, 50 units).

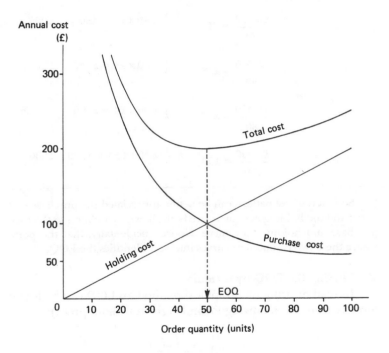

Figure 2.1 *Identifying the economic order quantity*

NOTES:
(1) Illustrative figures (*see* **10**):

$P = £5$; $H = 20$ per cent; $N = 1,000$; $U = £20$;
$\therefore HU = £4$ and $PN = £5,000$.

(2) Selected points for the graph (*see* **11**).

	Costs		
Order quantity (Q)	*Purchasing* $\left(\dfrac{PN}{Q}\right)$	*Holding* $(\frac{1}{2}QHU)$	*Total*
20	$\dfrac{£5,000}{20} = £250$	$\frac{1}{2}$ x 20 x £4 = £40	£290
40	$\dfrac{£5,000}{40} = £125$	$\frac{1}{2}$ x 40 x £4 = £80	£205
60	$\dfrac{£5,000}{60} = £83.3$	$\frac{1}{2}$ x 60 x £4 = £120	£203.3
80	$\dfrac{£5,000}{80} = £62.5$	$\frac{1}{2}$ x 80 x £4 = £160	£222.5
100	$\dfrac{£5,000}{100} = £50$	$\frac{1}{2}$ x 100 x £4 = £200	£250

(3) So that the cost pattern can be better appreciated the purchase cost curve and the holding cost curve are both shown in addition to the total purchase and holding cost curve. Notice, incidentally, that the point where these two component curves intersect identifies the EOQ.

12. Finding the EOQ by formula

Instead of using the graphical method an EOQ can be found directly from the following formula (given without proof):

$$EOQ = \sqrt{\frac{2PN}{S}}$$

where $S = HU$ in the previous paragraphs (i.e. S = annual cost of holding one unit in stock for a year).

So in the case of our illustration (where $S = HU = 20$ per cent of £20 = £4):

$$EOQ = \sqrt{\frac{2PN}{S}} = \sqrt{\frac{2 \times 5 \times 1,000}{4}} = 50 \text{ units}$$

13. Limitations of the economic order quantity computation

Although popular, the economic order quantity computation has distinct limitations in practice. These include the following.

(a) In normal circumstances the total annual cost curve is relatively flat in the vicinity of the economic order quantity and this means that quite significant divergencies from the quantity result in only minor cost increases. The economic order quantity, then, is rarely a critical figure.

(b) The actual optimum order quantity is often much more crucially dependent on the storage space and facilities available, work-load of the purchase office, economics of delivery and overall convenience of all involved in the purchase, than it is on the potential saving of a few pounds.

(c) The costs of purchasing and holding stock are often difficult to quantify with any accuracy. Consequently even when the economic order quantity has been calculated there is little certainty that the result is accurate.

(d) Changing prices or usage rates in theory require a recomputation of the economic order quantity, with the consequential need to alter all the relevant records in the purchase office and the stores office. If interest rates change then the order quantities and records of *all* materials bought and stocked will need to be changed.

(e) The formula presumes that the purchase of the material will continue for eternity. The shorter, then, the total time the material will be purchased the less valid the formula will be.

All in all, the technique is perhaps best used simply to check that some more convenient existing rule-of-thumb order quantity is not proving significantly more expensive than necessary.

Materials cost data — Pricing stores issues

When pricing materials issued from store there is always the problem as to whether the original purchase price or the immediate current price should be used. In times of inflation there is a danger that by using the original purchase price when costing a product the profit *from manufacturing* will be confused with the *paper profit* arising as a result of charging materials bought much earlier at a low price to a product whose market price reflects the newly inflated material price. If a radio is bought for £100 and the price then rises to £110, to sell it for £110 does not really bring in a £10 profit, since if the radio is to be replaced in stock this £10 cannot be distributed as a dividend. (This replacement involves no expansion, only a return to the original stock position.) If, on the other hand, issues are priced at current (replacement) prices many people may argue that this is not costing, since the original cost price is not being used.

This dilemma has led to a number of methods of pricing stores issues, all aimed at some form of compromise. The five most important of these are: FIFO; LIFO; weighted average; replacement price; standard price. Using the basic data given in Fig. 2.2 these five will be illustrated, discussed and compared.

The five main methods of pricing stores issues are illustrated together using the following data:

Date	Units purchased	Purchase price	Units issued	Replacement price
1/1	200	£10.25		£10.25
23/1	150	£12.00		£12.00
4/2			100	£12.25
16/2			130	£12.50
25/2	80	£12.50		£12.50
4/3			100	£13.00

(Standard price = £12)

The figures in bold type indicate the differences in each method. Note that under the LIFO and FIFO methods the storekeeper needs to amend the RECEIPTS column continually by crossing out quantities as units are issued so that the remaining balance in respect of each individual batch of material received can be identified. For the standard price method, the unnecessary figures are italicized (*see* **8**).

NOTES:
(1) Split issue: 100 at £10.25 + 30 at £12.00.
(2) Split issue: 50 at £12.00 + 80 at £10.25.
(3) Split issue: 80 at £12.50 + 20 at £10.25.
(4) Gain or loss on purchasing written off in the accounts.

Issue price method	Date	RECEIPTS			ISSUES			BALANCE	
		Quantity	Price £	Value £	Quantity	Price £	Value £	Quantity	Value £
FIFO	1/1	~~200~~ ~~100~~	10.25	2,050				200	2,050
	23/1	~~150~~ ~~120~~ 20	12.00	1,800				350	3,850
	4/2				100	10.25	1,025	250	2,825
	16/2				130[1]		1,385	120	1,440
	25/2	80	12.50	1,000				200	2,440
	4/3				100	12.00	1,200	100	1,240
LIFO	1/1	~~200~~ ~~120~~ 100	10.25	2,050				200	2,050
	23/1	~~150~~ ~~50~~	12.00	1,800				350	3,850
	4/2				100	12.00	1,200	250	2,650
	16/2				130[2]		1,420	120	1,230
	25/2	~~80~~	12.50	1,000				200	2,320
	4/3				100[3]		1,205	100	1,025
Weighted average	1/1	200	10.25	2,050				200	2,050
	23/1	150	12.00	1,800				350	3,850
	4/2				100	11.00	1,100	250	2,750
	16/2				130	11.00	1,430	120	1,320
	25/2	80	12.50	1,000				200	2,320
	4/3				100	11.60	1,160	100	1,160
Replacement price	1/1	200	10.25	2,050				200	
	23/1	150	12.00	1,800				350	
	4/2				100	12.25	1,225	250	Not
	16/2				130	12.50	1,625	120	used
	25/2	80	12.50	1,000				200	
	4/3				100	13.00	1,300	100	
Standard price (£12)	1/1	200	12	2,400[4]				200	2,400
	23/1	150	12	1,800[4]				350	4,200
	4/2				100	12	1,200	250	3,000
	16/2				130	12	1,560	120	1,440
	25/2	80	12	960[4]				200	2,400
	4/3				100	12	1,200	100	1,200

Figure 2.2   *Issue price methods*

14. FIFO (First in, first out).

The FIFO method uses *the price of the units in the first batch received* for all issues until all units from this batch have been issued — after which the price relating to the next batch received becomes the issue price. Once that batch has been fully issued the price of the units of the next batch received is used, and so on. Note the following (*see* Fig. 2.2):

(a) The need to record units left in each batch after issue.

(b) The balance cross-check: the 100 units left in stock at the end must comprise the last 80 received at £12.50 and the 20 remaining from the previous batch at £12, i.e.: 80 x £12.50 + 20 x £12 = £1,240 = amount in the balance-value column.

(c) The *advantages* of FIFO which are:

    (*i*) It is realistic, i.e. based on the actual physical issuing of items to the shop-floor in order of receipt.

    (*ii*) The valuation of the stock balance is a fair commercial valuation of the stock.

    (*iii*) No profits or losses arise (i.e. the value of issues after allowing for stock exactly equals the cost of purchases).

(d) The *disadvantages* of FIFO which are:

    (*i*) It is cumbersome.

    (*ii*) The issue price may not reflect current economic value.

(e) The *effect on costs and stock valuations:*

    (*i*) *Costs* lag behind current economic values.

    (*ii*) *Stock valuations* are based on the most recently acquired items.

15. LIFO (Last in, first out)

The LIFO method uses *the price of the units in the last batch received* for all issues until all units from this batch have been issued, when the price relating to the previous batch received is used. If, however, a new delivery is received before the relevant batch is fully issued, the new delivery price at once becomes the 'last-in' price and is used for pricing issues until either the batch is exhausted or a new delivery received. Note the following.

(a) The method can result in many batches being only partially 'written off'.

(b) This is a book-keeping method and must not be confused with the physical method of issue used by the store-keeper, who will always issue the oldest stock first.

(c) The balance cross-check (*see* Fig. 2.2): the 100 units remaining in stock must now relate to the very first batch received and the value, therefore, is:

100 x £10.25 = £1,025 = amount in balance-value column.

(d) The *advantages* of LIFO which are:

(*i*) It keeps the value of issues close to current economic values.

(*ii*) The valuation of the stock balance is usually very conservative.

(*iii*) No profits or losses arise.

(e) The *disadvantages* of LIFO which are:

(*i*) It is cumbersome.

(*ii*) It is not realistic, i.e. it implies that the physical issue principle is the opposite to that actually followed by the storekeeper.

(*iii*) The valuation of the stock balance is not acceptable under SSAP 9 (*see* **19**), and may not be acceptable for corporation tax assessments.

(*iv*) Should issues dip into 'old stock' then they will be valued at very out-of-date prices.

(f) The *effect on costs and stock valuations:*

(*i*) *Costs* lag only slightly behind current economic values.

(*ii*) *Stock valuations* are completely out of line with current economic values.

16. Weighted average

The weighted average method *averages prices after weighting* (i.e. *multiplying*) *by their quantities*. Thus, the weighted average for the first two prices in Fig 2.2 is:

$$\frac{(10.25 \times 200) + (12 \times 150)}{350} = £11.$$

Students are sometimes puzzled as to how to calculate a weighted average where there are units already in stock, but they need only remember that the average price *at any time* is simply the *balance-value* figure divided by the *balance-units* figure, e.g. in Fig.

2.2 after the February receipt there are 200 units, value £2,320, in stock and the weighted average, therefore, is:

$$\frac{£2,320}{200} = £11.60.$$

Note the following:

(a) Issue prices need only be computed on the *receipt* of new deliveries, not at the time of each issue as with FIFO and LIFO.

(b) The balance cross-check: the 100 in stock in Fig. 2.2 is at the average price of £11.60, i.e. the value is:

100 x £11.60 = £1,160 = amount in balance-value column.

(c) The *advantages* of Weighted Average which are:
   (*i*) It is logical, i.e. it assumes values of identical items are all equal.
   (*ii*) Since receipts are much less frequent than issues it is not so cumbersome as LIFO or FIFO.
   (*iii*) It smooths out fluctuations in the purchase price.
   (*iv*) No profits or losses arise.

(d) The *disadvantages* of Weighted Average which are:
   (*i*) Issues may not be at current economic values.
   (*ii*) The issue price is usually a fiction since it may never have existed in the market, e.g. the £11 in Fig. 2.2.
   (*iii*) Issue prices may run to a number of decimal places.

(e) The *effect on costs and stock valuations:*
   (*i*) *Costs* are in between FIFO and LIFO values.
   (*ii*) *Stock valuations* are usually satisfactory, though slightly out-of-date relative to FIFO.

17. Replacement price

This method simply uses the *current replacement price* to value issues. Note the following:

(a) The replacement price *at the time of each issue* must be found. This may involve considerable work.

(b) The *balance-value* column cannot be used in the same arithmetic way as the methods described above since such an attempt would quickly give rise to nonsensical figures.

(c) The *advantages* of Replacement Price which are:

(*i*) Issues are at current economic values.

(*ii*) The calculations are simple.

(d) The *disadvantages* of Replacement Price which are:

(*i*) It is difficult to be continually up to date with the replacement prices.

(*ii*) Profits and losses arise.

(*iii*) It is not a traditional 'cost' price.

(e) The *effect on costs and stock valuations:*

(*i*) *Costs* are at current economic values.

(*ii*) *Stock valuations* are at current economic values, but such valuations can only be used with a full understanding of inflation accounting.

18. Standard price

The standard price method uses the *planned purchase price (standard price) for all valuations.* Note the following:

(a) All purchases are also valued at standard, the gain or loss following such a valuation being written off in the accounts.

(b) Since all quantities are valued at the same price there is no need to record any money values at all (other than as a single statement of the standard price). This means the records can be kept in quantity figures only. (In Fig. 2.2 the unnecessary figures are italicized.)

(c) The value of the method is greatly improved if a complete system of standard costing is in operation (*see* Chapters 14–17).

(d) The *advantages* of Standard Price which are:

(*i*) It is very simple to apply and requires much less clerical effort than the other methods.

(*ii*) It provides a check on the efficiency of the Purchasing department.

(*iii*) It eliminates price fluctuations from costs enabling satisfactory manufacturing cost comparisons to be made.

(*iv*) It does not alter over the accounting period.

(e) The *disadvantages* of Standard Price which are:

(*i*) The initial standard price requires careful determination.

(*ii*) Profits and losses arise (although under standard costing this is not a disadvantage).

(*iii*) Issues may not be at current economic values.

(*iv*) It disregards price trends.

(f) The *effect on costs and stock valuations:* Costs and stock values are standardized and so not necessarily in line with current economic values or even past market values.

19. SSAP 9 and stock valuations

Note that when valuing stock, SSAP 9 lays down that such a valuation should always be at net realizable value where this is less than cost (and, indeed, SSAP 9 should always be referred to when computing any figures likely to form part of the enterprise's formal final accounts).

Labour cost data — Methods of remuneration

We turn next to labour cost data and find first that, although there are a multitude of different wage schemes, nearly all are variants of only three basic methods, namely, dayrate, piecework and premium bonus. These methods are discussed below, the following illustrative data being used to enable comparisons to be made:

Hourly rate	£5 per hour
Agreed rate of production	100 units per hour
Hours worked	8 hours
Production	1,200 units

20. Dayrate (daywork; time rate)

Under the dayrate method the employee is paid on the *basis of time worked*. The formula is:

hours worked x dayrate per hour.

Using our illustrative data the dayrate earnings would be 8 hours x £5 = £40.

21. Piecework (P/W)

Under the piecework method the employee is paid on a *basis of production*. The formula is:

units produced x rate per unit.

Sometimes each unit is given a 'piecework hours' value. This use of 'hours' is particularly applicable where units of production are varied. In these circumstances piecework earnings are the sum of all 'piecework hours' earned multiplied by the rate per 'piecework hour'. It should be appreciated that 'piecework hours' are in the nature of production 'points' and are *not* the same as worked hours.

Our illustrative figures indicate that management is prepared to pay £5 per 100 units produced.

∴ Piecework earnings = 1,200 units at £5 per 100 = £60.

Alternatively, from the P/W hours aspect, the figures show that management allows 0.01 hours per unit.

∴ P/W hrs earned = 0.01 x 1,200 = 12 P/W hours.

∴ Earnings = 12 P/W hrs at £5 per hr = £60.

22. Premium bonus

Under the premium bonus method a time allowance for a job is given, the time taken is recorded and *a bonus is paid on the basis of the time saved*. It is important to remember that this method relates to the *bonus*; the employee's basic pay is normal dayrate. The formula, therefore, for the employee's *total pay* is:

dayrate wage + bonus based on time saved.

If the time taken exceeds the time allowed, there is no time saved. There is, then, no bonus and dayrate only is paid for the time taken.

Example

(Based on our illustrative data)

Hours

Time allowed for 1,200 units = $\dfrac{1,200}{100}$ = 12

Time taken = 8

∴ Time saved = 4

If, now, the particular scheme in operation pays a bonus equal to half the time saved, then the wages calculation will be:

Bonus = $\dfrac{1}{2}$ x 4 x £5 = £10

∴ Total earnings = dayrate wage + bonus = (8 x £5) + £10 = £50.

NOTE: In some schemes the bonus is not calculated on the dayrate but on a separate *bonus rate*. Since there can be a number of dayrates in a department the use of a single bonus rate simplifies bonus calculations and ensures that bonuses paid out are independent of the dayrate of the employee.

---

23. Overtime (O/T) premium

An *overtime premium* (or *penalty*) is an extra amount over and above dayrate earnings paid to an employee who works longer than a normal working day. It is almost invariably calculated as a percentage of the extra hours worked, usually 50 per cent, called 'time and a half', or 100 per cent, called 'double time'.

For instance, if four hours of overtime is worked at time and a half, a total of six hours (4 + 50 per cent of 4) is paid, of which the payment for the *extra two hours* is called the overtime premium.

Labour cost data — Labour time and wage routines

Now we look at how labour time is recorded and wages compiled and paid. Recording labour time falls into two quite distinct categories: first, recording the time the employee is at work (gate timekeeping), and second, recording the time the employee is engaged on different activities.

24. Gate timekeeping

It is very important that the time an employee spends on the factory premises during any week is known. Employees on dayrate are obviously paid for all the hours they are on the premises, but even pieceworkers must record their hours, if only to be correctly paid for overtime. In practice, the actual hours spent on the premises by such workers are also needed to ensure regular and punctual attendance, for it is necessary to keep production not only at a high level but also flowing steadily. Irregular production by one employee, high though his or her overall production may be, leads to stresses at other parts of the production line which result in an unnecessary lowering of efficiency.

The recording of the time when employees enter and leave the premises is known as *gate timekeeping*. Such times are normally recorded on what is termed a *clock card*, albeit modern electronic time-recording may dispense with actual physical cards.

25. Time sheets

The most common method of recording labour times relating to different activities is for each employee to fill in a *time sheet*, i.e. a sheet detailing the employee's activities and the time spent on each. There are two kinds of time sheet, as follows.

(a) *Weekly time sheets.* These record the activities day by day of an employee for a complete week, each employee filling in one sheet a week. The *disadvantage* of weekly sheets is that, since most employees do not start to fill them in until they are to obliged to, i.e. at the very end of the week, the times spent earlier in the week on activities have often been forgotten, and consequently the sheets are inaccurate. Sometimes, in fact, the activity itself is forgotten and appears in the cost records as having been completed without the aid of any labour at all!

(b) *Daily time sheets.* These are similar to weekly time sheets except that they are completed and sent to the cost office each day. These do have the *advantage* that this risk of times being forgotten or manipulated is considerably lessened, but against that is the *disadvantage* that their use leads to a considerable volume of paper — in the case of a small factory with 100 employees, for example, some 2,000 pieces per month.

26. Job cards

Another method of recording labour times is by means of job cards. A job card is a card made out *for each job*, unlike time sheets which are made out for each employee. When an employee works on a job he or she records on the job card the time spent on that job. There are two kinds of job card.

(a) *One card per complete job.* In this method the card travels round with the job and labour times are recorded upon it after each operation. This has the advantage that when the card reaches the cost office all labour times are listed, and the cost clerks have merely to insert the labour rates, multiply and add to obtain the full labour cost. It has, however, a serious disadvantage: until the job is fully completed none of the times are known in the cost office. As some jobs may be weeks being completed, it is virtually impossible to reconcile the booked times with the gate times each week (*see* **27**).

(b) *One card per operation.* This method of recording means that a single job will have a number of job cards, one for each operation. This involves considerable paperwork, but it does enable time bookings to reach the cost office quickly.

> NOTE: Students should appreciate that no matter what method is used, there is always a possibility that in practice the times recorded are unreliable (*see* 1:**25**).

27. Reconciling booked time to gate time

Clearly, the total employee time booked to activities must equal the total gate time paid for (*see* **24**) and it is necessary to insert in the wages routine a check that ensures the two totals do, in fact, agree. As part of this routine each employee must make sure that the total hours he or she books in a period are equal to the total hours he or she is paid for. Such time booked will be within one or a combination of the following categories.

(a) Production jobs, each with its own job number (*see* 4:**2**).
(b) Process work (*see* 6:**1(a)**).
(c) Overhead activities (*see* 3:**1**).
(d) Idle (waiting) time. If employees have no work to do they must record the time they are 'idle' and indicate the reason (e.g. breakdown; waiting for materials, tools or instructions).

28. Wage computations

Once all the timekeeping records have been prepared the wages office can compute the wages of the employees. This computation is recorded on a *payroll* (or *wage sheet*) which lists all the employees and shows the major details relating to their pay.

Preparation of the payroll falls into the following two parts.

(a) *Computation of gross wages.* The gross wage of each employee is computed by reference to the following documents.
> (*i*) Clock cards: these are required, of course, for dayrate and premium bonus workers and also to compute overtime payments to pieceworkers.

(*ii*) Piecework tickets: these are tickets recording each pieceworker's production.

(*iii*) Job cards: These are needed in order to compute premium bonuses, since bonuses depend upon total time spent on individual jobs.

(*iv*) Employee's record card: this is a document recording remuneration details of the individual employee, e.g. rate of pay; holidays taken or outstanding; PAYE code number and earnings summary.

(b) *Computation of net wages.* From each employee's gross pay all the statutory and voluntary deductions are then made and the net pay for each employee is found.

29. Labour turnover

This refers to the rate at which employees who have to be replaced leave the enterprise. It is often closely linked to the level of remuneration — the lower the remuneration the higher the turnover. It can be measured in various ways, the simplest way being by use of the following formula:

$$\text{Labour turnover} = \frac{\text{No. of employees leaving}}{\text{Average no. of employees}}$$

Expenses cost data — General aspects

Finally we look at the cost data relating to expenses which are costs that are neither materials nor labour. They include, therefore, such items as rent, rates, power, royalties, advertising, depreciation, printing, telephones, heating, lighting, subcontracts, machine hire, freight, etc.

30. Direct and indirect expenses

In 1.18(a) a direct cost was defined as a cost that results solely from the existence of whatever is being costed. A *direct expense*, therefore, is an expense that results solely from the existence of whatever is being costed. An *indirect expense* is, of course, any expense that is not a direct expense.

31. Types of cost unit direct expenses

Cost unit direct expenses are relatively few, most expenses being indirect. However, the possibility of an expense being direct should always be kept in mind, and care taken not to form a habit of regarding all expenses as indirect. The following are examples of cost unit direct expenses.

(a) *Royalties*, since royalties charged are based on a rate per unit.
(b) *Plant hire*, if the plant is hired solely in order to manufacture a specific cost unit.
(c) *Subcontract or outside work*, if jobs are sent out for special processing, e.g. plating.
(d) *Salesmen's commissions*, since these are usually based on the sales value of units sold.
(e) *Freight*, if the goods are handled by an outside carrier whose charges can be related to individual units, e.g. rate per unit or per kilogram.

32. Minor direct expenses treated as indirect

In practice there are frequently a number of costs which are direct, but the amounts chargeable, particularly to different cost units, may be both small and difficult to ascertain. To avoid needless petty analysis such costs are usually treated as indirect expenses. Examples of such expenses are: sewing cotton; nails and glue; material-handling labour; and labour time spent on paperwork.

One direct expense which is often far from small but is nevertheless treated as indirect is *power*. The reason for this is that to charge out this cost as a direct expense would involve placing a meter on every machine and in every cost centre, and in the case of cost units, moreover, taking readings in respect of every unit processed. This, of course, is not practical, and so for convenience power is treated as an indirect expense.

33. The borderline between direct and indirect costs

Although we have carefully distinguished between direct and indirect costs (*see* 1:18(a)), in practice it is sometimes difficult to classify an individual cost. For example, a company may accept an order that requires a special tool which is bought and used. If no other work will ever require the use of the tool, then clearly it is a direct cost to the order. If, on the other hand, the tool is to be used on future work the cost cannot really be said to result solely from the existence of the order, since future work would ultimately have given rise to the cost. In this case the cost is indirect, and the current order should only bear at most a proportionate share of it. Sometimes, however, it is very difficult to determine whether or not the tool will be of use in future work, and so it is virtually impossible to say whether or not the cost is truly indirect.

34. Indirect costs that appear as direct costs

Sometimes what appears to be an indisputable direct cost turns out to be wholly or partially indirect. For instance, direct wages were earlier defined as wages paid to employees working on the direct materials (*see* 1.19(b)). Now assume that 200,000 such hours were booked against the first of a group of aircraft. Clearly this particular aircraft would be charged with 200,000 hours' direct wages. However, it could almost certainly be argued that part of this total included time spent clearing up production queries that would never be incurred again and which would, in fact, benefit all future aircraft (e.g. minor blueprint errors). Such labour costs would be akin to design costs, which are, of course, indirect. Thus part of the wages paid for the 200,000 hours is an indirect cost.

A similar case arises when a trainee works on a job. The labour cost here is, in fact, partially a training cost. Rather, then, than regard the whole wage cost as a direct wage cost it would be better to charge the job with the estimated direct wages which would otherwise have been incurred, and then charge the balance of the trainee's wage to training costs.

35. Effect of changes in cost analysis detail

If the cost unit is very large, say a new factory building, then many costs that are normally regarded as indirect become direct, e.g. supervision, site clerical labour, power, etc. However, if the cost accountant decides to cost each *part* of the building separately, such costs become indirect in respect of the individual parts.

Whether a cost is classified as direct or indirect, therefore, depends upon the extent of detail required in the cost analysis.

36. Financial costs traditionally excluded from expenses

It should be noted in passing that according to the traditional concept of cost expenses all financial costs are excluded. These costs include interest (which has already been referred to, *see* 1:17(f)), discounts both received and given, and bank charges.

Expenses cost data — Depreciation and obsolescence

37. Depreciation and obsolescence

Finally, we look at a special category of expenses cost data — depreciation and obsolescence. It is important to distinguish between depreciation and obsolescence. Note, then, that:

(a) *depreciation* is the *loss in value of an asset due to wear and tear and deterioration.* This loss in value is primarily due to wear and tear, but an unused asset will lose value as it slowly deteriorates, while on the other hand;

(b) *obsolescence* is the *loss in value of an asset due to its supersession,* i.e. the loss due to the development of a technically superior asset. There are degrees of obsolescence, since it is rare that the technical improvement is so dramatic that an existing asset is reduced to scrap value only (and needless to say, the major problem with obsolescence is predicting its occurrence).

In view of the fact that obsolescence involves loss of asset value, it is often considered to be a part of depreciation, which is then defined as 'loss of value due to effluxion of time', but as the loss of value is due to quite another reason than wear and tear and the circumstances are so very different, it is considered advisable to keep the two concepts quite separate.

38. Life of an asset

When discussing depreciation, reference is often made to the 'life' of an asset. This is often assumed to be its potential physical life. This is not always true; assets may well be used by the enterprise for a period less than their normal physical life (e.g. when bought for use on a particular contract only). To avoid error, therefore, the life of an asset should be regarded as *the length of time such an asset will be used.* It may be measured in years, production hours or units of production.

39. Revision of asset life.

As time passes the original estimate of asset life may well be seen to be erroneous. In such a case the asset life should be revised and depreciation amounts adjusted accordingly. Although this may well cause some alteration of previously accepted figures, it is better to admit an error and minimize its effects than to ignore the error and allow some future period to carry large and inappropriate losses or gains.

40. Asset cost

The full loss of value that must be accounted for by depreciation and obsolescence charges should be computed as follows:

$$\text{Total loss in value} =$$

$$
\begin{pmatrix}
\text{Asset} \\
\text{purchase} \\
\text{price}
\end{pmatrix}
+
\begin{pmatrix}
\text{Purchase and} \\
\text{installation} \\
\text{charges}
\end{pmatrix}
-
\begin{pmatrix}
\text{Scrap} \\
\text{value}
-
\begin{matrix}
\text{Dismantling} \\
\text{and removal} \\
\text{charges}
\end{matrix}
\end{pmatrix}
$$

This overall charge is normally simply referred to as 'asset cost'.

Example
> *Data:*
>
> | | |
> |---|---|
> | Purchase price | £10,300 |
> | Freight and purchase costs | £80 |
> | Installation costs | £320 |
> | Scrap value | £800 |
> | Disposal costs | £100 |
>
> *Method:*
> Asset cost is, therefore:
> £10,300 + £80 + £320 − £(800 − 100) = £10,000

41. Replacement value

Should depreciation charges for any given period be based on the original purchase cost of an asset or upon current replacement price? The answer to this perennial question hinges upon whether the object of the depreciation charge is to recover the cost of a capital outlay over the life of the asset, or to make an assessment of the true economic worth of the service given by the asset. In financial accounting one may well be primarily concerned with recovering the original cost, and therefore this figure will be used for calculating depreciation, but since the basic object of costing is to provide economic assessments, to adopt original cost in the depreciation calculations may well lead to serious error. In cost accounting, therefore, replacement values should be used.

Progress test 2

Principles

1. What are the functions of a *materials requisition?* **(1)**

2. What is the difference between a *stores record card* and a *bin card?* **(2)**

3. Distinguish between *perpetual inventory* and *continuous stocktaking.* **(3)**

4. What factors must be considered when setting the following stores control quantities: (*a*) *maximum level;* (*b*) *minimum level;* (*c*) *reorder level;* (*d*) *reorder quantity?* **(5)**

5. What are the costs of storage? **(6)**

6. What is meant by the *economic order quantity?* **(9)**

7. What is the EOQ formula and what are its limitations? **(12, 13)**

8. How does the value of the stores balance differ under each of the following issue pricing methods: FIFO; LIFO; weighted average; replacement price; standard price? **(14–18)**

9. What are the three basic methods of labour remuneration and how do they differ? **(20–22)**

10. How is *overtime premium* calculated? **(23)**

11. Why is gate timekeeping necessary? **(24)**

12. What are the relative advantages and disadvantages of (*a*) daily and weekly time sheets? **(25)**; (*b*) a job card per complete job and a job card per operation? **(26)**

13. Why are job cards sometimes needed to compute an employee's gross pay? **(28)**

14. How can labour turnover be measured? **(29)**

15. How can a direct expense be distinguished from an indirect expense? **(30)**

16. In what circumstances is plant hire a direct expense? **(31)**

17. Distinguish between depreciation and obsolescence. **(37)**

18. When considering depreciation charges what is meant by:

(*a*) asset life; **(38)** (*b*) asset cost? **(40)**

Practice

19. Calculate three normal control levels, which may be used in stock control systems, from the following information for a particular raw material:

Economic order quantity, 12,000 kilos
Lead time, 10 to 14 working days
Average usage, 600 kilos per day
Minimum usage, 400 kilos per day
Maximum usage, 800 kilos per day

(ACCA Dec 88. Part question)

20. From the following data compute the value of the 20 units closing stock under (*a*) the FIFO method, (*b*) the LIFO method, and (*c*) the weighted average method.

Receipts: 1/6/. . .   40 units at £25 each;
8/6/. . .   40 units at £30 each.
Issues: 2/6/. . .   30 units;
9/6/. . .   30 units.

21. A company uses 60,000 electronic units a year, each of which costs £10, although when orders of 14,000 units or more are placed a quantity discount of 2 per cent is given. If it costs the company £105 to place a purchase order for such units and the annual storage cost is 25 per cent of the value held, what is the economic order quantity?

22. Jobs are issued to operative X, to make 189 units, and to operative Y, to make 204 units, for which a time allowance of 20 standard minutes and 15 standard minutes per unit respectively is credited. For every hour saved, bonus is paid at 50 per cent of the base rate, which is £4 per hour for both employees. The basic working week is 42 hours. Hours in excess are paid at time and a half.

X completes her units in 45 hours and Y completes his in 39 hours (but works a full week). Because of defective material, six of X's units and four of Y's units are subsequently scrapped although all units produced are paid for.

You are required to calculate for each of X and Y:

(a) the amount of bonus payable;
(b) the total gross wage payable;
(c) the wages cost per good unit made.

(CIMA, adapted)

3
Absorption costing: overheads

Absorption costing is the traditional form of cost ascertainment. It is based on the principle that costs should be charged to (or 'absorbed into') whatever is being costed — be it cost unit, cost centre or enterprise function — on the basis of the benefit received from those costs. In this context direct costs give little in the way of theoretical difficulty since anything which gives sole rise to a cost must be the sole beneficiary. However, the indirect costs do create problems of analysis and in this chapter the traditional manner of solving these problems, by an overhead analysis and the creation of overhead absorption rates, is explained.

First, though, the term 'overheads' must be defined.

1. Overheads

Overheads are, broadly speaking, all those costs that are not charged directly to cost units. They equate, then, very closely to indirect costs — and, indeed, the CIMA Terminology defines overhead costs as being synonymous with 'indirect costs'. However, as we saw in 2:**32–35**, what is and what is not an indirect cost, i.e. an overhead, depends to some extent on the accountant, and past practice has usually limited direct cost unit charges to production costs involving materials booked on a material requisition, wages booked on a time sheet or job card, and expenses booked on a supplier's invoice, or other obvious source of direct charging — all other costs being regarded as overheads.

Allocation and apportionment of overheads

Since overheads are not charged direct to cost units, they must be shared equitably among them. Needless to say, cost accountants often have different opinions on what is equitable. Such differences of opinion are permissible, providing they are based on an intelligent understanding of the circumstances.

In this section the manner in which overheads are charged to cost units on the basis of benefit is explained.

2.   Summary of overhead charging procedure
The overhead charging procedure involves the following steps.

(a) Abstracting all the overheads (*see* **3**).
(b) Allotting overheads to cost centres (overhead analysis) (*see* **4–17**):
　　(*i*)   allocation of overheads to cost centres;
　　(*ii*) apportionment of overheads to cost centres;
　　(*iii*) allocation and apportionment of service cost centres' costs to production cost centres.
(c) Absorbing overheads into cost units (overhead absorption) (*see* **18–23**):
　　(*i*) computation of overhead absorption rates;
　　(*ii*) application of overhead absorption rates to cost units.

3.   Abstracting overheads
The first step is the abstraction of all the overheads of the enterprise. Traditionally these are divided into production, selling, distribution and administration overheads. Only the production overheads, however, then move on to the more elaborate overhead analysis and absorption routine, the other overheads being dealt with more simply, as indicated in **23**.

4.   Overhead analysis
Once the production overheads have been abstracted the next step is the preparation of an overhead analysis which allots these overheads to cost centres. It is essentially an analysis sheet listing the overheads vertically and the cost centres horizontally.

A complete worked example of an overhead analysis is shown in Fig. 3.1. Here the overheads are seen listed on the left-hand side together with the total amounts. In this example three service cost centres (Stores, Maintenance, and Production Control and Inspection) and two production cost centres (departments X and Y) have been assumed for the purpose of illustration.

When compiling an overhead analysis there are two ways of allotting overheads to cost centres, *allocation* and *apportionment*.

5. Allocation

This is allotting to a cost centre those overheads that result *solely* from the existence of that cost centre. (Note the similarity to the 'direct cost' definition, i.e. if the overhead is a direct cost to the cost centre it is allocated.)

Overheads should always be allocated if possible. However, allocation can be made only if the exact amount incurred is known without any need to have recourse to any form of sharing. Where the amount is not known in this unambiguous manner, the total amount must be *apportioned*.

In Fig. 3.1 only indirect materials and labour have been allocated (from the materials and wages analyses respectively, *see* 5:**19, 22**). If, however, a plant register is available then depreciation and possibly machine insurance can also be allocated.

6. Apportionment

This is allotting to a cost centre a fair *share* of an overhead on the basis of the *estimated benefit* received by the cost centre in respect of the facilities provided by the overhead.

If an overhead cannot be allocated to cost centres then it must be apportioned. This involves finding some basis, called the *basis of apportionment*, that will enable the overhead to be equitably shared between cost centres.

7. Bases of apportionment

The following are the most usual bases of apportionment and the overheads using them:

| Overheads | Total £ | Apportionment | | |
		Basis	Units	Rate per unit
Rent	8,000	Area	80	£100
Indirect materials	1,740	*Allocation*		
Indirect labour	54,630	*Allocation*		
Factory admin o'h'ds.	21,840	No. of employees	546	£40
Machine depreciation	4,400	Value £000s	400	£11
Power	5,500	kWh 000s	550	£10
Heat and light	800	Area	80	£10
Machine insurance	400	Value £000s	400	£1
Extraction (fumes) plant	1,200	No. of extraction points	40	£30
Total	98,510			
Service Depts.				
Stores		No. of material requisitions	1,750	£2
Maintenance		*Allocation*		
		Allocated wages	£6,300	£0.50 per £
Production Control and Inspection		No. of employees	500	£37
Total	98,510			

Figure 3.1   *Overhead analysis*

The italicized figures are allocations as opposed to
apportionments. Total of X and Y = £40,280 + £58,230 = £98,510,
i.e. the grand total of all overheads. This cross-check
proves the arithmetical accuracy of the analysis

Stores		Maintenance		Production Control and Inspection		Production Dept. X		Production Dept. Y	
Units	£	Units	£	Units	£	Units	£	Units	£
3	300	4	400	1	100	30	3,000	42	4,200
	110		*250*		*440*		*310*		*630*
	2,870		*6,710*		*16,600*		*10,400*		*18,050*
4	160	12	480	30	1,200	200	8,000	300	12,000
—	—	80	880	—	—	200	2,200	120	1,320
—	—	20	200	—	—	320	3,200	210	2,100
3	30	4	40	1	10	30	300	42	420
—	—	80	80	—	—	200	200	120	120
1	30	2	60	—	—	14	420	23	690
	3,500		9,100		18,350		28,030		39,530
	-3,500	175	350	—	—	1,000	2,000	575	1,150
	Nil		9,450		18,350		30,030		40,680
			-6,300		*100*		*1,900*		*4,300*
			-3,150	100	50	1,900	950	4,300	2,150
			Nil		18,500		32,880		47,130
					—18,500	200	7,400	300	11,100
					Nil		£40,280		£58,230

Figure 3.1 (cont'd)

Basis	Overheads apportioned on this basis
Area	Rent, rates, heat and light, building depreciation
Number of employees	Personnel office, welfare, administration, canteen, supervision, time and wages offices, safety
Book value	Depreciation, insurance
Weight of materials	Materials handling, storekeeping
Space (volume)	Heating, building depreciation
Number of radiators	Heating
Direct (to cost centres) maintenance costs	Indirect maintenance costs
Technical estimate	Power, steam consumption

NOTE: A *technical estimate* is an estimate of usage made by a technically qualified person.

8.   Choice of basis

Students will notice that some overheads in the above list can be apportioned on more than one basis. The choice of an appropriate basis is really a matter of judgement; it is necessary to ask oneself what factor is most related to the benefit received by the cost centres. For example, 'number of employees' is a good basis for apportioning time and wages office overheads, since the more employees there are in a cost centre the larger the proportional benefit received in respect of the clerical salaries and stationery necessary to arrange their wage payments.

The choice of basis, therefore, is left to the judgement of the accountant — who is not compelled, of course, to select one of the more conventional bases. If an unusual basis is more suitable, it should be chosen and, indeed, the bases that can be devised are limited only by human ingenuity.

9.   Illustrative example

Apportionments clearly depend on factory statistics, and in order that the student may be able to work through the overhead analysis given in Fig. 3.1 thoroughly, the statistics on which that analysis is based are given below.

Factory statistics

	Total	Stores	Main-tenance	Prodn. Control & Insp.	Prodn. X	Prodn. Y
Area — sq. ft. (000s)	80	3	4	1	30	42
Indirect material issues	£1,740	£110	£250	£440	£310	£630
Indirect labour bookings	£54,630	£2,870	£6,710	£16,600	£10,400	£18,050
Employees	546	4	12	30	200	300
Machine values	£400,000	—	£80,000	—	£200,000	£120,000
Estimated kWh (000s)	550	—	20	—	320	210
Fume extraction points	40	1	2	—	14	23
Materials requisitions issued	1,750	—	175	—	1,000	575
Maintenance labour bookings	£6,300	—	—	£100	£1,900	£4,300

10. Service cost centre costs

Once the overheads have been analysed to cost centres and totalled, the next step is to charge service cost centre costs to production cost centres. This is necessary since our ultimate object is to charge overheads to cost units, and as no cost units pass through service departments the costs of such departments are, in effect, themselves overheads and so must be charged to those cost centres where there are cost units, i.e. the production cost centres.

The method of analysing service cost centre costs is similar to that of the main analysis; where possible costs are allocated (e.g. wages of maintenance workers actually engaged in production cost centres), otherwise they are apportioned on some basis that reflects the work done by the service department for each of the production cost centres.

11. Service department charges illustrated

In Fig. 3.1 the first service department that must be charged out is Stores. A typical basis of apportionment for Stores, materials requisitions, has been selected and the £3,500 Stores cost charged in proportion to the number of requisitions used by each of the other cost centres.

In the case of Maintenance, £6,300 can be immediately allocated from the maintenance labour bookings. The balance of £3,150 must be apportioned on some basis that reflects the work done by Maintenance for other centres. Clearly, the maintenance labour bookings provide an excellent measure of work done by this centre, and the £3,150 is charged in proportion to the wages previously allocated. Since this allocation totalled £6,300, it can be seen that for every £1 maintenance wages allocated there must be £0.50 charged for apportionment of the remaining maintenance costs.

Finally, Production Control and Inspection overheads must be apportioned. A reasonable measure of the work done by this centre is the number of employees whose work is controlled and inspected. Since this centre only does work for the two production centres, the total overhead of £18,500 must be shared on the basis of the total of 500 employees engaged in the two production centres. This gives a charge of £37 per employee (£18,500 divided by 500).

12. Services working for other service departments

If a service department carries out work for a second service department, then clearly part of the former's costs are allotted to the latter department. Care should be taken, therefore, not to analyse the second department's costs until it has first been allotted its charges from all the other departments whose services it called upon (e.g. in Fig. 3.1 the Maintenance department is allotted its £350 share of Stores costs before its own charges are allotted).

13. Analysis by computer

Clearly, this form of analysis is ideal for a computer method of solution and in Fig. 3.2 a typical program is shown. After asking for the number of overheads and departments (instruction 20), the computer calls on the user to enter for each overhead the total overhead cost (instruction 25) and then the amount *allocated* to each department (instruction 26) and the number of base units applicable to each department where some apportionment is needed (instruction 27). Once entries have been made in respect of all the overheads, the computer automatically apportions the non-allocated costs for each overhead pro rata to the entered base figures, and adds up each department's costs — these totals being printed out department by department (instruction 30).

```
20   INPUT "No. of overhead costs to be allocated";n1: INPUT "No. of
     departments to be charged";n2
24   PRINT:PRINT "Total period costs to be allocated:"
25   FOR j=1 TO n1: PRINT:PRINT "Ohd";j;:INPUT "Total cost";c: t=0
26   FOR k=1 TO n2: a=0: PRINT "Department";k;: INPUT "allocation";a:
     d(k)=d(k)+a: c=c-a
27   a=0: INPUT "      Apportionment units";a: au(k)=a: t=t+a: NEXT k
28   FOR k=1 TO n2: IF t>0 THEN d(k)=d(k)+c*au(k)/t
29   NEXT k,j
30   PRINT "allotments:": FOR j=1 TO n2: PRINT "Department";j';" ";d(j):
     NEXT
```

Figure 3.2 *Overhead analysis computer program*

Reciprocal services

A problem arises when two or more service departments do work for each other. Thus, if the departments are A and B, then until B's charge to A is known, A cannot apportion any cost to B. But similarly until A's charge to B is known, B cannot apportion that initial cost to A.

There are three methods of breaking this vicious circle which are explained in **14–16** below. Worked examples are given using the following basic data.

The overhead analysis prior to allotment of service cost centre costs shows the following overhead charges:

Service department A	£3,200
Service department B	£4,100
Production department 1	£8,000
Production department 2	£6,000

These overheads are to be apportioned as follows:

	To A	To B	To Production 1	To Production 2
Dept. A's costs	—	10%	50%	40%
Dept. B's costs	50%	—	10%	40%

14. Continuous allotments

In this method the opening costs of the departments are apportioned according to the apportionment percentages. Then the newly apportioned costs are re-apportioned — again according to the apportionment percentages. And this step of re-apportionment is then continuously repeated until the apportionment figures become insignificant.

NOTE: By deferring apportionments to production cost centres until after the overall cost for each service department has been found, some saving of time can be made. This has been done in the example below.

Example

Step	Dept. A £	Dept. B £	Dept. 1 £	Dept. 2 £
(All amounts rounded to the nearest £)				
Opening centre costs	3,200	4,100	Ignore initially	
Apportionments (10% and 50%)	2,050	320		
Re-apportionments	160	205		
Re-apportionments	102	16		
Re-apportionments	8	10		
Re-apportionments	5	1		
Re-apportionments	1	0		
TOTAL CENTRE COSTS	5,526	4,652		
Final apportionments:				
Original centre cost	3,200	4,100	8,000	6,000
Apportionment A	− 5,526	552	2,763	2,211
Apportionment B	2,326	− 4,652	465	1,861
TOTAL	*Nil*	*Nil*	£11,228	£10,072

15. Algebraic method

Here the *total* service costs of each department are expressed as algebraic equations. The unknowns can then be found either by solving the simultaneous equations or by substitution, whichever is preferred.

Example ───

Let a = *total* overhead cost of Dept. A after apportionment
from B.

Let b = *total* overhead cost of Dept. B after apportionment
from A.

so $a = 3,200 + 0.5b$

$\therefore \quad a - 0.5b = 3,200$ . . . . . . (1)

and $b = 4,100 + 0.1a$

$\therefore \quad b - 0.1a = 4,100$ . . . . . . (2)

Solving: (1) x 2: $\quad 2.0a - b = \cdot 6,400$
(2) x 1: $\underline{-0.1a + b = 4,100}$

Add: $\quad 1.9a \quad\quad = 10,500$

$\therefore \quad a \quad\quad = £5,526$ (to nearest £).

Substituting in (2): $b - 0.1 \times 5,526 = 4,100$

$\therefore \quad b = 4,100 + 553 = £4,653$ (to nearest £).

(Alternatively, using substitution, $a = 3,200 + 0.5b = 3,200 + 0.5 \times (4,100 + 0.1a)$, and solve for a.)

Knowing these amounts, the formal apportionment can be made as in the previous method of continuous allotment.

16. Specified order of closing

The order of closing departments is carefully determined so that the services that do the most work for other service departments are closed first. The departments are then closed off in this order in the normal manner, and *no return charges from other service departments are made.* Although this method gives a theoretically inaccurate result, it has the advantage of ease. Moreover, the word 'accuracy' has little meaning within the context of apportionment so objections under this head tend to be pedantic.

Example ───

B, apportioning 50 per cent of its cost to A, affects A more than A,

apportioning only 10 per cent of its costs to B, affects B. Therefore, B is
closed off first, and A's apportionment to B omitted.

Step	Dept. A	Dept. B	Dept. 1	Dept. 2
Opening centre costs	3,200	4,100	8,000	6,000
Apportion B	2,050	–4,100	410	1,640
Apportion A	–5,250	—	2,917 *	2,333 *
Total	Nil	Nil	£11,327†	£9,973†

*Since the 10 per cent apportionment to B is omitted, Depts. 1 and 2
must share all A's costs in the ratio of 50:40.

†Note that the relative error in this instance is only 1 per cent.

17. Reciprocal services computations and the computer

Once again the nature of the problem calls for a computer
solution — though in this instance it must be appreciated that the
best approach is not necessarily the most obvious one for at first
glance it would seem sensible to hand over to the computer the
complexities of the algebraic method. But in actual fact the method
of continuous allotment is the best. True, in an extensive problem
there will be a great deal of allotting but computers love this kind
of work. And it is much easier to write a continuous allotment
program than an algebraic program.

Such a program is, then, reproduced in Fig. 3.3. In that
program n is the number of service departments and the d array
holds the total cost of each service department. The s array holds
the step amounts since after each allotment step of all the
departments there will, of course, be new amounts which have
been apportioned to departments and require re-apportioning.
And the c array holds the cumulative re-apportioned costs for each
department as the step proceeds (the final c amounts of one step
being the s amounts of the next step).

Briefly, the data is entered in instructions 20–50. In 60, f, a
flag which signals if any apportionments have been made during
the allotment step, is set at 0 (f = 0 signalling no apportionments made; f = 1 signalling at least one apportionment made)
and, in respect of each department from which an apportionment
is to be made and each department to which an apportionment is
to be made, the apportionment figure t is computed. If this figure

```
20   INPUT "No. of service departments";n: PRINT
25   DIM d(n),s(n),c(n),a(n,n): PRINT "Total period costs to be allocated:"
26   FOR j=1 TO n: PRINT "Department";j;:INPUT d(j): NEXT: PRINT
40   PRINT "% apportionment of costs:": FOR j=1 TO n: FOR k=1 TO n:
     IF j=k THEN 49
42   PRINT "Department";j;"to department";k;: INPUT z: a(j,k)=z/100
49   NEXT k,j: PRINT
50   FOR j=1 TO n: s(j)=d(j): NEXT j
60   f=0: FOR j=1 TO n: FOR k=1 TO n: t=s(j)*a(j,k): IF t < 0.0001
     THEN 68
62   c(k)=c(k)+t: f=1
68   NEXT k,j
69   FOR j=1 TO n: d(j)=d(j)+c(j): s(j)=c(j): c(j)=0: NEXT j: IF f=1 THEN
     60
70   PRINT: PRINT "Total service department costs after reciprocal
     apportionments:"
71   FOR j=1 TO n: PRINT "  Service department";j;"=";d(j): NEXT j
```

Figure 3.3 *Computer program for reciprocal service computations*

is less than 1/100th of a penny the apportionment is ignored (without this the computer would stay in the 60–68 loop forever). If it is more, the apportionment is made to the receiving department and f is set at 1 (62). At the end of this step (69) the departments' costs are increased by the c amounts, the new amounts for re-apportionment entered in the s array, the c array initialized and, if f is 1, a new step taken. When the whole step has been completed with no apportionments made the computer moves to instructions 70 and 71 where, for each service department, the overall totals after the reciprocal charges have been made are printed out.

Absorption of overheads

Once overheads have been analysed to production cost centres they can be charged to cost units. In essence, the procedure is to take each centre and *share its overheads among all the cost units passing through that centre*. This procedure is clearly akin to apportionment, only in this case cost units are charged and not cost centres. The technical term for this is *absorption*, and can be defined as the *charging of overheads to cost units*.

As we saw in **2(c)**, there are two steps to be taken: first, computing an overhead absorption rate, and second, the application of this rate to cost units.

18. Computation of overhead absorption rate

To compute the overhead rate some basis of absorption is first selected in a similar manner to the selection of an apportionment base (*see* **7, 8**). The overhead rate is then found by means of the following formula:

$$\text{Overhead absorption rate} = \frac{\text{Total cost centre overheads}}{\text{Total units of base used}}$$

Since there are a number of different bases that can be selected for absorption, in practice one comes across a number of different kinds of rates. The six most common rates have been listed below, together with their individual formulae and an illustrative

	Overhead rate	Cost centre 101	
Title	*Formula*	*Statistics*	*Rate*
Units of output	$\dfrac{\text{TCCO}^*}{\text{Units of output}}$	200 units	$\dfrac{£4,000}{200} = £20$ per unit
Direct labour hr	$\dfrac{\text{TCCO}}{\text{Total direct labour hours worked o.a.p.}\dagger}$	500 direct labour hrs	$\dfrac{£4,000}{500} = £8$ per hr
Machine hr	$\dfrac{\text{TCCO}}{\text{Total machine hours engaged o.a.p.}}$	1,600 machine hrs	$\dfrac{£4,000}{1,600} = £2.50$ per hr
Wages percentage	$\dfrac{\text{TCCO}}{\text{Total direct wages paid o.a.p.}}$	£4,000 direct wages	$\dfrac{£4,000}{£4,000} = 100\%$
Materials cost percentage	$\dfrac{\text{TCCO}}{\text{Total direct material used o.a.p.}}$	£12,000 direct materials	$\dfrac{£4,000}{£12,000} = 33\tfrac{1}{3}\%$
Prime cost percentage	$\dfrac{\text{TCCO}}{\text{Total prime cost incurred o.a.p.}}$	£16,000 prime cost	$\dfrac{£4,000}{£16,000} = 25\%$

*TCCO = Total cost centre overhead. (TCCO charged to cost centre 101 in overhead analysis = £4,000.)

†o.a.p. = on all production, i.e. in cost centre 101 production.

example of the computation of the rates for a typical cost centre, 101, which, it is assumed, has been allotted £4,000 overheads and has experienced the figures given in the *Statistics* column.

It is important to appreciate that only *one* rate will be computed for any single group of overheads. The table above shows the rates from which a selection can be made; it is not meant to suggest that all the rates given are to be computed simultaneously.

19. Applications of rate to cost units

Overheads are charged to individual cost units by simply multiplying the overhead rate by the units of the base that apply to each cost unit, i.e. the formula is:

Cost unit overheads = Overhead rate x Units of base in cost unit.

Example _____

Apply the different overhead rates computed in **18** to a cost unit, Job X, passing through 101 and having the following bookings:

	£	
Direct labour hours (which	3 hrs at £4.00 per hr	12.00
included 2 hrs' work	1 hr at £4.80 per hr	4.80
on a machine)	4 hrs	16.80
Direct materials		24.00
	Prime cost	£40.80

Solution _____

	OVERHEAD RATE		JOB X	
Title	*Rate*	*Units of base*	*Overhead charged £*
Units of output	£20 per unit	1 unit*	20.00
Direct labour hour	£8 per hr	4 hours	32.00
Machine hour	£2.50 per hr	2 hours	5.00
Wages percentage	100%	£16.80 wages	16.80
Materials cost percentage	33 1/3%	£24.00 materials	8.00
Prime cost percentage	25%	£40.80 prime cost	10.20

*In the case of this particular rate it must be assumed that all the cost units are identical units.

20. Choice of overhead rate

As with apportionment, sound absorption hinges on finding an appropriate basis for sharing the overheads. In the case of most overheads, *time* is the factor associated with cost units that is most closely related to overhead costs. It is logical, therefore, to charge those products that utilize factory facilities for the longest time with the largest share of the overheads, and so overheads are best absorbed on a time basis, i.e. using a direct labour hour, machine hour or wages percentage rate.

The following points should be noted in connection with the six methods of absorption.

(a) *Units of output.* This is the best of the rates, but unfortunately can be used only when all the cost units passing through the cost centre are identical.

(b) *Direct labour hour.* This is a good all-round rate. Students should use this rate in their answers unless there is a good reason for selecting a different one.

(c) *Machine hour.* When production is carried out on machines this rate is appropriate. Beware, however, of using this rate simply because most of the production is put on machines; using a machine hour rate in such circumstances would mean that any *non-machine* production would be charged no overheads at all! Indeed, where this rate is adopted it should be used to absorb only what are essentially the machine overheads — a second rate being applied in parallel to absorb all the other production overheads.

(d) *Wages percentage rate.* This rate will give identical results to the direct labour hour rate if there is only one rate of pay in the cost centre. If otherwise, then when times are the same overheads charged to cost units worked on by the more highly-paid employees will exceed those charged to units worked on by the more lower-rated employees. This is not strictly logical (since the overheads incurred per hour are the same whether the employee is highly paid or otherwise), but as this method is clerically simpler than the direct labour hour method (for which direct labour hours must be separately recorded and added on job cards), it is a good practical rate.

(e) *Materials cost percentage rate.* Overheads are in no way related to the cost of material used. A large, expensive piece of material could be on the factory floor for only a few minutes, utilizing virtually nothing of the factory facilities, and yet it would be given an overhead charge proportional to its material cost. This is clearly unsatisfactory, and students should almost always avoid its use.

(f) *Prime cost percentage rate.* Again overheads are not often related to prime cost, and so usually this rate is quite unsuitable. One notable exception to this, however, arises with certain kinds of contract work where the rate is acceptable (*see* 4:**10(d)**).

21. Predetermined overhead rates

In order to enable costings to be made from the first day of operations, overhead rates are almost invariably calculated on a basis of future overheads and production. Such rates are called *predetermined overhead rates,* and the use of such rates gives rise to the following points:

(a) *Calculation of predetermined overhead rates.* These rates are calculated from the following formula:

$$\text{Predetermined overhead rate} = \frac{\text{Budgeted overheads for the next year}}{\text{Budgeted units of base for the next year}}$$

(b) *Under- and over-absorption of overheads.* It is most unlikely that the actual overheads and units of base will exactly equal the budgeted amounts. Consequently, using predetermined overhead rates will result in actual production being charged somewhat more or less than the actual overheads incurred. The difference between the overheads charged and the overheads incurred is called the *under-* (or *over-*) *absorption of overheads.*

For example, assume:

Budgeted overheads	£15,000
Actual overheads	£15,160
Budgeted direct labour hours	10,000
Actual direct labour hours	9,820

$$\text{Predetermined overhead rate} = \frac{£15,000}{10,000} = £1.50 \text{ per hour.}$$

Therefore, since 9,820 hours were worked, a total of £1.50 x 9,820 = £14,730 would be charged to production. However, actual overheads were £15,160.

∴ Under-absorption of overheads = £15,160 – £14,730 = £430.

In other words, £430 of the overheads incurred were not charged to production.

(c) *Disposal of under- and over-absorbed overheads.* Monthly under-or over-absorption can be disposed of in one of two ways, as follows.

> (*i*) If seasonal, transfer to a suspense account since the under-absorption in the slack months should in all fairness be carried by the over-absorption in the busy months. Over the year under- and over-absorptions should, of course, virtually cancel out. At the year end any balance should be transferred to the annual profit and loss account.
>
> (*ii*) If not seasonal, transfer at once to monthly profit and loss account.

In *no* circumstances should any under- (or over-) absorption be included in the overhead of following periods (a basic costing principle, *see* 1:17(e)).

NOTE: Sometimes 'u/o' is used as an abbreviation for 'under or over'.

22. Blanket overhead rate
This is a single overhead rate computed for the entire factory, i.e. total factory overheads divided by total units of base throughout the factory.

Blanket overhead rates should never be used (other than in output costing, *see* 4:4), since cost units passing through centres with high overhead costs (e.g. machine shops) will be undercosted and those passing through low overhead centres (e.g. an assembly department) will be overcosted.

23. Absorption of non-production overheads
Traditionally non-production overheads have been treated in a very cursory manner — indeed early cost accountants would probably have included them among the production overheads were it not for the fact that this would have resulted in cost units being charged with selling and distribution overheads *before* the

units had incurred any such costs. This, of course, would be a serious breach of one of the fundamental costing principles (*see* 1:17(b)). In the event the following absorption methods were usually adopted.

(a) *Selling overheads*. Since the benefit received by a cost unit in respect of selling overheads is usually in proportion to the value of the unit, these overheads were usually absorbed as a percentage of the cost unit value, the overhead rate formula being:

$$\begin{matrix} \text{Selling overhead rate} \\ \text{(factory cost percentage)} \end{matrix} = \frac{\text{Total selling overheads}}{\text{Total factory cost of all sales}} \times 100$$

By applying this percentage to the factory cost of individual cost units, the selling overheads applicable to each unit were found.

(b) *Distribution overheads*. A distribution department is very similar to a production department from the point of view of costs. Thus, there are direct materials (packing cases, wood-wool), direct labour (packers, van drivers), direct expenses (freight), departmental overheads (supervision, heat and light) and 'machines' (vans, lorries, packing machines). It followed therefore that it could be treated in a similar way to a production department, with material requisitions, time sheets and overheads absorbed by means of overhead absorption rates. The overhead rates for vans and lorries would be based on miles, tonnes or hours, or a combination of these (*see* 4:5).

(c) *Administration overheads*. These overheads are so divorced from both production and selling that any basis of absorption must necessarily be very artificial. In practice the overheads were often apportioned between production, selling and distribution prior to preparing any other overhead analyses on a basis of common sense — and in the overhead analyses further apportioned on the basis of the number of employees.

24. Activity based costing (ABC)
In this chapter the conventional view that overheads should be apportioned on the basis of *benefit received* (*see* 6) has been adopted. However, an alternative basis is *the factor that has caused the cost* — i.e. the more an 'activity' (function, cost centre or cost unit) causes an overhead, the more of the overhead cost should be

charged to it. In other words, if activity X causes 50 per cent of overhead Y then activity X should be charged 50 per cent of the overhead cost of Y. This approach to overhead apportionment is called *activity based costing* (ABC) and the activities that cause the overheads are called *cost-drivers*. (Note that while the CIMA terminology defines 'cost-driver' as 'an activity which generates cost' and as being particularly related to activity based costing, the technique of ABC is defined as the attribution of costs 'on the basis of benefit received').

Without question, ABC is more consistent with modern views on cost charging than the conventional benefit-based approach. Since manufactured units are wholly charged with the direct materials they use, then activities should be charged with the costs they generate, regardless of benefit. Thus, while everyone may benefit by having a medical emergency service in a factory (the cost of which conventionally would be apportioned on the basis of number of employees), if the service is provided only because one department is involved in high-risk work, then the whole of its cost will be charged to that department. Similarly, computers bought simply to record data for the Accounts department should be wholly charged to that department despite the fact that the Personnel department may use some of its spare capacity to produce labour statistics. The following points should be noted in connection with ABC.

(a) The apportionment procedure involves collating all costs relating to the overhead to be apportioned by the identified cost-driver (e.g. if 'Inspection' were the overhead, then all the costs of inspection would be collated) and these costs then apportioned to activities pro rata to the number of cost-driver units each activity incurs (e.g. if inspection costs correlated highly with the number of components incorporated into the cost units inspected, the charge to a given unit would be pro rata to the number of components it incorporated).

(b) The technique helps to ensure that activity costs better reflect their true costs. Thus, if sales orders varied greatly in value while the cost of processing such an order was relatively constant, an equal charge per order for processing would better reflect the true cost incurred than a conventional selling overhead percentage charge based on sales value (with the result that the lower profitability of a small order relative to a large order would be highlighted).

(c) Knowing more realistically the potential cost of a newly-envisaged product helps the Design department to produce a more economic design.

(d) The efficiency of overhead activities can be better monitored by looking at the cost per unit of the cost driver than the more conventional cost per direct labour hour. (Thus, if direct labour hours doubled as a result of increased staff, then the cost per hour of, say, factory lighting maintenance could easily halve without any improved efficiency at all. Conversely, a reduction per metered hour of lighting — the probable cost-driver — would more accurately reflect improved efficiency.)

To summarize, ABC embodies the principle of charging a cost as nearly as is possible to the activity that generates it. The difficult part, of course, is identifying the cost-driver — a problem that calls for its solution for a sound understanding of the behaviour of costs (*see* Chapter 8).

25. Objections to overhead absorption

Students should be warned that nowadays many cost accountants regard overhead absorption as a discredited technique. Their objections are based on the fact that many overheads, such as rent and audit fees, are completely independent of whether an individual cost unit (or even a product line) is made or not. The sharing out of such overheads among cost units does not therefore provide any useful information to management. Moreover, since such apportionments are very often arbitrary, different cost accountants often arrive at different cost unit costs. Such procedures hardly form satisfactory bases for making intelligent management decisions.

Progress test 3

Principles

1. What are overheads? **(1)**

2. List the steps in the overhead charging procedure. **(2)**

3. Distinguish between allocation and apportionment. **(5, 6)**

4. Which overheads would usually be apportioned on the basis of the number of employees? **(7, 23(c))**

5. Name three ways of apportioning service costs to reciprocal services. **(14–16)**

6. What are the main absorption rates and which are the most satisfactory? **(18, 20)**

7. How should under- and over-absorbed overheads be disposed of? **(21(c))**

8. What is a blanket overhead rate? **(22)**

9. What is *activity based costing*? **(24)**

Practice

10. XY Ltd. operates a factory whose quarterly budget is given below:

	£	£	£	£
Selling value of goods produced				6,800,000
Production cost:				
Direct wages		1,200,000		
Direct material cost		4,200,000	5,400,000	
Indirect wages and supervision:				
Machine department X	38,000			
Machine department Y	43,500			
Assembly department	41,250			
Packing department	23,000			
Maintenance department	22,500			
Stores	11,500			
General department	24,250			
		204,000		

	£	£	£	£
Maintenance wages:				
Machine department X	10,000			
Machine department Y	20,000			
Assembly department	5,000			
Packing department	5,000			
Maintenance department	5,000			
Stores	2,500			
General department	4,500			
		52,000		
Indirect materials:				
Machine department X	27,000			
Machine department Y	36,000			
Assembly department	18,000			
Packing department	27,000			
Maintenance department	9,000			
Stores	6,750			
General department	· 4,000			
		127,750		
Power		60,000		
Rent and rates		80,000		
Lighting and heating		20,000		
Insurance		10,000		
Depreciation (5%)		200,000		
			753,750	
				6,153,750
	Budgeted factory profit			646,250

The following operating information is also available:

Department	Effective HP	Area occupied (sq. ft.)	Book value: machinery and equipment £	Direct labour Hours	Direct labour Cost £	Machine hours
Productive:						
Machine X	40	10,000	1,200,000	100,000	409,000	50,000
Machine Y	40	7,500	1,600,000	75,000	321,000	60,000
Assembly	—	15,000	200,000	75,000	293,000	
Packing	10	7,500	200,000	50,000	177,000	
Service:						
Maintenance	10	3,000	600,000			
Stores	—	5,000	100,000			
General	—	2,000	100,000			
		50,000	4,000,000			

The general department consists of the factory manager, and general clerical and wages personnel.

(a) **Prepare a quarterly overhead analysis sheet for the departments of the factory. (Show clearly the bases of apportionment.)**
(b) **Calculate hourly cost rates of overhead absorption for each productive department. Ignore the apportionment of service department costs among service departments.**

(CIMA, adapted)

11. A company produces several products which pass through the two production departments in its factory. These two departments are concerned with filling and sealing operations. There are two service departments, maintenance and canteen, in the factory.

Predetermined overhead absorption rates, based on direct labour hours, are established for the two production departments. The budgeted expenditure for these departments for the period just ended, including the apportionment of service department overheads, was £110,040 for filling, and £53,300 for sealing. Budgeted direct labour hours were 13,100 for filling and 10,250 for sealing.

Service department overheads are apportioned as follows:

Maintenance	— Filling	70%
	— Sealing	27%
	— Canteen	3%
Canteen	— Filling	60%
	— Sealing	32%
	— Maintenance	8%

During the period just ended, actual overhead costs and activity were as follows:

	£	Direct labour hours
Filling	74,260	12,820
Sealing	38,115	10,075
Maintenance	25,050	
Canteen	24,375	

Required:

Calculate the overheads absorbed in the period and the extent of the under/over absorption in each of the two production departments.

(ACCA June 90, Part question)

4

Absorption costing: costing methods

Although the *principles* of cost ascertainment remain unchanged in the different production circumstances, the actual application does depend very much upon these circumstances. The various applications can be said to constitute different costing *methods* and these will be described in this chapter (*see* Fig. 4.1).

1. Specific order costing
Specific order costing is the application of the principles of cost ascertainment in situations where *all the cost units are separately identified and costed individually* (or 'where the work consists of separate contracts, jobs or batches', CIMA terminology). The basic formula for this method is:

Specific order cost = Direct costs of specific order + Overheads absorbed by specific order cost unit.

The direct costs in this formula are charged from the documents recording the direct materials, wages and expenses used on the order, and the overhead absorbed is computed under one of the absorption methods given in Chapter 3.

2. Job costing
This is the form of specific order costing used where the *cost units are relatively small* (e.g. making furniture to customers' specifications). Being small units the work is normally carried out within the walls of the factory. This, however, need not always be the case. Plumbing repairs in private households will, for example, be costed using the job costing method. The method involves the following procedure.

Costing methods:	Specific order		Unit				Batch
Features:	Cost units separately identifiable		Cost units all identical				Identifiable batches each containing identical units
Formulae:	Order cost = (Direct costs + overheads absorbed) of order		Cost centre unit cost = (Direct costs + overheads charged) of cost centre ÷ No. of units produced in cost centre. Total unit cost = Total of all cost centre unit costs				Cost per unit = Batch cost ÷ No. of units in batch
Sub-methods:	Job	Contract	Output	Operating	Process		
					Discrete unit	Continuous unit	
Features:	Small cost units	Large cost units	Single cost unit and single process	Service	Discrete units (i.e. counted)	Continuous units (i.e. measured)	
Examples:	Furniture made to customer's specification; Plumbing repairs	Ship-building; Civil engineering projects	Quarry; Dairy	Railway; Hospital; School; Telecommunications	Light bulbs; Tennis balls; Computer disks	Refinery; Steelworks; Paper mill; Brewery	Bakery; Pottery; Printing

Figure 4.1 *Tabular summary of the main costing methods*

Job 707:	Usage	Price	£	£
		£		
Direct materials: X 312	32 m[a]	1.50 m[b]	48.00	
P 99/8	44 kg[a]	1.24 kg[b]	54.56	102.56
Direct labour: Dept. 1	3 hr[c]	5.80 hr[d]	17.40	
	6 hr[c]	4.20 hr[d]	25.20	
Dept. 4	$1\frac{1}{2}$ hr[c]	6.00 hr[d]	9.00	
Dept. 6	8 hr[c]	5.00 hr[d]	40.00	91.60
Direct expenses:				
Royalty (units)		10.00[e]	10.00	
Plating charge (sub-contract)	As invoice 913[f]	28.28	28.28	38.28
Factory overheads:				
Dept. 1	9 Direct labour hr[c]	4.40 hr[g]	39.60	
Dept. 4	3 Machine hr[h]	13.00 hr[i]	39.00	
Dept. 6	£40 Direct Wages[j]	150%[k]	60.00	138.60
	Factory cost			371.04
Selling overheads:				
10% factory cost			37.10	
Distribution costs:				
job 707D[l]			18.20	55.30
	Total cost *			426.34
	Profit			23.66
	Selling price[m]			£450.00

Figure 4.2 *Example of a job cost preparation*

*Administration overheads have already been apportioned to production, selling and distribution (*see* 3:23(c)). Therefore no separate charge is shown here.

Sources of data:

(a) Materials requisition.
(b) Stores records card.
(c) Time sheets.
(d) Employee record card.
(e) Royalty agreement.
(f) Subcontractor's invoice.
(g) Direct labour hour overhead rate.
(h) Machine time sheet.

(*Notes continued on page 85*)

(a) Each job:

    (*i*) is given a *job number* (or works order number) that identifies it from every other job, and

    (*ii*) has a *job card* (*see* Fig. 4.2) prepared for it that bears the job number and which is used to collect all the cost data relating to the job.

Job cards must be carefully designed so that they effectively and logically collect all the cost data involved.

(b) During production:

    (*i*) direct costs are charged to the job;

    (*ii*) a share of the overheads of each cost centre that the job passes through is charged by means of overhead absorption rates.

(c) When the job is completed and put in the finished goods store it will not be valued at more than the sum of the two charges specified in **(b)** above. This sum is the *factory, production* or *works cost*.

(d) Later, when the job is sold and delivered:

    (*i*) a share of the selling overheads is charged;

    (*ii*) the cost of delivery is charged.

This now brings the cost up to the *total cost*. The difference between this and the selling price is the profit (or loss).

3. Unit costing

This is the application of the principles of cost ascertainment in situations where *all the cost units are identical*. The basic formulae for this method are:

Cost centre unit cost =

$$\frac{\text{Direct costs of cost centre} + \text{Overheads charged to cost centre}}{\text{No. of units produced in cost centre}} \; ;$$

Total unit cost = Total of all cost centre unit costs.

(*Notes to Figure 4.2 continued*)

(*i*) Machine hour overhead rate.

(*j*) Department 6 direct labour cost entry on this cost card.

(*k*) Wages percentage overhead rate.

(*l*) Subsidiary job card prepared in distribution department.

(*m*) Original sales quotation.

Unit costing divides into three sub-methods: output, service and process costing.

4. Output costing
This is used where the enterprise essentially produces only *one product in a single process* (e.g. a quarry). It is a very simple method of costing. Since there is only one product and one cost centre there is no point in making complex calculations. Cost ascertainment will involve, therefore, little more than collecting and analysing all the costs and then dividing each cost by the total production to find the unit cost. Figures for the previous period may also be given for comparison.

5. Service costing
This is used where the cost unit is a unit of service (e.g. railways). The units of service may be sold by the enterprise (as railways sell transport) or used within the enterprise (as in the case of a factory canteen or boiler-house). It is a common form of costing in local government offices.

The method of costing is similar to output costing. All the costs incurred during a period are collected and analysed and then expressed in terms of a cost per unit of service.

Probably the most important aspect of service costing is the selection of the unit of service, for it is frequently difficult to find any wholly satisfactory form of cost unit. In practice the following are some of the units used:

Enterprise	*Unit*
Bus companies	Passenger-kilometres; seat-kilometres
Hospitals	Patient-days; operations
Electricity companies	Kilowatt-hours
Boiler-houses	Kilograms of steam raised
Canteens	Meals served; cups of tea sold
Road maintenance	Kilometres of road maintained
Transport departments	Tonne-kilometres; kilometres travelled

In service costing, two-part units such as the passenger-kilometres and tonne-kilometres mentioned above are very useful measures. A tonne-kilometre, for example, represents 1 tonne carried for 1 kilometre. Thus, if 5 tonnes were carried 3 kilometres this would represent 5 x 3 = 15 tonne-kilometres. (Note that if a second similar load were carried there would be a total of 15 + 15 = 30 tonne-kilometres, *not* (5 + 5) x (3 + 3) = 60 tonne-kilometres.)

Frequently, too, costings are improved if two or more cost units are used simultaneously, and two or more sets of costs-per-unit figures computed. For example, in the field of higher education, costs can be expressed in terms of cost per student, cost per student-hour, cost per course, cost per lecture-room, and cost per class-hour.

6. Process costing

This is used when identical cost units *pass through two or more cost centres*. It is the commonest form of unit costing.

Although conventional theory recognizes only the one sub-method it pays to distinguish a division of this method between the situation when the units are discrete and when the units are continuous. We can say, then, that we have:

(a) *discrete units process costing* which is used where the *cost units are physically separate* and the production measured by counting (e.g. light bulbs);

(b) *continuous units process costing* which is used where the *cost units are units of measurement* such as tonnes, litres, or square metres (e.g. a refinery).

Although process costing is conceptually simple, in practice complications often arise. Consequently this method warrants a chapter to itself and is covered in Chapter 6.

7. Batch costing

This is the application of the principles of cost ascertainment in situations where a batch of identical units is initially treated as a single identifiable job cost unit (e.g. book production). It is no more, in fact, than the application of job and unit costing methods in sequence. As long as a batch remains unbroken it is treated as a job cost unit and costed by the job costing method. On break-up of the batch, the cost per unit is found from the formula:

$$\text{Cost per unit} = \frac{\text{Total batch cost}}{\text{No. of units in batch}}$$

If the units are subsequently rebatched, the new batch cost card commences with the batch cost found by multiplying the number of units rebatched by the cost per unit.

8.   Uniform costing

Finally a mention must be made of uniform costing, which is not a costing method but merely the name given to a system which *standardizes costing methods and procedures over a group of factories, regional service centres or enterprises*, the object being to make all costings comparable. Installing such a system involves specifying carefully the way in which all the participating units must treat their costings, and in particular standardizing stores issue pricing, depreciation methods, cost classifications, overhead apportionment bases, overhead absorption rates, costing periods and the format of costing statements. As will be appreciated, when a system of uniform costing is in operation, the diversity of the various operating units frequently calls for the application of notional costs (*see* 1:**13**).

9.   Costing method and the valuation of stocks

Finally, note that whenever any cost method (pricing stores issues, absorption of overheads, etc.) affects the valuation of stock *for balance sheet purposes*, the SSAP 9 should be consulted as a matter of course and of importance.

Contract costing

Contract costing is really nothing other than ordinary job costing except that it is applied to relatively large cost units, particularly units that take a considerable length of time to complete and are constructed away from the enterprise's premises (e.g. buildings, road construction and other civil engineering works). However, because there are a number of factors that are unique to this kind of situation the method warrants a complete section to itself.

10. Features of contract costing

Where contract work is carried out away from the enterprise's premises it generally shows the following features:

(a) Most of the materials ordered are specifically for contracts. They will, therefore, be charged direct from the supplier's invoices. Any materials drawn from a main store will be drawn on materials requisitions in the normal way.

(b) Nearly all labour will be direct, even though it is a type of labour not usually regarded as direct, e.g. night-watchmen and site clerks.

(c) Most expenses are direct, e.g. electricity (meters will be installed on the site), insurance, telecommunications (the site will have its own communication equipment and, therefore, telecommunications invoices), postage, sub-contracts, architects' fees, etc.

(d) Nearly all overheads are head office costs. These obviously form only a small proportion of the total costs and so, since errors of overhead absorption are not likely to be as serious as in other costing methods, only simple absorption methods are called for.

NOTE: Many head office costs will arise in preparing tenders and material procurement as well as labour administration. This means head office costs will tend to vary with the *prime cost* of contracts, and therefore the prime cost percentage absorption rate may well be the most appropriate.

(e) Plant and machinery may be charged to contracts in one of two ways:

(*i*) An hourly rate for each item of plant is calculated in a similar way to a machine hour rate (*see* 3:18) and contracts charged on a basis of hours of use.

(*ii*) If plant is at the contract sites for long periods of time contracts are charged with the full plant value on arrival and credited with the depreciated value on departure.

11. Architects' certificates and retention moneys

In the construction trade progress payments are often made. Periodically the architect inspects the work and issues *architects' certificates* to the contractor detailing work satisfactorily completed. It is important to note that these certificates show the value of the work completed at *contract* price (i.e. 'selling' price), not cost price. The contractor then submits to his customer invoices claiming these amounts as progress payments and encloses the certificates as evidence of work done.

Also in the trade there is frequently a contract clause that entitles the customer to withhold payment of a proportion of the contract value (e.g. 10%) for a specified period after the end of the contract. This is called *retention money*, and during this period and before these retained moneys are paid the contractor must make good all constructional defects that appear. The prudent contractor will therefore hold in suspense part of the contract profit until all the retention moneys have been received. Any costs of remedying defects during the retention period would then be debited against this profit-in-suspense.

12. Contract cost accounting: basic procedure

The basic procedure for costing contracts is to open a separate account for each contract, debit it with all contract costs and credit it with the contract price. This means each contract account becomes a small profit and loss account, the profit or loss being transferred to a Profits and Losses on Contracts Account.

A summary of the procedure for an individual contract is as follows:

(a) Open an account for the contract.

(b) Debit all contract direct costs (including cost of plant transferred to site if this method of charging plant is being used).

(c) Credit materials, plant and other items transferred *from* the contract.

(d) Debit head office overheads charged to the contract.

(e) Credit contract price.

(f) Transfer balance, profit or loss, to the Profits and Losses on Contracts Account.

13. Uncompleted contracts

When a contract is uncompleted at the year end the simple procedure given in **12** is, unfortunately, complicated somewhat since the profit earned during the year is not really known. We are faced with the problem, then, of subjectively estimating the appropriate figure.

Now, cost accounting aims to measure performance as accurately as possible and it is as unacceptable to err, on grounds of prudence, on one side of an impartial measurement as it is to err on the other side. However, running parallel to this is the fact that the cost accountant must be able to provide year-end values for the final accounts and this work is controlled by the accounting requirements in respect of published figures. This means that when it comes to valuing year-end uncompleted contracts and contract profits it is necessary to make the computation in line with accepted accounting conventions — though for *management* a set of alternative informal computations can, of course, be prepared. And current accepted conventions are embodied in SSAP 9.

14. SSAP 9 and uncompleted contracts

The more important points in SSAP 9 as it relates to uncompleted contracts can be summarized as follows:

(a) *Turnover* is regarded as the appropriate proportion of total contract value as the contract actively progresses.

(b) A key term is *attributable profit* which the standard defines as 'that part of the total profit currently estimated to arise over the duration of the contract, after allowing for estimated remedial and maintenance costs and increases in costs so far as not recoverable under the terms of the contract, that fairly reflects the profit attributable to that part of the work performed at the accounting date.' The standard also lays down that there can be no attributable profit until the outcome of the contract can be assessed with reasonable certainty.

Attributable profit, therefore, is turnover less matched costs — and so the attributable profit transferred to the Profits and Losses on Contract Account for any period is the turnover relating to that period less its matching costs. Note, incidentally, that any such profit must be reduced by any *foreseeable losses*.

(c) The balance sheet should show (*see* Fig. 4.3):

(*i*) Excess of cumulative turnover over cumulative payments received on account — shown as *Amounts recoverable on contract*.

(*ii*) A figure computed as follows: An 'interim stock' figure is found by subtracting the matched costs from the actual costs incurred. Then, where appropriate, this figure is reduced by the sum of foreseeable losses and the excess of cumulative payments on account over cumulative turnover. The final balance can be shown on the balance sheet as:

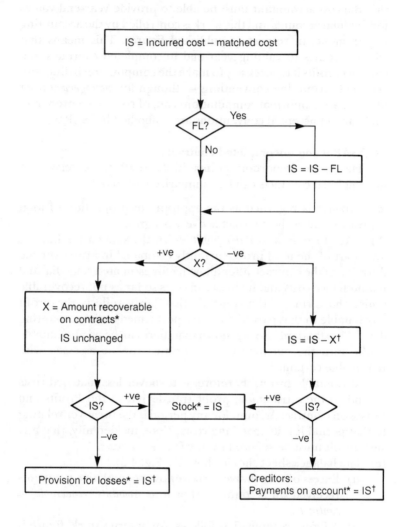

*Items actually shown Balance Sheet.
†Absolute value of item (i.e. negative value converted to
positive value).

Figure 4.3 *Balance Sheet entries relating to uncompleted contracts.*
Abbreviations: IS = Interim stock; FL = Foreseeable losses; X = Cumulative
turnover – cumulative payments on account.

if positive, then as *Stock at net cost, less foreseeable losses and payments on account*;
if negative, then as *Provision for foreseeable losses* or as *Payments on account* under 'Creditors' — whichever is appropriate.
(d) If any *loss* is anticipated, then the entire loss should be taken.

As can be appreciated, SSAP 9 lays down a valuation procedure which accords closely to the one that a cost accountant applying normal costing principles would adopt.

15. Contract accounts — uncompleted contract

Where a contract is incomplete the procedure given in **12** needs some amendment. First, steps **(e)** and **(f)** become inappropriate and the following steps should be inserted in lieu:

(e) Mark off two blank spaces in the Contract Account. (For reference purposes the first of these will be termed the Cost matching section and the second the Future section. The part of the account already containing the period costs will be referred to as the Costs incurred section.)

(f) Debit the Costs incurred section and credit the Future section with any accruals.

(g) Credit the Costs incurred section and debit the Future section with:

    (*i*) prepayments;
    (*ii*) stock on hand at site;
    (*iii*) plant remaining on site at written-down values.

(h) Credit and close off the Costs incurred section with the balance now remaining — which must be the cost of work done.

(i) Complete the Cost matching section by:

    (*i*) crediting the cost of the work done but not certified and carry this amount down into the Future section;
    (*ii*) computing and debiting the share of the cost of the future remedial work estimated to be applicable to the current period while crediting the Future section with this provision;
    (*iii*) Transferring the balance on the section — which must be the matched costs for the work certified — to the Profits and Losses on Contracts Account.

The first two sections of the Contract Account are now closed while the Future section details the opening figures for the next period.

(j)   Finally, to complete the accounting, the Profits and Losses on Contracts Account is credited with the sales value of the work certified, any foreseeable losses are provided for (by debiting the account and crediting a provision account) and finally the balance is transferred — the profit on the contract to date — to the P/L Account.

16. Contract cost accounting — illustration

The book-keeping procedure applicable to a contract can be illustrated using the following data:

Basic data:

    (*i*)   Details of Contract 158, for Customer AZA, begun during the year and having a total contract value of £9.5M:

Item	£000s
Materials purchased and delivered to site	4,421
Materials issued from store	374
Materials returned to store	86
Site wages	1,440
Site direct expenses	195
Plant sent to site	480
Plant returned from site	130
Architect's fees	200
Sub-contract work	680

Head office overheads to be charged at $12\frac{1}{2}\%$ of site
   wages

    (*ii*)   At the year end valuations were:

Item	£000s
Materials on site	124
Plant on site	205
Cost of work done but not yet certified (work in progress)	371
Prepayments	11
Accruals	37
Estimated remedial costs	800
Foreseeable loss on part of contract	50

(*iii*) During the year architects' certificates to the value of £8,100,000 were issued and AZA made payments on account of £8,500,000.

Account entries:

The letters in brackets in the accounts below refer to the steps detailed in **12(a) – (d)** and **15(e) – (j)**.

CONTRACT 158 A/C$^{(a)}$ (CLIENT AZA)

[*Costs incurred section*]

	£000s		£000s
Materials purchased$^{(b)}$	4,421	Materials returned$^{(c)}$	86
Materials ex store$^{(b)}$	374	Plant returned$^{(c)}$	130
Site wages$^{(b)}$	1,440	Materials on site c/d$^{(g)}$	124
Site direct expenses$^{(b)}$	195	Plant on site c/d$^{(g)}$	205
Plant sent to site$^{(b)}$	480	Prepayments c/d$^{(g)}$	11
Architect's fees$^{(b)}$	200	Bal: Total cost	
Sub-contract work$^{(b)}$	680	incurred c/d$^{(h)}$	7,451
Head office overheads$^{(d)}$	180		
Accruals c/d$^{(f)}$	37		
	£8,007		£8,007

[*Cost matching section (i)*]

	£000s		£000s
Total cost b/d	7,451	WIP — work not	
Provision for		certified c/d	371
remedial work*	682	Matched costs to	
		P/L on Contracts a/c	7,762
(Cost deemed incurred)	8,133		8,133

[*Future section*]

	£000s		£000s
Materials on site b/d$^{(g)}$	124	Accruals b/d$^{(f)}$	37
Plant at site b/d$^{(g)}$	205	Provision for	
Pre-payment b/d$^{(g)}$	11	remedial work b/d	682
WIP b/d	371		

*Share of estimated £800,000 remedial work:
    800,000 x proportion of contract complete = 800,000 x 8.1M/9.5M = £682,105
    The standard makes no recommendation as to the method of calculation or the actual accounts to be used to record this cost so an alternative treatment is quite acceptable.

PROFITS AND LOSSES on CONTRACTS A/C (j)

	£000s		£000s
Contract a/c: matched costs	7,762	Value work certified	8,100
Provision for			
Foreseeable Losses a/c	50		
Bal: Contract profit to P/L a/c	288		
	8,100		8,100

CUSTOMER AZA A/C (CONTRACT 158)

	£000s		£000s
P/L on Contracts a/c	8,100	Cash payment on account	8,500

Balance sheet items

Following the procedure shown in Fig. 4.3, the resulting computations are as follows (£000s):

   IS = Incurred cost – matched cost = 8133 – 7762 = 371
   Since there are foreseeable losses of 50, then IS = 371 – 50
      = 321
   X = Cumulative turnover – cumulative payments on account
      = 8100 – 8500 = – 400
   Since this is negative X becomes 400 and IS = 321 – 400
      = –79
   And since this is negative, too, the balance sheet will show:
      'Creditors: Payments on account £79,000'

Note that in effect the 'Payments on account' reflects the fact that despite there being £371,000 worth of WIP, £50,000 of this is expected to be utilized for foreseeable losses, which means there is a net value of £321,000. However, since AZA has paid £400,000 over and above the value of the work invoiced, then not only has the customer paid off this cost but has paid an extra £79,000. Although hopefully future work and invoices will more than liquidate this amount, as at the date of the balance sheet this sum can be regarded as owing to AZA, and hence constitute a creditor sum.

17. Previous periods' figures
 If the contract was running in a prior period, then additionally it will be necessary to first compute the figures for the whole contract and then deduct from these any amounts already taken into the accounts so as to leave net period figures for current inclusion.

Progress test 4

Principles

1. Distinguish between the following: (*a*) specific order costing; **(1)** (*b*) job costing; **(2)** (*c*) unit costing; **(3)** (*d*) output costing; **(4)** (*e*) service costing; **(5)** (*f*) process costing: (*i*) discrete units; (*ii*) continuous units; **(6)** (*g*) batch costing; **(7)** (*h*) uniform costing; **(8)** (*i*) contract costing. **(10)**

2. Outline the procedure followed when preparing a job cost. **(2)**

3. State two methods of charging plant to contracts. **(10(e))**

4. What are (*a*) architects' certificates; (*b*) retention moneys? **(11)**

5. What has SSAP 9 to say about profit on an uncompleted contract? **(14)**

6. What are the following balance sheet contract items and how are they calculated? (*a*) Stock; (*b*) Payments on account;

(*c*) Amount recoverable on contracts; (*d*) Provision for losses.
(14(c))

7.   Distinguish carefully between the three sections into which an uncompleted contract account divides at the end of a trading period.   **(15)**

Practice

8.   (a)   A long-term contract is one that will usually extend for
         longer than one year.
         Required:
           (*i*) Give two examples of long-term contract work.
                  (Fig. 4.1)
          (*ii*) List three characteristics of a long-term contract other
                  than its length.   **(10)**

     (b)   In order to overcome the problem of profit recognition
         with a contract that extends over a number of years,
         attributable profit is allowed to be recognized before
         the contract is completed.
         Required:
           (*i*) Explain the problem of profit recognition that is
                  associated with long-term contracts.   **(13)**
          (*ii*) Outline what you understand by attributable profit
                  and in what circumstances it should and should not be
                  taken.   **(14(b))**
         (*iii*) If it is thought that a loss might arise as a whole on a
                  contract how should this be treated?   **(14(b))**
     (c)   A long-term contract to build a factory in Radley was
         started up in November 1989 and is expected to be
         completed in February 1991. The value of the contract
         is at £1,400,000 and is at the stage that profit can be
         attributed to it. When work has been certified, the
         Company that issued the contract for the factory is
         sent an invoice for progress payments. You are given
         the following information relating to the year ended
         31 October 1990:

	£
Materials issued to Site from Store	600,000
Materials returned to Store	50,000
Materials remaining on Site 31 October 1990	20,000
Wages paid	250,000
Wages accrued	30,000
Sub-contractors' charges	25,000
Plant purchased at cost	100,000
Value of plant on site at 31 October 1990	60,000
Overheads allocated to contract	25,000
Value of work certified at 31 October 1990	900,000
Progress payments received at 31 October 1990	1,000,000
Costs to completion	150,000
Work in Progress	120,000

Required:
Prepare the following for the year ended 31 October 1990:
  (*i*) The Radley contract account.
  (*ii*) The Contractee's account.
  (*iii*) Contract profit and loss account.

(*AAT Dec 90. Part question adapted*)

9. Show how the balance sheet items relating to the contract in question 8 would appear as at 31 October 1990.

5
Cost accounts

There are two basic types of cost accounting: *integral accounts* and *interlocking accounts*. They exist separately for purely historical reasons and not because their use depends upon different circumstances. Integral accounts evolved after and from interlocking accounts and is the better and more efficient system. However, interlocking accounts are still used in industry, and are still examined upon, and therefore both types are outlined here.

It should, perhaps, be appreciated that the current level of computer technology does, in fact, render the traditional form of double-entry book-keeping obsolete. Today the most effective accounting technique is database accounting which incorporates set theory mathematics. However, it will no doubt be some time before accountants accept this newer form of computer accounting and probably even longer before double-entry is abandoned in examinations. This chapter, then, concerns itself only with the older traditional form of cost book-keeping.

Cost accounts

The cost accounts are those accounts which relate to all the transactions involving enterprise costs and are physically held in the cost ledger. And whichever system is adopted, integral or interlocking accounts, those *cost accounts* are essentially the same — it is only the way they relate to the financial accounts that is different.

1. Basic cost ledger data flow
There is a fundamental difference between the structure of

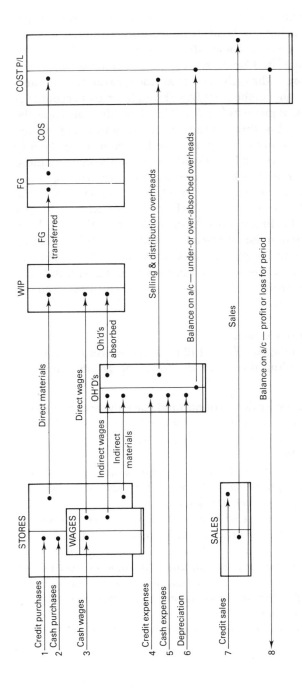

Figure 5.1 *Chart of accounts in the cost ledger*
Note that in this and the following two figures accounts having a double line at the bottom
are those which are in principle closed off at the end of each accounting period

financial accounts and that of cost accounts in that, whereas the financial accounts aim to classify transaction data by 'what' the data relates to, in the cost accounts the aim is to classify the data by 'where' the data is. Consequently, as the benefits from any expenditure spread through the organization, so the cost accounts reflect that spread, i.e. the costs flow through the cost accounts. A chart of the flow is given in Fig. 5.1. This chart illustrates how the cost of materials flow through the cost accounts by being debited to the Stores account on receipt of materials, then charged out to the Work-in-Progress and the Overhead accounts on issue, those costs which enter the Work-in-Progress account then being joined by the production wages and overheads before moving on to the Finished Goods account, after which the cost-of-sales is charged out to the Cost Profit and Loss. At the same time other overhead costs are collected in the Overhead account before being charged out to the Work-in-Progress or the Cost Profit and Loss. Then in the Cost Profit and Loss account the costs meet up with the sales so that the cost profit can be computed and then transferred out of the cost accounts.

2.   Chart of cost accounts

As already indicated, Fig. 5.1 illustrates the basic chart in cost accounts. In reading that chart the following points should be noted:

(a) Cost figures enter the accounts (and leave the accounts in the case of the balance on the Cost Profit and Loss) on the left of the chart. In 7–16 these entries are linked up with the rest of the accounting system.

(b) The direct and indirect materials figures, and the direct and indirect wages figures, are abstracted from the materials and wages analyses respectively (*see* 19, 22).

(c) The debit in respect of overheads to the Work-in-Progress account is the *absorbed* overheads and is found by multiplying the total units of base (e.g. direct labour hours) for the period by the overhead absorption rate. For instance, if 20,000 direct labour hours were booked to cost units and the overhead rates were £4.50 per hour, then £90,000 would be debited to the Work-in-Progress account for overheads.

(d) Selling and distribution overheads are *not* included in the charges to the Work-in-Progress account (*see* 3:**23**). As these overheads are incurred at the time of sale and delivery, they are charged to the Profit and Loss Account in the same period as the sales to which they relate are credited.

(**e**) The final balance on the Overhead account must be the under- or over-absorbed overhead (*see* 3:**21(b)**), and this, of course, is transferred to the Cost Profit and Loss account (unless the business is seasonal, *see* 3:**21(c)**).

(**f**) The balances on the Stores account, Work-in-Progress account and Finished Goods account are all closing stock values. An analysis of these figures can always be found in the subsidiary records (*see* **18**).

(**g**) Since the cost-of-sales transferred into the Cost Profit and Loss account is the total production cost of sales, it only remains to set this off against the sales and deduct the selling and distribution costs (either the actual costs or the absorbed costs) for a profit figure to be found (although this profit is often adjusted by under- or over-absorbed overheads).

3. Further analysis of chart

Our chart is inevitably a highly simplified version of a full set of cost accounts in practice. In a more practical context the following account sub-divisions will normally be found:

(**a**) The Stores account may well comprise an account for each physical store or class of store held.

(**b**) There will be a Work-in-Progress account for each department (and even perhaps classes of work within each of the departments) and as work is .physically transferred from department to department, so the associated Work-in-Progress accounts are debited and credited to reflect the movement of the corresponding values.

(**c**) The Overheads account is made up of a number of sub-accounts. Firstly, there may be a group of overhead accounts which collate the expenses under a 'nature' or 'what' classification (e.g. heating, rent and rates, security). The costs accumulated in these accounts would then be transferred to a set of overhead accounts relating to locations, i.e. cost centres or departments. In the case of service departments, the overall costs of these departments would in turn be transferred to the overhead accounts of the locations which benefit from those services. And, finally, the costs incurred by these latter locations would be transferred to the work-in-progress accounts using one of the methods of absorption. (For details of the mathematics of these cost apportionments, *see* Chapter 3.)

(d) Although in the chart the overhead account is shown as being closed off at the period end in principle, nevertheless in practice there is often a small residue of expense accruals and prepayments which will be carried down on this account into the next period.

4.   Cost account sub-systems
Within the accounts as a whole there are often sub-systems — particularly in respect of materials and labour (*see* **17–22**).

5.   Cost accounting trading periods
Because of the role costing plays in providing day-to-day management with vital cost data, in cost accounting a one-month trading period is adopted far more often than it is in financial accounting. Indeed, it is difficult to conceive of a worthwhile cost accounting system which adopted a trading period longer than one month.

6.   Cost audits
As will be appreciated, just as financial accounts can be audited so can cost accounts — and a *cost audit* is, of course, simply the verification of the correctness of the cost accounts and of the adherence to proper cost accounting procedures. Clearly, this will involve checking that:

(a) the figures themselves are correct;
(b) the cost accounts, cost centres and cost units are correctly charged.

It should be appreciated that the purpose of a cost audit is essentially to check that the various systems can be relied upon to operate in the intended manner rather than to locate and correct individual errors.

Cost audits generally follow the same procedural approach as normal financial audits.

Interlocking accounts

Interlocking accounts is a term relating to a system of cost accounting in which the cost accounts have no double-entry connection with the financial accounts, but use the same basic data. With interlocking accounts, therefore, the cost ledger is kept quite independently from the financial ledger but, since the basic data is the same, the two ledgers should be essentially in accord with each other.

7. Chart of interlocking accounts

Since under interlocking accounts the actual ledger accounts have no connection with each other, the financial accounts in the financial ledger are in no way affected by the existence of the cost accounts and so, in principle, can be ignored. However, since both sets of accounts use the same *data* there is a link between the financial and cost data figures. This link is illustrated in Fig. 5.2 where it can be seen that, as regards the *financial accounts:*

(a) There is a total block on any double-entry crossing from the financial ledger to the cost ledger, and vice versa.
(b) The financial accounts are essentially the accounts of any normal book-keeping system.
(c) The financial ledger account entries which use the interlocking data have been shown aligned against those same entries in the cost accounts — i.e. the left hand side of Fig. 5.1 — so that the link between the two sets of ledger accounts can be seen.
(d) The financial ledger sometimes records data which is not incorporated into the cost accounts — and the Financial Expenses account illustrates this point in Fig. 5.2.
(e) The Financial Profit and Loss account is identical to the normal book-keeping Profit and Loss account.

8. Cost Control account — interlocking accounts

Looking at the cost ledger side of Fig. 5.2 it will be seen that a new account appears in this ledger — the Cost Control account (also referred to as the *Financial Ledger Control account*) — and that apart from this account the cost accounts are simply those shown in Fig. 5.1. This new Cost Control account has only one function — to accept the second part of the double-entry of all the otherwise

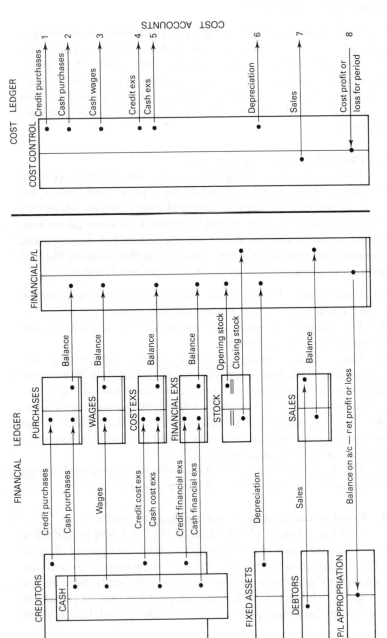

Figure 5.2 *Chart of interlocking accounts*

uncompleted cost ledger entries. It acts, in fact, rather like a dustbin — if, on introducing cost data into the ledger, one has to find some account where the second half of the double-entry can be dumped, then the Cost Control account is the place.

As will be quickly appreciated, the sole reason for the Cost Control account is to enable the cost ledger to be self-balancing. The figures within it are rarely revealing and the end-of-period balance is a rather uninformative amalgam of stock values, cumulative profits and losses, notional costs (*see* **9**), accruals and pre-payments (i.e. a total of all the cost account balances, and displayed on the 'wrong' side of the account).

9. Notional accounts

Just as it is possible to have financial data that appears only in the financial ledger (*see* **7(d)**), so it is possible to have cost data that appear only in the cost ledger. Typically notional costs record such data. Where accounts for notional costs exist the double-entry is quite straightforward — the cost account bearing the cost is debited and the Cost Control account is credited.

10. Interlocking accounts — illustration

An illustration of the workings of an interlocking system of accounts is given in **16** where a single set of data is used to illustrate the accounts prepared under both interlocking and integral accounts techniques.

11. Reconciliation of financial and cost profits

If all the data in the overall system is both the same and treated the same then the cost and financial profits will inevitably be identical. However, values and treatment are often not the same. Sometimes, as we have seen, there are accounts in one ledger which are not in the other. Also stock is frequently valued more conservatively in the financial accounts than in the cost accounts, and on occasion the two sets of accounts use different depreciation figures. As a result of all this the financial and cost profits do *not* agree. This being so, it is a worthwhile exercise to reconcile the two — both so that the differences in the data treatment can be highlighted and, more importantly, so that the correctness of the system is checked (e.g. such a reconciliation may reveal that certain data is improperly being included in, or excluded from, one or the other set of accounts). To reconcile the financial and cost profits, the following procedure should be adopted:

(a) Start with the cost profit.

(b) Adjust for differing views.

    (*i*) Ascertain all the points where the financial accountant viewed a transaction or value differently from the cost accountant.

    (*ii*) Compute for each point the money difference between the two views.

    (*iii*) Ask yourself, 'If the cost accountant had adopted the financial accountant's view, would the *cost* profit have been increased or decreased?' If increased, add the money difference, and vice versa.

(c) After taking into consideration all the points the resulting figure should be identical to the financial profit. If it is not, the two profits have not been reconciled and further differences must be sought.

Example

Data:

Cost P/L account	£12,800 profit
Financial P/L account	£11,300 profit

In the cost ledger: a £5,000 charge was made for depreciation, and the closing stock of raw materials was valued at £23,600.

In the Financial Ledger: depreciation was £4,400 and closing raw materials stock was valued at £21,500.

Method of reconciliation	£
Profit as per cost P/L account	12,800
Change if cost accountant had adopted financial accountant's depreciation charge	+600
	13,400
Change if cost accountant had adopted financial accountant's raw materials stock value	– 2,100
Profit as per financial P/L account	£11,300

NOTE: 1. The narrative for change entries can be abbreviated to the name of the difference, e.g. 'depreciation', raw materials stock value'. 2. Where there are more than two differences the layout is improved if all the additions are collected together and subtotalled, and similarly the subtractions.

12. Reconciliations in general

It should be appreciated that the technique of reconciling profits can be extended to any other book-keeping reconciliation (or 'analysis of differences' as it is sometimes referred to in examination questions). If we designate the figures to be reconciled in the two sets of accounts A and Z respectively, the general procedure is as follows.

(a) Start with A.
(b) Adjust for each item that shows different amounts in the two sets of accounts by considering how A would have altered if the figure in the Z set of accounts had been used in lieu of the figure actually used in the A set of accounts.
(c) At the end, check that Z is the resulting figure.

Example
_____
The estimated cost of job 1001 was £3,500 but the actual cost was £3,850. Using the information below reconcile (analyse the differences between) these costs.

    (a) The estimate specified among other things 100 units of material at £10 each less a quantity discount of 4 per cent, labour of 500 hours at £1.90 per hour and an overhead absorption rate of £2.50 per direct labour hour.
    (b) The actual cost included a material cost of 100 units at £10 less a quantity discount of 10 per cent and a labour charge of 580 hours at £2 per hour.

Solution

			£
(a)	Estimated cost		3,500
(b)	Effect of extra quantity discount:		
	(10–4)% of 100 x £10		–60
			3,440
	Effect of extra labour time:		
	80 hours labour at £1.90 per hr	£152	
	80 hours overhead at £2.50 per hr	200	+352
			3,792
	Effect of higher wage rate: 580 hrs at		
	10p		+58
(c)	Actual cost		£3,850

Integrated accounts

Integrated accounts is a term relating to a single accounting system which contains both financial and cost accounts and which uses a common input of data for all accounting purposes. In theory, all accounts are in a single ledger, though for practical purposes the accounts are usually kept in two physically separate ledgers.

13. Chart of integrated accounts

Figure 5.3 illustrates the essential accounting flow in the system of integrated accounts. The chart shows a dotted Cost Control account. Since such an account is purely optional the chart should initially be looked at as if the account did not exist, and on this basis the following points should be observed:

(a) The double-entry flows from the financial accounts to the cost accounts (it will be seen that the double-entries for the accounts in Fig. 5.3 are to be found in Fig. 5.1). In the pure book-keeping theory there is no distinction between the accounts in the two ledgers and so the demarcation line between them is shown in the chart as a dashed line.

(b) All the old nominal accounts and the Stock account disappear entirely from the financial accounts with the exception possibly of the occasional account relating to expenses or income which it is

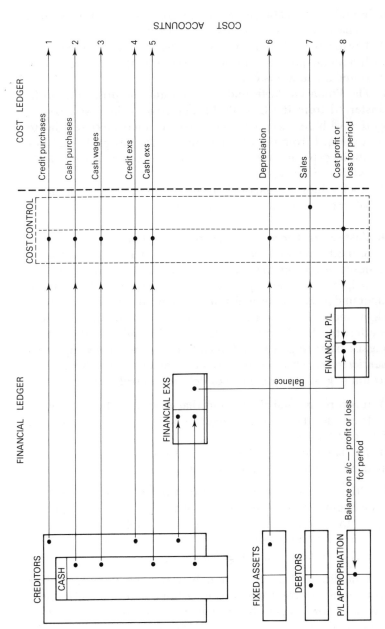

Figure 5.3 *Chart of integrated accounts*

not intended should be entered in the cost accounts (represented in the chart by the Financial Expenses account).

(c) The assets and liability accounts (other than the Stock account which disappears) are in no way affected by the adoption of an integrated accounts system.

(d) The Financial Profit and Loss account comprises the profit transferred from the Cost Profit and Loss in the cost accounts together with the exceptional nominal account balance relating to data excluded from the cost accounts. Since this profit and loss account incorporates the cost profit there is *no need to reconcile the cost and financial profits*.

(e) Stock values, accruals and pre-payments are all to be found in the balances on the various cost accounts.

14. Cost Control account — integrated accounts

As has been mentioned, in practice it is generally found to be physically inconvenient to keep all the accounts in a single ledger. The ledger is, therefore, physically divided into two, the financial ledger under the responsibility of the financial accountant, the cost ledger under the responsibility of the cost accountant. This does *not* affect the double-entry given in Figs 5.1 and 5.3 but, in order to assist balancing, a Cost Control account is opened up *in the financial ledger*. This control account is similar to any other control account (e.g. creditors control or debtors control) in that:

(a) It records in total all amounts that enter into the cost ledger;

(b) It enables the financial ledger to be balanced independently of the cost ledger;

(c) The balance on the Cost Control account must equal the net balance in the cost ledger as a whole.

Although the operation of the Cost Control account is identical to the operation of any other control account, it does sometimes appear to be more complicated, and so the following rules may prove helpful (and these rules are illustrated in the dotted Cost Control account shown in Fig. 5.3).

(a) Establish a clear distinction between the financial ledger accounts and the cost ledger accounts. Students often find it useful to imagine the ledgers being divided by a distinct line. Which accounts are to be in which ledger is purely a matter of choice by the accountant, although a division similar to that shown in Figs 5.1 and 5.3 is usual.

(b) The double-entry shown in Fig. 5.3 is adhered to without change, but in addition *whenever the double-entry spans the two ledgers* (and therefore crosses the dividing line) *the entry made in the cost ledger account is duplicated in the Cost Control account.*

NOTE: This results in *all* entries within the financial ledger being balancing entries. Hence this ledger is self-balancing.

15. Notional costs
The easiest way to handle notional costs in an integrated accounts system is to debit the notional cost account in the cost ledger and credit the Financial P/L account in the financial ledger (*see* **16** for an illustrative example).

16. Cost book-keeping illustration
To illustrate the book-keeping involved in both interlocking and integrated accounts the following problem will be solved:

A company has the following balances on the accounts in its financial and cost ledgers (all figures 000s):

Financial ledger: Stock £120; Debtors £91; Cash £30; Creditors £40; Fixed Assets (w/d value) £100; Cost Expenses (accrual) £1; Capital & Reserves £300.

Cost ledger: Stores £38; Work-in-Progress £40; Finished Goods £62.

During the trading period the following transactions took place (000s):

Credit trading:	Purchases £62; Sales £145; Cost expenses £24.
Cash payments:	Purchases £8; Wages £35; Cost expenses £12; Financial expenses £3; Creditors £80.
Cash receipts:	Debtors £132.
Stores issues:	Direct materials £75; Indirect materials £4.
Transfers:	Work-in-progress to finished goods £151; Cost of sales from finished goods £115.

You also have the following information:

> Production overheads are absorbed at 200% direct wages.
>
> £10,000 of the overheads related to selling and distribution.
>
> The wage analysis disclosed that there were £26,000 direct wages and £9,000 indirect wages.
>
> Depreciation: Financial accounts — 10% written down asset value; Cost accounts — £8,000.
>
> Closing stocks: All classes were conservatively valued in the financial accounts in total at £153,000.
>
> Financial expenses are never incorporated into the cost accounts.
>
> A notional charge of £3,000 was made for rent in the cost accounts.
>
> At the period end there was a cost expense prepayment of £5,000 which was carried forward in the financial accounts but not in the cost accounts.

(a) On the basis of an interlocking accounts system prepare all the financial and cost accounts and reconcile the financial and cost profits.

(b) Re-write all the financial and cost accounts on the basis of an integrated accounts system, given the following changed circumstances:

> (i) The stock values and depreciation are those to be found in the cost accounts, but a Stock Provision account, which adjusts the total stock valuation to that previously recorded in the financial accounts, is kept in the financial ledger.
>
> (ii) The accruals and pre-payments are now incorporated in the cost accounts (although the financial expenses continue to remain outside the cost accounts).

FINANCIAL LEDGER

CREDITORS

Cash	80	Bal b/d	40
Bal c/d	46	Purchases	62
		Cost exs	24
	46		46
		Bal b/d	46

PURCHASES

Creditors	62	P/L	70
Cash	8		

WAGES

Cash	35	P/L	35

FINANCIAL P/L

Purchases	70	Sales	145
Wages	35		
Cost exs	30	Close stock	153
Fin exs	3		
Deprec.	10		
Open stock	120		
Profit c/d	30		
Bal b/d	24	Profit b/d	30

COST EXS

Creditors	24	Bal b/d	1
Cash	12	P/L	30
		Bal c/d	5
Bal b/d	5		

FINANCIAL EXS

Cash	3	P/L	3

STOCK

Bal b/d	120	P/L	120
P/L	153		
	153		

SALES

P/L	145	Debtors	145

APPROPRIATION

Approp.	30	P/L	30

CASH

Bal b/d	30	Purchases	8
Debtors	132	Wages	35
		Cost exs	12
		Fin exs	3
		Creditors	80
		Bal c/d	24
Bal b/d	24		

DEBTORS

Bal b/d	91	Cash	132
Sales	145	Bal c/d	104
Bal b/d	104		

FIXED ASSETS

Bal b/d	100	P/L	10
		Bal c/d	90
Bal b/d	90		

CAPITAL

		Bal	300
		Bal	300

COST LEDGER

COST CONTROL

Sales	145	Bal b/d	140
		Cr. pur	62
		Cash pur	8
		Wages	35
		Cr. ohds	24
		Cash ohds	12
		Deprec.	8
Bal c/d	169	Not. rent	3
		Profit	22
	169		169
		Bal b/d	169

NOTIONAL RENT

C.C.	3	Ohds	3

WAGES

C.C.	35	WIP	26
		Ohds	9

SALES

P/L	145	C.C.	145

OH'D'S

C.C.	24	WIP	52
C.C.	12	P/L	10
Stores	4		
Wages	9		
Deprec.	8		
Rent	3		
P/L	2		

STORES

Bal b/d	38	WIP	75
C.C.	62	Ohds	4
C.C.	8	Bal c/d	29
Bal b/d	29		

WIP

Bal b/d	40	FG	151
Stores	75	Bal c/d	42
Wages	26		
Ohds	52		
Bal b/d	42		

F.G.

Bal b/d	62	P/L	115
WIP	151	Bal c/d	98
Bal b/d	98		

COST P/L

FG	115	Sales	145
S & D	10	Ohds	
Profit c/d	22	O-absorb	2
C.C.	22	Profit b/d	22

Note: C.C. = Cost Control

Figure 5.4(a) Solution (a) Interlocking accounts (all figures in £000s)

FINANCIAL LEDGER

CREDITORS

Cash	80	Bal b/d	40
Bal c/d	46	Stores	62
		Ohds	24
		Bal b/d	46

CASH

Bal b/d	30	Stores	8
Debtors	132	Wages	35
		Ohds	12
		Fin exs	3
		Creditors	80
		Bal c/d	24
Bal b/d	24		

FIXED ASSETS

Bal b/d	100	Ohds	8
		Bal c/d	92
Bal b/d	92		

DEBTORS

Bal b/d	91	Cash	132
Sales	145	Bal c/d	104
Bal b/d	104		

FINANCIAL EXS

Cash	3	P/L	3

NOTIONAL RENT

Fin P/L	3	Ohds	3

COST CONTROL

Bal b/d	139	Sales	145
Creditors	62		
Creditors	24		
Cash	8		
Cash	35		
Cash	12	Bal c/d	174
FA	8		
Rent	3		
P/L	28		
Bal b/d	174		

STOCK PROVISION

P/L	20	Bal	20
		P/L	16

FINANCIAL P/L

Fin exs	3	Cost P/L	28
Close stock prov.	16	Not. rent	3
Approp.	32	Open stock prov.	20

APPROPRIATION

		P/L	32

CAPITAL

		Bal	300

COST LEDGER

STORES

Bal b/d	38	WIP	75
Creditors	62	Ohds	4
Cash	8	Bal c/d	29
Bal b/d	29		

WAGES

Cash	35	WIP	26
		Ohds	9

SALES

P/L	145	Debtors	145

WIP

Bal b/d	40	FG	151
Stores	75	Bal c/d	42
Wages	26		
Ohds	52		
Bal b/d	42		

OH'D'S

Creditors	24	Bal b/d	1
Cash	12	WIP	52
Stores	4	P/L	10
Wages	9	Bal c/d	5
Deprec.	8		
Rent	3		
P/L	8		
Bal b/d	5		

F.G.

Bal b/d	62	P/L	115
WIP	151	Bal c/d	98
Bal b/d	98		

COST P/L

FG	115	Sales	145
S & D	10	Ohds	10
Profit c/d	28	O-absorb	8
Fin P/L	28	Profit b/d	28

Notes:
1. Treatment of Notional Rent:
(a) Amount credited to Notional Rent a/c in the Financial Ledger and debited to Overheads (and Cost Control).
(b) Amount released to profit via credit to the Financial P/L.
2. Stock Provision a/c: If desired (and as called for in this question), a Stock Provision a/c can be held in the Financial Ledger and a provision equal to the difference between the cost stock value and the more conservative financial stock value can be made by adjustments to the Financial P/L.

Figure 5.4(b)   *Solution (b) Integrated accounts (all figures in £000s)*

Solution ────────────────────────────
(a) For the accounts — *see* Fig. 5.4(a)
Reconciliation:

	£
Cost profit	22,000
Depreciation: Difference £10,000 and £8,000	–2,000
Stocks: Value change:	

	Financial a/cs:	120,000 to 153,000	=	£+33,000
	Cost a/cs:	140,000 to 169,000	=	£+29,000

Difference	£4,000	+4,000
Accruals: Opening £1,000 in financial accounts only		+1,000
Prepayments: Closing £5,000 in financial accounts only		+5,000
Financial expenses: £3,000 in financial accounts only		–3,000
Notional rent: £3,000 in cost accounts only		+3,000
Financial profit		£30,000

(b) *See* Fig. 5.4(b).

Accounting for material and labour costs

With the financial and cost accounting framework now in place we can look in this and the following section at how the specific and more detailed routines for accounting for materials and labour may be handled. To the extent that it is relevant an integrated accounting system will be assumed.

17. Chart of material accounts

Figure 5.5 shows the accounting flow chart for materials. The lower half shows in slightly more detail than Fig. 5.1 the ledger accounts involved, while the top half shows the parallel subsidiary records and accounting procedure required for individual transactions.

18. Subsidiary records

Study of Fig. 5.5 shows that each of the three main ledger accounts acts as a control account for a particular set of subsidiary records — the Creditors Control account controlling the Creditors

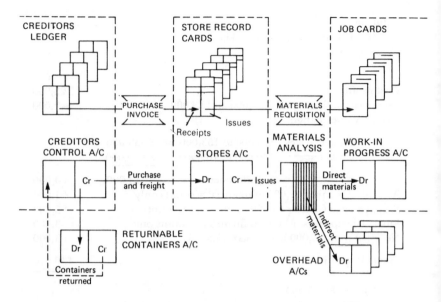

Figure 5.5   *Material accounting flow chart*

This chart shows the flow of data and the pattern of record-keeping
necessary in materials cost book-keeping.

ledger (as in normal book-keeping practice), the Stores account
controlling the stores records cards, and the Work-in-progress
account controlling the job cards. This results in the following:

(a) All details relating to figures in the main accounts can be
obtained by referring to the subsidiary records.

(b) The overall balance on any set of subsidiary records *will equal
the balance on the control account*. Thus the balance on the Stores
account will equal the total of all the value balances on the stores
records cards, and the balance on the Work-in-progress account
will equal the total of the costs shown on all the job cards. (It should
be appreciated that once a job is complete the job card is removed
from the job card file, the total of the cost of all such jobs removed
during a period being *credited to the Work-in-progress account.*)

19. Materials analysis
A *materials analysis* is an analysis of materials drawn from stores
to job numbers and overhead accounts. It ensures that all materials

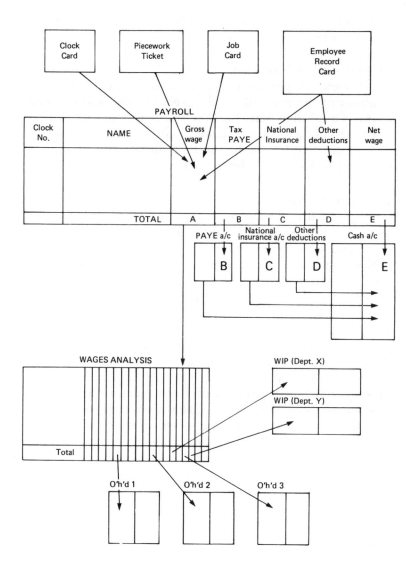

Figure 5.6 *Wage accounting flow chart*

This chart shows the accounting entries involved in accounting for labour costs

issued are charged to some part or other of the cost accounts and are not overlooked.

20. Finished goods account

Though not part of the material accounting system, the similarity of the Finished Goods account to the Stores account warrants a mention here. Like the Stores account, the Finished Goods account is a control account controlling, in this case, the *stock* records cards, the balances on these cards collectively equalling the balance on the account.

21. Chart of labour accounts

Figure 5.6 shows the accounting flow chart for labour and wages. It can be seen that the first step is the computation of gross wages and subsequent deductions. The total gross wage is then analysed and debited to the appropriate work-in-progress and overhead accounts, while credits to the appropriate financial accounts complete the double-entry.

22. Wages analysis

A *wages analysis* is similar to a materials analysis and analyses the total gross wages to the various cost activities, i.e. jobs and overheads. Essentially the object is to examine each employee's gross wage and compute how much is chargeable to the individual jobs and overhead activities the employee was engaged upon. It is prepared by consulting the same sources of data that were used for preparing the payroll (*see* 2:**28**), together with the labour time records discussed in 2:**25** and **26**.

Progress test 5

Principles

1.   Distinguish between interlocking and integrated accounts. (7–9, 13–15)

2.   What is a *cost audit*?   (6)

3. What are the rules for operating a Cost Control account? **(8, 14)**

4. Explain why the cost and financial profit and loss accounts in integrated accounts do not need to be reconciled. **(13(d))**

5. What detailed records (subsidiary ledgers) do the following accounts control: (a) stores; (b) work-in-progress; (c) finished goods? **(18)**

Practice

6. Tiny Ltd. started the year with the following trial balance:

			£	£
Capital: authorized and issued:				
10,000 £1 ord. shares				10,000
Fixed assets			3,000	
Debtors			1,000	
Cost control:	stores	£2,000		
	work-in-progress	£2,000		
	finished goods	£3,000		
			7,000	
Creditors				2,000
Bank			1,000	
			12,000	12,000

During January the following transactions took place:

	£
Stores purchases on credit	2,000
Sales on credit	2,500
Creditors paid (cash)	1,500
Wages	1,000
General operating expenses (cash)	1,000
Discounts allowed	150
Discounts received	100
Payments by debtors (cash)	2,000
Issues from raw materials store	3,000
Issues from finished goods store	2,000
Finished production transferred to finished goods store	4,000
Finished production kept in factory as an addition to fixed assets	500

In the cost accounts £100 was charged to overheads for notional rent and depreciation was taken at 1 per cent for the month on fixed assets (no depreciation on the addition). The company operates an integrated accounting system that incorporates a cost control account.

PREPARE:

    (*a*) all ledger accounts;
    (*b*) Cost Profit and Loss Account;
    (*c*) Financial Profit and Loss Account;
    (*d*) the company trial balance as at the month end.

NOTE: The capital expenditure should be transferred to the financial accounts.

7. A company's trading and profit and loss account for January 19–9 was as follows:

	£		£
Purchases	25,210	Sales: 50,000 units at	
Less Closing stock	4,080	£1.50 each	75,000
		Discounts received	260
	21,130	Profit on sale of land	2,340
Direct wages	10,500		
Works expenses	12,130		
Selling expenses	7,100		
Administration			
expenses	5,340		
Depreciation	1,100		
Net profit	20,300		
	77,600		77,600

The cost profit, however, was only £19,770. Reconcile the financial and cost profits, using the following information.

    (*a*) Cost accounts value of closing stock: £4,280.
    (*b*) The works expenses in the cost accounts were taken as 100 per cent of direct wages.
    (*c*) Selling and administration expenses were charged in the cost accounts at 10 per cent of sale and £0.10 per unit respectively.

(*d*) Depreciation in the cost accounts was £800.

(*e*) Purely financial transactions were excluded from the cost accounts.

6
Process costing

Process costing relates essentially to processes where all units are identical. A better term would be 'unit costing' but historically 'process costing' is the term used.

General considerations

Before turning to the different aspects of process costing one or two general points should be considered.

1. Basic process costing procedures
In all contexts of process costing the following principles should be adhered to:

(a) *All* costs, direct and indirect, incurred during the period are charged to each process so that a total process cost for each is obtained.
(b) The total process cost of each process is then shared equally among all the cost units processed in that process. The basic process costing formula, therefore, is:

$$\text{Cost per unit (CPU)} = \frac{\text{Total process cost incurred during period}}{\text{Total units processed during period}}$$

For instance, if the total process cost incurred in processing 1,000 units were £5,000, the CPU would be £5,000/1,000 = £5.
(c) The cost unit cost is built up cumulatively as the cost units pass through the different processes.

2. Discrete and continuous units
As was indicated in 4:6, process cost units are either discrete

(i.e. physically separate such as light bulbs) or continuous (when units are expressed in measurement terms, e.g. a liquid where the cost unit is a litre). For the first part of this chapter discrete unit costing will be explained while in the second part we look at continuous costing.

3. Process costing and standards

Although it will be assumed that all process unit costs are computed from the actual figures for the period, it is doubtful if this is the best approach to process costing. After all, if identical units are being produced then identical unit costs should be incurred over the year (inflationary effects excepted) and any differences between the costs of one period and another should arise from random or abnormal events and not from any real differences between the units. For this reason it is better to base the unit costs on standards and regard any deviations from the standards as being untypical and so to be written off against the profit for the period. Moreover, such an approach simplifies the computations since once the initial standards are set the CPU figures will hold for a year or so and will no longer need to be recomputed each period. The significance of this will not be lost on any student who works carefully through this chapter.

Principles of discrete unit costing

First, then, we examine discrete unit costing.

4. Equivalent units

Where discrete units are involved it is rare for every unit in a process to be fully processed by the end of the period. Frequently some units are still in-process and so the figure for the number of units processed in the basic formula must include an allowance for these as some of the process costs were incurred in their partial processing. This allowance is made by adding to the units fully processed an *equivalent units* figure which is computed by the formula:

Equivalent units = No. of units in process x % complete.

This is logical, since a cost that enables, say, two units to be each half completed may be regarded as the cost needed to complete fully one unit.

The basic formula given earlier now becomes:

$$CPU = \frac{\text{Cost incurred during period}}{\text{Units completed + Equivalent units in process}}$$

Using the earlier data, assume that of the 1,000 units, 600 are complete and 400 are in process and 50 per cent complete. Then:

Equivalent units in process = 400 x 50% = 200.
∴   Total equivalent production = 600 + 200 = 800 units.

$$\therefore \quad CPU = \frac{5,000}{800} = £6.25.$$

It should be appreciated that this CPU figure gives the cost incurred for a *fully completed unit*.

5.   Cost elements

When we consider the degree of completion of any units in process we may well find that the degree differs according to the cost element. To take a domestic example, if one is making a cake, then just before it is put in the oven the cake may well be complete as regards all materials, nearly complete as regards labour, but only just started as regards overheads since the oven heating costs will be the largest part of this element. In order to allow for this, therefore, it is necessary to treat cost elements separately and calculate a cost-per-unit figure for each element. Again note that the resulting calculation gives the cost-per-unit for each element for a *complete* unit. This means that the *total* cost of a complete unit can be found by simply adding the separate element costs-per-unit.

For example, assume that our £5,000 illustrative cost was made up of: materials £1,000; labour £2,500; overheads £1,500. 600 units are complete and the 400 in process are 75 per cent complete in materials; 50 per cent in labour and 25 per cent in overheads. The CPU for each element can be computed as follows, using the formula in 4 above:

Cost element	£	WIP equivalent units	Total equivalent units produced	CPU £
Materials	1,000	400 x 75% = 300 + 600 = 900		1.111
Labour	2,500	400 x 50% = 200 + 600 = 800		3.125
Overheads	1,500	400 x 25% = 100 + 600 = 700		2.143
Total	£ 5,000		Total cost per unit	£ 6.379

6. **Valuation of completed units and work-in-process**
The value of completed units is simply:

Number of completed units x Total CPU

From the figures given in 5 it can be seen that the value of the completed units = 600 x £6.379 = £3,827 (to nearest £).

On the other hand, work-in-process is valued by multiplying *each element cost-per-unit* by the number of *equivalent units* and then adding the products as follows:

Materials:	300 equivalent units at £1.111 =	333.3
Labour:	200 equivalent units at £3.125 =	625.0
Overheads:	100 equivalent units at £2.143 =	214.3
	Total WIP value	£ 1,173 (to nearest £)

7. **Input–output cross-check**
Note that since the output value of production must account for all the input costs, the combined values of the completed units and the work-in-process must equal the total process cost, i.e. in this case our £3,827 + £1,173 must equal the total cost of £5,000 — which it does.

This is clearly a valuable cross-check on the accuracy of the calculations.

8. **Units transferred from a previous process**
In process costing, units pass through a number of processes in sequence. Consequently, many processes start with units from a previous process. Now it is logical that cost units should be transferred to later stages at their cumulative cost, and therefore these costs must brought into the figures of the new process. It is also logical to treat such a cost as a separate cost element termed

'previous process' and restrict the term 'materials' to material added to production during processing.

'Previous process' is treated no differently from any other cost element. However, its degree of completion is *always 100 per cent*, since it is that part of the unit cost relating to the cost of previous operations which, clearly, must be fully complete.

Assume now that our 1,000 units were transferred from a previous process at a cost of £5 a unit. This element will appear in the computations as follows:

1 Cost element	2 Costs	3 Com- pleted units	Work-in-process		6 Equiv- alent units	7 Total equiv- alent units	8 CPU	9 WIP value
			4 Units	5 % complete				
	£						£	£
Previous process	5,000	600	400	100	400	1,000	5.000	2,000
Materials	1,000	600	400	75	300	900	1.111	333
Labour	2,500	600	400	50	200	800	3.125	625
Overheads	1,500	600	400	25	100	700	2.143	214
Total £	10,000						11.379	3,172

Input–output check:
Value of completed units
= 600 x £11.379   =   £6,827
Value of work-in-process
(Col. 9)   =   3,172
                         £9,999 total costs

NOTE: The £1 difference in the total costs is due to rounding. It is usual to adjust one of the valuations slightly to bring the output total into line with the total costs. This aids subsequent double entry.

9.   The 9-by-4 layout

The layout of nine columns and four rows used above (8) has been devised for the solution of unit costing problems, and the student is advised to learn it thoroughly. Columns 2–5 reproduce the given data (the previous process cost will, of course, always be

100 per cent complete as regards work-in-process). Columns 6–9 are computed as follows:

> Column 6 = column 4 x column 5
> Column 7 = column 3 + column 6
> Column 8 = column 2 ÷ column 7
> Column 9 = column 6 x column 8

Note that column 3 records the total *completed* units, i.e. it will include units transferred to the next process and also any units completed but lost at the end of the process (*see* **13**).

The layout should, of course, always be balanced using the input-output check described in **7**, i.e. by ensuring that:

> Total value of completed units + WIP value =
> Total cost of all elements (column 2)

10. Work-in-process at beginning of period

Where there is work-in-process at the beginning of the period, two different methods of treatment are open to the accountant, depending upon whether the processed units are to be valued on a FIFO basis or an average price basis. The two methods of treatment are as follows.

(a) *FIFO.* The overall object under the *FIFO* method is to find the CPU of processing all units during the period, use this CPU to determine the cost of *completing* the opening in process units and then assume that the first units transferred from the process are the old in process units which will be valued at their opening value plus the cost of completion. This is done by taking the following steps (*see also* example below).

    (*i*) Insert three more 'work-in-process' columns in the 9-by-4 layout to accommodate the opening WIP data (be careful to distinguish between opening WIP and closing WIP).

    (*ii*) Head the middle column '% to complete' (in lieu of '% complete'), i.e. if the units are already 70 per cent complete at the beginning of the period then a further 30 per cent is needed to complete and this is the figure that should be entered in this column.

    (*iii*) The last of the three columns, then, will show the equivalent units processed during the periods in respect of the opening in process units.

(*iv*) Amend the heading of column 3 of the 9-by-4 layout to 'Units started and completed' and insert the total units completed in the period *less the number of units in the opening work-in-process.*

(*v*) Complete the 9-by-4 layout, by adding the opening WIP equivalent units as found in (*iii*) to the other equivalent units and finding the CPU in the normal manner.

(*vi*) To value the units transferred, follow the steps outlined below.

(1) Take each element of cost and multiply the element CPU by the equivalent units in the opening work-in-process column. Then add these products. This gives, of course, the total cost of completing the opening work-in-process.

(2) Add the figure in (1) to the opening work-in-process value to give the total value of the completed opening work-in-process units.

(3) Apply the following formula:

$$\text{Value transferred units} =$$
$$[(\text{Total units transferred} - \text{No. opening WIP units}) \times \text{Total CPU}]$$
$$+ \text{Value in 2 above.}$$

In other words, the value of the units transferred is the value of the completed in process units together with the balance of units transferred valued in the normal way.

(**b**) *Average price method.* Under the average price method all costs, i.e. period and opening work-in-process, are averaged. All that is necessary, therefore, is the addition of the opening work-in-process element values to the period element costs to give a combined column 2 'Costs' figure. All other computations then proceed as usual.

Example

Find the value of the transferred units from the following process data which relates to an opening work-in-process of 30 units and a transfer during the period of 70 units from the previous process at a cost of £750:

	Opening WIP			Period costs (£)
	Units	% Complete	Value (£)	
Previous process	30	100	400	750
Materials	30	80	100	300
Labour	30	50	150	800
Overheads	30	33⅓	80	700
Total			£730	£2,550

100 units were completed and 55 of these transferred to the next process. There was no closing work-in-process.

FIFO method of valuation.

Cost element	Costs (£)	Units started and completed	Opening work-in-process			Total equiv-alent units	CPU (£)
			Units	% to complete	Equiv-alent units		
Previous process	750	70	30	0	0	70	10.714
Materials	300	70	30	20	6	76	3.947
Labour	800	70	30	50	15	85	9.412
Overheads	700	70	30	66⅔	20	90	7.778
Total	£2,550						31.851

		£
Value transferred units:		
30 units opening WIP – cost to complete:	6 x £3.947	23.682
	15 x £9.412	141.180
	20 x £7.778	155.560
		320.422
	Opening value	730.000
Total cost of opening WIP units		1,050.422
25 units started and completed: 25 x 31.851		796.275
55 units transferred		£1,846.697

Check:

Total input   = Opening WIP + Period costs
               = £730 + £2,550 = £3,280

Total output   = Units transferred + Closing stock
               = £1,846.697 + (45 x £31.851)
               = £3,280 (rounded).

Average price method.

Cost element	Costs (£) Opening WIP	Period	Total	Units completed	CPU (£)
Previous process	400	750	1,150	100	11.50
Materials	100	300	400	100	4.00
Labour	150	800	950	100	9.50
Overheads	80	700	780	100	7.80
Total	£730	2,550	3,280		32.80

Value of units transferred = 55 x £32.80 = £1,804

Check:

Total input, as before £3,280.

Total output = Units transferred + Closing stock
            = £1,804 + 45 x 32.80 = £3,280.

Normal losses in process

So far it has been assumed that no units have been lost during the processing. In practice this would be extremely rare.

11. Costing principle regarding normal losses
   It is a process costing principle that the cost of normal losses should be borne by the good production. The logic of this lies in the fact that such losses are one of the normal costs of production and therefore chargeable to whatever production emerges. Where discrete units are involved the large majority of losses arise, of course, from rejection on inspection.

12. Units lost at the beginning

If units are lost right at the beginning before any materials, labour or overheads have been incurred, then the 9-by-4 layout can be used as it stands without any adjustments.

For example, assume that in the illustration given in 8, 100 units are lost at the very beginning of the process, resulting in only 500 good units being completed. This will produce the following computations:

| Cost element | Costs | Completed units | Work-in-process | | | Total equiv-alent units | CPU | WIP value |
			Units	% complete	Equiv-alent units			
	£						£	£
Previous process	5,000	500	400	100	400	900	5.556	2,222
Materials	1,000	500	400	75	300	800	1.250	375
Labour	2,500	500	400	50	200	700	3.571	714
Overheads	1,500	500	400	25	100	600	2.500	250
Total £	10,000						12.877	3,561

Check:

	£
Value of 500 completed units = 500 x £12.877 =	6,439
Value of work-in-process =	3,561
	£ 10,000

13. Units lost at the end

In unit costing it is vital to remember that costs must not be charged until they are incurred (*see* 1:17(b)). This means that if units are lost at the end the cost of such losses can be charged only *to units which have reached the end,* i.e. completed units, and *not to any units still in process.* The procedure then is as follows.

(a) Complete 9-by-4 layout as normal remembering that column 3 shows completed units, i.e. total units completed, good and bad.

(b) Using the total cost-per-unit figure, find the cost value of the lost units.

(c) Divide this cost by the number of good, completed units. This gives the charge per good unit for the losses. Add this charge to the original cost-per-unit figure to give the final cost-per-unit of good production.

If, then, the 100 units were lost at the end the 9-by-4 layout would show the computations given below:

Cost element	Costs £	Completed units	Work-in-process			Total equiv- alent units	CPU £	WIP value £
			Units	% complete	Equiv- alent units			
Previous process	5,000	600	400	100	400	1,000	5.000	2,000
Materials	1,000	600	400	75	300	900	1.111	333
Labour	2,500	600	400	50	200	800	3.125	625
Overheads	1,500	600	400	25	100	700	2.143	214
Total £	10,000						11.379	3,172

The 600 completed units comprise 500 good and 100 lost but completed units.

Cost value of 100 lost units = 100 x £11.379 = £1,138

This cost shared between 500 good units = $\dfrac{£1,138}{500}$ = £ 2.276

Final CPU £ 13.655

Check:

Value of 500 completed good units = 500 x £13.655	=		6,828
Value of work-in-progress	=		3,172[*]
		£	10,000

[*]Note that this is the same WIP value as in **8**. This is logical. The WIP units have not reached the point of rejection and so cannot incur any costs of rejection arising at this point.

14. Scrap: normal losses

If any units classed as 'normal loss' have scrap value, it is necessary that the value of such scrap is deducted from both:

(a) the costs of the process; and

(b) the valuation of the lost units before dividing that valuation by the number of good units.

Example

The 100 units lost in **13** above were sold for a scrap value of £128. This sale of scrap means that the cost of the 100 lost units now becomes £1,138 − 128 = £1,010. This cost shared between 500 good units results in a unit cost of £1,010/500 = £2.020. So the final CPU in this case would become £11.379 + 2.020 = £13.399, say £13.4.

New check figures:

Input = £10,000 − 128 = £9,872

Output:

Value of 500 completed good units = 500 x £13.4 =	£ 6,700
Value of work-in-process (unchanged) =	3,172
	£ 9,872

Abnormal losses in process

A further principle to be carefully observed in process costing asserts that only *normal* costs are to be charged to production (*see* 1:**17(d)**). Consequently any abnormal losses must be written off against the profit and not included in the CPU figure for the good production.

15. Ascertaining units lost that are to be classified as abnormal
The following steps outline the method for ascertaining how many lost units are to be classified as abnormal losses.

(a) Predetermine a normal loss rate to be applied at *a given point in the process.*
(b) Compute the normal loss for all production that reaches this given point.
(c) Then Abnormal loss = Actual − Normal loss.
(Note that if the actual loss is *less* than the normal loss an 'abnormal gain' is made.)

It is absolutely essential in this calculation to be quite clear as to where the physical point of rejection is, since *normal loss can only be computed on a basis of the number of units that pass that point.* For instance, if the normal loss rate is 10 per cent, units are lost at the *end*, and a total of 500 units, good and bad, have reached the end, then the normal loss is 50 units. This figure is quite independent of the input, whether it was 1,000 or 10,000. Similarly, if the loss occurs in the *middle* of the process and 800 units have reached this point, then the normal loss would be 80, regardless of how many entered, completed or remained in the process.

16. Valuing abnormal losses

When pricing abnormal losses it is important to remember that such losses must carry a share of the cost of *normal losses*.

To appreciate this, consider the following extreme example: 100 total units are completed; the actual loss is 99; the normal loss is 20 per cent. The total good production, then, is only 1 unit, and the normal loss 20 units. Now, if the abnormally lost units do not carry a share of the normal loss, then the 1 good unit will have to carry the whole cost of the 20 units normal loss, a cost 'normally' shared between 80 units. This great burden is, then clearly, a non-normal charge arising on account of the abnormal loss. To keep the charge normal it is necessary to share the 20 units normal loss among all 80 other units so that the one good unit takes an eightieth part of the cost of the normal loss and the 79 abnormally lost units the remainder of the cost. In other words, abnormal losses must carry a share of the normal loss.

We can now give the procedure for valuing abnormal losses where such losses occur *at the end of the process*.

(a) Complete the 9-by-4 layout, remembering that column 3 includes *all* completed units: good units, normal loss and abnormal loss.

(b) Having done this, complete the following steps to obtain the final cost-per-unit.

    (*i*) Compute the units of normal loss on the basis of this column 3 figure, i.e. col. 3 × normal loss rate.

    (*ii*) Value the normal loss by multiplying these units by the initial total cost-per-unit figure.

    (*iii*) Divide this value by the total number of good and abnormal loss units to give a cost-of-normal-loss-per-unit figure (but *see* **17(b)**(*i*) *re* scrap value).

    (*iv*) Add this figure to the initial total cost-per-unit figure to obtain the final cost-per-unit.

(c) Multiply the final cost-per-unit figure by the number of units of abnormal loss to obtain the value of the abnormal loss.

NOTE: (1) The value of the good production is simply good units x final CPU. (2) The value of the work-in-process is unaffected, since the lost unit costs are incurred at the end of the process, i.e. they have not yet been incurred by work-in-process units, and therefore such units must carry no charge for such losses. (3) The abnormal loss value is transferred to an abnormal loss account. (4) The overall formula for finding the final cost-per-unit figure to be applied to both good and abnormal loss units can be written:

Final CPU = Initial CPU +

$$\frac{\text{No. of completed units x Normal loss rate x Initial CPU}}{\text{Good units completed + Abnormal loss units}}$$

Example _____

Using the computations given above (*see* **13**), where the actual loss is 100 units, assume that we now have a pre-determined normal loss rate of 6 per cent. Since the total units completed of all kinds is still 600, and since the work-in-process is unaffected by the losses, the 9-by-4 layout in **13** remains unaltered down to the initial total CPU of £11.379. The abnormal loss value is computed as follows:

The normal loss of 6 per cent must relate to the total units passing the loss point (in this case the end), i.e. 600 units.

∴   Normal loss = 6% of 600 = 36 units.
The actual loss is 100 units.
∴   Abnormal loss = 100 – 36 = 64 units.
Cost of the normal loss is 36 x £11.379 = £410.
This loss shared between remaining 564 units

(i.e. good units + abnormal loss) = 410/564 = £0.727 per unit.

∴   Final CPU = £11.379 + £0.727 = £12.106.
∴   Value of abnormal loss = 64 units x £12.106 = £775.

Check:		£
Value of 500 completed good units = 500 x £12.106 =		6,053
Value of abnormal loss charged to Abnormal Loss a/c =		775
Value of work-in-process =		3,172
	£	10,000

17. Scrap: abnormal losses

Where scrap arises in a process experiencing abnormal losses then deduct:

(a) the total scrap value from the cost of the process;

(b) (*i*)   the scrap value of the normal loss units from the cost of these normal loss units before dividing by the total good and abnormal loss units;

(*ii*)   the scrap value of the abnormal loss units from the cost of these abnormal loss units.

NOTE: If there is in fact an abnormal gain, the scrap value of the units *not* scrapped must be deducted from the abnormal gain figure. This is necessary, since the initial apparent gain must be reduced to allow for the loss of scrap income that would otherwise have been received if the full normal loss had been suffered.

18. Units lost part-way through the process

(*see* layout in Fig. 6.1)

If units are lost part-way through a process, the costs incurred relate only to partial completion. This means that two complete sets of three columns need to be added to the 9-by-4 layout. These sets record normal and abnormal units lost and are both similar to the three work-in-process columns (units lost; % complete; equivalent units lost). The equivalent units lost are added to the completed units (note that the lost units are *not* completed units, so must not be included in this figure) and the equivalent work-in-process units to obtain the total equivalent units figure (column 7 of 9-by-4 layout (*see* 8)). The layout is then completed, and after this the procedure continues as follows.

(a) The work-in-process and lost units degrees of completion are compared to ascertain whether the work-in process units lie before or beyond the point of loss.

(b) The value of the normal loss is found by multiplying normal equivalent units lost by the relevant element cost-per-unit (column 8 of 9-by-4 layout) and totalling products.

(c) This loss value is divided equally between all good completed units, abnormal loss units and if, but only if, the work-in-process lies beyond the point of loss, the work-in-process units. (All actual units, not just equivalent units, are counted, since each unit passing the point of loss shares equally in this loss regardless of the degree

Cost element	Complete units*	Cost	Work in process Units	% complete	Equivalent units	Normal loss Units	% complete	Equivalent units	Abnormal loss Units	% complete	Equivalent units	Total equivalent units	CPU	Normal loss	Abnormal loss	WIP
		£											£	£	£	£
Previous process	500	5,000	400	100	400	60	100	60	40	100	40	1,000	5.000	300	200	2,000
Materials	500	1,000	400	75	300	60	50	30	40	50	20	850	1.176	35	23	353
Labour	500	2,500	400	50	200	60	25	15	40	25	10	725	3.448	52	34	690
Overheads	500	1,500	400	25	100	60	25	15	40	25	10	625	2.400	36	24	240
		10,000											12.024	423	281	3,283
Scrap: 100 units at £1		–100												–60	–40	
Total		£9,900											12.024	363	241	3,283
													0.386		15	154
													12.410		256	3,437

Normal loss of £363 shared equally between all units that passed the loss point, i.e. all units except normal loss units.

$$\therefore \text{CPU loss} = \frac{363}{1,000 - 60} = £0.386$$

Final CPU £ 12.410

Charge for lost units: Abnormal loss of 40 units at £0.386
WIP: 400 units at £0.386

* If units are lost before completion, the costs incurred relate only to partial completion, so this column records *fully* completed units only.

Check:

		£
Value of completed units = 500 × £12.410	=	6,205
Value of abnormal units transferred to Abnormal Loss a/c	=	256
Value of work-in-process	=	3,437
		£9,898
Total cost was		£9,900
(Difference due solely to rounding)		

Figure 6.1 *Process cost computations: units lost part-way through the process*

of completion.) The resulting 'cost-per-unit loss' figure is added to the total cost-per-unit (column 8) to give the final cost-per-unit figure. This figure is then used to value the completed good units. **(d)** The value of the abnormal loss is found by multiplying the equivalent abnormal loss units by the relevant element cost-per-unit (column 8), totalling the products and adding a full 'cost-per-unit loss' charge for each abnormal unit lost.
(e) Work-in-process is valued as usual, but if it lies beyond the point of loss, then in addition each unit is given a full 'cost-per-unit loss' charge.

For example, keeping the data used in previous computations above (e.g. in **13** and **16**), assume also that the lost units completion was: materials 50 per cent, labour 25 per cent, overheads 25 per cent and the scrap value of lost units was £1 each.

A comparison of the completion figures of work-in-process and lost units clearly indicates that the units in-process lie *beyond* the loss point.

∴ Normal loss = 6 per cent of all units beyond loss point
        = 6 per cent of 1,000 = 60 units.
∴ Abnormal loss = 100 − 60 = 40 units.

The layout and computations in this instance are shown in Fig. 6.1.

19. Abnormal gains

When an abnormal gain arises the easiest way of handling the computations is to enter the units' abnormal gain in the 'Abnormal loss — Units' column as *negative numbers*. Do not forget, though, that where there is an abnormal gain more units are completed. To ensure that all the unit columns have been filled in correctly the following cross-check should be made:

Units transferred from previous process + opening WIP units = Completed units + closing WIP units + actual lost units (where actual lost units = normal loss + abnormal loss, and where the '+' converts to a '−' if there is an abnormal gain).

It should also be appreciated that having negative numbers in the abnormal gain column means that all subsequent mathematical computations must be carried out with due regard

to the minuses. Thus, the first four figures in the 'Values —
Abnormal gain' column will all be negative and the 'Scrap' figure
will be positive (since all the income which would have arisen from
the sale of these lost units will not now be received). So, if the loss
in our illustration had actually been only 40 units, the total scrap
sales credited would show on the layout as £ – 40, which would be
apportioned £ – 60 for the normal loss of 60 units and £+20 for
the abnormal gain units. Note, too, that the charge to the
abnormal gain for the lost units will also be negative, as will be the
value of the abnormal gain units transferred to the Abnormal Loss
(Gain) account.

While the adoption of this procedure will give a correct
answer, students should nevertheless try and see for themselves
the logic of the various values that arise in the course of the
computations.

20. Book-keeping for discrete unit costing

Once the cost figures have been computed they should be
incorporated in the cost accounts. This aspect of process costing
work will be explained at the end of this chapter after continuous
unit costing has been covered, and the process account relating to
the figures in Fig. 6.1 is given in **35**.

Principles of continuous unit costing

So far we have examined process costing only in the context of
discrete units which are all physically separate. Now we must look
at the method of costing adopted where the product is often an
unending flow, production being only measurable in terms of
tonnes or litres or (as in the case of a gas) cubic metres.

To a large extent costing such units follows much the same
line as costing discrete units. However, there are some important
differences.

21. Discrete unit *v.* continuous unit costing

The difference between discrete unit costing and continuous
costing arises from the differences between the product and its
production (as do all method differences). It is the following

features of continuous units and their production which create these differences.

(a) *By-products and joint products.* Continuous unit production almost invariably gives rise to by-products and joint products. So significantly do these products affect the costs that they are given a complete section to themselves (*see* **25–31**).

(b) *Changes in units of measurements.* A process can often start with units of one measurement and end with units of another. Indeed, it is possible to have three different kinds of units in a single process as, for instance, where an acid (measured in litres) reacts with a solid (measured in kilograms) to give a gas (measured in cubic metres). This means that the units input will not always balance the units output — such a balance is an almost invariable feature of discrete units accounting (although it should be noted that units can occasionally change in discrete units production, as, for example, when two or more separate units are assembled to make a larger unit).

(c) *Unobserved losses.* Where continuous units are processed, often the losses may be unobserved, at least in terms of direct measurement. For example, there can be losses from evaporation or spillage which can only be detected by the difference between the input and the output (and only then if the input and output units are the same).

(d) *Work-in-process.* Where continuous units are being processed, more often than not work-in-process can be ignored, since production is usually on a flow basis and the quantity actually in process at any moment between the input and output points is both very small relative to throughput and also constant from period to period. Only where the product is processed in separate containers, each of which undergoes treatment for a number of days, does work-in-process become a significant factor. On those occasions when work-in-process does arise the computations involved (e.g. ascertainment of equivalent units) follow the principles discussed earlier in this chapter.

22. Normal and abnormal losses

The principle put forward on page 140 that normal losses are charged to the process and abnormal losses to profit and loss still holds where there are continuous units, although the calculations usually prove simpler since normally losses are measured at the end of a process. This means, of course, that the valuation of in process losses is avoided and a simple division of the actual process cost by the expected output gives the CPU figure required for valuing transferred and untransferred units and abnormal losses (*see* 23).

23. Illustrative example

The following example illustrates a typical continuous unit process costing in which no by-products or joint products arise.

Data: Material from a previous process is heated with A and B to give product Z. The normal loss is 30 per cent of input, this loss being sold at £7 per tonne. During a given month there was an input of 300 tonnes costing £5,000 from the previous process, 200 tonnes of A at £5 per tonne and 100 tonnes of B at £10 per tonne. The process direct labour amounted to £2,000, the process direct expenses to £600 and the process overheads to £3,000. The actual output was 380 tonnes of which 350 tonnes were transferred to the next process.

Method: The following layout adequately caters for a costing exercise of this nature:

	Tonnes	Price (£)	£
Previous process cost	300	–	5,000
Materials: A	200	5	1,000
B	100	10	1,000
Process labour			2,000
Process direct expenses			600
Process overheads			3,000
Total input	600		12,600
Normal loss: 30% input	–180	7	–1,260
Expected output of Z	420		11,340

$$\therefore \text{CPU} = \frac{£11,340}{420} = £27 \text{ per tonne}$$

	Tonnes	Price (£)	£
Abnormal loss	–40	27	–1,080
Actual output of Z	380		10,260
Transferred to next process	–350	27	9,450
Held in stock	30	27	£810

24. Book-keeping for continuous unit costing

Again, discussion of the book-keeping subsequent to the costing will be covered at the end of this chapter (*see* **32–36**).

By-products and joint products

Next we consider how by- and joint-products should be costed.

25. By-products

A *by-product* is any product of value that is produced *incidentally* to the main product. For example, basic slag, a useful fertilizer, is obtained in the process of converting iron into steel. The following are the four basic cost treatments of by-products.

(a) *By-product sales regarded as 'other income'*. This method is convenient if the value is small.

(b) *By-product sales value deducted from joint cost*. Here the sales value of the by-product is deducted from the joint cost of producing both main and by-product. The resulting figure is then termed the 'main product cost'.

(c) *By-product sales added to the main product sales*. In this method the combined sales figure for all products is computed and the total costs then deducted, the difference being the combined profit or loss on operation. This approach is based on the view that since it is physically impossible to produce one product without the other, accounting statements must reflect this by producing *combined* figures.

(d) *By-product treated as if it were a joint product*.

26. Joint products and joint costs

Joint products are 'two or more products separated in the course of processing, each having a sufficiently high saleable value to merit recognition as a main product', and *joints costs* are 'the costs of a process which results in more than one main product' (CIMA Terminology). Joint products and costs are a particular feature of the butchery trade.

In any situation where joint costs are incurred the problem arises as to how to charge those costs to the joint products. The following two solutions have been put forward to solve this:

(a) *Apportionment on a physical units basis.* In this method the output relating to all the joint products is measured in some common physical unit (e.g. tonnes, litres) and the joint costs apportioned in proportion to these outputs.

(b) *Apportionment on a sales value basis.* Here the *sales values* of the joint products are used to apportion joint costs. Note that the basis is sales value, *not* selling prices. Use of selling prices results in completely invalid apportionments.

Example

Data: 100 tonnes of Alpha is processed to give 70 tonnes of Beta and 30 tonnes of Gamma. Total joint cost (i.e. process costs and cost of 100 tonnes of Alpha) = £900.

Selling prices: Beta, £12 per tonne; Gamma, £8 per tonne.

Method of apportionment (physical units basis):

	Total	Beta		Gamma	
Sales	£1,080	70 tonnes at £12	= £840	30 tonnes at £8	= £240
Joint cost	£900	£900 x 70/100	= £630	£900 x 30/100	= 270
Profit	£180		£210	*Loss*	£30

Method of apportionment (sales value basis):

	Total	Beta		Gamma	
Sales	£1,080	70 tonnes at £12	= £840	30 tonnes at £8	= £240
Joint cost	£900	£900 x 840/1080	= £700	£900 x 240/1080	= £200
Profit	£180		£140		£40

27. Assessment of methods

As can be seen, these two methods give quite different results and the question arises as to which is the better.

The short answer to such a question is, neither. The fact is, joint costs are in reality wholly indivisible. Since one product cannot be produced without the other it is just not possible to determine what it costs to produce only that one. Certainly such an exercise provides no help to management — it is clearly ridiculous to stop producing Gamma in the example above on the grounds that apportionment on a physical units basis shows that it is making a loss since stopping Gamma means also stopping Beta which is making a good profit.

Careful thought can lead to only one conclusion — that joint costs must be set against joint income and no attempt made to carry the analysis further. In our example Beta and Gamma together give a profit of £180. If this is satisfactory, production should be continued. If not, an alternative should be sought. Nothing is gained by trying to apportion the profit.

This said, however, it must be pointed out that year-end stocks of Beta and Gamma would need to be *valued*. In this context it may be that the apportionment of joint costs is acceptable, though very probably a net realizable sales value (*see* **30**) less a judiciously chosen profit margin would be a better basis of valuation.

28. Split-off point and subsequent processes and costs

It is important to appreciate that the methods discussed relating to by-products and joint products relate only to that production where the products are being processed jointly. Once

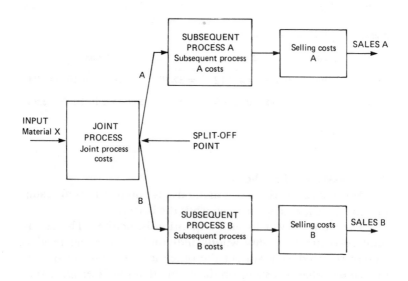

Figure 6.2 *Joint and subsequent processes and costs*

a product separates out and becomes independent, it is treated by the usual cost methods. The point of separation is called the *split-off point* and all events that come after the split-off point are termed *subsequent* events. Thus, the terms *subsequent processes* and *subsequent costs* relate to processes and costs that come after the split-off point. Events prior to split-off are termed 'joint'.

These definitions are illustrated in Fig. 6.2.

29. Treatment of subsequent costs

It is very necessary when preparing by-product and joint-product cost statements to ensure that all subsequent costs are charged only to *the appropriate product, and are not regarded as joint.* For example, where the by-product value is to be deducted from the joint cost (*see* **25(b)**) above) the subsequent costs of the by-product must first be deducted from the by-product sales value before attempting to deduct the sales value from the joint cost, e.g.:

	£	£
Joint cost		5,000
Less By-product value, i.e.:		
By-product sales	1,000	
Less By-product subsequent costs	−200	800
Main product cost		£4,200

It should be noted and remembered that selling and distribution costs are virtually always subsequent costs.

30. Net realizable value

When subsequent costs are deducted from the sales value of a product, the resulting figure is called the *net realizable value*. In the above example, therefore, the £800 is the net realizable value of the by-product.

Net realizable values are particularly relevant if a joint-costs apportionment on the basis of sales value is required, for in such a case it is essential that the apportionment is made on the basis of the *net realizable values of the joint products at the split-off point* and not on the full sales value. As a moment's thought will indicate, using full sales value would bias the apportionment illogically against any product having a relatively high subsequent cost, since much of the sales value would arise as a result of the added economic value of the subsequent processes, which, of course, is wholly unconnected with the other, now separate, joint products.

31. Illustrative example

To illustrate the points made above the following example is worked.

Data: Assume that in the example given in **23** there was, in fact, no *normal* loss at all, but instead 180 tonnes of J was jointly produced with 400 tonnes of Z. Of this production 100 tonnes of J and 360 tonnes of Z were processed in subsequent processes, the process costs being £200 and £4,860 respectively. By the period end 80 tonnes of the fully processed J and 300 tonnes of the fully processed Z had been sold at prices per tonne of £30 and £40 respectively. Selling costs amounted to 10 per cent of the sales values and the joint costs were apportioned on a sales value basis. Prepare the profit and loss account.

Method:

Step 1. Computation of the net realizable value (NRV):

	J			Z		
	Tonnes	Price (£)	Value (£)	Tonnes	Price (£)	Value (£)
Sales	80	30	2,400	300	40	12,000
Selling costs (10% sales)	—	-3	-240	—	-4	-1,200
NRV: Cost of sales	80	27	2,160	300	36	10,800
NRV: Completed production	100	27	2,700	360	36	12,960
Subsequent costs*	—		-200	—		-4,860
NRV: Completed production at split-off point	100	25	2,500	360	22½	8,100
NRV: Joint process production	180	25	4,500	400	22½	9,000

*Note that the subsequent process unit costs are £200/100 = £2 and £4,860/360 = £13.50 respectively.

Step 2. Joint costs:

	Tonnes	Price (£)	£
Total joint process costs (as before, *see* **23**)	600	—	12,600
Normal loss: Nil	—	—	—
Expected output	600		12,600
$\therefore$ CPU = $\dfrac{£12,600}{600}$ = £21 per tonne			
Abnormal loss	20	21	–420
Actual output	580 *	21	12,180

*180 tonnes of J and 400 tonnes of Z.

Step 3. Apportionment of joint costs on sales value basis:

	Total	J	Z
NRV: As above	£13,500	£4,500	£9,000
Joint costs (as in step 2)	12,180	$\dfrac{4,500}{13,500}$ x 12,180 = £4,060	$\dfrac{9,000}{13,500}$ x 12,180 8,120
Cost per unit		£4,060 ÷ 180 = £22.56	£8,120 ÷ 400 = £20.30

Step 4. Closing stock valuations (at cost):

	J			Z		
	Tonnes	Price (£)	£	Tonnes	Price (£)	£
Stocks at split-off point*	80	22.56	1,805	40	20.30	812
Finished goods stocks	20	24.56	491	60	33.80	2,028
Total			£2,296			£2,840

*Note that the finished goods unit costs are the unit costs at the split-off point + costs per unit of the subsequent processes — i.e. here £22.56 + £2 = £24.56 and £20.30 + £13.50 = £33.80 respectively.

Step 5. Profit and loss account:

	J		Z		Total	
	£	£	£	£	£	£
Sales		2,400		12,000		14,400
Costs: Joint (excluding abnormal loss)	4,060		8,120		12,180	
Subsequent	200		4,860		5,060	
Selling	240		1,200		1,440	
	4,500		14,180		18,680	
Less Closing stocks	2,296	2,204	2,840	11,340	5,136	13,544
Product profits		£196		£660		£856
Less abnormal loss						420
Net profit						£436

Process cost book-keeping

So far we have only looked at process *costing* and have ignored the book-keeping side of this costing method. However, on the whole process cost book-keeping entries follow those shown in Fig. 5.1, except that the Work-in-progress account takes the name 'Process account'. In practice there are, of course, often a number of processes and each has its own process account. Despite this close adherence to Fig. 5.1 there are a few book-keeping points special to process costing.

32. Units column

It is a feature of process accounts that they have columns for units as well as values. Where discrete units are involved the debit and credit units columns in a process account must balance, although in the case of continuous units the inputs are sometimes of different kinds (e.g. kilograms of material are added to litres of liquid) so no balancing of inputs and outputs is possible.

33. Scrap

Scrap sales are usually credited to the process account. If, however, abnormal losses are computed, *only the sales of normal scrap are credited*, the scrap sales of the abnormal loss being credited to the Abnormal Loss account (*see* **34**). This is a logical requirement for it is clear that if the normal loss is a legitimate charge to the process then the income from the normal loss should be a credit to the process, while if the abnormal loss is *not* to be charged then neither should the income from that loss be credited.

34. Abnormal loss account

Where abnormal losses are to be accounted for then an Abnormal Loss Account is opened. Operating such an account simply involves:

(a) debiting the cost of the abnormal loss (prior to deducting the abnormal loss sales);
(b) crediting the abnormal loss sales;
(c) writing off the balance on the account to profit and loss as an abnormal loss.

35. Process cost account illustrated

To illustrate process accounts, the process costs detailed in **23** and **18** are shown as book-keeping entries below. It should be appreciated that the data in these two examples appear in the form of practical working sheets and the accounting entries given below would be picked up from such sheets.

We start with the easier example — that relating to continuous units costing.

(a) *Illustrative process accounts relating to continuous units costing* (*see* **23**). Here the Z Process Account is as follows:

Z Process Account

	Tonnes	£		Tonnes	£
Previous process	300	5,000	Next process	350	9,450
Materials: A	200	1,000	Losses: Normal	180	1,260
B	100	1,000	Abnormal	40	1,080
Labour		2,000	Closing stock c/d	30	810
Direct expenses		600			
Overheads		3,000			
	600	12,600		600	12,600
Stock b/d	30	810			

NOTE: In the following period the treatment of the stock held would depend upon whether the FIFO or average price method were adopted. In either case it is advisable to regard the account entry as being equivalent to a purchase entry on a stores record card (*see* Fig. 2.2), the next period's costed output as being a second purchase, and the transfer to the next process at the end of that period as a subsequent issue. This should ensure a valid transfer price whichever pricing method is adopted.

(b) *Illustrative process accounts relating to discrete units costing (see* **18**). Here the accounts are as follows:

Process Account

	Units	£		Units	£
Transferred from previous process	1,000	5,000	Transferred to next process	500	6,205
Materials	—	1,000	Abnormal loss to Abnormal Loss a/c	40	*298
Labour	—	2,500	Scrap sales, normal loss	60	60
Overheads	—	1,500	Work-in-process c/d	400	3,437
	1,000	£10,000		1,000	£10,000
WIP b/d	400	£3,437			

*This figure is the value of the abnormal units lost (£256) with their scrap sales value (£40) written back, since this amount is credited in the accounts to the Abnormal Loss Account and not the Process Account (*see* **33**). In addition, the £2 adjustment to allow for the rounding error in the working sheet (Fig. 6.1) has been made to this figure.

Abnormal Loss Account

	Units	£		Units	£
Process account, abnormal loss	40	298	Scrap sales, abnormal units	40	40
			Net loss to P/L a/c	—	258
	40	298		40	298

36. Abnormal Gain account

It should be appreciated that in the case of abnormal gains the scrap value of the full normal loss is *still* credited to the process account, the difference between this and the actual scrap sales received being debited to the Abnormal Loss Account (which should now take the name Abnormal Gain Account).

For example, if the actual loss in the process account above (35) had only been 40 units, i.e. an abnormal gain of 20 units, the book-keeping entries would have been:

(a) Dr. Cash account 40 units at £1   £40
    Dr. Abnormal Gain account 20 units at £1   £20
    (i.e. scrap value of the 20 units which were *not* scrapped)
    Cr. Process account 60 units at £1   £60
    (i.e. scrap value of the normal loss)

(b) Dr. Process account 20 units   £276
    Cr. Abnormal Gain account   £276
    Transfer of gain to Abnormal Gain account

As will be appreciated, changing the abnormal units in Fig. 6.1 changes a large number of other figures and particularly the total of the *Abnormal loss* column which will now be negative. However, if we assume this total was £–256 then this entry shows how the figure is incorporated into the accounts — after, of course, writing back the £20 added in the layout to allow for the scrap sales *not* received as a result of the gain.

The Abnormal Gain Account would, therefore, ultimately appear as follows:

Abnormal Gain Account

	Units	£		Units	£
Process a/c, units not lost	20	20	Process a/c, cost of units gained	20	276
Net gain to P/L a/c	–	256			
	20	276		20	276

Progress test 6

Principles

1. What are the basic principles of process costing? **(1)**

2. How is scrap handled in process costing? **(14, 17, 33)**

3. Distinguish between by-products and joint products. **(25, 26)**

4. What are the four methods of cost treatment for by-products? **(25)**

5. Which is the best way of apportioning joint costs to joint products? **(27)**

6. Define: (*a*) split-off point; (*b*) subsequent process; (*c*) subsequent cost. **(28)**

7. What is meant by 'net realizable value' in the context of joint products? **(30)**

8. What entries are found in an Abnormal Gain account? **(36)**

Practice

9. The following figures relate to a single industrial process:

Quantity of work-in-process at commencement: 8,000 units
Costs of work-in-process at commencement:

Material:	£29,600
Wages:	£6,600
Overhead:	£5,800

During the period under review, a further 32,000 units were introduced, and the additional costs were:

material: £112,400; wages: £33,400; overhead: £30,200

At the end of the period, 28,000 units were fully processed, and 12,000 units remained in-process. This closing stock was complete as regards material cost, and one-third complete as regards wages and overhead.

Using the average method of valuation, tabulate these production and cost figures to give quantities, unit values, and total values for completed output, and for each of the three elements comprising the closing work-in-process. Attention should be paid to the form of presentation.

(*CIMA*)

10. Using the information given in question 4 above, recompute the cost per unit of the completed units and the value of the closing work-in-process if 8,000 units are lost at the end of the process.

11. C Limited manufactures a range of products and the data below refer to one product which goes through one process only. The company operates a thirteen four-weekly reporting system for process and product costs and the data given below relate to Period 10. There was no opening work-in-progress stock.

5,000 units of materials input at £2.94 per unit entered the process.

	£
Further direct materials added	13,830
Direct wages incurred	6,555
Production overhead	7,470

Normal loss is 3% of input.

Closing work-in-progress was 800 units but these were incomplete, having reached the following percentages of completion for each of the elements of cost listed:

	%
Direct materials added	75
Direct wages	50
Production overhead	25

270 units were scrapped after a quality control check when the units were at the following degrees of completion:

	%
Direct materials added	66⅔
Direct wages	33⅓
Production overhead	16⅔

Units scrapped, regardless of the degree of completion, are sold for £1 each and it is company policy to credit the process account with the scrap value of normal loss units.

You are required to prepare the Period 10 accounts for the
(*i*) process account; and
(*ii*) abnormal gain or loss.

(*CIMA Nov 90, Part question*)

12. From the following information, find the profit made by each product, apportioning joint costs on a sales value basis:

	A	B
Sales	£38,000	£42,000
Selling	£5,000	£20,000

Joint costs: Materials £31,200, Process costs £13,800.

Part two

Cost analysis

7

Estimation

Cost and management accounting very much involve the manipulation of data. On the majority of occasions this involves either actual figures or figures estimated by reference to some subjective factors (i.e. essentially using a feel for the situation as in the case of estimating the first year's sales of a new product). Sometimes, however, estimates can be obtained by the mathematical analysis of given information (which may in turn be either actual figures or a subjective estimate of future figures). In this chapter two such estimating techniques are examined — those that can be made from regression analyses and learning curves — together with a technique that allows the estimator to test how sensitive his estimate is to error.

Regression analysis

Regression analysis exploits the fact that very often two sets of figures (variables) have a mathematical relationship with each other. Often this is because there is a cause and effect relationship (e.g. advertising expenditure and sales revenue) but sometimes only because there is an underlying common factor (e.g. car ownership and foreign travel, since both are affected by changes in the standard of living). In business these relationships can be useful if one such figure is known, or can be reasonably estimated, whereas the second isn't, for in this case this unknown second figure can be estimated from the first by means of the mathematical relationship. Of course, this relationship must be worked out in advance and for this we adopt a technique called *regression analysis*. In order to illustrate a simple regression analysis we will assume that we wish to estimate the future cost of a facility when we know we will be working 5,500 labour hours in a particular part of an organization. Past figures relating to this facility (after allowing for inflation by adjustment to constant prices) are available and are as follows:

Period	Labour hours worked	Facility cost (£s)
1	4,100	54,000
2	3,400	45,000
3	5,300	64,000
4	4,600	55,000
5	4,900	59,000
6	3,900	50,000
7	5,900	63,000
8	4,600	62,000

1. Scattergraph

Although by no means essential for a regression analysis, nevertheless it often pays first to depict the data graphically so that a 'feel' is obtained for the situation. In preparing such a graphical depiction the normal principles of graphical presentation (*see* Chapter 5 of *Statistics*, 6th edn., W. M. Harper, Pitman Publishing, 1991) must be observed — particularly that of allocating the horizontal (*x*) axis to the independent (*x*) variable. Here, of course, the independent variable is the labour hours worked (since the cost depends upon the hours worked and not the hours worked on the cost) and the resulting graph is shown in Fig. 7.1(*a*). This graph is called a *scattergraph* and it helps to show the relationship between the two variables. If the points on the graph fall more or less in a straight line the relationship is said to be *linear* — and at this level our regression analyses will be restricted to linear relationships. In Fig. 7.1(*a*) the relationship is clearly linear and, indeed, a straight line that approximates to the slope of the points can be drawn by eye (*see* Fig. 7.1(*b*)). This line is called the *line of best fit*, and it can be used to estimate what value one variable takes if the other variable is given a particular value (e.g. if labour hours worked are 3,000 then the facility cost would be £44,000). It should be observed that in drawing a line of best fit the deviations of the points from the line must be kept to a minimum.

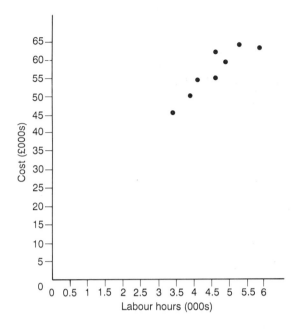

Figure 7.1(a) *Scattergraph*

2. Regression lines

While a line of best fit drawn by eye is often quite acceptable, there are advantages to constructing the line mathematically. First, it replaces a subjective line drawing technique by one that is objective (which means that the line will always be in the same place no matter who draws it), and secondly, the figures that follow such a mathematical analysis can be used in further statistical analysis of that data (although such further analysis is beyond the scope of this book). For both these reasons a computed line of best fit — referred to as a *regression line* — is better than one drawn by eye.

3. The regression lines of *y on x* and *x on y*

Although the principle underlying the computation of a regression line is always to minimize the deviation of the points from the line, two factors arise in making such an analysis:

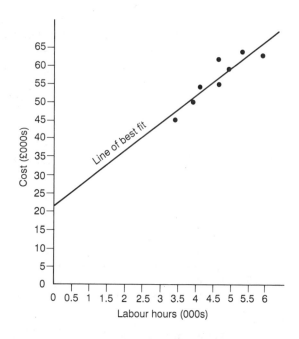

Fig. 7.1(b)   *Scattergraph with line of best fit*

(a) The deviations are *not* found by measuring the deviations of the points from the nearest places on the line but by measuring the deviations either vertically or horizontally.
(b) The line is more effectively centred if the deviations are first *squared* before being used in the computation. And this method of finding regression lines is called the *method of least squares*.

From the point made in **(a)** it will be appreciated that in any analysis *two* regression lines can always be found — the one that is obtained by measuring the deviations vertically and the one that is obtained by measuring them horizontally. Students often find this confusing and wonder which of the two lines they should be using in any given situation. The answer is quite simple: if the value of the *y* variable is to be estimated from the *x* variable then the deviations are measured vertically, while vice versa the deviations are measured horizontally. Note that the line obtained in the first case is called the *y on x* regression line and can be interpreted as the line that enables the *y* variable to be estimated from the *x* variable, while the other regression line is called the *x on y* line and can be interpreted as the line that enables the *x* variable to be estimated from the *y* variable. However, it should be appreciated that since a properly drawn graph has the independent variable on the horizontal axis then in the vast majority of cases it is the former, *y on x* line, that is needed, so only in the rare case where we want to estimate what value the independent variable must be to result in a specific value of the dependent variable is the *x on y* regression line used.

4. Regression line formulae

Since any straight line takes the algebraic form of *y = a + bx* (or *x = c + dy*), computing a regression line simply involves finding what values in a given case must be substituted for *a* and *b* (or *c* and *d*) in this formula. As already indicated, there are two regression lines that can be found in every regression analysis and so there are two sets of formulae. However, as these two sets are virtually identical we will combine them into a single set in which the symbol *z* relates to *the variable from which the estimate is to be made*. This set is as follows (where *n* is the number of points in the analysis):

$$b \text{ (or } d) = \frac{n\Sigma xy - \Sigma x \Sigma y}{n\Sigma z^2 - (\Sigma z)^2}$$

$$a \text{ (or } c) = \frac{\Sigma(\text{variable to be estimated}) - b^*\Sigma z}{n}$$

*or *d*

5. The *y on x* regression line of the illustrative data

Using this formula we can now find the *y on x* regression line (predicting cost from time worked) of the illustrative data given in the opening paragraph of this section.

Since in this instance the variable from which the estimate is to be made is *x* (the hours worked), our formula in **4** becomes:

$$b = \frac{n\Sigma xy - \Sigma x \Sigma y}{n\Sigma x^2 - (\Sigma x)^2} \quad \text{and} \quad a = \frac{\Sigma y - b\Sigma x}{n} \quad \text{where } n = 8$$

And the values that need to be slotted into these formulae can be found by using the following layout (where all workings are in thousands):

x	y	xy	x^2
4.1	54	221.4	16.81
3.4	45	153.0	11.56
5.3	64	339.2	28.09
4.6	55	253.0	21.16
4.9	59	289.1	24.01
3.9	50	195.0	15.21
5.9	63	371.7	34.81
4.6	62	285.2	21.16
Σ 36.7	452	2,107.6	172.81

$$\therefore \ b = \frac{8 \times 2107.6 - 36.7 \times 452}{8 \times 172.81 - 36.7^2} = \frac{272.4}{35.59} = 7.65$$

$$a = \frac{452 - 7.65 \times 36.7}{8} = 21.4$$

$$y = 21.4 + 7.65x$$

6.   Use of a regression line

As has already been said, a y *on* x regression line is used to estimate the value y will take given any value of x. Thus, we can estimate the cost of the facility that would follow 5,500 hours worked by substituting 5.5 into the regression line formula, i.e.:

$$y = 21.4 + 7.65x = 21.4 + 7.65 \times 5.5 = 63.475$$

In full this is £63,475.

7.   Reliability of estimates from regression line formulae

Although we can apparently produce very exact estimates — in **6** the formulae estimate was to £1 — it should be appreciated that this exactitude follows simply from the number of decimal places to which we choose to work. In practice the actual value experienced may be significantly different from our estimate. For instance, although we estimated that a cost of £63,475 would follow from working 5,500 hours we can see from the original data that working only 5,300 hours gave rise to a cost of £64,000 (period 3) while working 5,900 hours resulted in a cost of only £63,000 (period 7). This indicates that one has to be very cautious of putting undue reliance on any estimate arising from a regression analysis. And in this regard the scattergraph can assist us, for the closer the points lie to the line of best fit then the more reliable an estimate will be. Indeed, if all the points actually lie on the line — or virtually on the line — then considerable confidence can be placed in the estimate, whereas if the points are widely spread on either side of the line then the estimate should be treated as being very provisional. Note, incidentally, that if all the points lie on the line of best fit then there can be no deviations and so our two regression lines will lie on top of each other.

8. Regression coefficient
   Sometimes the term *regression coefficient* is used in connection with regression analyses. This is simply the *b* value in the regression formulae. So in our illustrative example the regression coefficient is 7.65.

Learning curves

It is a feature of life that the more often you repeat a sequence of operations, the faster you are able to perform the sequence. If this improvement is plotted on a graph then you see that at first there is a considerable improvement between performing the first and the second sequence and that this improvement continues, albeit at a diminishing rate, throughout all the subsequent sequences. The curve so formed is called a *learning curve*, and is the subject of this section.
   Students are not required to study the mechanics of learning. They may, however, be struck by the similarity these curves have to cooling curves and radioactive product decay curves. This similarity is not really surprising as it is very likely that one underlying mechanism in all cases is a probabilistic one. However, here we take the phenomenon for granted and merely look at its mathematical features in the operating context of unit production.

9. Measuring learning improvement
   Before we can discuss learning in such a context we need to select a method of measuring improvement. We could, for

instance, compare the time each unit took with the time taken for the first unit, or the time taken for the previous unit. But working unit by unit leads to a very large number of calculations where there is a large number of units. Instead it is more practical to base improvement measurement on the *average time per unit for all units produced,* and this form of measurement is met with far more than other forms.

10. The *x* per cent learning curve

When a large number of units are produced then the improvement towards the end of the run is very slight. We do not, therefore, look at improvements per unit at all points on the curve. Rather, we usually look at the improvement that follows successive doubling of production, i.e. we look at the average unit time after production has reached 2, 4, 8, 16, 32, 64, 128 etc. units. And the extent to which the average unit time drops at each level gives us the basis for expressing a learning ratio. Look, for instance, at the following figures relating to products A and B:

	Product A		Product B	
Units produced	Cum. time	Average unit time	Cum. time	Average unit time
1	1,000	1,000	1,000	1,000
2	1,800	900	1,600	800
4	3,240	810	2,560	640
8	5,832	729	4,096	512
16	10,496	656	6,560	410
32	18,880	590	10,496	328
64	33,984	531	16,768	262

If the average unit times for product A are examined it will be seen that at each doubling of production the time drops to 90 per cent of the previous average unit time whereas in the case of B each doubling results in the average unit time being 80 per cent of the previous average. Conventionally, therefore, we say that product A has a 90 per cent learning curve and product B an 80 per cent learning curve (*see* Fig. 7.2). More generally we can say:

'If the average unit time reduces to *x* per cent for each doubling of output of a product, then that product is subject to an *x* per cent learning curve.'

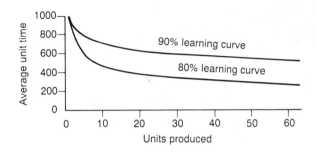

Figure 7.2 *Learning curves*

Note, incidentally, that the *cumulative* times increase at a lower rate than *x* per cent. In the case of A each increase is 80 per cent of the previous cumulative time (80% of 1,000 = 800; 80% of 1,800 = 1,440; 80% of 3,240 = 2,592) and in the case of B it is 60 per cent (60% of 1,000 = 600; 60% of 1,600 = 960; 60% of 2,560 = 1,536). It is possible, then, to measure the learning rate in terms of these percentages but, as has been said, it is usual (though not invariable) to measure learning in terms of reduced average unit times.

11. The learning index

The more mathematically minded student may recognize the learning curve as being a negative exponential curve and suspect that the whole of the curve — and not just those parts of it marked out by the doubling of output — can be described as a continuous function. And as this is often the case many learning curves can be described by the expression:

$$y = ax^i$$

where y = average time per unit after x units
a = time of first unit
x = cumulative number of units produced
and i = learning index

In practice i has to be found by a careful labour time analysis. At the start of the analysis the average unit times have to be recorded for the initial units produced and only if these show that a constant learning curve exists can i be computed. Where this is so then i can be computed as follows:

Since $y = ax^i$ then $x^i = y/a$
∴ $i \times \log x = \log y - \log a$
∴ $i = (\log y - \log a)/\log x$

Example

For product A in **10**, a is 1,000 and when x is 64 then y is 531. So:

$$i = (\log 531 - \log 1,000)/\log 64$$
$$= (2.7251 - 3)/1.8062 = -0.152$$

So the full learning curve expression for product A is $y = 1,000x^{-0.152}$.

Knowing this mathematical expression means, of course, that we can find what the average unit time for any number of units will be. Thus, if 200 units are produced then $y = 1,000 \times 200^{-0.152}$ $= 1,000/200^{0.152}$ (since $x^{-0.152} = 1/x^{+0.152}$) $= 446.934$. Moreover, this in turn means we can find the *actual* time of the xth unit by subtracting successive average times. For example, to find the time taken to produce the 200th unit:

As average unit time for 200 units $= 446.934$, then cumulative time for 200 units $= 446.934 \times 200 = 89,387$
And average unit time for 199 units $= 1,000 \times 199^{-0.152} = 447.275$
∴   Cumulative time for 199 units $= 199 \times 447.275 = 89,007$
∴   Time taken to produce 200th unit $= 89,387 - 89.007 = 380$

12. Cumulative and incremental learning curves

The student should, perhaps, be aware that the expression '80 per cent learning curve' can mean either:

(a) the average unit time of *all* production reduces to 80 per cent for every doubling of output — the *cumulative* interpretation; or
(b) the average unit time of the *extra* production reduces to 80 per cent for every doubling of output — the *incremental* inter-pretation.

In this chapter we have adopted the definition given in **(a)**. This is by far the commonest interpretation, and the one normally to be assumed. Nevertheless, the other should be understood in principle and to illustrate very briefly the mathematics of the incremental interpretation we will look at the product B 80 per cent learning curve given in **10.** In that paragraph the mathematics of the cumulative interpretation was shown and illustrating the incremental interpretation we have the following figures:

Units produced	Extra units produced	Time for extra units*	Total time for all units	Average unit time for units
1	1	1,000	1,000	1,000
2	1	800 x 1 = 800	1,800	900
4	2	640 x 2 = 1,280	3,080	770
8	4	512 x 4 = 2,048	5,128	641
16	8	410 x 8 = 3,280	8,408	525
32	16	328 x 16 = 5,248	13,656	427
64	32	262 x 32 = 8,384	22,040	344

*Time for initial unit progressively reduced to 80 per cent and multiplied by the number of extra units produced to reach the stated level of total output.

As can be seen by comparing the times in the right-hand column of the table in **10,** the average unit times for all production under the incremental interpretation are significantly different from the average unit times adopting the cumulative interpretation.

13. Conclusion

While learning curves do genuinely exist they do not often form quite the smooth curve that the theory suggests. Indeed, being probabilistic, they tend to be a little erratic in practice, and they are, of course, always subject to change due to external factors (e.g. lighting intensity, fatigue). Also, surprising as it may seem, an element of forgetting is essential to learning, for if you cannot forget how you performed an operation in the sequence in a sub-optimum time then you will repeat the sub-optimum time on each subsequent occasion with no chance of correction. Finally, very few learning curves are 'pure' for nearly always when we start learning a new operation we already have some skills in similar operations. Indeed, were we to start learning wholly from scratch our learning curve would not immediately show any dramatic improvement since in such a situation we must spend time learning just what precisely it is we are supposed to be learning.

So much for the theoretical weaknesses of learning curves. On the practical side, however, there is a much more serious problem and that is that the learning index for a given set of operations can never be known in advance. (The index values given in examination questions are, of course, concocted by the examiner purely for the question — and the student, incidentally, is advised not to write a note to him asking him how he knows!) This means that the index can only be accurately ascertained after a considerable number of units have been produced. But, of course, by this time the curve is fast approaching the point where future improvements are marginal, and so the information gained is only of limited use. And where only a relatively few units are produced then often the information does not come (if it comes at all) until close to the end of the run.

All in all, however, learning curves do exist and anyone who wishes to estimate future operation times in a situation where there is a long run of production of identical units must take these curves into account and not project the times of the initial fumbling steps onto his future time estimates.

Sensitivity analysis

All decisions are made on the basis of estimates and at the back of any manager's mind is the knowledge that estimates can be wrong. Where the decision is an important one he may well feel that before committing himself fully he should have some idea how the figures which determine the decision would actually appear if one or more of the estimates were wrong by some potential margin, i.e. how sensitive to possible error are the estimates on which the decision is based. An analysis of such sensitivity is naturally referred to as a *sensitivity analysis*.

14. Making a sensitivity analysis

The principle underlying a sensitivity analysis is simple enough — you merely list all the alternative values for the estimated figures and then, taking each alternative value in turn, recompute the consequences. Though simple in principle the work volume can be extensive — a decision involving a mere five twice-estimated figures will call for thirty-one recomputations if all the possible combinations of the alternative values are to be tested.

15. Illustration
The technique of sensitivity analysis can be demonstrated by means of a simple illustration.

Assume there are two different companies, Safe and Sorry, which have made the following estimates about their separate operations during the coming year:

Company	Sales	Cost of sales	Selling costs
Safe	£100,000	£80,000	£10,000
Sorry	£100,000	£10,000	£80,000

As can be quickly verified, each company anticipates making £10,000 profit.

The managers of the two companies both feel it is quite possible for any one, two or all three estimates to be over-optimistic by about 10 per cent. They have, therefore, called for a sensitivity analysis which will reveal what will happen in all the potentially different circumstances.

Now the easiest way to make this particular analysis is to draft a table so that the changed estimates can be slotted into a framework which mirrors the repeated calculation, i.e. in this case sales – cost of sales – selling costs = profit. Such a table, when completed, will look as shown on the next page (changed estimates in italics; the effects of each change on each company shown together for comparative purposes).

The manager of Safe, looking at his analysis, may perhaps be relieved to see that even in the unlikely event of all three estimates being over-optimistic the company only stands to lose £200. The manager of Sorry, on the other hand, sees that his company stands to lose £7,900 if all three estimates are wrong, and not much less if only two — the sales and selling costs — are in error. Indeed, Sorry suffers more than Safe as a result of an estimate error in every set of circumstances save that in which the error lies in the cost of sales alone. Clearly Sorry is very much more sensitive to error than Safe. Note, incidentally, that Sorry's sensitivity extends to *over-pessimistic* estimates, too, as the student may well like to verify for himself.

Changed prediction	Company	Sales (£)	–	COS (£)	–	SC (£)	= Profit (£)
Original prediction	Safe	100,000		80,000		10,000	10,000
	Sorry	100,000		10,000		80,000	10,000
Sales down 10%	Safe	90,000		72,000*		10,000	8,000
	Sorry	90,000		9,000*		80,000	1,000
Cost of sales up 10%	Safe	100,000		88,000		10,000	2,000
	Sorry	100,000		11,000		80,000	9,000
Selling costs up 10%	Safe	100,000		80,000		11,000	9,000
	Sorry	100,000		10,000		88,000	2,000
Sales + cost of sales	Safe	90,000		79,200 **		10,000	800
	Sorry	90,000		9,900 **		80,000	100
Sales + selling costs	Safe	90,000		72,000		11,000	7,000
	Sorry	90,000		9,000		88,000	–7,000
Sales + cost of sales	Safe	90,000		79,200		11,000	–200
+ selling costs	Sorry	90,000		9,900		88,000	–7,900

*NOTE: that if sales fall, the cost of sales will fall, pro rata, even though the cost per unit remains unchanged.
**10 per cent reduction to match reduced sales + 10 per cent increase to allow for changed cost of sales estimated.

16. Other forms of sensitivity analysis

Sensitivity analyses can take other forms to that illustrated above. These include:

(a) Analysing the consequences of over-pessimistic estimates as suggested, since the failure to grasp a possibly profitable opportunity as a result of over-pessimistic estimates, though not crippling as the opposite error might be, nevertheless can mean that a business fails to achieve the success that its talents warrant.
(b) Computing in respect of each estimate the margin of error (*see* margin of safety, 11:31) that would result in a project breaking-even instead of making the estimated profit. For example, in the illustration above, Safe sales could be 50 per cent

in error before the company would be reduced to a break-even level, though its cost per unit would only need to be 12½ per cent in error for the company to suffer such a fate. This difference, then, is a measure as to how much more sensitive the unit costs are to error than the sales (in Sorry the sensitivity rankings would, of course, be reversed).

(c) Although the two contexts indicated below are not covered in this book, for the record it should be noted that we can also engage in analysing sensitivity in the contexts of:

  (i) investment decisions, where the possibility of error in the estimate of future cash flows will affect the net present value figure;

  (ii) linear programming. It is interesting to note that a linear programming decision is usually relatively insensitive to small estimate errors since in most cases there needs to be a very significant error in any figure before the optimum mix switches from one corner of the area of feasible solution to another, whilst minor changes in the position of the optimum corner make very little difference to the overall optimum value.

All in all, sensitivity analysis can be used to draw management's attention to the factors in a decision which must be both accurately estimated and carefully controlled, while at the same time indicating those other factors where estimate error or control weakness is of much less consequence.

Progress test 7

Principles

1. What is a scattergraph and how is it constructed? **(1)**

2. Why is a computed line of best fit better than one drawn by eye? **(2)**

3. Why are there always two regression lines in any regression analysis? **(3)**

4. How reliable are any estimates made from a regression analysis? **(7)**

5. What is a regression coefficient? **(8)**

6. How can learning improvement be measured? **(9)**

7. Explain what is meant by:

(a) the x per cent learning curve, **(10)**
(b) the learning index. **(11)**

8. Distinguish between cumulative and incremental learning curves. **(12)**

9. What is the purpose of a sensitivity analysis, how is it carried out and what forms can it take? **(14–16)**

Practice

10. In the context of the data given in the introduction to the section on regression analysis on page 160, a period is experienced in which the actual cost was £63,000. The records detailing the actual hours worked have been mislaid and you are asked to make your best estimate as to what the total of these hours might have been.

11. An engineering department is considering undertaking a customer order for 100 units of a new product X. To date, 30 units of X have been produced for a total production time of 5 hours — the first unit taking 20 minutes to produce.

(a) Draw the learning curve appropriate to this product.
(b) Estimate the total operation cost of filling the customer order if operating costs run at £10 per hour.
(c) Estimate the average unit operation time of completing the last 10 units of the customer's order.

12. The following data relating to cost x and potential cost drivers A, B, C, D and E has been abstracted from the trading

figures of XYZ Manufacturing Company Ltd for the last six
half-yearly period figures (adjusted for inflation) — a period
when the company's structure and operations remained
essentially stable:

		Potential cost-drivers				
Period	Cost x – £s	A	B	C	D	E
1	10,645	141,818	216	8,631	988	32,197
2	14,236	197,830	584	6,842	611	530
3	11,518	170,729	306	5,386	895	11,730
4	13,291	181,976	810	8,834	698	65,290
5	15,055	199,809	751	7,919	504	3,469
6	12,427	162,568	498	7,690	806	28,648

Determine which of the potential cost-drivers is the more
likely actual cost driver of cost x and suggest the possible nature
of both the cost and the driver.

8
Cost behaviour

We have already seen that there is more than one way of classifying costs. When cost behaviour is being considered a further type of classification is required, this time based on the pattern of behaviour of the cost in respect of changes in the activity level.

Behaviour classification

1. Costs and activity

Costs are dependent upon, and change with, activity — the greater the activity the greater, usually, the cost. Making an accurate prediction of a cost involves both:

(a) a realistic identification of the activity upon which the cost is primarily dependent, and

(b) an accurate assessment of the mathematical relationship between the cost amount and the level of activity.

For explanatory purposes the problem of identifying the appropriate activity will be left until the section on measuring activity (*see* **17**). For the present any activity element will merely be either asserted without question or assumed to be physical units of production.

2. Relevant activity range

To know only that a cost is dependent upon a particular activity is not in itself of very much help. More useful is knowing just how a cost behaves in relation to that activity. Now, not only will the cost amount differ at different levels of activity, but if the difference between these levels is large the behaviour *pattern* will differ as well. It was this phenomenon which, of course, underlay the extensive fall in the cost of microprocessors, the cost patterns prevailing when just a few were being produced being very different from those prevailing when thousands were being produced. To predict costs in practice within a specific organization it is necessary therefore to limit consideration solely to the range of activity anticipated. This range is called the *relevant activity range* and can be defined as the *range of activity over which predictions are required in practice.*

3. Fixed costs

There are some costs that remain the same whatever the level of activity. These include rent, local government taxes, debenture interest, audit fees, etc. Such costs are called fixed costs. Another typical fixed cost is the cost of top management salaries. Note, however, that this particular cost is very dependent upon the scale of operations, any large increase or, conversely, decrease down to shut-down level almost certainly affecting this cost significantly. So the concept of the relevant activity range is often very important in the case of a fixed cost.

A *fixed cost*, then, can be defined as a cost which *remains unchanged regardless of the level of activity within the relevant range.*

Note that this does not mean that a fixed cost within this range cannot alter. It most certainly can — local government taxes alter every year. All the definition lays down is that the cost is unaffected by *changes in activity*. Other factors can, and do, change a fixed cost.

4. Time and specific project costs

The student should note that other definitions of fixed cost often include a reference to a period of time (e.g. CIMA *Terminology*), and, indeed, the term *period cost* is often used as an alternative to 'fixed cost'. In other words, such a cost is defined as being incurred on a time basis. While in the majority of contexts this is factually correct, there are still occasions when no time basis is involved. For instance, in predicting the cost of a specific project such as printing a book the term 'fixed cost' can relate to any cost that will be incurred regardless of the number of copies to be printed and without reference to any time period (e.g. set-up costs). This use of the term in respect of a specific project is too convenient for it to be excluded by the narrower, though more common, definition.

5. Variable cost

The opposite of a fixed cost is a *variable cost* which is a cost which *varies in direct proportion to the level of activity* (although the CIMA Terminology merely specifies 'tends to vary'). A good example of a variable cost is the raw materials cost since a 10 per cent increase in production usually results in a 10 per cent increase in this cost. Again, strictly speaking, a reference to the relevant activity range should be included in the definition since the greater this range the less it may be true to say that the cost is in direct proportion to the activity (e.g. quantity discounts on materials above a given level can lower the cost per unit so that the cost of producing five times as many units is not five times as much). However, in practice this point is much less important in the case of the variable costs than it is in the case of the fixed costs.

6. Semi-variable costs

Unfortunately there are a good many costs which neither remain unchanged nor vary in direct proportion to activity. These costs change with changes in activity but not in direct proportion.

Careful examination of a cost of this nature often shows that it is a combination of a fixed cost element and a variable cost element. Thus, the cost of a telephone expense comprises a fixed rental charge plus a variable charge for calls. Similarly, the cost of maintenance is often made up of the costs of regular maintenance (e.g. weekly servicing) which tend to be fixed and the costs of breakdown maintenance which tend to vary with machine running time. A cost having this dual nature is called a *semi-variable* (or *semi-fixed*) *cost* and can be defined as *a cost which is partly fixed and partly variable*. The total semi-variable cost is, of course, the sum of these two parts.

In practice it will generally be found that most indirect labour costs are semi-variable.

7. Unit costs

It is important to appreciate that the definitions of costs being developed relate to the total of a cost and not the unit cost. So if material costing £1 per kg was used and 5,000 and 6,000 kg respectively were processed we would say that the variable cost was £5,000 and £6,000 respectively. A variable cost, therefore, increases as activity increases although the variable cost *per unit* remains unchanged. Conversely, if the fixed cost of the process were £30,000 the fixed cost *per unit* would fall from £6 to £5 as the activity changed from the lower to the higher level.

8. Decision driven costs
   In 1:14 it was suggested that decision-driven costs are best excluded from most cost analyses. If they are included, however, then they are probably best regarded as fixed costs, although it should be noted that they differ from normal fixed costs in so far as the latter costs are a distinct consequence of the activities of the enterprise even though they remain unaffected by the level of those activities.

9. Costs in the long and short term
   Finally it should be noted that the classification of a cost into fixed or variable sometimes depends upon the time-span involved. For instance, with a time-span of a day even direct wages must often be classified as a fixed cost since staff cannot be discharged (or engaged) at such short notice. Conversely, a twenty-year time-span means that even debenture interest may become a variable cost (since increased activity over this period may result in further debentures being issued). It is this feature of cost behaviour that underlies the saying 'In the long run all costs are variable'.

Behaviour patterns

One of the best ways of understanding the behaviour pattern of a cost is by means of a graph showing the effect of activity on the cost.

10. The economist's total cost curve (*See* Fig. 8.1).
   If the total cost of running an organization is plotted against activity, it is usually found that at the lowest activity levels the cost rises sharply (though progressively less sharply) as the initial activity calls into being necessary but grossly under-employed

facilities (curve of increasing returns). The curve then straightens out and rises steadily and consistently (curve of constant returns). Ultimately, at the higher activity levels the curve begins to rise more and more steeply as facilities are progressively more and more overloaded (curve of diminishing returns).

This is the traditional cost curve of the economist. However, since an enterprise normally operates between the extremes of under-employment and over-employment of facilities, the relevant activity range usually includes only the straight part of the curve. So in practice many of the accountant's cost curves are straight lines and, provided these curves are not read outside the relevant range, the oversimplification that depicts them as straight *across the whole graph* can be employed — and will be employed in the rest of this book.

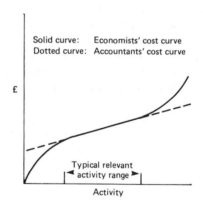

Figure 8.1   *Total cost curve*

11. Fixed, variable and semi-variable cost curves

(*See* Fig 8.2.) The three fundamental and commonest patterns of cost behaviour are as follows.

(a) *The fixed cost curve* (Fig. 8.2(*a*)). Since a fixed cost does not change with activity a fixed cost curve is no more than a horizontal straight line across the graph.

(b) *The variable cost curve* (Fig. 8.2(*b*)). Since a variable cost varies in direct proportion to the activity, the variable cost at zero activity must be zero and the cost must rise at a constant slope reflecting the constant cost increase per unit of activity.

(c) *The semi-variable cost curve* (Fig. 8.2(c)). At zero activity only the fixed cost element of the semi-variable cost has any value and so the cost curve starts from the cost axis at a point equal to the fixed cost element, and then rises at a constant slope which reflects the variable cost increase per unit of activity.

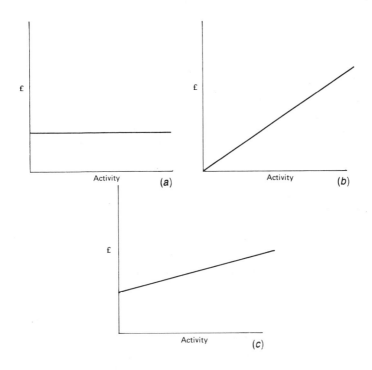

Figure 8.2   (a) *Fixed cost curve*
(b) *Variable cost curve*
(c) *Semi-variable cost curve*

12. Stepped fixed costs

(*See* Fig. 8.3(a).) It is a feature of fixed cost curves that in practice they often produce a step pattern. This arises because usually a fixed cost can only increase in jumps. For example, up to a certain level of activity it may be that three people can service that activity (e.g. storekeepers) but above that level a fourth person is required. Engaging this fourth person results in the fixed cost rising at once by the whole of that person's salary and so the fixed cost curve rises vertically at this activity level. At a yet higher activity level the process may well repeat itself.

Note that if the engagement of a new employee can be postponed by paying overtime or other diminishing returns costs, the kind of pattern shown in Fig. 8.3(*b*) results.

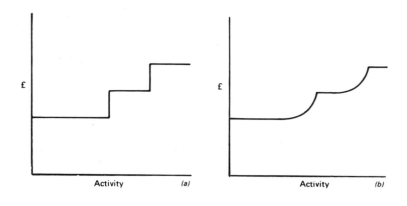

Figure 8.3 (*a*) *Stepped fixed cost*
(*b*) *Stepped fixed cost with diminishing returns expenditure incurred between steps*

13. Variable cost patterns

(*See* Fig. 8.4.) Although the underlying feature of all variable cost curves is a rising slope, the pattern of the slope can vary according to the circumstances. The following are some of the variations.

(a) *The variable cost per unit increases at different activity levels* (Fig. 8.4 (*a*)). This situation can arise where, for example, the work for the first eight hours is paid at, say, £5 per hour, the next four hours at £10 per hour and the four subsequent hours at £20 per hour.

(b) *The variable cost per unit decreases at different activity levels* (Fig. 8.4(*b*)). This is the opposite to (a), when, say, the first four hours

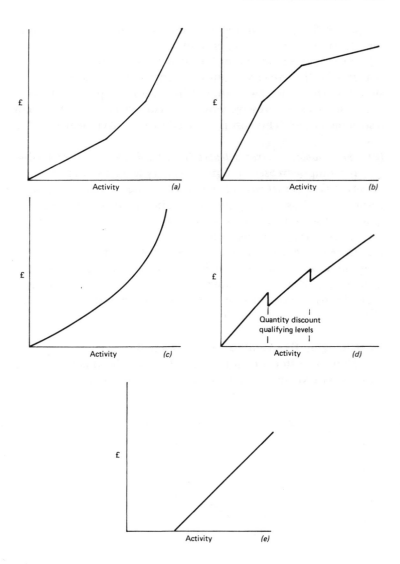

Figure 8.4 (a) *Increasing variable cost*
  (b) *Decreasing variable cost*
  (c) *Curvilinear variable cost*
  (d) *Stepped variable cost, e.g. quantity discount curve*
  (e) *Penalty variable cost*

are paid at £20 per hour, the next four hours at £10 per hour and the remaining hours at £5 per hour.

(c) *The cost curve is curvilinear* (Fig. 8.4(*c*)). Where the variable cost per unit itself increases steadily as activity increases (i.e. in any situation where the law of diminishing returns applies), the cost curve steepens progressively to give a curved 'curve' rather than a straight 'curve'. This cost is referred to as a curvilinear variable cost.

(d) *The variable cost curve is stepped* (Fig. 8.4(*d*)). Where the variable cost per unit decreases at a given activity level and the decrease affects *all the lower activity costs*, a kind of stepped variable cost curve results. The classical example of this kind of behaviour relates to quantity discounts when, at the quantity discount level, all units purchased carry the lower unit cost.

(e) *There is a penalty variable cost* (Fig. 8.4(*e*)). If a certain basic minimum of service is provided free but additional service requested is charged pro rata to requirements, the result is a variable cost curve which only starts to rise from the activity axis at the critical basic activity level.

14. Changing fixed and variable costs patterns

There are often occasions when a fixed cost becomes a variable cost and vice versa. The following are two typical cases.

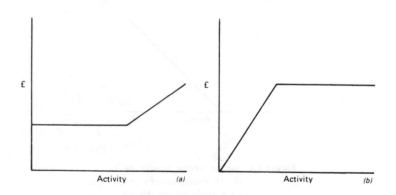

Figure 8.5   (*a*)   *Fixed cost changing to variable cost*
(*b*)   *Variable cost changing to fixed cost*

(a) *Fixed cost changes to variable cost* (*see* Fig. 8.5(*a*)). This arises when, for example, an indirect worker (e.g. storekeeper) is required to work overtime once a given level of activity is exceeded.

(b) *Variable cost changes to fixed cost* (*see* Fig. 8.5(*b*)). This arises when there is a charge per unit up to a given activity level after which no additional charge is made. For example, some car hire agreements incorporate a daily or weekly charge per mile up to a stipulated mileage after which all additional miles are 'free'.

Analysing cost behaviour

Knowing the potential patterns of costs is, of course, quite different from knowing the particular pattern of a specific cost in a specific organization. This pattern can only be discovered by means of a careful analysis of the immediate past costs incurred.

In this section the approach to analysing costs is outlined, though it must be emphasized that only the simplest situation albeit the commonest, will be considered, i.e. where a semi-variable cost can be broken down into a non-stepped fixed element and an unchanging linear variable element.

15. Individual costs analysed
Different costs behave in different ways. To try and analyse the total cost of a combination of individual costs risks unsolvable complications. Sometimes a total cost includes only costs which all respond in the same way to activity (e.g. the costs of milk bottle tops and of washing bottles both vary directly with the number of bottles handled), but this is often far from the case. Consequently when analysing cost behaviour it is important to *analyse each individual cost separately.*

16. Steps in a cost behaviour analysis
The following steps are taken in order to analyse the behaviour pattern of an individual cost.

(a) A measure of activity is selected.
(b) The appropriate time period and the relevant activity range are determined.
(c) The cost is analysed graphically or mathematically.

(d) The results of the analysis are used to predict future costs.

These steps are considered in more detail in **17–23**.

17. Measuring activity

In analysing cost behaviour the first step is to decide on the measure of activity. Where factory production is closely associated with the cost this is usually the obvious candidate.

However, it should be noted that whereas production is often an excellent measure when dealing with the usual direct costs, this is not necessarily so in the case of overheads. Most overheads that vary at all vary more with *hours worked*. For instance, power, light, heat, shop-floor administration costs (including supervision) and many indirect labour costs, such as canteen wages, all tend to vary far more in relation to actual working hours than to actual production. For this reason hours worked are often employed as the measure of activity when dealing with variable overheads.

In the case of non-production costs factory production is not usually appropriate. It is therefore necessary to find some activity having a major influence on the cost to be analysed, i.e. a cost driver, and itself capable of being accurately predicted. Thus, vehicle costs will be very much affected by distances travelled and so distance travelled may well prove an effective activity measure. For the costs of some offices, numbers of invoices or some other suitable document produced may prove an equally effective measure.

It could be that in some situations there is no natural activity measure; for instance, where there is a despatch department that packs various types of parcels. In this situation the creation of an artificial *activity unit* made up of the essential cost drivers may be warranted. Thus, a carefully determined number of units could be assigned to each kilogram despatched and each type of parcel as well. The activity in the department would then be measured by the total activity units experienced during the period.

Example ───────────────────────────────────

A despatch department assigns 4 units of activity to each kilogram despatched, 3 units to each A-type parcel and 7 units to each B-type parcel packed. During the month 2,000 A-type parcels and 1,000 B-type parcels weighing respectively 1,200 and 1,800 kg were despatched. What was the activity of the department for the month?

Solution:

	Activity units
A-type parcels: 2,000 x 3 units	6,000
B-type parcels: 1,000 x 7 units	7,000
Weight: (1,200 + 1,800) x 4 units	12,000
Total activity for month	25,000 units

When deciding upon an activity measure never forget that the object of the exercise is to predict costs. The measure that gives the best prediction should therefore be selected. The quality of a measure for this task can be judged by how closely actual results come to the line of best fit (*see* 7:1). In other words, the closer the fit of the actual points to this line, the better the measure.

18. Time periods and the analysis

It was pointed out that cost behaviour is to some extent dependent on the time-span involved. It is, then, necessary to select an appropriate time period for observations to be used in any analysis. Ideally, this should be as short as possible since the value of an analysis increases not only with the number of past observations but also the extent to which cost observations are up to date. Unfortunately, however, a very short time period often results in slightly abnormal events (and no time period ever comprises typical events only) while unmatched costs and activity (as regards timing) can also seriously bias the figures.

The time period selection must, therefore, be something of a compromise. Under normal circumstances observations involving monthly time periods are found to be both the best compromise and the most convenient.

19. Determining the relevant range

Having decided upon the activity measure and the time period the next step is to determine the relevant activity range. This essentially is the range over which predictions are required, though it is also necessary that the organization should have some not too out-of-date experience at both ends of this range if the analysis is to prove satisfactory.

Note that the actual range taken as relevant may well have a profound effect on the resulting curve (*see* Fig. 8.6 where the selection of two differing ranges from a single comprehensive curve results in wholly different cost curves, both equally valid within their ranges). This is immaterial so long as it is never forgotten that the curve must only be read inside its relevant range.

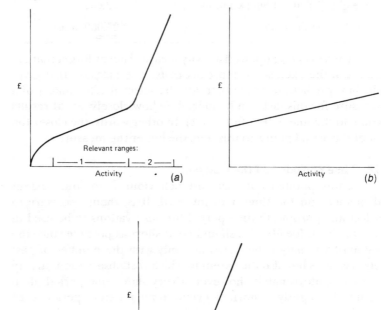

Figure 8.6   (a)   *Total cost curve*
                 (b)   *Relevant range 1 cost curve*
                 (c)   *Relevant range 2 cost curve*

20. Mathematical analysis of cost

Given that the cost to be analysed broadly involves no more than a non-stepped fixed cost combined with an unchanging linear variable cost, an analysis of the cost into its fixed and variable components can be made by employing the scattergraph technique or a regression analysis (*see* Chapter 7), whichever is judged to be the more suitable. From this analysis a straight line

formula will result that can be used to estimate costs on the basis
of the activity involved.

21. Other factors determining cost

Sometimes other factors besides activity affect a cost, e.g.
heating costs are also affected by the season of the year. As far as
possible such factors must be allowed for in the analysis and also
in the prediction subsequently made from the analysis.

22. Inflation

One major factor that can seriously distort any cost analysis is
the effect of inflation on the cost. To remove this influence it is
important that inflation is 'edited out' of all figures (e.g. by dividing
the figures by the appropriate inflation indices).

23. Use of analysis in prediction

Knowing in relation to a given cost the fixed element and the
variable cost per unit of activity prediction simply involves
multiplying this variable cost by the predicted units of activity and
adding the fixed cost (or even, more simply, by reading the cost
directly from the graph). However, when making such a prediction
the following points should be borne in mind.

(a) The prediction must be adjusted to allow for other factors (e.g.
season of the year, inflation, etc.).

(b) The prediction will be valid only to the extent that:
  (*i*) the future behaviour of a cost is consistent with its past
      behaviour — this whole analysis does assume a stable and
      continuing relationship between cost and activity;
  (*ii*) it is made within the relevant activity range.

Progress test 8

Principles

1. Define: (*a*) relevant activity range; (2) (*b*) fixed cost;
(3) (*c*) variable cost; (5) (*d*) semi-variable cost; (6)

2. Why is it important to know the relevant activity range and
on what basis is this range selected? (2, 19)

3. How does the economist's total cost curve differ from a cost curve produced by an accountant?   **(10)**

4. What are the steps taken when making a cost behaviour analysis?   **(16)**

5. What is an artificial activity unit?   **(17)**

6. How can a cost behaviour analysis be used for prediction and how valid will such a prediction be?   **(23)**

Practice

7. It is necessary to predict a crucial future cost in a market research department. Two measures of activity have been suggested for this department: interviews conducted and pages of analyses prepared. The following are the figures for the eight most recent periods:

Period	Interviews conducted (no.)	Analyses prepared (pages)	Cost (£)
1	6,290	310	23,200
2	4,550	200	19,500
3	6,200	600	23,600
4	4,630	480	20,220
5	6,200	400	23,600
6	3,800	440	18,480
7	3,560	440	16,200
8	4,770	330	20,200

The relevant activity range is considered to be 25 per cent either side of the mean activity of these eight periods.

The first cost prediction required is in respect of period 9 when it is estimated that there will be 4,000 interviews conducted and 480 pages of analyses prepared.

Predict the departmental cost for period 9.

9

Introduction to decision-making

To make a right decision a manager must make a correct judgement as to how the people affected will react to the decision, make a correct prediction as to the future values of the economic figures involved in the decision, and make a correct analysis of these figures. The latter task is usually delegated in its entirety to the management accountant.

Although most of the principles below are explained as they are introduced, one or two rely for their full appreciation upon aspects that have not so far been discussed. For completeness these principles are included in this chapter, although later chapters may need to be read before all their implications can be grasped. This also applies to some of the terminology. Ideally, having read this introduction so as to have some appreciation as to what will be covered in the next three chapters, at the end of those chapters you should re-read this one in order to bring together all the principles involved.

1. All alternatives must be identified

The first thing that must be appreciated is that decision-making involves *choice between alternatives* — even if these solely comprise doing what is proposed or not. Indeed, to do or not to do is, perhaps, the most common of all decision-making exercises. But whatever the circumstances all the alternatives must be identified, for it is quite impossible to select the best alternative if that alternative is not included in the analysis. The first task of any decision-maker, therefore, is to identify all the viable alternatives. In the majority of decisions this is often the hardest part of the whole decision-making exercise. Although analysing the figures may not be easy, it is rarely as difficult as marshalling the viable alternatives. All too often the full range is not considered because of either ignorance of the existence of an alternative (e.g. of unadvertised equipment) or lack of forethought, or even because the selection of some alternatives is outside the authority of the decision maker (e.g. when purchasing materials a buyer is rarely allowed to amend the design of the product even slightly). Nevertheless, in principle *all* alternatives must be formally identified.

2.　Relevant costs

In most decision-making situations costs abound. It is, however, a fundamental principle that only the *relevant* costs should be considered.

In itself this statement is something of a tautology since the test of relevance is the need for consideration. However, emphasizing the very need to identify which costs are relevant and which are not is itself very useful in decision-making. Note, for instance, that an associated cost is not necessarily a relevant cost. Thus, it may cost £50 to transport a unit to a customer. This cost is a cost associated with the unit, but if the decision lies between painting the unit black or white it is not a relevant cost since it has no bearing on the decision.

It should, perhaps, be made clear that to include an irrelevant cost will not of itself give rise to an error in the decision analysis. An irrelevant cost is, in effect, neutral and in no way alters the analysis. However, what happens in practice is that the analyst incorporates an irrelevant cost incorrectly simply because he feels it *should* have some influence on the result. By first carefully identifying which costs are relevant and which are not, the danger of wrongly incorporating an irrelevant cost is considerably reduced.

Virtually all the other decision-making principles relate to determining the relevance of a cost.

3.　Future costs only are relevant

Since the past cannot be changed, then all decisions relate to future events. This means that *all past and sunk costs are irrelevant* and the use of such costs in decision making must be wholly restricted to their value in making predictions. Indeed, were it not that cost-behaviour patterns analysed from past costs often prove the soundest basis for predicting future costs, they would be totally excluded from decision-making.

Ignoring past costs is often psychologically difficult. After all, if you had just paid £100,000 for some equipment, this amount would appear to be a very relevant cost should you be faced with the choice of retaining it or replacing it with more efficient equipment. Yet retain or replace, the £100,000 remains spent and is, therefore, wholly irrelevant. For the purpose of any retain-or-replace decision the only relevant value is the net realizable value, i.e. the *future* 'cost'.

4. The differential principle
Of all the decision-making principles perhaps the most important is the differential principle. This asserts that when deciding between alternatives *only those factors which differ between alternatives should be considered.* From this it follows that the only relevant costs are those which differ between alternatives.

To apply this principle in an analysis it is necessary to look at each factor that has a bearing on the overall profit of the enterprise, and decide if selecting one alternative rather than another would alter that factor's effect on the profit. If it would, it is relevant — if not, it isn't.

Close adherence to this principle will not only guide the student towards the correct solution of a problem but also often lessen the work load. In many decision-making examination questions there are a number of irrelevant figures and being able to ignore these almost invariably simplifies the whole problem.

A frequent difficulty in applying the differential principle lies in selecting a base from which differences can be measured. If, for example, only four out of five products can be manufactured, which do you compare with which? To break this deadlock it often pays to select arbitrarily any alternative as a base and test the other alternatives against it. When another alternative proves better, the first is discarded and this other becomes the new base (*see* question 19 in progress test 11).

5. Common costs and common incomes are irrelevant
It follows from the differential principle that any costs or

incomes which are shared in total between the alternatives and will remain unchanged regardless of which alternative is selected are irrelevant and should not be included in the analysis. However, if it is desired to give additional background material such costs and incomes may be added at the end of the analysis, providing that their irrelevance to the decision is made very clear.

6. Interest as a relevant cost
Interest is only a relevant cost where the alternatives have cash-flow differences involving significant amounts and, in addition, significant timing differences, i.e. when the interest payable by the enterprise will differ significantly depending upon the alternative selected. Note that if interest *is* a relevant cost in a decision the decision is called a 'long-term decision' and as such falls outside the scope of this book.

7. Tax as a relevant cost
It should not be forgotten that tax also becomes a relevant cost if the tax payable by the enterprise differs significantly depending on the alternative selected.

8. Existing conditions
If one of the alternatives being considered involves the use of existing equipment or any loss of an existing advantage, then:

(a) if an *asset*, charge its opportunity cost, i.e. net realizable value (*see* **11 (b)**), to the alternative requiring the use of the asset;
(b) if an *advantage*, charge the cash loss which would be suffered by giving up the advantage. (For example, if adopting alternative X will result in the loss of bulk discounts then X must be charged with the value of lost discounts for purpose of making the decision.) It is under this heading that consideration should be given to the contribution per unit of key factor (*see* **11:18**).

9. Principles of data presentation
Analysing the data correctly is only part of the management accountant's responsibility in decision-making. Equally important is the presentation of the data in an appropriate manner.

(a) Always comply with the general principles of data presentation. (These principles are essentially statistical in form and the student is advised to refer to any of the appropriate texts on this subject, e.g. *Statistics*, W. M. Harper, M & E Handbook series.)

(b) Always bear in mind *the use to which the figures will be put*. (This, of course, is a fundamental cost accounting rule — *see* 1:22.) Do not include any figures which may mislead, e.g. a cost-per-unit figure based on full capacity when full capacity cannot be attained.

(c) Always present figures in a comparative form. This enables managers to see how, why and where differences between alternatives arise and gives them insight into, and confidence in, the final conclusions.

(d) Always present the conclusion clearly. State the obvious — to the uninitiated in management accounting it could well be the most perfectly camouflaged data in the whole presentation.

10. Decision-making advice

When involved in decision-making bear in mind the following advice:

(a) *Irrelevance of book values.* Don't forget that book values, being past costs are *never* relevant in decision-making (and even if the book value is an up-to-date replacement value it is still rarely the value required in decision-making — *see* 11).

(b) *Time span.* It is often advisable to calculate all figures in an analysis in respect of the total time-span involved. Although this may result in large figures, this is preferable to combining figures computed for shorter terms when errors of principle may arise in the combination process. For example, to take a trivial case, if 300 and 100 units are produced in the first and second halves of the time span at costs of £6 and £4 a unit respectively, the overall cost per unit is *not* £5.

(c) *Fixed and variable costs.* Do not assume that fixed costs are always irrelevant nor that variable costs are always relevant. As will be seen, it is always possible that some fixed costs will differ between alternatives and sometimes there are variable costs which do not differ, e.g. if the decision lies between buying the raw material at £5 a ton from one supplier or £4 a ton from another, the other unit variable costs are clearly all irrelevant.

(d) *Standing alternatives.* It should be remembered that there are always two standing alternatives with which any new plan can be compared. These are:

(*i*) do nothing, i.e. carry on as currently engaged.

(*ii*) place the funds required for the plan in an outside investment.

This means in the case of (*i*) a comparison of the consequences following from the operation of the plan with continued current operations, and in the case of (*ii*) a comparison of the return on capital with outside investment possibilities.

It should be noted that *at any time* a comparison can be initiated between (*i*) and (*ii*) for *any project*, i.e. between carrying on as currently engaged, as against the liquidation of current operations, and the subsequent investment of the funds released elsewhere.

(e) *Inflation.* Where inflation is likely to complicate the figures, then it is advisable to edit out its effects. This, however, requires the employment of a statistical technique and so the student is again referred to the texts that illustrate such a technique.

(f) *Decisions involving multi-alternatives.* When the number of alternatives to be considered is large, it is often advisable to split the alternatives into small groups (sometimes even pairs). Each group is then considered in turn, and the best alternative singled out. Subsequent comparisons between these preferred alternatives will indicate the best one to adopt. In other words, in effect, run a knock-out competition between the alternatives.

Such a course is advisable because the relevance of a factor often depends upon which alternatives are being compared. To try to compare all alternatives simultaneously will involve so many factors that the comparison will be very complicated. Initial rejection of inferior alternatives within given groups very much lessens the complexity of the final analysis.

(g) *Applying the differential principle.* Finally, remember that in a decision-making analysis it is necessary to:

(*i*) introduce any and every factor that will differ between alternatives and which will have an effect on the profit of the enterprise, e.g. changes in incomes, changes in fixed costs, interest;

(*ii*) ignore every factor that will remain the same whichever alternative is selected.

This can, perhaps, be summarized by saying that the costs that are relevant to decision-making are *the future costs that differ*.

11. Historical, net realizable and replacement values

At this point the student may be uncertain as to the role in decision-making of the different ways of valuing existing assets.

(a) *Historical values.* These should *never* be used.

(b) *Net realizable values.* The net realizable value (i.e. what would be received on disposal of an asset less the costs of the disposal) should always be taken as the true measure of the worth of an asset. It follows, therefore, that the depreciation cost of using such an asset over the decision period is the difference between its net realizable value at the beginning and its net realizable value at the end of that period.

(c) *Replacement values.* The function of a replacement value is to provide a measure of the economic worth of an existing asset outside the particular circumstances of the enterprise, and in these kinds of circumstance it should be used to reach a decision. For instance, in setting a price a manager may not be so much concerned with the minimum level that follows from using net realizable value as the average economic price that the market would regard as reasonable. For this, replacement value serves best.

12. Full cost *v.* differential cost

It is here advocated that only differential costs should be used in decision-making and never full costs (i.e. costs resulting from common costs being apportioned between alternatives). However, where there is a disturbing element of uncertainty about the behaviour of future costs — particularly where there has been experience of so-called 'fixed' costs creeping upwards with increasing activity — many managers feel it is safer to use a full cost approach. While the accountant may, and should, try to allay the manager's fears, he must nevertheless respect his feelings. After all, if the accountant's evidence fails to convince then it is probable that some valid doubt does exist.

Progress test 9

Principles

1. What is a relevant cost? (2)

2.   How are the following to be classified in terms of relevance for decision-making: (*a*) future costs;   **(3)** (*b*) common costs; **(5)** (*c*) common income;   **(5)** (*d*) interest;   **(6)** (*e*) tax.   **(7)**

3.   What is the differential principle?   **(4)**

4.   What are the principles of data presentation?   **(9)**

5.   When do you use historical, net realizable and replacement values in a decision-making situation?   **(11)**

10
Short-term decision-making

There is really only one decision-making technique and that is differential costing. However, in different circumstances some kinds of cost differences are more significant than others. As a result there are a number of different decision-making techniques, although since all do no more than emphasize different aspects there is inevitably no clear distinction between one technique and another. In selecting a technique, therefore, it is not so much a matter of selecting the correct technique as selecting the most appropriate technique. Correctness relates only to the application of the decision-making principles given in Chapter 9.

The decision-making techniques can initially be divided into short- and long-term techniques, again with no hard-and-fast dividing line. The criteria for the division is no more than the relevance of interest — if interest is a significant cost then a long-term technique is needed while if it is not significant a short-term technique can be used. These latter techniques include marginal costing (*see* Chapter 11), cash flow and opportunity costing and conventionally fall within the ambit of costing — long-term decision-making being regarded as an essentially management accounting topic.

Differential costing

First, we look at the most fundamental of the decision-making techniques.

1. **Scope of differential costing**
    This technique identifies the most profitable of a group of

alternatives by *identifying the cost differences between the alternatives and ignoring those costs that remain unaffected by the decision* (cost here includes income). While variations in this technique give rise to techniques that exist in their own right, e.g. marginal costing (*see* Chapter 11), there are occasions when none of these specialist techniques is wholly suitable. Analyses that use a direct application of the differential principle are frequently termed *differential cost analyses*.

2.   Common differential costing circumstances

Differential costing is most commonly used where two alternatives are, in cost differential terms, nearly identical. Thus, selecting which out of a number of suppliers should be given an order rarely involves more than comparing prices — nothing more complicated is needed. Similarly, if two schemes will result in identical variable costs and incomes and only certain fixed costs will be different, then a direct comparison of these fixed costs will at once identify the more profitable alternative.

It should be appreciated that there are occasions when alternatives appear more at variance than they really are. Thus, if there is a decision involving a critical resource then the cost of this resource will remain unchanged whichever alternative is selected (if it won't, then the resource is not being fully exploited). Consequently in a differential cost analysis this cost will be ignored. For example, if the critical resource were labour hours, of which there were only 1,000, to be paid at £5 an hour, then, since the full number available will inevitably be used, the total labour cost will always be £5,000 whichever alternative is selected. Since such costs do not alter they will be excluded from the differential cost analysis.

Example _____

	Product A	Product B
Selling price	£30	£70
Material	£4	£20
Labour (at £5 hr)	5 hr	10 hr

Labour is the critical resource. Should A or B be produced?

Solution

Relevant figures:	A	B
Production per 10 hours:	2 units	1 unit
Sales	£60	£70
Materials	£8	£20
Net differential income per 10 hours	£52	£50

A should be selected since £2 more profit will be earned every 10 hours of the crucial resource than would be earned if B were selected.

NOTE: (1) Labour costs, being the same for both alternatives, are excluded. (2) The figures show only the *differences* between the alternatives and in no way measure actual profit, only profitability.

3. Unchanged income decisions

There are sometimes occasions when the total income remains unaffected by the decision. This is particularly the case where a decision has to be made as to which products should be sub-contracted where demand exceeds capacity. On these occasions the income can be ignored and the decision based on a cost minimization analysis.

4. Absolute and relative costs

When a comparison is required between two alternatives only, then the presentation of differential costs can be made using either absolute costs or relative costs.

(a) *Absolute costs.* Using this approach the full costs and incomes that differ are listed for each alternative so that the two net differential figures can be compared and the more profitable alternative identified, as in **2** above.

(b) *Relative costs.* Using this approach one alternative is taken as 'base' and the gain or loss in respect of each item of income and cost that would result if the other alternative were selected instead is detailed. This results in a final figure that indicates the net total gain or loss that would follow if the second alternative were substituted for the 'base' alternative, and so indicates whether or not such a substitution is profitable. If this method had been adopted for the problem in **2** above the presentation would have been as follows.

Example
_____

Taking the production of A as base, the substitution of B would have the
following consequences:

Extra sales every 10 labour hours: £70 — £60	£10
Extra costs producing B: £20 — £8	£12
Net difference	£2 loss

Producing B will lose £2 per 10 hours of labour. Therefore A should
be produced.

_____

Cash flow technique

The differential approach in decision-making can be applied to
cash alone in many situations — which needless to say simplifies
much of the work involved in assessing the alternatives.

5. Definition of cash flow
   Cash flow is the actual movement of cash in and out of an
enterprise. Cash flow in (or *positive cash flow*) is cash received, and
cash flow out (*negative cash flow*) is cash paid out. The difference
between these two flows is termed the *net cash flow*.

6. When to use the cash flow technique
   The circumstances in which a cash flow decision-making
technique can be employed are those in which the prime
differences can be measured in terms of the future cash flows of
the alternatives. In essence the underlying principle of the
technique can be stated as follows: *the most profitable alternative is the
one that will, over the period for which a solution is required, most
favourably affect the bank balance of the enterprise, other things being
equal.* In other words, the most profitable alternative is that
alternative which makes one richest.

7. Application of the cash flow technique
   To apply the cash flow technique for decision making:

(a) For each alternative compute:

(*i*) the *future* cash flows both in and out that would result from
the selection of the alternative;

(*ii*) the overall net cash flow.

(b) Select the alternative having the most favourable net cash
flow.

Example _____

A finished goods stock item that cost £200 to make is in danger of
becoming completely obsolete. There are two alternative ways of
disposing of it: sell it to X for £200 or to Y for £216. Y is situated twice as
far away as X (although owing to road conditions the delivery time will
be the same) and the cost accountant has supplied the following cost
estimates for delivery:

X — petrol and oil £10; wages £12; share of licence, insurance and
depreciation (based on mileage) £14;

Y — petrol and oil £20; wages £12; share of licence, insurance and
depreciation £28.

Should the item be sold to X or Y?

Solution

	X	Y
Cash flow in: Sales	£+200	£+216
Cash flow out: Petrol, oil and wages	−22	−32
Net cash flow	£+178	£+184

Since Y has the most favourable net cash flow the correct decision is
to sell to Y.

NOTE: (1) The £14 and £28 share of the licence, insurance and
depreciation are not included as there is no actual future outflow of
cash in respect of these costs. This exclusion is, of course, as it should
be since the actual amounts incurred by the business remains
unchanged whichever delivery is undertaken — or even if neither
is undertaken. (2) The net cash flow does not measure the profit
(there is a loss whichever alternative is selected) but only indicates
which alternative is the more profitable.

_____

8. Qualification to the cash flow principle

Despite the unarguable logic of the cash flow principle,
students are often concerned at the total disregard of those costs
which are not represented by actual future cash flows. In one
respect their concern is justified, for the principle does contain a

vital qualification, *other things being equal*. In other words it is necessary that, whichever alternative is selected, at the very end the enterprise will be in exactly the same position except as regards its bank balance. Sometimes this is not so: under one alternative the enterprise may be left with goods in stock, or a plot of land, or an old machine. In such cases the net cash flow figures emerging as a result of employing the pure cash flow technique must be adjusted to allow for such left-over items.

9. Past flows irrelevant

In another respect — that involving past flows — the concern of students is unfounded. If an enterprise had earlier paid out a sum of money for some item, then this amount does *not* enter the calculations, for no matter which alternative is selected the payment cannot be eliminated and, therefore, under the decision-making principles it fails to be relevant. It may be difficult to accept that a sum of £1m paid last week for a piece of equipment has absolutely no bearing on the decision to dispose of that piece of equipment this week, but it is nevertheless a correct statement of principle.

10. Depreciation and cash flow

It was noted in the example in **7** above that since depreciation does not involve a flow of cash it does not appear in a cash flow analysis. This does not mean that it will be overlooked completely. For instance, where one alternative calls for the purchase of an asset the purchase price of the asset will enter the analysis as a negative cash flow while the anticipated receipt for the final residual value will enter as a positive cash flow. Since the difference between these amounts is, in fact, the asset depreciation, the depreciation is taken into account, though not as a single specified sum.

This inclusion of depreciation also occurs in respect of an existing asset in a replacement decision (*see* Progress test, q. **7**) albeit in a somewhat roundabout way. Careful study of the cash flow analysis made in such a case will show this depreciation to be allowed for by the combined effects of:

(a) recording the positive flow that would arise from the *ultimate* sale of the asset as part of the case for retaining the asset; and

(b) recording the higher positive flow that would arise from the *immediate* sale of the asset as part of the case for replacing the asset.

Again, the difference between these two figures is the asset depreciation.

11. Absolute and relative cash flows
Cash flows can be presented as absolute flows or relative flows in exactly the same way as costs (*see* **4**).

In **7** above a statement using absolute flows was given. The same problem can be reworked using relative flows as follows.

Example

Taking the sale to X as base, the substitution of the sale to Y gives the following relative cash flows:

Sales — extra cash flow	£+16
Costs — extra cash flow	–10
Net relative flow	£+6

Selling to Y will improve the overall cash flow by £6. Therefore the sale should be to Y.

12. Advantages of using the cash flow technique
The advantages of using the cash flow technique are as follows.

(a) It is a relatively simple technique — only actual cash flows in and out have to be considered. There are no complications involving the matching of costs and revenue, no temptations to apportion fixed costs to alternatives, and no problems of depreciation.
(b) By concentrating on future cash flows it automatically prevents past costs being unnecessarily included in the calculations and so avoids the possibility of erroneous treatment of such past costs.
(c) It avoids misguided attempts to saddle particular alternatives with unrecovered past costs. For example, some managements believe they cannot discontinue a specific product until it has 'recovered' its tooling costs. They fail to appreciate that continued production of an inferior product often makes less profit than the introduction of a better product, despite heavy unrecovered costs.
(d) It is needed if a discounted cash flow analysis is required

(although the analysis then becomes a long-term one and as such falls outside the scope of this book).

Opportunity costing

In many ways the concept of opportunity cost is the hardest of all the costing concepts to apply, both in practice and in theory. It is difficult in practice because the opportunity costs are all too often not known and not accessible, and it is difficult in theory because opportunity costs are not absolute — as will be shown, they depend very much on the probability that the opportunity can be taken.

13. Opportunity cost

An *opportunity cost* is an economic concept that can perhaps be most simply defined as *the value of a benefit sacrificed in favour of* (or as a result of) *taking an alternative course of action*. For instance, if you have a material that you can sell at £1 a kilo, then the opportunity cost of using that material in your own production is £1 a kilo, *regardless of how much you paid for it*. Again, if you could earn extra net income of £200 by travelling to London instead of Manchester, then the opportunity cost of your travelling to Manchester instead is £200.

As can be seen, the concept of an opportunity cost is not difficult. Problems do begin to arise, however, when there are doubts about the validity of the opportunity, e.g. if it is only possible, and not certain, that you can sell your material at £1 a kilo or that you would earn an extra £200 by travelling to London.

14. Opportunity costing

In opportunity costing all the costs involved in an analysis are opportunity costs. In principle opportunity costs should always be used in decision-making since decision-making aims at maximizing profit and such profit maximization depends upon the up-to-date economic valuation of all resources and capacity used. Thus, if you bought a gallon of solvent for £1.10 and then sold it for £1.20 when the market price was £1.30 it could be argued that as far as the book-keeping went you had made a profit of 10p, but as far as the decision-making went you had made a loss of 10p. In other words, since the cost objective in decision-making is to find the relative profit of one alternative over another, all competing resources and activities must be valued on the basis of their own maximum profit potential rather than on any other basis.

15. Resources and activities
Although there is no theoretical distinction between the opportunity cost of a resource and that of an activity it probably pays in practice to be aware of the difference between these two factors. They can be defined roughly as follows:

(a) An *activity* is anything that the enterprise *will* 'produce' (or process), be it a product or a service.
(b) A *resource* is anything that the enterprise holds that can be disposed of without further processing. Timber and screws are obvious examples, but contracted labour, too, is a resource, as is land. Plant and equipment are resources which must not be overlooked.

The crucial distinction is that an activity, as against a resource, will make a future demand on the capacity of an enterprise. Whereas resources can be sold in whatever quantities the enterprise happens to possess without affecting other aspects of the enterprise's work, selling an activity does affect those aspects and these must be assessed.

16. Zero and negative opportunity costs
It is a feature of opportunity costs that in many instances they are zero. This can arise, for instance, when an employee is engaged for 40 hours at an inescapable £150 but there is only 30 hours work for him to do. Here the remaining 10 hours are free as regards valuing his time for any other work. Even if a net income of only £5 (excluding any charge for other than labour) is earned, that is £5 more profit than would otherwise be made. Thus, the opportunity cost of the 10 hours is zero (though note that once this £5 net income work exists the opportunity cost to any other alternative now rises to £5).
Although labour is probably the commonest example of a zero opportunity cost, instances also arise where, through obsolescence, a machine is completely worthless. Clearly, in using such a machine an enterprise suffers no sacrifice and the opportunity cost, therefore, is zero.

There are also, though rarely, cases where the opportunity cost is negative, e.g. where an obsolete machine not only has no residual value but would even incur costs in its disposal. Regrettably, in such a case the opportunity cost of the 'depreciation' would not be negative since disposal would be no cheaper after use than before. However, if a project actually resulted in the disposal of the machine as a spin-off then the opportunity cost could be included in the project analysis as a negative figure.

17. Complications in determining a resource opportunity cost
Strictly speaking, it could perhaps be argued that to find the value of a resource opportunity cost it is necessary to ascertain the highest net receipt that could be obtained if the resource were sold on the same day as it was to be used in the proposed alternative. However this runs contrary to the spirit of the definition, for if it were known that the disposal value of the resource would be doubled a week later then this doubled value should really be adopted as the opportunity cost — it is certainly the opportunity cost of disposing of the resource now as against holding it for a little longer. But if *future* disposal values are valid opportunity costs, where does the process of looking to the future end? And how sure must one be that the value will rise for a future value to be a valid opportunity cost?

This is not all, for it can also be queried as to whether an opportunity cost has to be based on a disposal value. For example, if, because of transport complications, a resource would cost an enterprise twice as much to buy as it would to sell, is the disposal value or the replacement value the correct opportunity cost? The answer seems to depend upon whether the resource would in fact be replaced. If it would, then the replacement value should be taken. If not, the disposal value is used. But if the replacement value is to be used, should that be the current replacement value or the known future value, or even the suspected future value?

18. Opportunity costs and uncertainty
As is doubtless becoming clear, an opportunity cost is by no means a certain cost, even where the problems of future values and replacement costs do not arise, for it depends very much on making an economic valuation in a world that is notoriously

lacking in economic certainty. So it is often very difficult to say just what you would receive if you sold some of a given material held in stock. You may get the ruling market price or you may not. Indeed, you may get above the market price if you were to sell to a financially insecure customer, but would the higher price really be the opportunity cost? These problems can become even bigger if the resource is your own product, and your product is unique. You *may* be awarded a contract for £200,000 if you really made the effort but if you decide to select a different alternative you will never know if you would have succeeded or not. So how can you value the sacrifice made by not making the attempt to win the contract at £200,000? And if you don't value it at £200,000 what *do* you value it at?

19. Conclusion
From all this it can be seen that determining an opportunity cost is not always a straightforward exercise. In practice it may also be difficult even to find disposal values on the day in question, let alone future replacement values in what is possibly a very imperfect market. An opportunity cost, therefore, is often far more of a subjective than an objective valuation. How, then, should one proceed?

Unfortunately, no firm criteria can be laid down. Given the concept that the opportunity cost to be charged to a given alternative is the maximum sacrifice that an enterprise would suffer in giving up some other alternative, then all the practitioner can do is to test each item against that concept. When your figures are certain you can proceed with confidence. When uncertainty and doubt begin to enter you must be more cautious of the interpretation of your results.

Progress test 10

Principles

1. What is: (*a*) differential costing? (**1**) (*b*) cash-flow technique for decision-making? (**7**) (*c*) opportunity costing? (**14**)

2. Distinguish between: (*a*) absolute and relative costs; **(4)** (*b*) absolute and relative cash flows. **(11)**

3. How does depreciation enter into a cash flow analysis? **(10)**

4. What is an opportunity cost? **(13)**

5. Explain when an opportunity cost can be: (*a*) zero? (*b*) negative? **(16)**

6. What problems arise in using opportunity costs? **(17–19)**

Practice

7. A company is considering replacing a sound but somewhat old-fashioned machine by a more up-to-date special purpose one. Unfortunately, in five years' time the work done on these types of machine will end. The facts are as below and you are to determine whether or not to replace the existing machine.

	Existing machine	*New machine*
Book value	£24,000	—
Resale value now	10,000	—
Purchase price	40,000	£30,000
Residual value in 5 years	4,000	2,000
Annual cash running costs	9,000	6,000
Annual receipts from production	10,000	12,000

8. The company of which you are the management accountant has obtained a contract to supply 200,000 metal fittings at £5 each.

To undertake this work a special purpose machine has been purchased for £22,000 which at the end of the contract will have a residual value of £2,000.

Estimated production costs are:

Direct material, per unit	£1.50
Direct labour, per unit	£1.00
Variable production overhead, of direct labour costs	60%
Fixed production overhead, excluding depreciation, for the contract	£40,000
Variable selling overhead, per unit	£0.30
Fixed selling overhead, for the contract	£80,000

Although the contract has not yet started a second machine of more advanced design has been offered to the company for £36,000. This machine will produce 25 per cent more units per operator hour but will use 5 per cent more material. The machine will have no residual value at the end of the contract. The makers are prepared to buy back the first machine for £5,000.

The works manager has in the circumstances asked if the second machine should be purchased. You are required to advise the works manager of the action to be taken.

(CIMA adapted)

9. A company incurred a tooling cost of £200,000 for a product whose manufacture and sales were planned to be 5,000 units a year for five years. The total cost build-up per unit is as follows:

Direct materials	£4
Direct labour (2 hr at £4 hr)	8
Share of tooling cost	8
Fixed overheads (at £8 hr)	16
	36
Profit	4
Selling price	£40

After only six months' production the company learns there is a good market (lasting at least 4½ years) for another type of product which has a direct material cost of £6, a selling price of £16 and requires 1/2 hour's labour to make. Unfortunately labour is in short supply and to make this product would mean permanently abandoning the first product, scrapping the tools, and switching all labour over to the second product. This second product would, in addition, require an extra expenditure of £12,000 p.a. on fixed costs.

Which product should the company manufacture?

10. A foundry sells for £200 a unit a product which is essentially two halves assembled together, a right-hand half and a left-hand half. The casting requirements to make either half are:

Material, 1 tonne at £40 a tonne;
Labour, £10

The assembly cost for joining the two halves together is £20 per finished unit, i.e. per pair of halves.

Unfortunately material is in scarce supply and the foundry has only 200 tonnes available for the forthcoming period. It has, however, been offered a supply of completed right-hand halves. What is the maximum price the foundry would be prepared to pay to buy these halves if all units made could be sold and if a total cost of £400 would be incurred in transporting the load of purchased halves to the foundry?

11. AB Limited has just completed production of an item of special equipment for a customer, ST Limited, only to be notified that the customer has gone into liquidation.

After much effort, the sales manager has managed to locate one potential buyer, VW Limited, which has indicated that it might be prepared to buy the machine if certain conversion work could be carried out.

The selling price of the machine to the original buyer had been fixed at £101,200 and had included an estimated normal profit mark-up of 10 per cent on total costs. The costs incurred in the manufacture of the machine were:

Direct materials	£38,000
Direct wages	24,000
Overheads:	
variable	6,000
fixed, production	20,000
fixed, selling and administration	4,000
	£92,000

If the machine is converted, production management assesses that the following extra work would be needed.

Direct materials, at cost, £6,400
Direct wages:
Department L: 3 men for 4 weeks at £300 per man/week
Department M: 1 man for 4 weeks at £240 per man/week
Variable overhead:
20 per cent of direct wages
Fixed production overhead:
Department L: 83⅓ per cent of direct wages
Department M: 25 per cent of direct wages.

The following additional information is available.

(a) In the original machine there are three types of basic materials:
  (i) type P could now be sold to a scrap merchant for £6,000;
  (ii) type Q could be sold to the scrap merchant for £4,000, but it would take 120 hours of labour paid at £3 per hour to put it into a suitable condition for sale;
  (iii) type R would need to be scrapped at a cost to AB Limited of £1,200.
(b) The materials for the conversion are at present in stock. If not needed for the conversion, they could be used in the production of another machine in place of materials that would currently cost £7,600.
(c) The conversion would be carried out in two departments. Department L is currently extremely busy and it is estimated that its contribution to overhead and profits is £2.50 per £1 of labour.
  Department M is very short of work. For organizational reasons its labour force cannot be reduced below its present level of four employees, all of whom are paid at the standard wage of £240 per week. The load of work on these employees is, however, only 40 per cent of their standard capacity.
(d) The designs and specifications of the original machine could be sold overseas for a sum of £3,000 if the machine is scrapped.
(e) An additional temporary supervisor would have to be

engaged for the conversion work at a cost of £1,800. It is the company's normal practice to charge supervision to fixed overhead.

(f) Customer ST Limited paid a non-returnable deposit to the company of 12 per cent of the selling price.

You are required to:

(a) calculate the minimum price that AB Limited should accept from VW Limited for the converted machine, explaining clearly how you have arrived at your figure;

(b) state briefly any assumptions that you have made in arriving at your conclusions.

(CIMA adapted)

11
Marginal costing

In Chapter 3 total absorption costing was shown to adopt the principle of *sharing* each cost between cost units and cost centres on the basis of benefit received. The underlying objective of that technique was to obtain an overall average economic cost of carrying out whatever activity was being costed. However, overall averages are of only limited use where day-to-day management is involved — as many people paying income tax will confirm, for if they are given the chance of overtime it is their marginal rate of tax that is of significance and not their average rate. In this chapter, therefore, a more immediately useful technique of ascertaining costs will be outlined.

1. Marginal cost ascertainment

Marginal cost ascertainment is based on the view that in many practical short-term situations the cost of any given activity is the cost that that activity specifically generates — and no more. Put another way, it is the difference in cost between carrying out and not carrying out that activity. To achieve this the following principle is adopted in respect of all cost data:

> In *marginal cost ascertainment* each cost unit and each cost centre is charged with only those costs that are generated as a consequence of that cost unit and that cost centre being a part of the enterprise's activities.

2. Marginal costs

The costs which are generated solely by a given *cost unit* are the variable costs associated with that unit (the variable cost here including the variable cost element of any associated semi-variable cost). Ascertaining these costs simply involves ascertaining:

(a) all the unit direct costs;
(b) the variable overhead cost per unit incurred by the cost unit.

Costs ascertained on this basis are termed *marginal costs,* and the marginal cost of a cost unit can be defined as the *additional cost of producing one such unit.* It follows as a matter of course that the marginal cost of a number of units (similar or otherwise) is the sum of all the unit marginal costs.

> NOTE: The difference between the terms 'variable cost' and 'marginal cost' is primarily one of context. We normally talk of the marginal cost of a cost unit, but the variable cost of a cost centre.

3. Preparation of a unit marginal cost
To prepare a unit marginal cost, therefore, involves ascertaining the unit direct costs and the variable overhead costs per unit. Finding the unit direct costs in marginal costing is no different from finding these costs in absorption costing. Finding the variable overhead cost per unit for each overhead cost, however, calls for the following steps.

(a) The variable cost per unit of activity (e.g. direct labour hours) is found from a cost behaviour analysis.
(b) The number of units of activity per cost unit are ascertained.
(c) The variable overhead cost per cost unit is found by multiplying **(a)** by **(b)**.

Example
_____
If a cost behaviour analysis showed that the variable cost element of a certain overhead was £2 per direct labour hour and that a cost unit required 4 hours of direct labour, the cost unit variable overhead would be 4 x £2 = £8.
_____

Once all the individual variable costs per unit, direct and variable overhead, have been found they are added together to give the marginal cost of the cost unit.

Example
_____
Odds and Ends. The Odds 'n' Ends Department manufactures Odds and Ends. Each Odd requires £15 of direct material and 3 direct labour hours while each End requires £10 of direct material and 5 direct labour hours. Direct labour is paid at £3 per hour and an analysis of the overheads shows

there is a variable overhead cost of £2 per direct labour hour. Ascertain the marginal cost per unit of each product.

Solution

		Odd	End
		£	£
Marginal cost: Direct material		15	10
Direct labour	3 x £3 =	9	5 x £3 = 15
Variable overhead	3 x £2 =	6	5 x £2 = 10
Marginal cost per unit		£30	£35

4. Marginal costing

This is the name given to any system of costing which is based upon the preparation and use of the marginal costs of cost units. Formally it has been defined as 'The accounting system in which variable costs are charged to cost units and fixed costs of the product are written off in full against the aggregate contribution' (CIMA terminology). For contribution, *see* 9.

5. Identifiable fixed costs

A fixed cost has been defined as a cost which remains unchanged regardless of the level of activity within the relevant activity range. The word 'activity', however, can refer not only to *how much* is being done but also to *what* is being done. So if an employee made screws one day and washers the next we could say that the *nature* of the activity had changed. Now, as a little thought will indicate, there will be some fixed costs which will still stay unchanged in this situation regardless of changes in the nature of the activity (e.g. audit fees) and there are some which will not stay unchanged (e.g. the hire charge per day for a tool that can only be used to make screws). A fixed cost that *changes with the nature of the activity* is called an *identifiable fixed cost*. To identify such a cost it is only necessary to ask oneself if the cost would disappear if the activity were different. If it would, then the cost is identifiable.

In marginal cost ascertainment the cost of any identifiable fixed cost is added to the *total* marginal cost of the activity with which it is identified.

Example
Odds and Ends (continued). In the Odds 'n' Ends Department the production of Odds requires an Odd Moulding machine, which is hired at £100 per week, while the production of Ends requires an End Moulding machine at a hire charge of £60 a week. Ascertain the weekly costs of Odds and Ends for a week in which 30 Odds and 20 Ends were produced.

Solution

	Odds	Ends
	£	£
Marginal costs for the week	30 x £30 =900	20 x £35 = 700
Identifiable fixed costs:		
Moulding machine hire	100	60
Product costs for week	£1,000	£760

It should be appreciated that fixed costs may not only be identifiable with products. They can also be identifiable with cost centres. Thus the salary of the Odds 'n' Ends foreman would be an identifiable fixed cost in respect of that department.

6. Unidentifiable fixed costs

Fixed costs that cannot be identified with either a product or a cost centre are called *unidentifiable fixed costs*. Such costs must never be charged out to products or centres.

The student should carefully note that fixed costs which are unidentifiable at one level may well be identifiable at another. Thus, while the Odds 'n' Ends foreman's salary is unidentifiable as regards the products it is identifiable as regards the Odds 'n' Ends Department. On the other hand, the managing director's salary is not identifiable with any of the departments but only with the company as a whole.

Example
Odds and Ends (continued). Further analysis of the costs in the Odds 'n' Ends Department reveals that the departmental fixed cost element amounts to £600 per week. Ascertain the departmental cost for the week specified in **5**.

Solution

	£
Product costs for week:Odds	1,000
Ends	760
Fixed cost unidentifiable with products but identifiable with department	600
Departmental cost for week	£2,360

7. Contribution per unit

Having seen how costs are ascertained under the marginal costing technique we can now turn to see how sales enter the marginal cost statements.

First of all it should be realized that there is a very direct link between unit marginal cost and selling price since the selling price is a price per unit. On the one hand, therefore, the unit marginal cost will show the *additional cost* of producing one more unit, while on the other hand the selling price will show the *additional income* from selling one more unit. Clearly the difference will be the *additional profit* to the enterprise that will result if just one more unit is made and sold. This direct linkage is the most important consequence that flows from using a marginal cost technique, and this additional profit figure is so important that it is given its own name: the *unit contribution.*

In view of the importance of this concept it is worth reiterating the logic behind it. This asserts that since all fixed costs remain unchanged by the production of one more unit, the only cost increase resulting from the production of one more unit is the increase in the variable cost. This variable cost increase is measured by the marginal cost of the unit and so the difference between the selling price and this marginal cost, the unit contribution, must measure the increase in the profit of the enterprise that arises from the production and sale of that one unit.

Example

Odds and Ends (continued). The selling prices of Odds and Ends are £50 and £75 respectively. What are the unit contributions?

Solution

	Odd	End
	£	£
Selling price	50	75
Unit marginal cost	30	35
Unit contribution	£20	£40

8. Net contribution

Where more than one unit is made and sold the total contribution is obviously the sum of all the unit contributions. Where the units are all identical this is equal to the number of units multiplied by the unit contribution. However, if the number of units is the total units of the product then any product identifiable fixed costs can be deducted to give the additional profit that arises from the production and sale of the product itself. This figure, which is obtained by deducting the identifiable fixed costs from the total contribution, can be called the *net contribution*.

Note that the net contributions at one level can be added together and then the identifiable fixed costs at a higher level can be deducted to give the net contribution at that higher level (e.g. product net contributions can be added and then the departmental identifiable fixed cost deducted to give the departmental net contribution, and this procedure repeated at a higher level so that a yet more all-inclusive contribution is found).

Example

Odds and Ends (continued). From the earlier figures find the weekly product net contributions and the departmental net contribution.

Solution

	Odds	Ends
	£	£
Product contributions:		
Total cost unit contributions 30 x £20 =	600	20 x 40 = 800
Less Product identifiable fixed costs	100	60
Product net contribution	£500	£740

Departmental contributions:	£
Product net contributions: Odds	500
Ends	740
Total product net contribution	1,240
Less Departmental identifiable fixed	
costs (*see* **6**)	600
Departmental net contribution	£640

9. Interpreting contributions

Contributions must be interpreted correctly if the cost information is to prove useful. Though such interpretation is essentially a matter of common sense, the contributions so far discussed will be briefly reinterpreted as follows:

(a) The unit contribution shows how much additional profit will be earned if just one more unit is made and sold, e.g. if one more Odd were made and sold the profit would increase by £20. This profit increase repeats for each additional unit up to the point where there is a change in the pattern of the cost behaviour — usually when fixed costs increase as a result of additional facilities being required.

(b) The product net contribution shows how much additional profit is earned as a result of the product being made and sold in its entirety, e.g. in the case of Odds, £500 per week. To put it the other way round, discontinuing a product would result in the enterprise profit falling by the product net contribution.

(c) The departmental (or cost centre) net contribution shows how much additional profit is earned as a result of the activities of the department, e.g. in the case of the Odds 'n' Ends Department, £640 per week. Again, putting it the other way round, if the department closed down the enterprise profit would fall by the departmental net contribution.

From these interpretations it can be seen that the term *contribution* can be defined generally as *the additional profit resulting from carrying out a specified activity.* More formally it has been defined as 'Sales value less variable cost of sales' (CIMA terminology).

10. The irrelevance of the enterprise overall profit position

When interpreting contributions the interpretation is usually made in terms of increasing or decreasing the enterprise profit. Note, however, that the interpretation is essentially unaffected if the enterprise, is, in fact, making a loss. In such a case any contribution lessens the enterprise loss by the amount of the contribution. Phrasing the interpretation more generally still it can be said that a *contribution directly measures the effect of an activity on the overall profit and loss position of the enterprise.*

11. Worked example

A processing plant, producing 30- and 50-litre drums of solvent, has the following costs and sales:

	30-litre drums	50-litre drums
Direct cost per drum	£5	£8
Selling price per drum	£26	£40

Activity: Drums processed and sold:		
Period 1	200	100
Period 2	150	150

Overheads (semi-variable): Period 1 – £6,200; Period 2 – £6,600. Litres are an excellent measure of activity.

(a) How much profit would the plant earn if 100 30-litre and 200 50-litre drums of solvent were processed and sold?

(b) How much more profit would be earned if the output in **(a)** were increased by 10 per cent?

Solution

(a) (i)   If the overhead is a semi-variable, the difference in cost between the two periods must represent the variable cost change (since the fixed cost element does not change at all) as a result of the activity change. Therefore:

	Period 1 Litres	Period 2 Litres	Difference
Activity: 30-litre drums	30 x 200 = 6,000	30 x 150 = 4,500	
50-litre drums	50 x 100 = 5,000	50 x 150 = 7,500	
	11,000	12,000	1,000
Overheads	£6,200	£6,600	£400

∴ 1,000 litres have a variable cost of £400.

∴ Variable cost per unit of activity (litre) = $\dfrac{£400}{1,000}$ = £0.40

In addition, if the variable cost is £0.40 per litre, the variable cost element in period 1 would be 11,000 x £0.40 = £4,400. Since the total cost was £6,200, the fixed cost element must be £6,200 – £4,400 = £1,800.

(*ii*) Knowing the variable overhead cost per litre, the unit contributions can be found:

	30-litre drum	50-litre drum
	£	£
Direct costs	5	8
Variable overheads	30 x £0.40 = 12	50 x £0.40 = 20
Unit marginal cost	17	28
Selling price	26	40
Unit contribution	£9	£12

(*iii*) Knowing the unit contribution, the profit can be found:

Product contributions:		£
30-litre drums	100 x £9	900
50-litre drums	200 x £12	2,400
Total contribution from products		3,300
Less total fixed costs		1,800
Profit		£1,500

(b) If output were increased by 10 per cent the total contribution from products would increase by 10 per cent. Moreover, this whole increase would be additional profit.

∴ Additional profit = 10 per cent of £3,300 = £330.

12. Marginal cost accounting

While marginal costing is often employed outside the formal book-keeping system, it is possible to keep all the accounts on a marginal costing basis. When marginal cost book-keeping is practised the system differs from the accounting systems discussed in Chapter 5 only as regards the fixed costs. Since in marginal cost accounting it is argued that fixed costs are time and not activity based, they should be charged only against time and not activities, i.e. written off to profit and loss in the period they are incurred, and never charged to cost units. Application of this principle has the following effects.

(a) Fixed costs are charged to a fixed overhead control account, and then *written off* to the profit and loss account at the period end (accruals and prepayments being carried down in the overhead account in the normal way, of course).
(b) No cost units carry any fixed overhead and so *all stocks are valued at marginal cost only.*

The essential distinguishing features of marginal cost accounting are show diagrammatically in Fig. 11.1.

Marginal cost decision-making

As we saw in 9:**3**, in decision-making it is only future costs that are relevant. And to prepare an analysis that uses future costs means that it is necessary to be able to predict costs, and this, as has been seen, requires a knowledge of the behaviour of costs. A costing technique that is based on cost behaviour, as marginal costing is, is therefore a logical technique to adopt for decision-making. Moreover, the fact that marginal costing is also based on the view that only costs *specifically* generated by a cost unit or centre should be charged to that unit or centre gives it a particularly valuable decision-making feature.

13. Testing product economic viability
    A commonly recurring decision involves testing to see if an existing product should be discontinued or, alternatively, a new product initiated. As this is achieved by ascertaining whether the existence of the product increases the profit of the enterprise or not, marginal costing is the logical technique. For instance, assume three products, A, B and C, are made in a department having identifiable fixed costs of £60,000. The sales of these products are expected to be £50,000, £100,000 and £150,000 respectively and the marginal costs £20,000, £70,000 and £130,000. Setting out the figures in a marginal cost format results in the following:

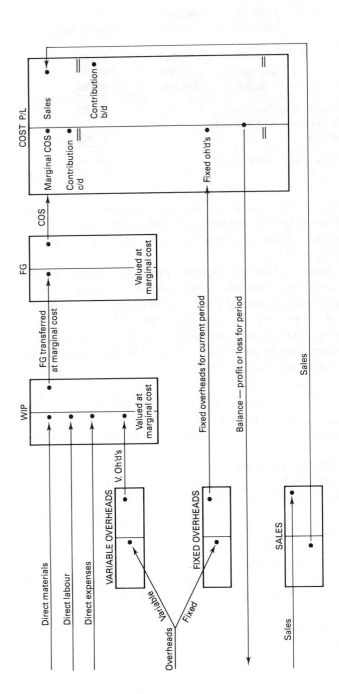

Figure 11.1 *Chart of marginal cost accounting*

This chart indicates how the Overheads, Work-in-Progress, Finished Goods and Profit and Loss accounts differ in a marginal costing system from the same accounts in a normal absorption accounting system (see Fig. 5.1)

Product	Predicted sales (£)	Marginal costs (£)	Contribution (£)
A	50,000	20,000	30,000
B	100,000	70,000	30,000
C	150,000	130,000	20,000
Total product contributions			80,000
Less Departmental identifiable fixed costs			60,000
Departmental net contribution			£20,000

Clearly, if any product is discontinued the whole of its contribution will be lost, and the enterprise profit will be reduced by the amount of that contribution. A, B and C, then, are all economically viable.

Note, however, how the apportionment of the departmental fixed costs can lead to possible errors in decision-making. If in the above example departmental fixed costs were apportioned on the basis of sales turnover (i.e. initially in the ratio of 1 : 2 : 3 respectively), and if it were a rigid policy rule that any product that failed to make a profit on its total cost must be discontinued, the following decisions would result:

	A £	B £	C £
Departmental fixed costs: £60,000			
Predicted sales	50,000	100,000	150,000
1st analysis: All three products:			
Contribution	30,000	30,000	20,000
Fixed cost apportionment	1/6 10,000	2/6 20,000	3/6 30,000
Profit	20,000	10,000	(10,000)
Decision: Discontinue C			
2nd analysis: C discontinued:			
Contribution	30,000	30,000	—
Fixed cost apportionment	1/3 20,000	2/3 40,000	—
Profit	10,000	(10,000)	—
Decision: Discontinue B			

3rd analysis: B and C discontinued:

Contribution	30,000	—	—
Fixed cost	60,000	—	—
Profit	(30,000)	—	—

Decision: Discontinue A

As can be seen, the final decision is that all the products will be discontinued and even if this resulted in all the departmental fixed costs ceasing there would still be an overall loss to the enterprise of £20,000 (the departmental net contribution computed earlier).

Naturally, where the situation is as simple as this the absurdity of discontinuing any of the three products is clear. However, in a more complex case, and particularly where the fixed and marginal costs are not segregated so that only a single total cost figure is set against product sales, it would not be surprising if an economically wrong decision resulted from such an analysis.

Finally, the student is reminded that should a product have an identifiable fixed cost (which was not the case in the above example), then since discontinuing the product would bring the cost to an end such a cost must be deducted from the product contribution (to give the product *net* contribution) before deciding upon the viability of the product.

14. Testing departmental viability
The economic viability of a department can be tested in the same way as product viability, the only difference being that, whereas product identifiable fixed costs are unusual, there will almost always be departmental identifiable fixed costs to be deducted from the sum of the product net contributions. As can be seen, in the example above the department is economically viable — and this is so regardless of any share of the unidentifiable fixed costs that the accountant may decide to apportion to the department.

15. The relevance of substitution
Underlying the analysis just made has been the assumption that nothing could be substituted for the products under review. Where substitution is possible (as it usually is) and some new

product could replace an existing product or, alternatively, production of one of the remaining products could be expanded to fill the capacity left by the discontinued product, a more complex analysis needs to be made. Such an analysis often adopts the differential costing technique which was discussed in the previous chapter.

16. Acceptance of a special contract

Another type of decision often relates to the acceptance or otherwise of a special contract under which units are sold below normal selling prices. In such circumstances the contribution is the relevant figure to be considered, since the whole of any contribution must be extra profit. From this it follows in principle that it is always better to take a special contract if there is some contribution, no matter how small, than to reject the contract and have no contribution.

Note, however, the following two qualifications to this.

(a) It is assumed that the fulfilment of the contract will not affect normal sales. Nothing is gained by selling units at £4 which otherwise would have been sold at £5.

(b) It is also assumed that nothing better is likely to come along. A business that fills its workshops with many low-contribution contracts and then has to turn away high contribution work is not making the best decisions. Judging whether or not anything better may come along is, of course, the responsibility of management.

17. Key factors

There is always something that limits an enterprise from achieving an unlimited profit. Usually this is sales, i.e. the enterprise cannot sell as much as it would like. Sometimes, however, an enterprise can sell all that it can produce, but output is limited by the scarcity of some economic factor of production, e.g. materials, labour, machine capacity or cash. Such a factor is called a *key factor* (or *limiting factor*) — although the term *constraint* is now becoming increasingly used instead.

18. Contribution per unit of key factor

If a key factor is operating, then it is important that the enterprise makes as much profit as it can each time it uses up one of its scarce units of key factor. Since fixed costs do not alter, this means *maximizing the contribution per unit of key factor*.

Example

Data: Materials are limited to 1,000 tonnes. A choice must be made between two jobs requiring such materials, A and B. Job details are as follows:

	Job A	*Job B*
Selling price	£3,000	£2,000
Marginal cost	£1,000	£1,200
Contribution	£2,000	£800
Tonnes required	4	1

Method: On the face of it A is in all respects the more profitable; it has a higher selling price, lower marginal cost and contribution over twice that of B. But in using 4 tonnes of materials it earns a contribution of only £500 a tonne, i.e. if all jobs were of this type our 1,000 tonnes would allow us to earn only £500,000 contribution. B, on the other hand, earns a contribution of £800 a tonne, so if all jobs were of this type it would allow us to earn £800,000 contribution. Type B jobs are therefore more profitable in these circumstances, and so should be selected in preference to type A jobs.

Where a key factor is involved, then, the work giving the highest contribution per unit of key factor used should be selected.

19. Make-or-buy decisions

This kind of decision typically arises when the product being manufactured has a component part that can either be made within the factory or bought from an outside supplier. On the face of it, since the only extra cost to make the part is the marginal cost, the amount by which this falls below the supplier's price is the saving that ariscs on making. However, this may not be so as it is also important to consider what work would otherwise be carried out using the relevant facilities if the part were not made. Clearly, if other work has to be displaced so as to make the part, the business will *lose the contribution this work would otherwise have earned*. Such a contribution loss must be added to the marginal cost of the part.

So, in a make-or-buy decision there are two factors which must be compared, namely:

(a) the supplier's price;
(b) the marginal cost of making, plus the loss of contribution from displaced work.

This loss of contribution is usually best found by use of the contribution per unit of key factor (*see* **18** above). It should also be appreciated that this lost contribution is an opportunity cost of the kind previously discussed in 10:**13–19**.

Example
_____

Data: An X takes 20 hours to process on machine A6. It has a selling price of £300 and a marginal cost of £180. A Y (a component part used in production) could be made on machine A6 in 3 hours for a marginal cost of £15. The supplier's price is £30. Should one make or buy Ys?

Method: Contribution per X = 300 – 180 = £120.

∴ Contribution earned per hour making X on machine A6 is $\frac{120}{20}$ = £6

If then a Y is made in 3 hours, £18 contribution is lost.
∴ Real cost to make Y = £15 + £18 = £33.
This is more than the supplier's price of £30, and so it is better to buy than make.

_____

Note that this decision assumes that machine A6 is working to full capacity. If this were not so and the machine were frequently idle, no loss of contribution would result from using it to make the component. In such circumstances the sole cost of making would be the marginal cost of the component — in this example £15 — which, being less than the supplier's price of £30, would indicate that the component should be made rather than bought.

20. Profit planning

Very often an enterprise first decides its sales, costs and activity and then computes what profit will emerge. In profit planning this is reversed; the enterprise first decides what profit it wants and then works *backwards* to see what sales, costs and activity are needed to produce that profit.

In practice, certain factors are usually determined before planning begins (e.g. capacity may be limited, or selling prices determined by competitors' activities) and then profit planning indicates the value that the remaining factors must take to achieve the profit target.

Example

Data: A company manufactures a single product having a marginal cost of £3 a unit. Fixed costs are £48,000. The market is such that up to 40,000 units can be sold at £6 a unit, but any additional sales must be made at £4 a unit. There is a planned profit of £80,000. How many units must be made and sold?

Method: Contribution from first 40,000 units = 40,000 x (6 – 3) = £120,000. Deducting the fixed costs from this contribution shows that these units would generate a profit of £120,000 – 48,000 = £72,000. However, this is £80,000 – 72,000 = £8,000 shortfall on the required profit. So enough extra units have to be sold at a unit contribution of £4 – £3 = £1 to generate an additional £8,000 contribution.

∴ Additional units = £8,000/£1 = 8,000
∴ Total number of units to be made and sold = 40,000 + 8,000 = 48,000 units.

21. Differential costing and marginal costing

In marginal costing one looks at the difference between the costs and incomes that would result if an activity were carried out and the costs and incomes that would result if the activity were not carried out. It employs, then, the differential costing principle and so is a differential costing technique. However, marginal costing is a narrower technique since it does not concentrate solely upon differences. For instance, if two kinds of materials could be used to make a product, the choice in no way affecting the conversion cost, then under marginal costing one should in theory compare the product marginal costs whereas only the material cost difference is really relevant.

Example

Data: A product uses 2 kg of material and 5 hours of direct labour at £3 per hour. Variable overheads are £2 per direct labour hour. 1,000 units of product are to be made. Currently material at £5 per kg is being used but a substitute material at £4 per kg may become available. What would the saving be if this new material were used? (This is a very trivial example and is intended to do no more than illustrate the difference between marginal costing and differential costing.)

Method:
Marginal cost analysis:

	Current material	*New material*
	£	£
Unit cost: Material	2 x £5 = 10	2 x £4 = 8
Direct labour	5 x £3 = 15	5 x £3 =15
Variable overheads	5 x £2 = 10	5 x £2 =10
Unit marginal cost	35	33
Marginal cost of 1,000 units	£35,000	£33,000

∴ Saving using new material = £35,000 – £33,000 = £2,000.

Differential cost analysis:
Difference in material price = 5 – 4 = £1 per kg.
Material usage = 1,000 units x 2 kg = 2,000 kg.
∴ Saving using new material = 2,000 x £1 = £2,000.

---

22. Incremental costing
   A form of differential costing which is very similar to marginal costing is *incremental costing*. This is a cost technique which shows the *cost change associated with each incremental change in activity*, i.e. a change in either the level or the nature of the activity. The similarity to marginal costing follows from the logical consequence that a marginal cost is, in fact, the incremental cost of producing one more unit.
   In most circumstances the terms marginal cost and incremental cost can be used interchangeably.

Marginal versus absorption costing

Should marginal or absorption costing be adopted? Here we look at the points to be considered when making this decision, along with the distinctions between the two.

23. Advantages of marginal costing
The following advantages are claimed for marginal costing over absorption costing.

(a) No attempt is made to relate fixed costs, which are incurred on a time basis, with products, since such costs are independent of production. This avoids complicated and misleading statements (*see* **13**).

(b) Significant under- or over-absorption of overheads cannot arise. (Note that some under- or over-absorption arises since the variable costs often have to be charged on an overhead rate basis to cost units before the actual variable overheads for the period are known.)

(c) Fictitious profits cannot arise due to fixed costs being absorbed and capitalized in unsaleable stock. (For example, assume 100 units are produced for a cost, all fixed, of £1,000, i.e. £10 a unit. Twenty only are saleable and are sold for £15 each. If the remainder are valued in stock at £10 each the profit and loss account will show a profit of £100, whereas a loss of £700 would be a truer figure.)

(d) Marginal costing avoids the false sense of security that absorption costing can give when all products show a satisfactory profit, but owing to the activity level being lower than that planned, such profits are unknowingly being more than offset by under-absorbed overheads.

(e) Contribution is a more correct measure of the effect of making and selling a product than the product profit figure obtained from absorption costing, which is not only incorrect when the activity level is different from that planned but may even indicate quite the reverse of the true situation.

(f) Marginal costing is simpler and less ambiguous than absorption costing, and avoids the complexities of apportionments which are really only arbitrary divisions of indivisible fixed costs.

(g) If a variety of products is offered to customers, marginal costing enables the planned profit to be made (assuming the activity is as planned) regardless of sales mix (e.g. if a contribution of £1 per hour is obtained in respect of all products, then if the planned number of hours are worked, the contribution and hence the profit obtained will be that planned, no matter which products are actually produced).

(h) Pricing can be done more intelligently since the contribution to be added onto any cost unit will:

(*i*) be based on the total contribution required from all production (i.e. planned profit and fixed costs);

(*ii*) take account of the use made by the unit of any relevant key factor.

24. Advantages of absorption costing

The following advantages are claimed for absorption costing over marginal costing.

(a) Since production cannot be achieved without incurring fixed costs, such costs *are* related to production, and absorption costing attempts to make an allowance for this relationship. This avoids the danger inherent in marginal costing of creating the illusion that fixed costs have nothing to do with production.

(b) Fictitious losses cannot arise as they can in marginal costing owing to fixed costs being written off in a period when merchantable goods are produced and stocked for sale in a later season (e.g. fireworks).

(c) Use of absorption costing avoids the stock valuation anomalies associated with marginal costing. For example, a manufacturer may pay a fixed monthly rental for a machine. Under marginal costing such a charge would not be included in the stock value. If, though, he renegotiates to pay a rental based on his *production,* this charge will be included in the stock value. Thus, although an article remains exactly the same, and is made in exactly the same way, nevertheless under marginal costing its stock value increases.

(d) When pricing, finding the marginal cost alone is not sufficient, since it is essential that the added contribution should relate to fixed costs; otherwise an enterprise with a high fixed cost could set prices that gave too small a contribution and so resulted in an inadvertent loss. In absorption costing an addition is automatically made based on the utilization of the fixed cost facilities by the different products.

> NOTE: This claim is valid only if the cost accountant is not setting prices as outlined in **23(h)** but is simply adding an arbitrary contribution to the marginal cost.

(e) Use of marginal costing in pricing tends to lead to low prices being quoted at a time of slack demand. Customers may then expect the business to maintain such prices on future occasions.

(f) If a wide range of goods involving differing fixed cost requirements are offered to customers and no pre-knowledge of likely demand is available, then absorption costing enables a more consistent profit to be earned.

(g) In a situation where the enterprise has a monopoly and wishes to charge its customers for its different products on a basis of average economic cost, absorption costing enables the enterprise to achieve this object better than marginal costing.

25. Choice of technique
The paragraphs above indicate that the choice of technique is not easy to make. Unfortunately, no rules can be given; all that can be said is that the technique which is most appropriate to the circumstances should be chosen.

At the heart of the controversy lies the implication that since fixed costs are incurred on a time basis and are irrespective of the volume of production, they cannot form part of the individual cost of units produced. This is not so. Without the fixed costs the units could not be produced at all. The relationship between fixed costs and cost units may be tenuous and changing, but the problem cannot be solved by denying the relationship entirely.

In the ultimate analysis the two techniques are not really contradictory; they simply represent the extremes of this elusive relationship, and cost accountants serve management best by ensuring that their statements reflect the appropriate relationship existing in any given circumstances.

26. Reconciliations of absorption and marginal profits
Sometimes examiners call for a reconciliation of the two different profits that emerge from applying absorption and marginal costing principles. Such a reconciliation simply follows the procedure already given in 5:**12**, and will be illustrated by the following question relating to a single period in a small company's trading:

Sales, production, opening and closing stocks: 620, 800, 220 and 400 units respectively. Selling price: £20 per unit. Direct costs of production, fixed and variable overheads: £8,000, £892 and £2 per unit respectively. Under his absorption costing procedure the financial accountant charges

overheads to production at £4 per direct labour hour (600 being booked
during the period) and values stock at £13 per unit. Under his marginal
costing procedure the cost accountant charges actual overheads in all
cases and values stock at marginal cost. Reconcile the financial
accountant's profit of £4,340 with the cost accountant's profit of £4,068.

Solution

First, reproduce the two respective profit and loss statements:

Cost method:	Absorption		Marginal	
	£	£	£	£
Sales: 620 units @ £20		12,400		12,400
Direct costs	8,000		8,000	
Overheads charged to production*	2,400		1,600	
Manufacturing cost (800 units)	10,400		9,600	
Plus opening stock (220 units)	2,860		2,640	
	13,260		12,240	
Less closing stock (400 units)	5,200		4,800	
Cost of sales	8,060	8,060	7,440	7,440
Contribution				4,960
Less Fixed costs				892
Profit		£4,340		£4,068

*600 hours @ £4 per hour and 800 units X £2 per unit.

Now prepare the reconciliation as in 5:**12**:

(a) Absorption cost profit   £4,340

(b) Affect on absorption profit if marginal cost
     principle had been applied:

Overheads: Absorption: Charged to production	2,400 }	−92†
Marginal: Actual = 1600 + 892	2,492 }	
Opening stock: Absorption	2,860 }	+220
Marginal	2,640 }	
Closing stock: Absorption	5,200 }	−400
Marginal	4,800 }	

(c) Marginal cost profit   £4,068

†Under-absorption of overhead.

Break-even analysis

One of the spin-offs from marginal cost theory is that it enables us to compute the level of activity at which neither a profit nor a loss is made. An analysis involving such a computation is called a *break-even analysis*.

27. Break-even definitions
Break-even analysis uses the following definitions:

(a) *Break-even:* any situation which results in neither a profit nor a loss being made.

(b) *Break-even point:* the level of activity at which neither a profit nor a loss is made.

(c) *Break-even chart:* a graph depicting the break-even point together with its associated income and costs.

NOTE: (1) It should be appreciated that break-even situations can arise in respect of enterprises, divisions, cost centres nad specific projects. At a further level the concept of break-even can also be used whne comparing two alternatives (*see* **42**). (2) Frequently 'break-even' is abbreviated to 'B/E'. (3) In break-even theory it is an *activity* which is being costed and priced. It is not merely an analysis of how a cost behaves relative to activity.

28. Fundamental break-even principles
The basic principle which underlies the whole of break-even theory is that at the very lowest level of activity costs exceed income but that as activity increases income rises faster than costs and eventually the two amounts are equal, after which income exceeds costs until diminishing returns bring costs above income once again.

This very general statement on the relationship between costs, income and activity merely states the obvious. To be of practical value break-even theory must incorporate information relating to cost behaviour and sales policy. So as to enable a theory having practical value to be developed the following simplifying assumptions are usually made.

(a) That within the relevant activity range the *total* cost of whatever *activity* is being costed behaves as a simple straight-line semi-variable cost.

(b) That the unit selling price remains constant throughout the relevant activity range.

(c) That costs and income are matched, i.e. there is no build-up or run-down of stocks.

Although rather sweeping, these assumptions are valid in the majority of cases. Even where they are not, in most instances the error resulting is either of small practical importance or can be allowed for in a short subsidiary analysis (e.g. where there is a stock build-up the cost of the build-up can, for analytical purposes, be excluded from the total cost).

29. The traditional break-even chart (*See* Fig. 11.2)

Given these assumptions it is quite easy to show the total cost curve on a cost-activity graph. Such a curve shows as a semi-variable cost having a fixed cost equal to the point where the curve cuts the cost axis and a straight curve rising at an angle reflecting the variable cost per unit of activity. This, of course, is a normal cost behaviour curve, albeit for the total cost of the activity. However, it is now possible to add the income curve. Since at zero activity there will be zero income this curve starts at the origin of the graph and is a straight line rising at an angle reflecting the constant unit selling price. Where cost and income curves cross, cost and income must be the same and the crossing must, therefore, mark the break-even point.

Example

A total cost has a fixed element of £90,000 and a variable cost element of £500 per 1 per cent activity. Sales are made at a price equal to £2,000 per 1 per cent activity. These figures give the break-even chart shown in Fig. 11.2 where it can be seen that the total cost curve starts at £90,000 and by 100 per cent activity rises to 90,000 + 100 × 500 = £140,000 while the income curve starts at zero and by 100 per cent activity rises to 100 × 2,000 = £200,000. Since the curves cross at 60 per cent activity, the break-even point is 60 per cent activity (when cost and income are both £120,000).

It should be noted that the *vertical* distance between the cost and income curves at any given level of activity measures the profit or loss (depending upon which curve is the higher) at that activity level.

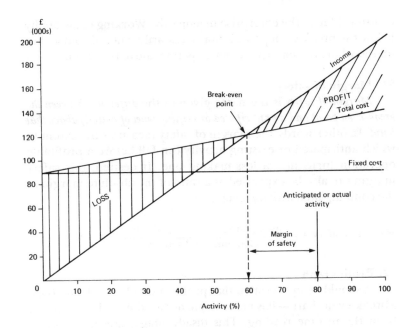

Figure 11.2 *Traditional break-even chart*
The break-even point is measured in terms of activity. This chart shows that if
the anticipated activity is 80 per cent, then:

Expected income   = £160,000;
Expected total cost = £130,000;
Expected profit   = £30,000;
Margin of safety   = 20 per cent.

30. The significance of the enterprise break-even point

A break-even point is always of importance in so far as it indicates the lowest activity level at which the activity under analysis is economically viable. The point has, however, even greater importance when it relates to a whole enterprise for then it is virtually a life-and-death measure. This arises because if an enterprise continually operates below its break-even point (i.e. makes losses), no matter how fractionally, then without question its life is limited. On the other hand, if it continually operates above its break-even point (i.e. makes profits), again no matter how fractionally, then it may live indefinitely. The break-even point, therefore, marks very clearly for the management of an enterprise the very lowest level to which activity can fall without putting the continued life of the enterprise in jeopardy. Working occasionally below the break-even point is not necessarily fatal, of course, but on the whole the enterprise must operate above this level.

31. Margin of safety

Margin of safety is the name given to the *difference between the break-even point and an anticipated or existing level of activity above that point.* In other words, the margin of safety measures the extent to which anticipated or existing activity can fall before a profitable operation turns into a loss-making one. If desired, this safety margin can also be expressed as a ratio of the absolute margin to the contemplated activity level, i.e.:

$$\text{Margin of safety} = \frac{\text{Contemplated activity} - \text{B/E activity}}{\text{Contemplated activity}} \times 100$$

32. Profit graph

It should be appreciated that profit cannot be read *directly* off a break-even chart — it is necessary to deduct the total cost reading from the income reading. This disadvantage, however, can be overcome by plotting the profit directly against activity, the resulting chart being referred to as a *profit graph* (*see* Fig. 11.3 which reproduces our earlier illustrative figures in the form of a profit graph). As a moment's reflection will indicate, on such a graph at a level of nil activity a loss equal to the fixed cost will be suffered (£90,000 in Fig. 11.3) and at break-even (i.e. nil profit) the profit curve will cut the activity axis (at 60 per cent in Fig. 11.3).

Break-even mathematics

It is not necessary, of course, always to draw graphs to find break-even figures. They can be found mathematically.

33. Total contribution and profit

First the relationship between total contribution and profit must be made clear. Note that:

Profit = Sales – Total cost.

Now according to our simplifying assumptions, the total cost is made up of a fixed cost element and a variable cost element, i.e.:

Total cost = Variable cost + Fixed cost.

∴ Profit = Sales – (Variable cost + Fixed cost)
    = Sales – Variable cost – Fixed cost.

But Sales – Variable cost = Total contribution.

∴ Profit = Total contribution – Fixed cost.

Note that in a break-even situation, Profit = 0.

∴ 0 = Total contribution – Fixed cost.

∴ Fixed cost = Total contribution.

Or, in other words, at the break-even point the total contribution is equal to the fixed cost.

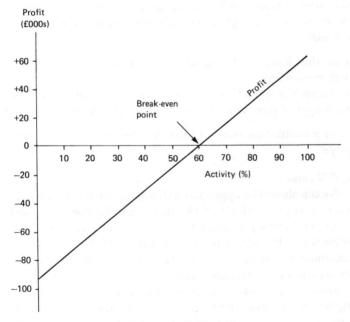

Figure 11.3 *Profit graph*

34. Unit contribution is a constant

It was explained earlier (*see* **7**) that the difference between the marginal cost of a unit and its selling price gives the unit contribution. Given the simplifying assumption that the marginal cost (i.e. the variable cost element of the total cost) and the selling price are unchanged with changing activity, then the difference, too, must remain unchanged, i.e. the unit contribution is the same at all levels of activity (within the relevant activity range, of course). From this a number of logical consequences flow.

35. Unit contribution and profit

First, assume that we have a product with a selling price of £12 and a marginal cost of £8. It has, therefore, a unit contribution of £12 – £8 = £4. This means that every time we make and sell a unit we receive £12 from the customer, pay £8 for the marginal cost and have £4 over. This £4 is not, of course, profit, since the fixed costs still remain to be paid. Indeed, until we have sufficient lots of £4 to pay all these fixed costs there can be no profit. For instance, if the fixed costs are £400, then we need to make and sell 100 units before we have enough £4 contributions to pay the fixed costs. Note that:

(a) at this level we break even and this, then, must be the break-even point;

(b) if we make and sell one unit more the £4 contribution received is no longer required for the fixed costs, and is therefore all profit.

This means that *above the break-even point all earned contribution is profit*.

36. P/V ratio

Next it should be appreciated that sales and total contribution are in direct proportion to each other, i.e. if the sales increased by 20 per cent, the total contribution increases by 20 per cent, etc. For instance, if we sell 10 of the units discussed above our sales are £120 and our contribution is £40. Increase sales by 20 per cent (i.e. 2 units) and the contribution rises to £48, i.e. by 20 per cent.

Since sales and total contribution are always in direct proportion, dividing one by the other will always give the same figure, e.g. contribution divided by sales in the above examples gives:

$$\frac{4}{12} \; ; \; \frac{40}{120} \; ; \; \frac{48}{144} \; ; \quad \text{all of which cancel down to } \tfrac{1}{3}$$

This fraction is called the *P/V ratio* and can always be calculated as follows:

$$\text{P/V ratio} = \frac{\text{Total contribution}}{\text{Sales}}$$

This ratio is useful in as much as it enables the contribution to be quickly calculated from any given level of sales (or vice versa), since the formula can be turned round to:

$$\text{Total contribution} = \text{Sales} \times \text{P/V ratio}$$

(e.g. given a sales figure of £180, the contribution will be £180 × 1/3 = £60).

37. Break-even formulae

Next, the constant value of the unit contribution, together with the earlier defined cost and income relationships, enable a series of formulae to be developed which can be applied in marginal costing and break-even circumstances. The most useful of these formulae are the following:

(a) Sales – Marginal cost of sales = Total contribution.
(b) Profit (Loss) = Total contribution – Fixed cost.
(c) P/V ratio = Total contribution / Sales.
(d) Break-even point:
   (*i*) measured in units = Fixed cost / unit contribution
   (*ii*) measured in £ sales = Fixed cost × $\dfrac{\text{Sales}}{\text{Total contribution}}$

                   = Fixed cost / P/V ratio

Given sufficient initial data, use of the above formulae will enable any missing figures to be found.

Example 1
Data:

$$\begin{aligned}
\text{B/E} &= 1{,}000 \ \text{units} \\
\text{Sales} &= 1{,}500 \ \text{units at £6 each} \\
\text{Fixed cost} &= £2{,}000
\end{aligned}$$

Find the marginal cost per unit and the profit (using formulae (d)(*i*) and (b) above).

Method:

    B/E (units) = Fixed cost / Unit contribution

    ∴ 1,000 = 2,000 / Unit contribution

∴ Unit contribution = 2,000 / 1,000 = £2.
And since selling price is £6, the marginal cost per unit must be:

$$£6 - £2 = \underline{\underline{£4}}.$$

In addition, total contribution must be 1,500 x £2 = £3,000.

$\therefore$ Profit = Total contribution – Fixed cost
= £3,000 – £2,000 = <u>£1,000.</u>

Example 2
Data:
Fixed cost = £4,000
Profit = £1,000
Break-even is at £20,000

Find the sales and marginal cost of sales (using formulae (b), (d)(*ii*) and (a) above).

Method:

Profit = Total contribution – Fixed cost
$\therefore$ £1,000 = Total contribution – £4,000
$\therefore$ Total contribution = £5,000

And B/E = Fixed cost x $\dfrac{\text{Sales}}{\text{Total contribution}}$

$\therefore$ 20,000 = 4,000 x Sales / 5,000 = 4/5 Sales
$\therefore$ Sales = 5/4 x £20,000 = <u>£25,000.</u>

In addition, Sales – Marginal cost of sales = Total contribution
$\therefore$ 25,000 – Marginal cost of sales = 5,000
$\therefore$ Marginal cost of sales = <u>£20,000.</u>

38. Break-even logic
The formulae given help to provide insight into the various marginal cost and break-even relationships. However, you are strongly advised always to try and reach your answer in practice by logical argument. Not only is one's memory fallible but frequently slightly more sophisticated questions cannot be solved by the simple application of these formulae.

> NOTE: When using logical argument, one can often use the fact that the contribution at break-even exactly equals the fixed cost.

Example
Reworking Examples 1 and 2 in **37** using logical argument.

1. Contribution at break-even = fixed cost (i.e. contribution exactly

covers fixed cost), and since break-even is 1,000 units and fixed costs £2,000, then £2,000 is the contribution from 1,000 units.

∴ Unit contribution = 2,000 / 1,000 = £2.

∴ Since selling price is £6, marginal cost must be £6 – £2 = £4 per unit.
In addition the total contribution from 1,500 units at £2 per unit is £3,000.
Out of this, £2,000 fixed costs must be paid leaving profit of £1,000.

2. Since the total contribution is made up of fixed cost and profit, a total contribution of £4,000 + £1,000 = £5,000 is obtained here from the level of sales attained.

Now since contribution at break-even equals the fixed cost, then at break-even a contribution of £4,000 is obtained from the given break-even sales of £20,000.

In addition, sales and contributions are in proportion to each other, and so to have increased the contribution from £4,000 to £5,000 (i.e. a quarter) sales must have increased by a quarter — that is, from £20,000 to £25,000.

(Alternatively, contribution of £4,000 from £20,000 sales gives a P/V ratio of 4,000/20,000 = ⅕. Therefore sales required to give contribution of £5,000 is £5,000 x 5 =£25,000.)

Finally, since £5,000 of this £25,000 sales is contribution, the remainder, £20,000, must be the marginal cost of sales.

The practical use of break-even theory

39. The validity of break-even charts

Although break-even charts are very useful in giving visual insight into the relationship between fixed costs, variable costs, sales, contribution and profit when looked at in terms of activity, they must always be used with caution in any real-life situation. In such practical circumstances the validity of these charts should always be assessed in the light of the following possibilities.

(a) *That the total cost may not be akin to a simple semi-variable cost* because:

    (*i*) the fixed cost element may, in fact, contain stepped fixed costs;

    (*ii*) the variable cost element may not be made up only of unchanging linear variable costs.

(b) *That the income curve itself may not be linear* (e.g. as sales increase discounts may need to be given in order to bring in yet further sales).

(c) *That a required graphical reading may fall outside the relevant activity range.* Reading outside this range (or, in statistical terminology, extrapolating) can lead to serious errors.

(d) *That a required estimate may fall outside the selected time-span.* Remember, a change of time-span can affect the behaviour classification of a cost (*see* **8:9**).

(e) *That changed conditions may have altered the cost behaviour pattern.*

(f) *That managerial decisions may have interchanged fixed and variable elements.* Management can often interchange fixed and variable costs. For instance, it can replace a small labour team on piecework, a variable cost, by an automatic machine having mainly fixed costs. This means that a break-even chart can be completely outdated by a management decision. It is, then, usually necessary to prepare a new chart every time break-even data is required.

Possibly the greatest shortcomings of break-even charts lie in their inability to handle multi-product situations and also the difficulty at times of finding a valid measure of activity of the behaviour of all the costs involved, even when there is only a single product. This is particularly the case in the service industries. How, for example, would you measure activity in a dock which handles many varieties of ships and cargoes and uses a number of different freight-handling facilities? In such cases the use of break-even charts may well be extremely limited.

All this being said, however, it must be appreciated that there are a great many situations where break-even charts can be validly used — more, perhaps, than might be thought from the above list of potential disqualifying possibilities. Where they can be validly used such charts are without question of real value.

40. Break-even theory applied to proposed projects

Break-even theory does not only apply to enterprises. It applies also to projects. For instance, a project may have a fixed set-up cost of £5,000, a unit variable cost of £5 and a unit selling price of £7. Here it can quickly be seen that for the project to break even, sales of 5,000 ÷ (7–5) = 2,500 units (£17,500) are required. All the other break-even mathematics can similarly be applied, of course. Indeed, one is on firmer ground when applying break-even theory to projects, since the fewer the costs and the more homogeneous the product the more likely it is that the assumptions the theory needs will actually hold.

Note one trap that must be avoided for yet again no *apportioned* fixed overheads must ever be used in the analysis. Only the project identifiable fixed costs must be considered.

41. Break-even theory applied to profit planning

In simple circumstances break-even theory can be applied to profit planning. To apply it in this context all that is necessary is that the planned profit is regarded as a fixed cost and added to the fixed costs total. Finding the break-even point on this basis gives the required activity level needed for the desired profit.

Example
A company sells for £20 a product having a marginal unit cost of £12. The company has a fixed cost of £30,000 and plans to make a profit of £10,000. How many units must be made and sold?

Solution
Fixed cost and planned profit = £30,000 + £10,000 = £40,000. To break even at the equivalent of a £40,000 fixed cost (i.e. to obtain a contribution of £40,000) when selling a product having a unit contribution of £20 – £12 = £8 calls for sales of £40,000 ÷ £8 = 5,000 units.

42. The break-even point as a point of indifference

If the anticipated activity level of a proposed project proved to be the break-even point, it would be a matter of economic indifference whether the project was carried out or not since the enterprise profit would be unaffected. This concept is a useful one. For example, assume that a department can carry out a required task by incurring either a fixed cost of £10,000 and a unit variable cost of £10 or a fixed cost of £14,000 and a unit variable cost of £8.

In this case the chosen method will depend upon the anticipated level of activity — the higher the level the more the choice will tend towards the high-fixed/low variable cost alternative. If, however, there is considerable doubt as to just what level of activity can be anticipated it may be more acceptable to start by finding the point of indifference. In this case, since an extra £4,000 fixed costs must be spent to reduce the variable cost (i.e. increase the contribution) by £2 per unit, the point of indifference is the same as the break-even point in a parallel situation, i.e. it is £4,000 ÷ £2 = 2,000 units. At 2,000 units, then, it is a matter of indifference which alternative is selected since the overall cost will be the same. (*Check:* first alternative cost = £10,000 + 2,000 x £10 = £30,000; second alternative cost = £14,000 + 2,000 x £8 = £30,000.) Now the final decision may be made much more easily since even though there may be considerable doubt as to the actual future activity, it may be possiblé to predict with reasonable certainty *which side* of 2,000 units that activity will lie.

Progress test 11

Principles
1. What is the principle of marginal cost ascertainment?   (1)

2. What is: (*a*) a marginal cost;   (2)   (*b*) an identifiable fixed cost;   (5)   (*c*) a net contribution;   (8)   (*d*) a key factor;   (17) (*e*) profit planning;   (20)   (*f*) incremental costing?   (22)

3. How is a contribution figure to be interpreted?   (9)

4. How does marginal cost accounting differ from absorption cost accounting?   (12)

5. What is the relevance of key factors to decision-making? (18)

6. What factors enter a make-or-buy decision?   (19)

7. How does differential costing differ from marginal costing? (21)

8. Compare and contrast marginal costing and absorption costing. Are these techniques wholly contradictory? **(23–25)**

9. What are the assumptions that underlie break-even theory? **(28)**

10. What is: (*a*) the margin of safety; **(31)** (*b*) a profit graph? **(32)**

11. How is a P/V ratio calculated and why is it useful? **(36)**

12. A well-known writer commenting on the break-even chart said: 'It (the break-even chart) must be applied with an intelligent discrimination, with an adequate grasp of the assumptions underlying the technique and of the limitations surrounding its practical application.' Expand on this statement giving illustrations of the points which the writer had in mind. (*ACCA*) **(39)**

Practice

> NOTE: Although the principles of marginal costing are essentially simple, the permutations and combinations of these principles are so numerous that the technique provides a rich mine of questions for examiners. The student, therefore, is advised to work through all of this Progress test since more will probably be learnt in this way than by any detailed study of the chapter text.

13(*a*). A one-off order for 3,000 garden chairs has been received from an overseas customer for the coming period. Your budgeted production for the period is for 16,000 chairs, which represents 80% of your capacity to manufacture garden chairs. Budgeted data for the period is as follows:

	£	£
Sales		672,000
Materials	192,000	
Labour	196,000	
Overheads	200,000	
		588,000
Net profit		84,000

You ascertain that £20,000 of labour and 20% of overheads are fixed in nature and all the other costs are variable.

Required:

Prepare a cost statement to show whether the order should be accepted if the customer was prepared to pay:

(*i*)   £30 per chair
(*ii*) £36 per chair.

Give reasons for your decisions.

(*b*) What other factors need to be taken into consideration before the order is accepted or rejected?

(*AAT Dec 90,* Part question)

14. A company produces a standard product, each unit of which has a direct material cost of £48, requires 2 hours' labour and sells for £120. The company has no variable overheads, only fixed overheads of £128,000 a month. Labour, which is paid at £6 per hour, is currently very scarce, while demand for the company's product is heavy.

A contract worth £10,800 has just been offered to the company and the estimating department has ascertained the following facts in respect of the work.

(a) The labour time for the contract would be 200 hours.

(b) The material cost would be £2,280 plus the cost of a special component.

(c) The special component could be purchased from an outside supplier for £600 or alternatively could be made by the company for a material cost of £240 and an additional labour time of 12 hours.

Advise management regarding the action it should take.

15. As a cost consultant to a Mexican farmer who grows summer vegetables and exports them to USA, you are required, using the information given below, to:

(a) calculate the profit or loss per box of each type of vegetable that your client will obtain from operating the farm on the present basis;

(b) advise your client of:

(*i*) the area to be cultivated with each line to produce the largest total profit; and

(*ii*) the amount of the largest total profit.

The farmer owns 240 acres of land on which he grows: staked tomatoes, ground tomatoes, cucumbers and green beans. Of the land 70 acres are unsuitable for staked tomatoes or green beans but are suitable for cucumbers or ground tomatoes. On the remainder of the land any of the four crops may be grown. There is an adequate supply of labour for all kinds of farm work. Marketing policy requires that each season there is produced:

(*i*) all four types of vegetable; and

(*ii*) not less than 5,000 boxes of any one line.

It is decided that the area devoted to any one line should be in terms of complete acres and not in fractions of an acre. You may assume there are no other physical or marketing limitations.

Details relating to production, market price and direct and fixed costs are given below.

	Staked tomatoes	Ground tomatoes	Cucumbers	Green beans
Acreage at present devoted to each line	105	50	60	25
Summer season's yield, in boxes per acre	700	200	150	300
Weight, in lbs per box	60	60	80	36
	$	$	$	$
Market price per box	3.86	3.86	4.56	5.68
Costs:				
Direct:				
Materials per acre	189	74	63	108
Labour:				
Growing, per acre	224	152	93	132
Harvesting and packing, per box	0.80	0.72	1.00	1.20
Transport and export, per box	1.30	1.30	1.00	2.40

Fixed overhead, incurred each season:

	$	Basis of apportionment to products
Cultivation:		
Growing	36,000	Direct labour costs incurred
Harvesting	12,000	Direct labour costs incurred
Transport and		
export	12,000	Weight produced
General administration	40,000	Number of boxes produced
Notional rent	12,000	Number of acres cultivated

(*CIMA*)

NOTE: Suggested answer given in respect of Question (b) only.

16. Z Ltd is a retailer with a number of shops selling a variety of merchandise. The company is seeking to determine the optimum allocation of selling space in its shops. Space is devoted to ranges of merchandise in modular units, each module occupying seventy square metres of space. Either one or two modules can be devoted to each range. Each shop has seven modular units.

Z Ltd has tested the sale of different ranges of merchandise and has determined the following sales productivities:

	Sales per module per week	
	1 Module	*2 Modules*
Range A	6,750	6,250
Range B	3,500	3,150
Range C	4,800	4,600
Range D	6,400	5,200
Range E	3,333	3,667

The contribution (selling price – product cost) percentages of sales of the five ranges are as follows:

Range A	20%
Range B	40%
Range C	25%
Range D	25%
Range E	30%

Operating costs are £5,600 per shop per week and are apportioned to ranges based on an average rate per module.

Required:

(a) Determine the allocation of shop space that will optimise profit, clearly showing the ranking order for the allocation of modules.

(b) Calculate the profit of each of the merchandise ranges selected in (a) above, and of the total shop.

(c) Define the term 'limiting factor', and explain the relevance of limiting factors in planning and decision-making. **(17–18, 13:14)**

(ACCA June 90)

17. (a) Find the break-even point and the profit from sales of £40,000 when: selling price is £5; marginal cost £3; fixed cost £10,000.

(b) Find the profit when: sales are £80,000; marginal cost of sales £60,000; break-even point £60,000 sales.

(c) A company makes £5,000 profit from £60,000 sales. Its fixed costs are £15,000. What is its break-even point?

(d) A company has sales of £100,000, fixed costs of £20,000 and a break-even point of £80,000. What profit has it made?

(e) A company has a profit of £5,000, fixed costs of £10,000 and a break-even point of £20,000. What were its sales?

18. A company has abstracted the following data for the past two successive periods:

	Period 1	Period 2
Material costs	£30,000	£36,000
Labour costs	£21,200	£24,700
Overhead costs	£41,800	£45,300
Production	10,000 units	12,000 units

Sales throughout were made at £10 per unit.

(a) Use a break-even chart to find:
   (*i*) the company fixed costs;
   (*ii*) the current break-even point.

(b) A plan is proposed whereby: variable costs will be

reduced by £1 per unit; fixed costs will rise by £11,600. Find:

(*i*)   the new break-even point;
(*ii*) the minimum sales level that will justify changing from the current position to the proposed plan.

19. Your enterprise wishes to subcontract a job involving a number of identical units. You have received the following quotes from four subcontractors, A, B, C and D:

A: £20 per unit;
B: £1,000 + £15 per unit;
C: £3,000 + £10 per unit;
D: £5,000 + £5 per unit.

Which quote do you accept?

20. Earlier this year our company launched a new product — a special kind of 4-wheeled vehicle. Our selling price is £9,000 excluding tyres which can be bought from us for £90 and have a life of 6,000 miles.

We have just heard that our competitor has launched a similar vehicle, though his is 6-wheeled. His selling price is £9,990, excluding tyres which he sells at £80 each and which have a life of 10,000 miles. Despite the extra tyres required for his vehicle, he claims that in the long run his vehicle is the cheaper to run.

(a)   What life would the vehicles need to have to make customers indifferent as to which one they bought?
(b)   If the actual lives of both vehicles were 120,000 miles, what life must our tyres have in order to enable us to compete in respect of cost to the customer? What effect would an offer by the sales manager to sell our vehicle at £9,000 *inclusive* of a set of tyres have on the tyre-life figure?

21. A furniture company manufactures one type of lounge suite exclusively. This suite comprises the following seven components: one settee, two armchairs, four armless chairs. These components can either be manufactured by the company or subcontracted, and the relevant data relating to the components is as follows:

	Settee	Armchair	Armless chair
Direct material cost per component	£80	£40	£44
Direct labour cost per component	10	5	1
Sub-contract price per component	200	80	60

Suite sales are currently running at 8,000 per period, each suite selling for £600. Although the company would like to manufacture all its own components, a capacity limit of 50,000 direct labour hours obliges the company to sub-contract some components.

Cost studies have shown that variable overheads vary with direct labour hours worked and are incurred at a rate of £1.60 per hour. Fixed costs are £140,000 per period and labour costs £4.40 per hour.

(a) Which components, and how many, should be manufactured by the company?

(b) What is the maximum profit that could be earned:
   (i) at current sales?
   (ii) if sales were unlimited?

(c) If the selling price had to be reduced to £560 per suite, what is the maximum profit the company can obtain?

12
Decision-making: conclusion

We have now looked at various decision-making techniques. However, students may wonder how they are to decide on which technique to use.

1. General principles of selection

First it must again be emphasized that the fundamental principle in decision-making work is to examine *differences* between alternatives — or between undertaking a project and not undertaking it.

Applying this principle to short-term decisions, the following points become clear.

(a) If the alternatives under consideration *have no effect on the fixed costs*, then the break-even or marginal cost technique is indicated. Generally speaking, the *break-even technique* is limited to single-product situations and the *marginal cost technique* to decisions involving the selection of different products or projects.

(b) If *fixed costs are affected* then either the *differential cost* or the *cash flow technique* should be used. The actual choice between the two is often only a matter of preference, though probably cash flow will be somewhat easier to apply as long as the essential qualification of the technique, that all other things are equal, holds good in the given situation.

Finally, remember that the only costs relevant in decision-making are *future opportunity* costs. Though these will often be the same as the expected actual costs there will be times when they are not and it is important to always be alert for this possibility.

2. Solution independent of technique

Note that it makes no difference which technique is selected. If the technique is used correctly, then the correct solution will emerge.

To demonstrate the validity of this last point the following very simple problem will be solved using the marginal cost, differential cost and cash flow techniques.

Example ───

A factory has the choice of producing A, B or C. It has a total fixed cost of £150,000 per year, a total capacity of 40,000 hours and can always sell whatever it produces. Product details are as follows:

	A	B	C
Selling price per unit	£20	£50	£120
Marginal cost per unit	£12	£26	£70
Hours per unit	2	4	10

(a) *Using marginal cost technique*:

	A	B	C
Selling price	£20	£50	£120
Marginal cost	£12	£26	£70
Contribution	£8	£24	£50
Contribution per unit of key factor (hr)	£4	£6	£5

Decision: produce B.

(b) *Using differential cost technique:*

	A	B	C
Potential production (units)	20,000	10,000	4,000
Sales	£400,000	£500,000	£480,000
Total marginal cost	£240,000	£260,000	£280,000
Net differential income*	£160,000	£240,000	£200,000

Decision: produce B.

* As the fixed costs do not alter they are not entered into the differential cost analysis. As a result in this particular problem the net differential income is the same as the contribution.

(c)   *Using cash flow technique:*

	A	B	C
Cash in: Sales	£+400,000	£+500,000	£+480,000
Cash out:			
Marginal costs	−240,000	−260,000	−280,000
Fixed costs	−150,000	−150,000	−150,000
Net cash flow	£+10,000	£+90,000	£+50,000

Decision: produce B.

Note that if absorption costing (which is not, of course, a decision-making technique) is used without reference to the production capacity there is a danger that the higher unit profit earned from C will induce management to accept C rather than B (*see* below).

(d) *Using absorption costing technique:*

Overhead absorption rate = £150,000/40,000 = £3.75 per hour.

	A	B	C
Marginal cost per unit	£12	£26	£70
Fixed overheads at £3.75 per hour	7½	15	37½
Total absorption cost	19½	41	107½
Selling price	20	50	120
Profit	£ ½	£ 9	£ 12½

Possible (wrong) decision: produce C.

3.   Combining techniques

Techniques are essentially tools for solving problems and just as skilled tradespeople will often combine tools to make a product, so skilled cost accountants will combine techniques. For example, when employing the cash flow technique they may well ignore flows common to all alternatives, e.g. 'fixed' cash flows, so that 'net cash flow' is in effect a differential net cash flow. The same solution emerges, of course, as would if a 'pure' technique were used, but time and effort is saved.

4.   Conclusion

Applying decision-making principles is admittedly not always easy. However, if you bear in mind the fundamental differential principle, then your own common sense should enable you to pick a way through the figures successfully. Never forget that the object of presenting decision-making data to management is to enable managers to determine which is the best course to set for the business. Under some circumstances all courses are unwelcome but it is still management's task to find the least unwelcome, and the cost accountant must assist in this task.

This may be stated in another way by saying that in decision-making the cost accountant is concerned with *profitability*, not profit. It is essential that this distinction is absolutely clear to the modern accountant.

Above all, the emphasis on the future must never be forgotten. Today's decisions must be based on tomorrow's opportunities, not yesterday's errors.

Part three

Planning and variance analysis

13
Budgets

Introduction

Budgets are prepared for a variety of reasons and understanding the reason behind the preparation of any budget is essential to understanding the mechanics of that budget.

1. Definition
   A *budget* is a *quantitative economic plan in respect of a period of time*. Because this is an important definition it will pay us to look at each key word in turn.

(a) *Quantitative.* A budget must comprise quantities. An enterprise may plan to build up a reputation for fair trading but it is not possible to budget for such a reputation since this is an intangible that cannot be quantified.

(b) *Economic.* To be a budget a plan must be in economic terms. An enterprise may plan to make the strongest steel in the world but such a plan cannot be properly referred to as a budget.

(c) *Plan.* A budget is a plan. It is not a hope or a forecast (*see* **3**) but an authoritative intention.

(d) *Time.* A budget is always in respect of a period of time (*see* **4**). Budgets are five-yearly, yearly, quarterly, monthly, weekly, daily or other time period. Note that while quantitative economic plans can also relate to cost units such plans are *not* budgets (they are, in fact, termed standard costs, *see* 14:**18**).

Budgets can be divided into a number of different categories. These are shown diagrammatically in Fig. 13.1 and discussed in **5–8** below.

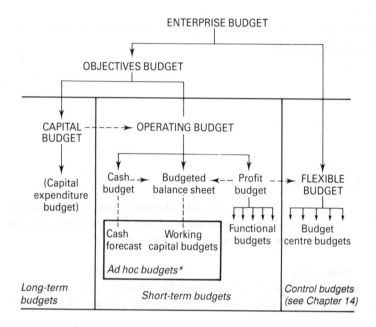

*These are budgets prepared for special periods or projects and rarely incorporated into the overall enterprise budget.

Figure 13.1 *Categories of budget*

2. Economic v. monetary plans

An economic plan is not one that is primarily prepared in narrow monetary terms. More fundamental than money are the *quantities* of economic resources and utilities involved, and it is these that must form the bedrock of all budgets. All that the monetary figures do is to express those quantities in a common economic measure.

3. Forecasts v. budgets

As was stated above, a budget is a plan and not a forecast. The difference may be put as follows.

(a) A *forecast* is a prediction of what will happen as a result of a given set of circumstances.

(b) A *budget* is a planned result that an enterprise aims to attain.

From this it follows that a *forecast* is a judgement that can be made by anybody (provided they are competent to make judgements), whereas a *budget* is an enterprise objective that may be specified only by the authorized management. (Moreover, note that the announcement of a budget is an implicit instruction to employees to work to achieve that objective.)

4. Budget period
This is the period of time for which a budget is prepared and used. Such periods depend very much on the type of budget involved and also on the circumstances. The following are typical periods.

(a) Operating budget: one year.
(b) Capital budget: many years.
(c) Research and development budget: some years.
(d) Control budgets: one month (*see* 14:**23**).

5. Objectives and flexible budgets
There are two forms of planning and they are fundamentally different. One form is based on determining the best way to achieve one's objectives and the other on identifying divergences from planned performances. On the face of it, it would appear that one planning exercise can result in a plan that will cover both functions, since it would seem reasonable to argue that comparison of actual performance with the plan would reveal the required divergences. However, for the reason explained in 14:**10**, this argument is invalid. As there are two different forms of planning there needs to be two different kinds of budget.

(a) *Objectives budget.* This lays down the manner by which the enterprise's objectives are to be achieved. It specifies in detail the planned quantities and values of each economic factor and also all the activity levels involved in the achievement of those objectives.
(b) *Flexible (or control) budget.* This lays down what should have happened in respect of each budget factor in view of the *actual* activity levels achieved.

This chapter will only be concerned with objectives budgets, flexible budgets being discussed in the next.

6. Capital and operating budgets

An enterprise has both long-term and short-term objectives, though naturally the short-term objectives are no more than the intermediate steps towards the enterprise's long-term objectives. In theory, planning for long-term objectives should be no different from planning for short-term ones. However, in practice there is a difference of emphasis. In long-term planning it is the viability of the capital structure that is management's primary concern while in short-term planning it is the day-to-day management of resources. Consequently two different kinds of objectives budgets have been developed.

(a) *Capital budget.* This plans the capital structure and liquidity of the enterprise over a long period of time. It is concerned, therefore, particularly with equity, liabilities and fixed and current assets, especially the year-end cash balances. A major sub-budget of the capital budget is the *capital expenditure budget* which plans the capital expenditure, especially expenditure on new plant and facilities.

(b) *Operating budget.* This plans the day-to-day use of resources and creation of utilities. It is particularly concerned, therefore, with materials, labour, overhead resources, sales and cash.

Capital and operating budgets are clearly interconnected since capital budgets can only be developed on the basis of planned operations over the years. However, at the end of the planning process the capital budget in effect lays down the objectives for each of the sequential operating budgets and Fig 13.1 therefore shows the connection in this form.

Since capital budgets relate more to long-term financing than costing, their preparation is not covered in this book.

7. Types of operating budgets

The following are the three most important operating budgets:

(a) *Profit budget.* This budget plans the resources (excluding cash) to be used and the utilities to be created and sold during the budget period. Planned prices are then placed on the resources and utilities so as to convert the budgeted quantities into costs and income, from which figures a budgeted profit can be found. In addition, the budget often shows the planned closing stocks. This budget is closely connected with the flexible budget for the period since if all actual activity levels accord with those planned the flexible budget will be identical to the objectives budget, though this event is rare in practice. On this point note that in order to distinguish the profit budget from its superficially similar flexible counterpart, the former is described as a *fixed budget*, i.e. a budget that employs a fixed level of activity. Note, too, that the profit budget divides into sub-budgets referred to as 'functional budgets' (which are further discussed in **15**).

(b) *Cash budget.* This budget simply plans the receipts and payments. The majority of the required figures can be abstracted from the profit budget but some important (and usually very large) amounts relating to capital expenditure and income are taken from that part of the capital budget that relates to the cash budget period. The prime function of a cash budget is to show the budgeted cash balances at various points of time throughout the budget period.

(c) *Budgeted balance sheet.* This budget plans the balance sheet for the end of the budget period. It embodies the budgeted profit from the profit budget, the budgeted closing cash balance from the cash budget and the planned changes in the other asset and liability values, in particular those relating to the working capital.

8. *Ad hoc* operating budgets

In addition to those budgets which form the overall enterprise operating budget there are two classes of budget which are normally prepared on an *ad hoc* basis for a selected period of time (rarely the normal operating budget period).

(a) *Working capital budget.* A working capital budget is a budget that is usually prepared in respect of a project, and plans the working capital requirements of the project.

(b) *Cash forecast.* Despite the term a cash forecast is usually a cash budget prepared in respect of the whole enterprise for a particular period of time with the object of enabling the enterprise's cash to be effectively managed over especially crucial moments arising during that period.

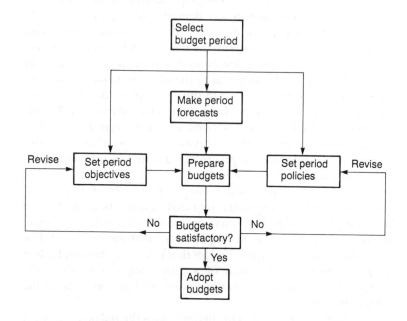

Figure 13.2   *Budget preparation procedure*

9. Steps in the preparation of a budget

Preparing a budget almost always involves taking the following steps (*see* Fig. 13.2).

(a) Selecting the budget period.

(b) Setting objectives to be reached by the end of the budget period or, where relevant, at points during the budget period.

(c) Either or both:

    (*i*) preparing forecasts for the period;

    (*ii*) abstracting relevant figures from budgets already prepared.

(d) Determining enterprise policies (e.g. product range; normal hours of work per week; channels of distribution, stocks; research and development appropriation; credit policy; investments).

(e) Computing from the forecasts or budgets already prepared the requirements in terms of the economic quantities needed to meet the objectives while complying with the policies — and subsequently converting these quantities into monetary values. This results in an initial provisional budget.

(f) Reviewing this initial budget with regard to the planned objectives and amending the objectives or policies or both repeatedly until an acceptable budget emerges.

(g) Formally adopting the budget which then becomes an executive order.

10. Functions of a budget

At first glance it does seem that a budget is no more than an accounting statement relating to future rather than past performance. However, the shift from the past (where events are known and cannot be changed) to the future (where events are uncertain and subject to manipulation) is crucial and the provision of accounting statements forms only a minor function of a budget — almost, in fact, no more than a spin-off. To view budgets realistically the student should fully understand that budgeting is primarily a *management* and not an accounting technique. However, in this chapter only the mechanics of budgeting will be discussed.

11. Other forms of budget

Note the additional two types of budget:

(a) *Rolling (continuous) budget.* This is a budget having an end-point in time always the same distance ahead in the future. Thus a five-year capital budget which is continually extended a year at a time as each year passes (so that the enterprise is always looking five years ahead) would be a rolling capital budget. Similarly an operating budget with a one-year budget period which at the end of each month incorporated a further month so that there was always a budget for the twelve immediate future months would be a rolling operating budget.

There are two reasons why a rolling budget is recommended. Firstly, it provides an opportunity to reassess in the light of up-to-date information the viability of the remainder of the budget. Secondly, since enterprises do not progress in a series of kangaroo hops but progress continuously, rolling budgets are more closely aligned to business reality than budgeting intermittently only as and when the end of the current budget period approaches.

(b) *Summary budget.* This is a budget that merely brings together all the summary data from a group of sub-budgets so as to provide management with all overall appreciation of the consequences that would follow the achievement of their more detailed plans.

12. Zero-base budgeting

In practice, budgeting is often done on the basis of taking existing costs as the starting point of the budget and adjusting these costs for changed circumstances and future planned activities. Under *zero-base budgeting* this approach is dismissed as being ineffective and instead all aspects of operations are looked at in critical detail and with a fresh eye. For each type of operation a case has to be made for its budgeted expenditure which will include a careful analysis of alternative ways of achieving the objectives of the operation. As in all forms of sound budgeting, budgets are first expressed in terms of resources needed and only subsequently converted into monetary terms.

An essential aspect of zero-base budgeting is an initial preparation of a 'minimum' budget which details the resources and costs needed to meet the minimum basic level of achievement and then the preparation of separate 'incremental' budgets that detail the resources and costs needed to reach higher levels of achievement. Subsequently, all budgets are ranked in compromise terms of necessity, advisability, desirability and financing requirements so that a final decision can be made as to which are to be accepted.

Zero-base budgeting is a budgetary method that adopts a thoroughly organized approach to preparing a comprehensive and exhaustive set of budget documents, themselves carefully designed, which detail the case for each individual budget proposal together with supporting figures and which ultimately enable a soundly-based final budget to be set by the organization. The technique is particularly suitable for non-profit-making bodies since its use of incremental budgets enables management — or government authorities — to compare the different levels of services and costs that are available to them and so be able to provide the best value for the money on hand in terms of a mix of services and efficiency standards.

Operating budgets

An operating budget is essentially a budget that lays down the planned requirements for the day-to-day operations of an enterprise over the budget period. Apart from the straightforward application of ordinary costing and receipts and payments procedures to future figures instead of past figures, the preparation of an operating budget requires two essentials: clear thinking and common sense. Unfortunately no book can help students with these, and so this kind of budgeting is the easiest technique to learn and the hardest to apply. In this section a few useful words will be defined and a logical approach suggested. In the majority of budget situations, however, you must use your own initiative.

13. Profit budget

The first operating budget is the *profit budget*. This specifies, both in quantities and in values, all the economic resources to be used (apart from cash) and utilities to be created and sold during the budget period. From these budgeted figures a budgeted profit statement can be prepared and the budgeted profit computed.

In the next three paragraphs some key points relating to the preparation of this budget are discussed.

14. Principal budget factor

Before any detailed planning for the profit budget can start it is necessary to identify the *principal budget factor* (or *limiting factor*), i.e. that factor which prevents an enterprise from immediately expanding to infinity. The principal budget factor is usually sales, the enterprise being unable to sell all it can produce. However, there are other possible factors which may limit enterprise activity, such as shortage of machinery, cash, labour, space, materials and managerial ability.

Clearly, the principal factor dictates the whole course of planning short-term operations. Indeed, part of the art of management is to make plans so that this factor is fully exploited. We have already discussed in connection with key factors this aspect of maximizing return from the use of a limiting factor (*see* 11:**18**).

The principal budget factor does not remain constant. If the limitations imposed by one factor are removed, another takes its place and becomes the principal budget factor. In practice, it is important that one is aware when this type of switch-over is imminent.

15. Functional budgets

The considerable detail and large number of managers usually involved in the preparation of a profit budget make it near-impossible for this to be prepared in the form of a single document. Instead the budget preparation task is divided up between the various functions and the sub-budgets prepared by these functions are called *functional budgets*. Each function is budgeted on the basis of the objectives of the enterprise and any relevant data from the other functional budgets. The inevitable dependence of one budget on another requires these budgets to be prepared in a hierarchical manner and Fig. 13.3 indicates a common form of budget hierarchy together with the necessary data flow between budgets.

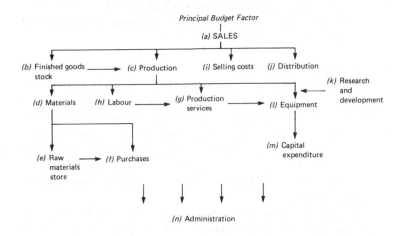

Figure 13.3   *Interrelationships of functional budgets*

It is assumed here that the principal budget factor is sales.
The letters in brackets refer to sub-paragraphs of **15**.

Essentially, preparing a functional budget involves providing answers to relevant questions relating to the role of the function within the enterprise and in respect of other budget objectives. Thus, on the assumption that sales is the principal budget factor, the basic information required for each functional budget would be given by the answers to the following questions.

(a) *Sales.* In view of this being the principal budget factor, what quantities can be sold and at what prices?

(b) *Finished goods stock.* What finished goods stock will be required to support the budgeted sales?

(c) *Production.* What production must be achieved to meet budgeted sales and secure the budgeted finished goods stock?

(d) *Materials.* What materials will be required to meet the budgeted production?

(e) *Raw material stores.* What raw material stocks will be required in view of the materials budget?

(f) *Purchases.* What purchases must be made to obtain the budgeted materials and raw material stocks, and at what prices?

(g) *Production services.* What production services will be required to support the budgeted production, and at what cost?

(h) *Labour.* What labour must be employed to achieve the budgeted production and staff the budgeted services, and at what remuneration rates?

(i) *Selling costs.* What selling services will be required to achieve the budgeted sales, and at what cost?

(j) *Distribution.* What distribution services will be required to distribute the budgeted sales, and at what cost?

NOTE: Students often make the error of basing these last two budgets on production instead of *sales*.

(k) *Research and development.* What research and development will be needed and at what cost?

(l) *Equipment.* What equipment will be needed to enable budgeted production to be achieved, budgeted research and development to be supported, and budgeted services to be set up?

(m) *Capital expenditure.* What capital expenditure will be needed in the budget period to acquire the budgeted equipment?

(n) *Administration.* What administration will be required, and at what cost, to administer effectively an enterprise engaged in achieving all the foregoing budgets?

16. Summary profit budget

Once the functional budgets have been prepared it only remains to collate the summary figures from these budgets so as to produce the summary profit budget and ascertain the budgeted profit figure that emerges as a result. If this profit is acceptable then the budget can be adopted, but if not then some or all of the functional budgets have to be revised — this revision continuing until an acceptable profit does finally emerge.

17. Cash budget

In addition to the budgeted profit figure the profit budget provides much of the data needed for the cash budget. Once, then, the profit budget is set the cash budget can be started.

In principle the cash budget involves no more than listing the planned receipts and payments. Though conceptually simple, care must be taken when preparing a cash budget. Note particularly that the cash pattern may differ considerably from the income and expenditure pattern, especially as regards timing. It is necessary to watch out carefully for such factors as credit trading (this will 'shift' the cash flow into a later period than the date of the sales or purchases), capital payments and receipts, tax and dividend payments, and non-trading income and expenditure. It should be appreciated, too, that cash fluctuations can be very rapid and involve large sums, and for this reason the cash budget should be prepared on the basis of a budget period of not more than one month at the longest. The preparation is essentially as follows.

(a) Begin with the cash balance at the start of the budget period.
(b) Add receipts and deduct payments for the period.
(c) Finish with the cash balance at the end of the period.

18. Cash budget illustration

To illustrate the layout of a typical cash budget the following very simple problem is solved.

Question

A company has been experiencing a £20,000 increase in sales each month for the past half year or so and it anticipates that this monthly increase will continue for the immediately foreseeable future. Its profit statement for last month was as follows:

		£	£
Sales			200,000
Costs:	Direct materials	100,000	
	Direct labour	40,000	
	Variable overheads	20,000	
	Fixed overheads (excluding rent)	20,000	
	Rent	5,000	
			185,000
Profit			£15,000

The company's sales are on credit, the debtors paying two months after the sale while the creditors for materials and overheads are paid after the company has taken one month's credit. Labour costs are, of course, paid as they are incurred and the rent is paid quarterly. Last month the rent was paid and the month-end cash balance was £10,000. £10,000 capital expenditure is planned for month 2. There are no stocks at any time.

Prepare the cash budget for the next four months.

Solution

NOTES:

(1) From the profit statement it can be seen that the marginal costs are: materials, 50 per cent of sales; labour, 20 per cent of sales; variable overheads, 10 per cent of sales.

(2) Since the fixed overheads are the same each month, the one month's credit does not affect the cash budget over the four months.

(3) Sales for the month before last (needed to compute month 1's receipts from debtors) must be £200,000 – 20,000 = £180,000.

(4) Since the rent is £5,000 a month the quarterly rent payable must be £15,000, and since this was paid last month it must be due again in month 3.

	Cash Budget (£000s)				
	Last month	*Month 1*	*Month 2*	*Month 3*	*Month 4*
Operating Data (Note 1):					
Sales	200	220	240	260	280
Materials, 50% sales	100	110	120	130	140
Labour, 20% sales	N/a	44	48	52	56
Variable overheads, 10% sales	20	22	24	26	28
Budgeted receipts:					
Debtors (2 months) (Note 3)	N/a	180	200	220	240
Budgeted payments:					
Materials (1 month)	N/a	100	110	120	130
Labour	N/a	44	48	52	56
Variable overheads (1 month)	N/a	20	22	24	26
Fixed overheads (Note 2)	N/a	20	20	20	20
Rent (Note 4)	15	0	0	15	0
Capital expenditure	—	—	10	—	—
TOTAL	N/a	184	210	231	232
Budgeted excess cash receipts over payments	N/a	(4)	(10)	(11)	8
Month end cash balance	10	6	(4)	(15)	(7)

N/a = Not applicable.

19. Budgeted balance sheet

Finally, with the profit and cash budgets completed it is possible to turn to the budgeted balance sheet which plans the assets and liabilities at the end of the budget period. Of all the operating budgets this is usually the simplest to prepare and, with the opening balance sheet at hand, involves no more than:

(a) Taking the budgeted profit from the profit budget and, after deducting the forecast tax and any intended dividends, adding the retained profit to the opening equity.
(b) Changing the opening long-term liabilities and fixed assets to

reflect any changes in these items (the cash budget will often be of help in identifying these, though events such as revaluations will need to be specifically noted). The asset depreciation for the year will, of course, be abstracted from the profit budget.

(c) Ascertaining the working capital items as follows.

(*i*) Current liabilities other than tax can normally be ascertained from the cash budget (operating data section) though reference to the purchases and sales budgets may be necessary to ascertain the full values of the creditors and debtors.

(*ii*) Stock values will be taken from the profit budget (though if this only indicates the stock *changes* reference will also need to be made to the opening stock values).

(*iii*) The cash amount is the closing cash balance in the cash budget.

In preparing a budgeted balance sheet it is unwise to find any missing figure by merely computing the amount needed to make the balance sheet balance. Since all the balance sheet figures must be ascertainable from the other operating data or must be implicit in management's plans (e.g. policy of reducing goodwill yearly), it is much better to utilize the balancing feature of balance sheets to confirm that all the balance sheet figures are both included and correct in amount.

Budget administration

Finally, a few brief observations on the administration of budgets, although many aspects of this topic more appropriately arise under the heading of management accounting.

20. Budget committee

Budgets are set by managers. Only managers can decide what utilities will sell, what resources will be necessary to create those utilities, and what prices should obtain throughout the budget period. In addition, budgeting involves considerable management coordination. For these reasons, and also because budgeting involves managers in all parts of the enterprise, it is essential that a budget committee is set up with representatives from all functions and that this committee is charged with the preparation and the administration of the enterprise budgets.

21. Budget officer

In addition to the committee, a budget officer should be appointed. His work is essentially that of secretary to the committee, and entails:

(a) ensuring that the committee secretarial work is carried out (e.g. agendas, minutes, notice of meetings);
(b) ensuring that committee instructions are passed to the appropriate people;
(c) collecting data and opinions for consideration by the committee;
(d) keeping managers to the budget time-table (*see* **22** below);
(e) coordinating and briefing the members of the committee.

Clearly, the management accountant is well suited for, and is often appointed to, this post.

22. Budget time-table

When preparing major budgets it is first necessary to prepare many of the smaller, but key, budgets. If these smaller budgets are not completed quickly, the preparation of the major budgets will be held up, which in turn will hold up the summary budget and therefore the ultimate budget adoption. Delay in adopting the budget is clearly serious, for a budget issued after the start of a period has very much reduced value, and may even result in the delay of vital projects. In order, then, that the budget can be adopted before the period begins, it is necessary to prepare a carefully thought-out time-table for all budget activities. Such a time-table must be rigidly adhered to, since delays in this type of work tend to snowball and quickly assume serious proportions.

23. Budget manual

To assist everyone engaged in budgeting and budget administration, a budget manual should be issued. This sets out such matters as the responsibilities of the people engaged in, the routine of, and the forms and records required for, budgeting (together with the control procedures that will subsequently follow any comparison of actual performance relative to the budget).

More generally, the budget manual will set out all information needed by all persons involved in budgeting and budgetary control to enable them to maximize both:

(a) their contribution to the budget compilation; and
(b) their benefit from the control data ultimately reported back to them.

Progress test 13

Principles

1. What is a budget? **(1)**

2. Distinguish between a budget and a forecast. **(3)**

3. What is a budget period? **(4)**

4. Define: (*a*) capital budget; **(6(a))** (*b*) operating budget; **(6(b))** (*c*) working capital budget; **(8(a))** (*d*) rolling budget; **(11(a))** (*e*) zero-base budgeting. **(12)**

5. What is a principal budget factor and why is it important in budgeting? **(14)**

6. What are the steps to be taken in the preparation of a budgeted balance sheet? **(19)**

7. What is the purpose of each of the following: (*a*) budget committee; **(20)** (*b*) budget officer; **(21)** (*c*) budget time-table; **(22)** (*d*) budget manual? **(23)**

Practice

8. (This question is an extensive budgeting exercise. However if you work through it you will find that in all probability you will have covered most aspects met in examination questions on operating budgets.) Untrue, a branch of Proverbs Ltd., makes silcpercys from sowzeers. Last year's accounts were as follows.

Profit and Loss

		£	£
Sales:	80,000 barrels of silcpercys at £50		4,000,000
Less:	discounts		140,000
			3,860,000

Costs of sales:	Production: 320,000 barrels of		
	sowzeers at £5	1,600,000	
	Direct labour	800,000	
	Variable overheads	400,000	
	Fixed overheads *	700,000	
Marketing:	Contract total	100,000	3,600,000
	Profit		£260,000

*Includes £90,000 depreciation and £110,000 rent.

Balance Sheet

	£	£
Plant and equipment (at cost)		900,000
Less depreciation: 4 years at 10%		-360,000
		540,000
Stocks: Raw materials, 100,000 barrels		
sowzeers at £5	500,000	
Finished goods, 15,000 barrels		
silcpercys at £45	675,000	1,175,000
Debtors: Entitled to 5% discount	200,000	
Other	30,000	
	230,000	
Less Provision for discount	-7,000	223,000
Prepayments: Rent	27,500	
Marketing	11,000	38,500
Cash		500,000
		£2,476,500
Head office account		2,014,833
Creditors: Purchases for month 2 production		400,000
Accruals: Fixed overheads		41,667
Variable overheads		20,000
		£2,476,500

From the following additional data prepare all the operating budgets for the first four months of the current year.

(a) The sales quantity for the current year is planned to be 25 per cent up on last year.

(b) Planned sales for the first five months are 10 per cent, 15 per cent, 20 per cent, 25 per cent and 5 per cent respectively of the planned annual sales.

(c) All prices and rates (excluding rent but including selling prices) are expected to be 20 per cent more than last year.

(d) To allow for settling, sowzeers have to be purchased two months before processing (which can be regarded as being instantaneous).

(e) Creditors allow one month credit. Debtors who pay one month after delivery receive a 5 per cent cash discount and 70 per cent of the debtors avail themselves of this discount. The remainder pay after two months.

(f) For policy reasons the settled stock of sowzeers at the end of month 5 must be sufficient for sales for the rest of the year. Apart from this, raw material stocks are to be kept to a minimum.

(g) Finished goods stocks at month end are to be equal to the month's sales, except at the end of month 4 when the planned stock is zero.

(h) Fixed overheads are incurred equally throughout the year but are absorbed into production on a direct wages basis.

(i) Apart from rent, which is paid at the end of month 3 for the whole year in advance, the fixed overhead payments are the same each month and these costs together with the variable overheads are paid one month in arrear.

(j) Most of the direct labour is casual (and hence variable).

(k) Marketing is undertaken by a different branch of Proverbs. Under a new contract this branch will charge monthly £5,000 plus 1 per cent sales, the amount due being payable one month in advance (budgeted sales being used initially and amounts subsequently adjusted in the light of actual sales).

(l)   Plant and equipment worth £100,000 will be purchased for cash at the end of month 4.

(m) The company prices stores issues on a FIFO basis.

9.   ZBB Ltd has two service departments—material handling and maintenance, which are in competition for budget funds which must not exceed £925,000 in the coming year. A zero base budgeting approach will be used whereby each department is to be treated as a decision package and will submit a number of levels of operation showing the minimum level at which its service could be offered and two additional levels which would improve the quality of the service from the minimum level.

The following data have been prepared for each department showing the three possible operating levels for each:

Material handling department
Level 1. A squad of 30 labourers would work 40 hours per week for 48 weeks of the year. Each labourer would be paid a basic rate of £4 per hour for a 35-hour week. Overtime hours would attract a premium of 50 per cent on the basic rate per hour. In addition, the company anticipates payments of 20 per cent of gross wages in respect of employee benefits. Directly attributable variable overheads would be incurred at the rate of 12p per man hour. The squad would move 600,000 kilos per week to a warehouse at the end of the production process.

Level 2. In addition to the level 1 operation, the company would lease 10 fork-lift trucks at a cost of £2,000 per truck per annum. This would provide a better service by enabling the same volume of output as for level 1 to be moved to a customer collection point which would be 400 metres closer to the main factory gate. Each truck would be manned by a driver working a 48-week year. Each driver would receive a fixed weekly wage of £155.

Directly attributable overheads of £150 per truck per week would be incurred.

Level 3. A computer could be leased to plan the work of the squad of labourers in order to reduce their total work hours. The main benefit would be improvement in safety through reduction in the time that work in progress would lie unattended. The computer leasing costs would be £20,000 for the first quarter (3 months), reducing by 10 per cent per quarter cumulatively thereafter.

The computer data would result in a 10 per cent reduction in labourer hours, half of this reduction being a saving in overtime hours.

Maintenance department

Level 1. Two engineers would each be paid a salary of £18,000 per annum and would arrange for repairs to be carried out by outside contractors at an annual cost of £250,000.

Level 2. The company would employ a squad of 10 fitters who would carry out breakdown repairs and routine maintenance as required by the engineers. The fitters would each be paid a salary of £11,000 per annum.

Maintenance materials would cost £48,000 per annum and would be used at a constant rate throughout the year. The purchases could be made in batches of £4,000, £8,000, £12,000, or £16,000. Ordering costs would be £100 per order irrespective of order size and stock holding costs would be 15 per cent per annum. *The minimum cost order size would be implemented.*

Overheads directly related to the maintenance operation would be a fixed amount of £50,000 per annum.

In addition to the maintenance squad it is estimated that £160,000 of outside contractor work would still have to be paid for.

Level 3. The company could increase its maintenance squad to 16 fitters which would enable the service to be extended to include a series of major overhauls of machinery. The additional fitters would be paid at the same salary as the existing squad members.

Maintenance materials would now cost £96,000 per annum and would be used at a constant rate throughout the year. Purchases could be made in batches of £8,000, £12,000 or £16,000. Ordering costs would be £100 per order (irrespective of order size) and stock holding costs would now be 13.33 per cent per annum. In addition, suppliers would now offer discounts of 2 per cent of purchase price for orders of £16,000. The minimum cost order size would be implemented.

Overheads directly related to the maintenance operation would increase by £20,000 from the level 2 figure.

It is estimated that £90,000 of outside contractor work would still have to be paid for.

Required:

   (a) Determine the incremental cost for each of levels 1, 2 and 3 in each department.

   (b) In order to choose which of the incremental levels of operation should be allocated the limited budgeted funds available, management have estimated a 'desirability factor' which should be applied to each increment. The ranking of the increments is then based on the 'incremental cost x desirability factor' score, whereby a high score is deemed more desirable than a low score. The desirability factors are estimated as:

	Material Handling	*Maintenance*
Level 1	1.00	1.00
Level 2 (incremental)	0.60	0.80
Level 3 (incremental)	0.50	0.20

Use the above ranking process to calculate which of the levels of operation should be implemented in order that the budget of £925,000 is not exceeded.

(ACCA Dec 88 Part question)

14
Flexible budgets and standard costs

It is one thing to make a plan — quite another to achieve it. If the plan is to be achieved — if *control* is to be maintained — it is essential that progress should be monitored, and monitoring calls for performance measurement in terms of the plan.

In the remaining chapters of this book the accounting aspects of performance measurement for control are outlined. In this particular chapter the method of formulating plans so that such measurement can be carried out is described.

Fundamentals

From here on we will, in the ultimate analysis, be concerned with economic control. First, then, we must look at a few fundamental points relating to this aspect of management work.

1. Control
The purpose of performance measurement in the context now being considered is to assist management to achieve the plans made when preparing the operating budgets, in particular the profit budget. They will, in other words, attempt to *control* costs and sales. The touchstone, then, of the success of the techniques employed is their ability to assist managers in maintaining such control.

2. A plethora of names
Although we are now primarily concerned with the technique

of controlling profit the student should be warned that this technique has many names. Historically it developed through the integration of the previously separate techniques of *standard costing and budgetary control*, and it is often still referred to by this composite title. It is also often loosely referred to as *cost control*, even though the control of income is an important facet of the technique. Sometimes the term *responsibility accounting* is used in recognition of the fact that control and responsibility are inseparably linked. More recently the term *variance accounting* has arisen, this title recognizing the importance of the measurement of the divergence of actual from plan.

Yet it is questionable if any of these terms is a good description of the technique as a whole. The latter two betray the dominance of an accounting approach over what is a management technique (*see* page 340), while 'cost control' implies that only costs are subject to control. But since at the end of the day the technique aims at enabling management to control profit, the term *profit control* does seem the more appropriate one to adopt.

3.   Control and the cost accountant

As we have said, control is primarily a management, not an accounting, technique. The cost accountant can, however, assist management in the operation of the technique by:

(a) drafting management proposals in the form of monetary statements that indicate the profitability of management plans; and

(b) making a comparison of actual with planned costs and preparing clear and meaningful statements detailing any divergences and their effects on the profit.

The accountant is in no way responsible for determining the necessary action to be taken to correct the divergences. This is wholly a line management responsibility.

4.   The influence of tradition

In the development of any technique it frequently happens that the early stages are to a greater or lesser extent misdirected because of initial misconceptions, with the result that the later development is burdened with out-of-date attitudes having their roots in history. This is so in the case of the current subject for historically the techniques involved were developed primarily as accounting techniques rather than control techniques. This early wrong emphasis is with us still so that today the accounting aspects are often stressed at the expense of the control aspects. Yet the fundamental objective of all work in this area is to help managers to control costs and sales. A modern approach, therefore, will reverse the priorities and subordinate the accounting aspect to the control aspect.

Regrettably it may be some time before this view is fully accepted. Until then examination papers will naturally tend towards questions reflecting the traditional view rather than the modern. It is necessary, then, for the student to learn both approaches to the subject. But it must be pointed out that, apart from emphasis, the two techniques have many more similarities than differences. Indeed, the modern technique leaves the bulk of the traditional one basically unchanged and differs primarily in the method by which it handles the fixed costs. And this difference, in turn, arises because the traditional method employs absorption costing and the modern method marginal costing.

5. **Features of the traditional (standard costing and budgetary control) technique**
The traditional technique has the following features:

(a) An emphasis on accounting as against control.

(b) The adoption of the absorption cost technique.

(c) Statement formats which reproduce the conventional historical cost statements with planned figures substituted for past figures.

(d) Performance analysis more in terms of products than economic factors and management responsibilities.

(e) The cost accounts prepared by grafting the new figures onto the traditional book-keeping pattern.

6. **Features of the modern (profit control) technique**

(a) An emphasis on profit control as against accounting conventions.

(b) The adoption of the marginal costing technique (and for the student this is the most distinctive feature of the modern technique).

(c) Statement formats specifically designed to aid management control (e.g. product cost statements will rarely be prepared since control is achieved by monitoring individual production activities, not the costs of individual cost units).

(d) Performance analysis in terms of economic factors and management responsibilities.

(e) The cost accounts relegated to a very minor role in the technique and then used primarily only to incorporate the overall result into the enterprise's monthly final accounts.

7.   Budget centre

Traditionally a budget centre has been defined as 'a section of an entity for which control may be exercised and budgets prepared' (CIMA terminology). However, it is now considered that because a crucial principle of control involves holding managers responsible for their decisions, control data should be based on managers rather than sections. Although the two are, in practice, all too often the same thing it is perhaps advisable to bear in mind a definition which reflects this principle. Under such a definition a *budget centre* can be regarded as *a part of the organization for which a given manager has responsibility and authority and to which profit control data can be assigned.*

Note, now, the distinction between a cost centre (which is used for cost ascertainment) and a budget centre, for what is chargeable to a cost centre isn't necessarily chargeable to a budget centre. For instance, under cost ascertainment an inspector's salary would be chargeable to the cost centre in which he worked but in a control system it would be chargeable to the budget centre of the manager to whom he was responsible.

8.   Budgetary control

Budgetary control can be defined as 'the establishment of budgets relating the responsibilities of executives to the requirements of a policy, and the continuous comparison of actual with budgeted results, either to secure by individual action the objective of that policy or to provide a basis for its revision' (CIMA terminology).

Note that from now on the word 'standard' will be increasingly employed. You should be aware that the word 'planned' can be substituted for 'standard' at all times.

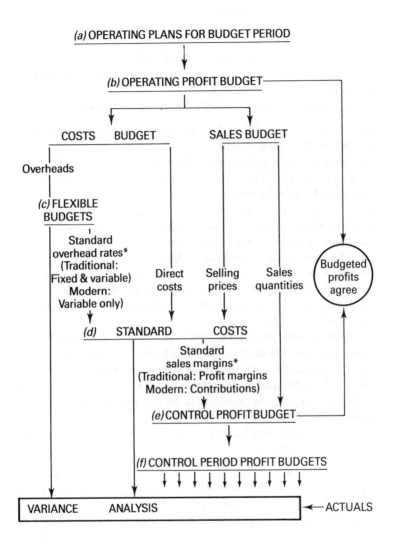

Figure 14.1 *Standard cost and budgetary (profit) control planning sequence*

(Letters in brackets refer to subsections of the example in 24.) This sequence is appropriate for both the traditional and the modern techniques except where marked with a *. At those points the sequence is appropriate for the traditional technique. In the modern technique the fixed overheads are taken direct from the flexible budgets to the control profit budget

9. The planning sequence

Like the functional budgets described in 13:15 the planning statements now to be considered are prepared in sequence, and, indeed, they follow on directly from the budgets looked at in Chapter 13. This planning sequence is shown diagrammatically and in its entirety in Fig. 14.1.

The sequence can be briefly described as follows.

(a) All the *operating plans* for the operating budget period are formulated by management.

(b) The operating plans are incorporated into an operating *profit budget* (*see* 13:13). This can be regarded as comprising a costs budget and a sales budget.

(c) The overheads in the costs budget are re-analysed through the medium of *flexible budgets* so that standard overhead rates for both fixed and variable overheads are found.

(d) The direct costs in the costs budget are re-analysed to give the *cost unit* direct costs and these are combined with the standard overhead rates and the cost unit selling prices detailed in the sales budget to give the *standard cost* for each cost unit. From this, the unit *standard profit* is found.

(e) By combining the unit standard profits and the budgeted unit sales quantities detailed in the sales budget a *control profit budget* can be prepared and the total budgeted profit found. This budgeted profit must be identical to that shown in the operating profit budget and the agreement of the two profits proves the accuracy of the overall re-analysis.

(f) The control profit budget is itself analysed into shorter *control period profit budgets*.

Although this last analysis brings the planning sequence to an end, Fig. 14.1 shows that when the control period plans and the actual results are brought together, a *variance analysis* can be prepared. This is the performance measurement device that the flexible budget and standard costs technique aims to provide (*see* Chapter 15).

10. The failings of a fixed budget

Chapter 13 showed that a profit budget calls for a quite thorough analysis of all the needed economic resources and at first glance it may appear that performance measurement involves no more than a comparison of the actual results with this budget. Unfortunately nothing is further from the truth. The profit budget discussed earlier is a *fixed* budget and fixed budgets have serious failings when it comes to using them for performance measurement. For instance, assume that a fixed budget laid down that a department was to make 1,000 units for a cost of £2,000. In the event, because of poor sales, the departmental manager was subsequently instructed to make only 500 units. This was done for a cost of £1,400. To what extent was the *cost* performance good or bad?

From the data given it is impossible to say. If all the budgeted £2,000 costs were variable costs then the manager has done badly since producing half the budgeted production should have resulted in a cost one-half of budget, i.e. £1,000. Conversely, if the £2,000 had represented fixed costs the manager has done well since the reduced activity should have left these costs unaffected. (Do not fall into the trap of assuming a fixed cost is an *unchangeable* cost. It is not. Local government taxes are a fixed cost but change yearly. Remember, what makes a cost a fixed cost is the fact that it does not change simply because *activity* changes — and certainly management incompetence can result in it changing.)

So a fixed budget is quite useless for performance measurement and should never be used for that. Indeed, it is in respect of this sort of budget that the old saying 'the budget is out of date before the period even begins' is often perfectly true. However, this saying is irrelevant since such a budget should never be used after the period begins anyway.

11. Allowances

Since a fixed budget is an inappropriate device for performance measurement the question arises as to what method is appropriate. This question can be answered by looking again at the example. Clearly, planning that there shall be a budgeted cost of £2,000 for 1,000 units is, as it stands, insufficient. In addition, the division of costs between fixed and variable must be known. Assume that of the total £2,000, £1,000 relates to fixed costs and £1,000 to variable costs. There is, then, a planned fixed cost of £1,000 for the period and a planned variable cost of £1 per unit. Since the manager produced 500 units we would, if he kept to his cost plan, expect him to incur a total cost of £1,000 + 500 × £1 =

£1,500. Since he has spent only £1,400 he saved £100, and this, of course, means the profit will be £100 more than it would have been if he had merely achieved his planned cost performance. He has therefore performed well.

In order, then, to measure a manager's cost performance it proves necessary to compute how much he should be allowed to spend in view of the actual circumstances surrounding his performance. Such a figure is called an *allowance* and is defined as the *figure one would expect to see achieved if the manager or factor being controlled had performed as planned after allowing for the actual performance on the part of other managers or factors.*

> NOTE: Traditionally an allowance as defined above is referred to as a standard cost, so that the £1,500 allowance above would be called the standard cost of 500 units. This means that in the traditional terminology 'standard cost' refers to a planned cost set for a single cost unit for an indefinite period and also the expected cost of a particular number of units for a single particular period. This can lead to confusion and so the use of two different terms is strongly advised. Students are, however, warned that in examinations the expression 'standard cost' may well be used where they would expect the word 'allowance'.

12. The comparison rule

Clearly, measuring the performance of a manager (or factor) will be based on the manager's (or factor's) performance in relation to the allowance. It is no use looking at the original fixed budget figure, for such a figure relates almost certainly to a quite different set of circumstances from those which appertain at the time of the actual performance. It follows, then, that it is a fundamental rule in performance measurement that actuals must only be compared with allowances — never with budgets.

13. Control plans

Obviously, in order to be able to compute allowances it is necessary to analyse the fixed budget in terms of fixed and variable costs. Furthermore, such an analysis must also be in terms of detailed economic factors, and prepared in such a way that allowances can be easily and unambiguously computed. As the ultimate objective is to help managers to control their performances the resulting statements can be called *control plans*.

Although in theory one single control plan should be possible, in practice this work is more effectively carried out by using two kinds of plan, as follows.

(a) *Flexible budgets.* These are plans that relate specifically to periods of time, overheads and budget centres.

(b) *Standard costs.* These are plans that relate specifically to single cost units.

When preparing control plans it is necessary to prepare the flexible budgets first since these provide the standard overhead rates which are needed to prepare the standard costs of the cost units.

14. Control periods

Fixed budgets are generally made for a relatively long period of time — normally one year. This, of course, is far too long a period for effective performance measurement where comparisons must be made at intervals of no more than a month at most. In consequence the final control plans must relate to such shorter control periods.

Flexible budgets

These budgets are prepared with the aim of providing both standard overhead rates for inclusion into the standard costs and also overhead allowances which can be compared with the actual overheads so that performance in respect of these overheads can be measured.

15. Flexible budget

This is 'a budget which, by recognizing the different cost behaviour patterns, is designed to change as volume of output changes' (CIMA terminology). As a by-product it also enables standard overhead rates to be calculated.

Essentially, preparing a flexible budget is simply a matter of analysing the overheads into fixed and variable elements and determining the extent to which the variable overheads will vary within the relevant range of activity. Either of the following two methods can be employed to prepare a flexible budget:

(a) *Formula method:*

    (*i*) *Before* the period begins:
        (1) budget for a normal level of activity;
        (2) segregate the fixed and variable overheads;
        (3) compute the variable overhead per unit of activity.

    (*ii*) At the *end* of the period:
        (1) ascertain the actual activity;
        (2) compute the variable overheads allowed for this level
        and add the fixed overheads to give the budget overhead
        allowance (this is known as 'flexing the budget').

This is expressed in the formula:

Allowed overhead for period =

$$\text{Fixed overhead for period} + \left(\begin{array}{c}\text{Actual units of activity}\\\text{for period}\end{array} \times \begin{array}{c}\text{Variable overhead per}\\\text{unit of activity}\end{array}\right)$$

Example

	Preparation of flexible budget before period begins:				Application of flexible budget at end of period:	
	Budgeted activity: 800 hours*				Actual activity attained: 900 hours*	
Overhead	Budget *	Fixed o'h'ds *	Var. o'h'ds *	Var. o'h'd per hr. of activity	Var. o'h'ds allowed	Total budget o'h'd allowance
	£	£	£	£	£	£
Power	400	—	400	0.5	450	450
Rent	800	800	—	—	—	800
Indirect labour	2,300	700	1,600	2.0	1,800	2,500
Maintenance	900	100	800	1.0	900	1,000
Heat and light	200	40	160	0.2	180	220
Supervision	1,000	760	240	0.3	270	1,030
Total	£ 5,600	2,400	3,200	4.0	3,600	6,000

*In this example these figures are assumed. In practice, they would be found by first preparing a fixed budget and then segregating the fixed and variable overheads by the analysis detailed in **7:1–6**.

The figures in the total budget overhead allowance column are then ready for comparing with the actual overhead costs for the period.

(b) *Multi-activity method:* The alternative method of preparing a flexible budget involves preparing a budget for every major level of activity. When the actual level of activity is known, the allowed overhead is found by interpolating between the budgeted overheads for the activity levels on either side.

Example

Overhead	50% £	60% £	70% £	80% £	90% £	100% £
Rent	500	500	500	500	500	500
Depreciation	400	400	400	450	500	500
Indirect labour	2,000	2,400	2,800	3,200	3,600	4,000
Indirect materials	100	100	120	140	150	160
Power	100	120	140	160	180	200
Supervision	1,000	1,000	1,000	1,100	1,400	1,500
Maintenance	300	300	350	450	600	900
Storekeeping	200	200	250	250	300	300
Administration	1,300	1,400	1,500	1,700	2,000	2,000
Total £	5,900	6,420	7,060	7,950	9,230	10,060

Activity level: % capacity

If, then, the actual activity level were, say, 72 per cent, the allowed overheads would be computed by interpolating between the 70 per cent and 80 per cent budget levels (i.e. adding two-tenths of the difference to the 70 per cent figures) as follows:

	£
Rent	500
Depreciation	410
Indirect labour	2,880
Indirect materials	124
Power	144
Supervision	1,020
Maintenance	370
Storekeeping	250
Administration	1,540
Total	£7,238

Again, these allowances are ready for comparing with the actual overheads.

16. Choice of method of preparation of the flexible budget

The choice of preparation method depends primarily upon how 'fixed' the fixed overheads are. If they are likely to change significantly over the relevant range of activity (due to large stepped fixed costs 8:12), the second method should be employed. If, on the other hand, fixed overheads remain relatively unchanged over this range, the first method is perfectly satisfactory and requires less work in preparation.

Note that whichever method is adopted care needs to be taken in selecting the measure of activity to be employed (*see* 8:17).

17. Flexible budgeting chart

Finally a chart summarizing the main steps taken in flexible budgeting is given in Fig. 14.2. The last step, the comparison of the actual overhead costs with the allowances, will be discussed in the next chapter.

Standard costs

The second stage in planning for control involves planning the unit direct costs and incorporating the unit overheads, i.e. preparing the standard costs.

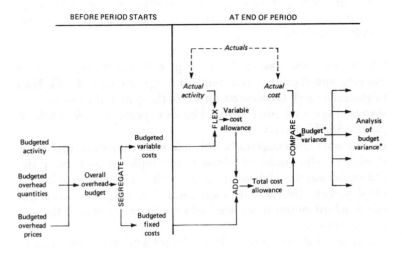

Figure 14.2 *Main steps in flexible budgeting*

Before the period begins, budgeted fixed and variable overheads must be segregated. At the end of the period the actual figures are compared with the budget allowances (not with the original budgeted figures). Determining the variable overhead allowances is called 'flexing the budget'.
*See Chapter 15.

18. Standard cost

A *standard cost* is a *cost plan relating to a single cost unit.* It covers all aspects of the cost plan including the planned sales margin and selling price.

19. Cost standards

As was explained in 1:9, every cost consists of a usage component and a price component. Consequently, when planning a cost, it is necessary to plan both usage and price. Often it is also necessary to plan other factors, such as the specification of material, or grade of labour, or loss in process. Such a planned figure is called a *cost standard* which can, therefore, be defined as *a usage, price or other standard upon which a standard cost is based.*

20. Setting a standard cost

Setting a standard cost for a cost unit follows much the same procedure as preparing a job cost, except that planned figures are used in lieu of actuals. For any given cost unit the following standards must be set.

(a) *Standard direct material costs.* This calls for setting standard material specifications, the standard usage per unit of each kind of material used, the standard price of these materials — and the standard material mix ratios and losses expected (*standard yield*) if process work is involved.

(b) *Standard direct wages costs.* This calls for setting standard labour grades (i.e. the grades of labour to be employed on making the units), the standard labour times per unit of each grade of labour employed and the standard wage rates of those grades. Note that the standard labour times are traditionally referred to as the *unit standard hours*.

(c) *Standard direct expenses.* This calls for setting the unit cost of any direct expenses incurred in producing (or selling) the units.

(d) *Standard factory overhead costs.* This calls for setting predetermined rates (*see* 3:21) in respect of the variable and fixed overheads and then using these rates to compute the variable and fixed overhead costs per unit of production.

> (*i*) *Standard factory variable overhead cost.* Setting this cost simply involves ascertaining how many units of activity the cost unit uses and multiplying this figure by the variable overhead rate per unit of activity (standard variable overhead rate) as given by the flexible budget. Thus, in the example in **15(a)** it can be seen that the variable overhead rate is £4 per hour. If, then, a given cost unit were planned to take 12 hours activity, the standard variable overhead cost would be 12 x £4 = £48.

> (*ii*) *Standard factory fixed overhead cost.* Setting this cost calls for a standard fixed overhead rate, which is determined by dividing the budgeted units of activity into the budgeted fixed overhead cost as given by the flexible budget. This rate is then multiplied by the units of activity used by the cost unit in the normal way to give the standard factory fixed overhead cost. Thus, in the example in **15(a)** a budgeted activity of 800 hours and fixed overheads of £2,400 gives a standard fixed overhead rate of £2,400/800 = £3 per hour. If the planned activity units used by the

cost unit were again 12 hours the standard factory fixed overhead cost would be £3 x 12 hours = £36.

Note that the procedure in (*ii*) only relates to the traditional method of standard costing since the modern method employs marginal costing.

(e) *Standard selling and distribution overhead costs.* The standard selling and distribution overhead costs of the unit are set in the same way as the unit standard manufacturing overhead costs.

(f) *Standard selling price and standard sales margin.* Finally the planned, standard, unit selling price is set, and by deducting from this the total unit standard cost, the unit standard sales margin is found. Under the traditional technique this margin is the *standard profit* and under the modern technique it is the *standard contribution*.

21. Standard cost cards

All the above standards should be recorded on a *standard cost card*. Such a card, which is very similar to a job card, is made out for each cost unit manufactured and forms a complete record of all the cost standards and standard costs relating to that unit. In practice it should be laid out in such a way that the standard cost of the unit when only partly completed can be quickly found. This is important for valuing work in progress.

NOTE: When solving standard cost problems the standard cost card is an invaluable source of data. If an examination question does not give a standard cost card, students are strongly advised to prepare their own before attempting to calculate any of the variances discussed in Chapter 15.

Control profit budget

Once the flexible budgets and standard costs have been prepared all the planning is essentially complete. However, if only to prove the arithmetical accuracy of the analysis, it is useful to make a summary of these control plans showing that adherence to them will in fact result in the budgeted profit given in the original fixed budget. Such a summary is called a *control profit budget*.

22. Preparation of a control profit budget

The control profit budget is prepared as follows:

(a) The budgeted units sales quantities as detailed in the operating profit budget are listed.

(b) Each budgeted quantity is multiplied by the unit margin as shown in the standard cost of the unit to give the budgeted product margin.

(c) The budgeted product margins are totalled to give the total budgeted margin. In the traditional method this is the total budgeted profit. In the modern method, however, it is the total budgeted contribution — and to obtain the budgeted profit all the budgeted fixed overheads in the flexible budgets must be added together and the total subtracted from the total budgeted margin.

If the analysis of the figures in the operating profit budget to the flexible budgets and the standard costs has been accurately made, the budgeted profit in (c) will be the same as the budgeted profit in the operating budget.

23. Subdivision of control plans into control periods

Since control budget periods are always very much shorter than operating budget periods it is necessary to subdivide the control plans accordingly. Fortunately this merely involves appropriately subdividing the sales in the operating sales budget and the fixed costs in the flexible budgets and then preparing short-term control profit budgets so that a control profit budget is obtained for each control period.

Often in examinations these short-term budgets are prepared on the assumption that the organization concerned has twelve identical control periods. Note, however, that identical control periods are neither necessary nor usual, for often seasonal factors result in sales differing from period to period. This means, of course, that the budgeted sales quantities opening the control profit budgets will be the quantities planned for *that specific budget period*. Fixed overheads can also be treated in the same way if necessary. In this manner seasonality can be eliminated from the analysis of the subsequent performance data.

24. Example of the preparation of control plans

This example illustrates the full planning sequence from a set of original management plans. For simplicity the example involves an organization manufacturing only one product and, since flexible budgets have already been illustrated, only two very truncated flexible budgets are shown. The figures will be prepared in accordance with the traditional technique but **25** shows the changes that would follow a marginal cost form of analysis.

(a) *Management operating plans — one year.*
  (*i*) Planned production operations:
    (1) output for the year — 120,000 cwt of Z;
    (2) Z produced by mixing X and Y in the ratio of 3 : 2;
    (3) normal loss of 20 per cent input;
    (4) 32 employees working a 1,875-hour year.
  (*ii*) Planned sales: 120,000 cwt of Z.
  (*iii*) Planned prices and rates:
    X — £4 per cwt; Y — £10 per cwt; Z — £20 per cwt;
    Direct labour — £6 per hour;
    Production royalty — 20p per cwt.
  (*iv*) Planned overheads:
    (1) Factory: Variable overheads — £120,000;
                Fixed overheads — £480,000;
                Measure of activity — direct labour hours.
    (2) Marketing: Variable overheads — £96,000;
                 Fixed overheads — £240,000;
                 Measure of activity — cwt sold.
  (*v*) Planned control periods: management plan to have twelve identical control periods during the year.
(b) *Operating profit (fixed) budget.* From the management operating plans the following operating budget can be prepared:

			£	£
Sales:	120,000 cwt Z at £20 cwt			2,400,000
Costs: Factory:	Direct materials:			
	X, 90,000 cwt at £4 cwt		360,000	
	Y, 60,000 cwt at £10 cwt		600,000	
	Direct wages:*			
	60,000 hrs at £6 hr		360,000	
	Direct expenses:			
	Production royalty at 20p cwt		24,000	
	Overheads: Fixed		480,000	
	Variable (with direct			
	labour hrs)		120,000	
Marketing:	Overheads: Fixed		240,000	
	Variable (with cwt sold)		96,000	2,280,000
	Budgeted profit			£120,000

*32 employees **x** 1,875 hrs.

(c) *Flexible budgets.* From the management operating plans and the operating profit budget the following flexible budgets can be prepared:

(*i*) Factory: Budgeted activity 60,000 direct labour hrs.

			Standard
Overheads	*Fixed*	*Variable*	*Variable per D.L. hr*
	£	£	£
All	480,000	120,000	2

Standard fixed overhead rate per direct labour hour = £480,000/60,000 = £8 per hr.

(*ii*) Marketing: Budgeted activity 120,000 cwt.

			Standard
Overheads	*Fixed*	*Variable*	*Variable per cwt*
	£	£	£
All	240,000	96,000	0.80

Standard fixed overhead rate per cwt = £240,000/120,000 = £2 cwt.

NOTE: Since there are twelve identical control periods during the year the fixed factory and marketing overheads per period will be £40,000 and £20,000 respectively.

(d) *Standard cost.* From the management operating plans, the operating profit budget and the flexible budgets, the following standard cost can be prepared:

Standard Cost Card–1 cwt Z				£
Standard direct materials:	X, (3/5),	0.75	cwt at £4 cwt	3.00
	Y, (2/5),	0.50	cwt at £10 cwt	5.00
		1.25	cwt (at £12.80 cwt)	8.00
Standard loss (20%)		–0.25	cwt	—
Standard yield (80%)	Z,	1.00	cwt	8.00
Standard direct wages: 1/2 D. labour hrs at £6 hr				3.00
Standard direct expenses: Production royalty per cwt				0.20
Standards factory variable o'h'ds: 1/2 D. labour hr at £2 hr				1.00
Standard factory fixed o'h'ds: 1/2 D. labour hr at £8 hr				4.00
Standard factory cost				16.20
Standard marketing variable o'h'ds: 1 cwt at £0.80 cwt				0.80
Standard marketing fixed o'h'ds: 1 cwt at £2 cwt				2.00
Standard total cost				19.00
Standard profit				1.00
Standard selling price				£20.00

(e) *Control profit budget.* From the operating profit budget (sales) and the standard cost the following control profit budget can be prepared:

	£
Budgeted profit: 120,000 cwt Z at £1 cwt	120,000

This budgeted profit agrees with that in the operating profit budget so confirming the mathematical accuracy of the analysis.

(f) *Control profit budget — first control period.* The management operating plans show that management planned to have twelve identical control periods during the year. As a result of this the control profit budget for each control period is easily prepared by dividing the overall control profit budget by twelve:

	£
Budgeted profit: 10,000 cwt Z at £1 cwt	10,000

NOTE: £10,000 per control period for twelve periods gives the

£120,000 year's profit as laid down in the overall control profit budget.

25. Control plans under marginal costing technique

If the control plans above were prepared on the basis of the modern, marginal costing, technique the only differences would be as follows:

(a) The standard factory and marketing fixed overheads of £4 and £2 would be excluded from the standard cost in **24 (d)** with the result that the standard total cost would be £13 and the standard margin (contribution) £7 cwt.

(b) The control profit budget in **24 (e)** would be prepared as follows:

		£
Budgeted contribution: 120,000 cwt Z @ £7		840,000
Less budgeted fixed overheads: Factory	480,000	
Marketing	240,000	720,000
Budgeted profit		£120,000

And, of course, the first control period budget would need to be similarly amended.

Progress test 14

Principles

1.   What are the main differences between the traditional and the modern techniques of profit control?   **(5, 6)**

2.   What is a budget centre?   **(7)**

3.   Why is a fixed budget inappropriate for performance measurement?   **(10)**

4.   What is an allowance?   **(11)**

5.   Distinguish between: (*a*) standard cost and flexible budget; **(13)** (*b*) standard cost and cost standard.   **(18, 19)**

6. What is the formula for calculating an overhead allowance? **(15(a))**

7. What cost standards are involved in setting: (*a*) a standard direct materials cost; **(20(a))** (*b*) a standard direct wages cost? **(20(b))**

8. How are standard overhead costs set? **(20(d)(e))**

9. What is: (*a*) a standard sales margin; **(20(f))** (*b*) a standard cost card? **(21)**

10. How is a control profit budget prepared? **(22)**

11. How do control plans prepared on the basis of the modern marginal costing technique differ from those prepared on the basis of the traditional technique? **(25)**

Practice

12. (a) From the information given in the following fixed budget prepare on an absorption cost basis all the necessary control plans:

Budgeted Profit and Loss Account for Year

	£	£
Sales: 1,000 15-gal containers of Z at £600 each		600,000
Costs:		
Dept. 1: 20,000 gal A at £3 gal	60,000	
15,000 hrs Grade I direct labour at £6 hr	90,000	
10,000 hrs Grade II direct labour at £3 hr	30,000	
Variable overheads (variable with process hrs)	125,000	
Fixed overheads	55,000	
Dept. 2: 1,000 empty containers at £8 each	8,000	
6,000 direct labour hrs at £4 hr	24,000	
Variable overheads (variable with indirect labour hrs)	8,000	
Fixed overheads	14,000	
Marketing: Variable overheads (variable with units sold)	50,000	
Fixed overheads	60,000	524,000
Budgeted profit		£76,000

NOTE: Department 1 produces Z and has 25,000 budgeted process hours. Department 2 fills the containers with Z and has 2,000 budgeted indirect labour hours.

(b) Given that there are ten control periods of equal activity in each year, prepare the control profit budget for the first control period.

15
Variance analysis

Once the control plans have been completed the next step in the performance measurement routine is to await the end of the first control period. Once this moment has passed all the *actual* operating figures should be collected as quickly as possible. As soon as this is done the actuals should be compared with their allowances and an analysis of the differences made. Such an analysis is called a *variance analysis*.

Mathematical principles of variance analysis

Differences between actuals and allowances should not be computed in a disorganized manner for the dangers of differences overlapping or failing to be analysed at all are too great to risk. So before looking at the various differences that can arise it is necessary to outline in this section a theoretical basis on which an analysis can be constructed.

1. **Profit variances**
    When comparing an actual and an allowed figure a difference is usually found to exist. If this difference is valued so that the effect on the profit is measured then the valuation is referred to as a profit variance. For instance, in the example earlier (*see* 14:11) the departmental manager's actual expenditure was £1,400 and his allowance was £1,500. Since the difference of £100 directly measured the effect on profit, the £100 is a profit variance. A *profit variance*, then, can be defined as a *measure of the effect on profit of a given manager's performance or factor diverging from plan*. Recollect that since in computing an allowance we adjust for all the actual

circumstances except those in relation to the manager or factor under consideration, the difference between actual and allowance must measure the effect of that manager or factor, *and no other*, diverging from plan.

To take a further illustration, assume we plan to use 5 kg of A at 10p per kg per cost unit produced and actually use 10,240 kg producing 2,000 units. Our allowed usage for 2,000 units is clearly 2,000 x 5 = 10,000 kg and so we used 240 kg of A too much. And 240 kg at 10p per kg means the profit would be reduced by £24 as a result of our performance. We would, therefore, have a variance of £24.

The following points should noted:

(a) A profit variance measures the effect on *profit*, not anything else. Thus, if sales were planned to be £5,000 and actually amounted to £4,000, the divergence of £1,000 would *not* be a profit variance since the profit would not be affected to the extent of £1,000 (in fact the £1,000 is known as a *sales* variance).

(b) A profit variance is a *monetary* figure. If sales were planned to be 300 units and only 200 were actually sold, the 100 units deficit would not be a profit variance. Not until this 100 deficit is valued in terms of the effect on profit is a profit variance produced.

Profit variances are not the only kind of variances (e.g. the difference between an actual and planned cash receipt would be a *cash* variance, and, as noted above, there are also sales variances). These, however, are virtually the only variances examined upon and so the only ones discussed in this book.

2. Variance computation

As already indicated, the computation of a profit variance essentially involves no more than the valuation of the difference between an actual and an allowance. However, to state it more explicitly, it can be said that to compute a profit variance for any given factor it is necessary to:

(a) compute the allowance for that factor on the basis of the planned factor details given in the operating plans;
(b) ascertain the actual figure;
(c) find the divergence between actual and allowance;
(d) value the divergence in terms of the effect on profit.

3. Direction and name of variance

All profit variances must meet the following criteria.

(a) *They must state the direction of the profit effect*, i.e. state if the divergence affects the profit favourably or adversely. Note that:

  (*i*) a *favourable variance* (denoted by an F) is one which on its own would result in the ultimate profit being higher than planned;

  (*ii*) an *adverse variance* (denoted by an A) is one which on its own would result in the ultimate profit being lower than planned.

The two variances illustrated earlier, then, would be reported as £100F and £24A respectively.

(b) *They must be named*. Naming a profit variance is simply a matter of identifying it to the people involved in the profit control system. The name can, then, be whatever people choose. Some variances have fairly obvious names — those that measure the effect on profit of material price divergences are commonly called material price variances. Others, such as the variance that measures the effect on profit of a particularly cold spell coinciding with a fuel shortage, do not have such obvious names. In general, however, an individual variance can be defined as follows:

> *An X profit variance* (where X is the factor under analysis) *is the variance arising due to the actual X diverging from the planned X* (e.g. a *materials price* profit variance is the variance arising due to the actual *materials price* diverging from the planned *materials price*).

Since all variances can be defined in this general form no variances will be specifically defined in the text.

4. All valuations to be at standard

It can be regarded as an absolute rule that all valuations in a profit control system *must be made at standard* (i.e. standard price or standard cost). This rule includes both the valuations of divergences which are initially in physical units and also valuations of stock in the 'actual profit' statement. Proving the validity of this rule would lead into deep water but essentially it arises from the fact that isolating variances adjusts for the difference between actual and standard values and to use actual values for valuing would therefore result in double counting. So failure to observe this rule will result in a non-balancing analysis and also in variances appearing in the wrong control periods.

It will be appreciated that this rule also meets the need of providing performance measurement data in logical management terms since a manager responsible for the *usage* of a resource will expect any divergence between the allowance and actual usage to be valued at the price he agreed to when the plans were made (i.e. at standard) rather than some subsequent actual price over which he had no control.

5.   'And every plan shall have its variance'

Every planned factor will have its associated variance since each factor plan will enable a factor allowance to be computed — and comparison of this with the factor actual will reveal the factor divergence. It must, however, be admitted that finding every factor variance does depend upon the actuals being reported in parallel with the control plans. This is not always possible, though an effective profit control system will be designed with this need in mind.

6.   Segregating an actual semi-variable

One instance in which it is often impossible to ascertain an actual factor in parallel with a planned factor relates to the semi-variable overheads. A semi-variable overhead plan sets both a budgeted fixed overhead and a variable overhead per unit of activity. It is, however, usually impossible to segregate an *actual* semi-variable into its fixed and variable components. As can be seen in Fig. 7.1, the segregation technique depends upon the existence of a number of points on a graph. Just one point is not sufficient. Of course, if the semi-variable is made up of two distinct costs (e.g. an electricity standing charge and a unit charge) its segregation is possible, but usually there is no way of breaking down the actual semi-variable into its two components (do *not* fall into the trap of arguing that the actual fixed component must, by definition, be the same as the budgeted fixed component). This means that the two semi-variable allowances — the fixed allowance and the variable allowance — cannot be compared with separate actuals but can only be added together and compared in total with the total actual semi-variable overhead.

It should be appreciated that in examinations this limitation on the provision of actual figures does not, of course, apply, and separate actuals may in fact be given in any particular question.

7. The total profit variance

Of all the variances, the most important is the one that measures the divergence of the actual profit from the allowed profit — the *total profit variance*. If the variance is favourable there is much good cheer. If adverse, then there is gloom in proportion to the size of the variance.

8. Variance analysis

Good cheer or gloom, once the profit variance is known, management will quickly wish to know in detail just how it arose. The analysis providing this is called a *variance analysis* and is prepared by finding the variance associated with each planned factor in the control plans. This involves taking the flexible budgets, standards costs and control profit budget together with the actual results and computing, factor by factor, the variances arising. Needless to say, the sum of all the variances identified in a variance analysis must equal the total profit variance.

9. Chart of profit variances

There is a virtually infinite number of differing kinds of profit variances that can arise in practice. Nevertheless there are some that are common to most organizations and these variances are shown in Fig. 15.1 in their hierarchical form. Note that the main effect of using absorption costing rather than marginal costing is to create an additional group of variances — though, as will be seen in **30**, the sales volume margin variances arising under the two techniques will differ, since under marginal costing the sales margin is measured in terms of unit contribution, while under absorption costing it is measured in terms of unit profit.

It should also be appreciated that any variance can be found by summing its sub-variances (so that, for example, the direct wages variance can be found by adding the wage rate and labour efficiency variances together).

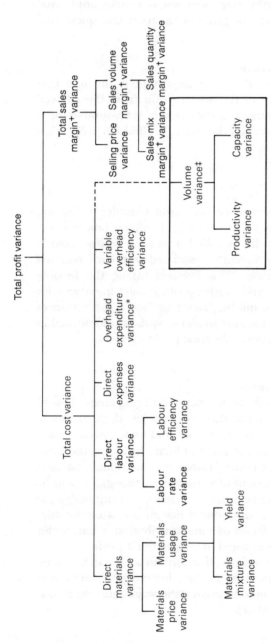

*If an examination question gives the actual fixed and variable overheads as separate figures, this variance can be analysed into a fixed overhead expenditure variance and a variable overhead expenditure variance.

†In standard absorption costing the sales margin is the profit margin, whereas in standard marginal costing it is the contribution.

‡This variance, and its sub-variances, only arises if standard absorption costing is employed.

Figure 15.1 *Chart of common cost variances*

Absorption variance analysis

We start by looking at the preparation of a variance analysis using the technique of standard absorption costing. To illustrate the mechanics of making the analysis the control plans in the example in 14:**24**, will be used in connection with an assumed set of actual figures for the first control period which are shown below. Whenever the text refers to an 'actual' amount, it is in the following actual Profit and Loss Account figures that the required amount will be found.

Actual Profit and Loss Account — Control Period 1

		X		Y		£	£
Sales:	7,000 cwt Z						136,400
Costs:	Materials	X		Y			
		cwt	£	cwt	£		
Purchases		6,600	27,840	5,000	49,560	77,400	
To stock (at standard)		−500	−2,000	−600	−6,000	−8,000	
Issues		6,100	25,840	4,400	43,560	69,400	
Direct wages: 4,425 hrs						26,800	
Factory overheads						46,200	
Production royalty						2,000	
Cost of production (8,000 cwt Z)						144,400	
Less Finished goods stock: 1,000 cwt at £16.20 cwt[*]						−16,200	
						128,200	
Marketing overheads						22,100	
Cost of sales						150,300	150,300
Actual loss							£13,900

[*]Note the valuation of stock at standard cost (14:**24(d)**).

10. Total profit variance

As indicated in **7**, the total profit variance is found by comparing the actual profit with the allowed profit. Now, since this variance relates to everything, no adjustment is called for in respect to 'outside' factors. Consequently the total profit variance is found by comparing the actual profit with the budgeted profit as shown by the control profit budget for the corresponding period.

In our illustration this involves comparing the actual loss of £13,900 shown above with the budgeted profit of £10,000 given in 14:24(f). The total profit variance for control period 1 is, therefore, £23,900A, and it is this amount we must now analyse. Below, then, each planned factor is taken in turn and its corresponding variance found so as to provide us with our required variance analysis.

11. Materials price variance

This variance arises on the purchase of materials and is found by comparing the actual purchase cost with the purchase cost allowance. This allowance is, of course, what the purchase would have cost if the planned (standard) price had been paid, i.e. it is the actual quantity at the standard price. Since every £1 over- or under-spent affects the profit by £1 the difference between the actual cost and this allowance gives the material price variance.

Example

	X	Y
Actual quantity purchased (cwt)	6,600	5,000
Standard price (per cwt) 14:**24(d)**	£4	£10
Purchase cost allowance	£26,400	£50,000
Actual cost	£27,840	£49,560
Materials price variance	£1,440 A	£440 F

This variance is the responsibility of the buyer.

> NOTE: No variance arises on the purchase of more or less materials than planned (other than perhaps minor stockholding cost variances which naturally are not material *price* variances) since the profit is unaffected by such divergences — the excess or deficit merely affecting stock levels.

12. Materials usage variance

This variance is found by comparing the actual materials

usage with the usage allowance and valuing any difference at the standard price of the material.

If the planned quantity of material had been used each time a unit was produced then the total material usage would be equal to the number of units produced multiplied by the standard usage. This, then, is the usage allowance and any usage above or below this allowance will affect the profit to the extent of the value of the over- or under-usage.

Example

	X	Y
Units produced, Z (cwt)	8,000	8,000
Standard usage (14:24(d))	0.75 cwt	0.50 cwt
Usage allowance	6,000 cwt	4,000 cwt
Actual usage	6,100 cwt	4,400 cwt
Difference	100A cwt	400A cwt
Standard price per cwt 14:24(d))	£4	£10
Materials usage variance	£400A	£4,000A

This variance is the responsibility of the manager of the production department concerned.

13. Materials mix and yield variances

Where materials are planned to be mixed in given proportions and a planned loss on process is laid down, it is useful if the materials usage variance is further analysed into mixture and yield variances which are computed as follows.

(a) *Materials mix variance.* The easiest way to compute this variance is to find the allowed mix value of the total *input* (in other words, ask yourself what the *actual input would have been* if the materials had been mixed in the planned proportions) and compare the value of this with the actual value of the input (using standard prices for valuing, of course). Clearly, if the materials had been mixed in exactly the planned proportions, these two figures would be identical and, almost equally clearly, every £1 extra of actual value is, in fact, an overspending of £1 and therefore a reduction of the profit by this amount.

So a materials mix variance is computed by taking the difference between the allowed mix value of the input and the actual value.

Example

Total actual input:	X	6,100	cwt at £4	= £24,400
	Y	4,400	cwt at £10	= 44,000
		10,500	cwt	£68,400

Standard cost of 1 cwt of input
mix (14:**24(d)**) = £8/1.25 = £6.40
∴ Allowed value of input mix of
10,500 cwt = 10,500 x £6.40   = 67,200

Materials mix variance   £1,200 A

(b) *Materials yield variance*. This variance is found by comparing the actual yield with the allowed yield and valuing the difference at the standard cost per unit of *output*. The allowed yield is quite simply the actual input multiplied by the standard yield. Note that the difference must be valued at the standard cost per unit of output since every unit lost (or gained) here is a unit of output and must be valued accordingly.

Example

Actual input (total)	10,500 cwt
Standard yield (14:**24(d)**)	80 %
Yield allowance	8,400 cwt
Actual yield	8,000 cwt
Difference	400 A cwt
Standard cost of output (14:**24(d)**)	£8 per cwt
Materials yield variance	£3,200 A

(c) *Cross-check*. Since the mixture and yield variances are sub-variances of the usage variance, the sum of the two former must equal the latter.

Example

Mix variance	£1,200A
Yield variance	3,200A
Total	£4,400A
Materials usage variance (**12**): X	400A
Y	4,000A
Total materials usage variance	£4,400A

The two totals agree and the analysis is therefore proved arithmetically accurate.

14. Labour rate variance

This variance is the difference between the actual and the allowed wages, and being in effect no more than a price variance in respect of the 'purchase' of labour, is found in exactly the same way as a price variance. The allowed wages, of course, are the wages that would have been paid if the standard rates had been paid and are computed by multiplying the actual hours worked by the standard wage rate.

Example

Actual hours worked	4,425
Standard wage rate (14:**24(d)**)	£6 per hr
Wage allowance	£26,550
Actual wages	£26,800
Labour rate variance	£250 A

The personnel manager will normally be responsible for this variance.

15. Labour efficiency variance

This variance is really a usage variance in respect of the 'usage' of labour time. It is called an 'efficiency' variance since the comparison of actual against planned times is a measure of labour efficiency. To compute a labour efficiency variance, therefore, merely find the allowed time (i.e. how long would have been taken if the planned times had been adhered to) and compare this with the actual time — and value the difference at the standard wage rate.

Example
_____

Units produced, Z	8,000 cwt
Standard time per cwt	
(14:**24(d)**)	$\frac{1}{2}$ hr
Time allowance	4,000 hrs
Actual time taken	4,425 hrs
Difference	425 A hrs
Standard wage rate (14:**24(d)**)	£6 per hr
Labour efficiency variance	£2,550 A

_____

The manager responsible for the supervision of the labour will be responsible for this variance.

16. Direct expenses variance

This variance is no more than the difference between the actual and the allowed direct expenses — the latter being simply the actual number of units produced multiplied by the standard direct expenses shown in the standard cost.

Example
_____

Units produced, Z	8,000 cwt
Standard direct expense	
— royalty (14:**24(d)**)	20 p per cwt
Direct expense allowance	£1,600
Actual direct expense	£2,000
Direct expenses variance	400 A

_____

17. Overhead expenditure variance

This variance is found by computing the allowed overhead from the relevant flexible budget and comparing this allowance with the actual overhead incurred.

The only difficulty that may arise in finding this kind of variance could be in computing the allowance. In this regard remember that an overhead expenditure allowance is made up of two parts — a fixed allowance and a variable allowance. The fixed allowance is quite simply the budgeted fixed cost for the period, while the variable allowance is found by multiplying the *actual* units of activity by the standard cost per unit of activity. Adding these two allowances gives the total overhead expenditure allowance and the difference between this and the actual expenditure gives the required overhead expenditure variance (since every £1 overspent is £1 less profit).

Example

	Factory	*Marketing dept.*
Actual activity	4,425 D.L. hrs	7,000 cwt Z
Standard cost per unit activity (14:**24(c)**)	£2 per hr	£0.80 per cwt
Variable overhead allowance	£8,850	£5,600
Fixed overhead allowance: one control period (14:**24(c)**)	£40,000	£20,000
Total overhead allowance	£48,850	£25,600
Actual overheads	£46,200	£22,100
Overhead expenditure variance	£2,650F	£3,500 F

The relevant departmental managers will, of course, be responsible for these variances.

As indicated earlier, it sometimes happens in examination questions that the actual fixed and variable overheads are given separately. When this occurs separate fixed and variable overhead expenditure variances can be computed by comparing the given actuals with the corresponding allowances.

Example

If the actual factory overheads had been given as £40,200 fixed and £6,000 variable, the following variances could have been computed:

Fixed overhead expenditure allowance (as above):	£40,200
Actual fixed overhead expenditure	40,000
Fixed overhead expenditure variance	200 A
Variable overhead expenditure allowance (as above)	8,850
Actual variable overhead expenditure	6,000
Variable overhead expenditure variance	£2,850 F

18. Variable overhead efficiency variance

This variance is perhaps the most complex of the variances. It arises because the expenditure allowance is based on the units of *activity* undertaken, *not* the units of production. Thus, if 10 units of activity having a standard cost of £2 per unit of activity are undertaken, there will be an expenditure allowance of £20. If then £20 is spent there will be no expenditure variance. But it may be that only 3 units of *production*, each having a standard activity of 2 units of activity, were produced. This means these 3 units of production should have required (have an allowance of) 6 units of activity. Since 10 units of activity were actually undertaken then 10 – 6 = 4 units of activity were in excess of plan. And, as variable costs are incurred on each and every unit of *activity* (as against unit of production), then an excess variable cost equal to the variable costs of these 4 units of activity will be incurred — which will reduce the profit by this amount. (In other words there was an under-recovery of the variable overhead cost of 4 units of activity.) This loss will be the variable overhead efficiency variance (since it arises on account of the inefficient use of overhead facilities).

To find a variable overhead efficiency variance, then, it is necessary to take the following steps.

(a) Find the *allowed* activity by multiplying the units of production by the standard activity as laid down in the standard cost.

(b) Compare this allowance with the *actual* units of activity undertaken.

(c) Value the difference at the *standard cost per unit of activity*.

Example

Actual production, Z	8,000 cwt
Standard activity (14:**24(d)**)	½ D.L. hr
Activity allowance	4,000 hrs
Actual activity	4,425 hrs
Difference	425 A
Standard cost (14:**24(d)**)	£2 per hr
∴ *Variable overhead efficiency variance*	£850 A

This variance will be the responsibility of the manager responsible for the efficient use of the overhead facilities.

NOTE: If activity is measured in cost units (as it is in the marketing budget centre), the allowed units of activity will, in fact, be the actual units involved and so no overhead efficiency variance can arise. In other words, the variance only arises where the overheads are incurred on a basis *other than* cost units and where, therefore, a divergence can arise between the overheads allowed on the basis of activity and the overheads allowed on the basis of cost units (indeed, the variance can be computed using just this approach: e.g. allowed variable overheads on basis of activity units — allowed variable costs on basis of cost units = (4,425 direct labour hours × £2 standard variable overheads per hour) — (8,000 cwt of Z produced × £1 standard variable costs per cwt) = £8,850 – £8,000 = £850A).

19. Volume variance

In **3:21(b)** it was pointed out that a predetermined overhead recovery rate could fail to recover exactly the actual overheads incurred. This failure arises because either the actual overheads are not identical in amount to that budgeted, or the actual production is not as budgeted, or both. In a variance analysis the first of these differences is measured by the overhead expenditure variance. This leaves the second of the differences still to be accounted for and it is the function of the volume variance to do this. In effect a *volume variance* measures the under- or over-recovery of fixed overheads due to the actual volume of production differing from the planned (note that only the *fixed* overheads are involved since the variable overheads automatically rise and fall with production so that a fall, say, in production is matched by a fall in these overheads — which, by definition, is not the case with the fixed overheads).

To compute the volume variance, the allowed volume (i.e. the budgeted production) is compared with the actual volume and the difference valued at the standard fixed overhead cost per unit of production.

Example

(a) Factory

Volume allowance (14:**24(f)**)	10,000	cwt
Actual production	8,000	cwt
Difference	2,000	A cwt
Standard fixed overhead cost (14:**24(d)**)	£4	per cwt
∴ *Factory volume variance*	£8,000	A

(b) Marketing

Volume allowance (14:**24(f)**)	10,000	cwt
Actual sales*	7,000	cwt
Difference	3,000	A cwt
Standard fixed overhead cost (14:**24(d)**)	£2	per cwt
∴ *Marketing volume variance*	£6,000	A

*Marketing overheads are recovered using a *sales* absorption rate (and the volume allowance is, of course, unit sales).

In the case of production a volume variance can arise either because more (or less) labour hours were worked than planned or because the labour force worked more (or less) efficiently, or both. A production volume variance can, therefore, be analysed into two variances measuring the effect of both these factors. The method of computation is shown below.

20. Productivity variance

A *productivity variance* (or *volume efficiency variance* or *fixed overhead efficiency variance* as it is sometimes called) measures the under- or over-recovery of fixed overheads due to the efficiency of direct labour. Since for every hour worked the labour force should produce its planned hourly production, then every hour worked during which production does not materialize results in the under-recovery of one hour's fixed overheads. The productivity variance can, therefore, be calculated by comparing the actual hours worked with the number of hours that should have been worked in view of the actual production (the allowed hours) and valuing the difference at the standard fixed overhead rate per hour.

Example

Allowed hours for 8,000 cwt Z				
= 8,000 x $\frac{1}{2}$ (14:**24(d)**)		=	4,000	hrs
Actual hours			4,425	hrs
Difference			425	A hrs
Standard fixed overhead rate per hour				
(14:**24(c)**)			£8	
∴ *Productivity variance*			£3,400A	

21. Standard hours production

It will be noticed that in calculating all three of the efficiency variances in the illustration (labour efficiency, variable overhead efficiency and productivity) an allowance of 4,000 hours was used. Whenever production overheads are recovered on an hourly basis (which is usually the case when absorption costing is used) it may be advantageous to measure production in terms of allowed hours — and this is particularly so where many different kinds of cost units are produced and a common measure is needed to find the overall production. In such circumstances the allowed hours are called *standard hours* and all production is measured in these hours. In our illustration, therefore, we can say that there were 4,000 standard hours of production.

In passing it may be worth noting that since all the efficiency variances arise from the performance of the direct labour, some authorities hold that all these variances should be referred to as labour efficiency variances.

22. Capacity variance

This measures the under- or over-recovery of fixed overheads due to the actual hours worked differing from the budgeted hours. In our illustration the allowance for this variance is the budgeted hours and the form of computation follows the previous pattern.

Example

Allowance: 60,000 hrs for year	
(14:**24(c)**) ÷ 12	5,000 hrs
Actual worked	4,425 hrs
Difference	575 A hrs
Standard fixed overhead rate per hour	
(14:**24(c)**)	£8
∴ *Capacity variance*	£4,600 A

Note that the sum of the capacity variance (£4,600A) and the productivity variance (£3,400A) equals the factory volume variance (£8,000A).

23. Total sales profit variance

This variance is found by comparing the actual sales profit with the allowed sales profit — where in our illustration the allowed sales profit is clearly the budgeted sales of 10,000 cwt at a profit margin of £1 per cwt (14:**24(f)**). Here the point to note is that in computing the actual sales profit then in accordance with the rule 'always value at standard cost' the actual cost of sales must be valued at the standard total unit cost. So:

Actual sales — 7,000 cwt	£136,400
Actual COS — 7,000 x £19 (14:**24(d)**)	133,000
Actual sales profit	3,400
Allowed sales profit	10,000
Total sales profit variance	£6,600 A

This variance is normally the responsibility of the sales or marketing manager, and as it arises on account of both a divergence of selling price and volume from plan, it can be analysed into two sub-variances in a manner described below.

24. Selling price variance

This sub-variance of the sales profit variance is just another instance of the ordinary price variances discussed earlier. It is therefore found by comparing the actual sales value with the allowed sales value. This allowance is simply the amount one would have obtained if all sales had been at the planned selling price and so is found by multiplying the actual sales quantity by the standard selling price. Again, since every £1 obtained above the planned selling price increases the profit by £1, the difference between the actual and allowed sales values is the sales margin selling price variance.

Example

Actual quantity sold, Z	7,000 cwt
Standard selling price (14:**24(d)**)	£20 per cwt
Sales value allowance	£140,000
Actual sales value	136,400
Selling price variance	£3,600 A

This variance is, of course, the responsibility of the sales manager.

25. Sales volume profit variance

This measures the effect on profit of actual sales quantities falling below or exceeding the planned quantities, i.e. budgeted quantities. Since the profit is affected by the profit margin associated with the deficient or excess units, the variance is found by comparing the actual sales quantities with the allowed (budgeted) quantity and valuing the difference at standard profit.

Example

Sales quantity allowance, Z (14:**24(f)**)	10,000 cwt
Actual sales quantity	7,000 cwt
Difference	3,000 cwt
Standard profit margin (14:**24(d)**)	£1 cwt
Sales volume profit variance	£3,000 A

Normally, this variance is the responsibility of the sales manager. If, however, for some reason he was not provided with sufficient units to sell (e.g. because of production failures), the variance will be charged to whoever and whatever caused the shortfall.

One final point — it should be appreciated that any sales margin variance relates to a *margin* variance and not a sales value variance (i.e. divergences from planned sales values) since the latter is not a profit variance and does not therefore automatically measure the effect on profit of a divergence from plan. As it happens, in the case of the sales margin selling price variance we can use sales values since fortuitously, as has been pointed out, every extra £1 we obtain on the selling price is £1 extra profit. But this, of course, is not so in the case of the sales volume profit variance for if, in our illustration, we compare the allowed quantity at the standard *selling price* with the actual quantity at the standard selling price we obtain sales values of 10,000 x £20 – 7,000 x £20 = 200,000 – 140,000 = £60,000. This £60,000 is the volume *value* variance and it certainly is not the sales volume profit variance.

26. Sales mix margin variance
Because volume of sales is so critical to an enterprise's ability to control profit, the desirability of a frequently (e.g. daily) assessment of the sales volume margin (profit or contribution) variance cannot be denied. However, if there are a large number of products, it is sometimes argued that a variance computed in respect of each product — the only way an accurate variance can be found — is impractical (although in view of the capability of today's computers this view can probably be challenged). As it happens there is a short alternative rough-and-ready procedure that can be adopted. This procedure rests on the fact that if the product mix of actual sales is as planned, then the sales volume margin variance can be computed by multiplying the difference between an actual sales volume (measured in units or sales as appropriate) by the standard average (weighted) sales margin per unit of volume. If, however, the actual mix is not as planned, then a variance error arises — and the difference between the true variance and the short-cut variance is, not surprisingly, called the *sales mix margin variance*.

Since the sales mix margin variance is not part of the overall integrated variance analysis, only a brief example is given here. Note, incidentally, that a rough-and-ready sales volume margin variance is called a *sales quantity margin variance*.

Product	Unit	Budgeted quantity	Standard price £	Budgeted value £	Standard margin £	Budgeted margin £	Actual sales Units	Actual sales £	Divergence Units	Volume variance* £
A	gal	10,000	2	20,000	1	10,000	12,100	24,200	2,100 F	2,100 F
B	bags	500	120	60,000	50	25,000	630	75,600	130 F	6,500 F
C	cwt	2,000	10	20,000	5	10,000	1,155	11,550	845 A	4,225 A
		12,500		£100,000		£45,000	13,885	£111,350	1,385 F	£4,375 F

* Divergence x Standard margin

Weighted average margin per unit = 45,000/12,500 = £3.6 per unit
Alternatively, weighted average margin per £ sales = 45,000/100,000 =
45p per £

Variances:	Based on units	Based on £s
Sales quantity margin variance	£4,986F [*]	£5,107.50F†
Sales volume margin variance	4,375F	4,375.00F
Sales mix margin variance	611F	732.50F

[*] 1,385 x £3.6
† (£111,350 − 100,000) x 45p

27. Summary of variances

At the end of the analysis the sub-variances should, of course,
equal the profit variance. This will prove the arithmetical accuracy
of the analysis.

Example

	Variance		£
Material price (11):	X		1,440A
	Y		440F
Material mix (13(a))			1,200A
Material yield (13(b))			3,200A
Labour rate (14)			250A
Labour efficiency (15)			2,550A
Direct expenses (16)			400A
Overhead expenditure (17):	Factory		2,650F
	Marketing		3,500F
Variable overhead efficiency (18):	Factory		850A
Production volume:		Productivity (20)	3,400A
		Capacity (22)	4,600A
Marketing volume (19(b))			6,000A
Selling price (24)			3,600A
Sales volume profit (25)			3,000A
Total profit variance (10)			23,900A

Marginal variance analysis

From the point of view of computing variances the modern
technique of variance analysis is not so very different from that of

absorption variance analysis. In this brief section those variances which are *not* the same under the two techniques are illustrated.

28. Total profit variance

An important point which must not be overlooked when working with marginal variance analyses is that all stocks are valued at standard marginal cost. In the case of the raw materials stocks, the valuations will be the same regardless of which technique is used, but this is not so when it comes to finished goods stocks. And changing the value of the finished goods stocks changes, of course, the *actual* profit for the period which in turn changes the profit variance.

Example

Finished goods:
1,000 units @ absorption factory standard
cost of £16.20 (14:**24(d)**)   £16,200
@ marginal factory standard
cost of £12.20*   £12,200

Reduction in stock value   £4,000

*£16.20 per unit — standard fixed overhead of
£4 (14:**24(d)**) = £12.20
So the actual profit for the period shown on page 313 will be reduced by £4,000, which in this case means the loss will increase from £13,900 to £17,900

∴   *Total profit variance* = 10,000 — 17,900 loss = £27,900A

29. Volume, productivity and capacity variances

Since under marginal costing fixed overheads are not charged in any way to cost units, in a marginal variance analysis the volume, productivity and capacity variances disappear completely. The disappearance of these variances means that the only overhead variances left are the variable overhead efficiency and the overhead expenditure. And in the case of these variances the method of computation remains unchanged.

30. Sales contribution and sales volume contribution variances

Under standard marginal costing the unit cost and sales margin is, of course, the standard unit marginal cost and contribution. In computing the sales contribution and sales volume contribution, then, this standard cost and contribution will be used. Apart from this, the computations are identical to those in **23** and **25.**

Example

Actual sales — 7,000 cwt	£136,400
Actual COS — 7,000 x £13[*]	91,000
Actual sales contribution	45,400
Allowed sales contribution: £840,000 (14:**25(b)**) ÷ 12	70,000
Sales contribution variance	£24,600A

[*]Absorption cost of £19 less fixed overheads absorbed of £4 and £2 (14:**24(d)**)

And the sales volume contribution variance is similar to that found in **25** except that the 3,000 cwt difference is valued at the standard contribution of £7 cwt — so *sales volume contribution variance* = 3,000 x £7 = £21,000A.

Note that the selling price variance is unaffected by the costing technique employed and therefore remains at £3,600A (which, together with the £21,000A variance just computed, gives the sales contribution variance of £24,600A).

31. Summary of variances

As will be appreciated, in view of the small number of differences the summary of the marginal cost variances will be substantially the same as that of the absorption variances.

Example

Summary as in **27** except that the two production volume variances and the marketing volume variance will be excluded (i.e. complete exclusion of variances totalling 3,400A + 4,600A + 6,000A = 14,000A) while the sales volume contribution variance will change from £3,000A to £21,000A, an increase of £18,000A. This means the summary total in **27** (£23,900A) will be adjusted by these amounts, i.e. 23,900A — 14,000A + 18,000A = £27,900A.

And this is the profit variance computed in **28** above.

32. The sales volume contribution variance

Before leaving discussion of the individual variances in a variance analysis the importance of the sales volume contribution variance under the modern control technique should be appreciated, for, measuring as it does the contribution gained or lost as a result of a divergence between the actual and planned sales volume, by its very nature it must measure (as its counterpart in standard absorption costing fails to do) the full impact on profits of the volume divergence.

This variance is very much a key variance since the success of an enterprise is closely bound up with the level of its sales. For this reason any adverse amounts should be carefully considered. Although the responsibility for the variance normally falls on the sales manager, this is not by any means invariably so. If, for example, sales quantities were down because production failed to produce the units to sell, then the variance must be charged to the production manager responsible. In such a case it would probably be worthwhile analysing the variance so that the contribution lost as a result of strikes, absenteeism, breakdowns, etc., could be reported to the production manager.

Progress test 15

Principles

1. What is a profit variance and what determines the name of any given profit variance? **(1,3)**

2. What is the general procedure for computing a profit variance? **(2)**

3. Why is it usually impossible to segregate an actual semi-variable cost into its fixed and variable components? **(6)**

4. What is the total profit variance, how is it computed and how does it relate to a variance analysis? **(7, 8)**

5. How is an overhead expenditure variance computed? **(17)**

6. Explain how a variable overhead efficiency variance can arise. **(18)**

7. What is meant by standard hours production and why is this measure useful? **(21)**

8. Which variances have different values according to whether the analysis is prepared along traditional or modern lines? **(28–30)**

9. What is the significance of the sales volume margin variance in a marginal costing analysis? **(32)**

Practice

10. Given that the cost standards are 20 gallons and £2.50 per gallon, compute the variances when the actuals are:

    (a) 24 gallons for a cost of £60;
    (b) 20 gallons for a cost of £70;
    (c) 24 gallons at £3.50 per gallon;
    (d) 18 gallons for a cost of £50.

11. Find the variances where the cost standards are 100 direct labour hours and £4 per hour and the actuals are:

    (a) 110 hours for a cost of £385;
    (b) 95 hours for a cost of £368.

12. Hydrogen pentoxide is prepared by mixing hydrogen and oxygen in the proportions of 1:5. The standard prices of these gases are £0.50 and £0.05 per cubic foot respectively. During the last production run 10,200 cubic feet of hydrogen was mixed with 57,600 cubic feet of oxygen. Compute the mix variance.

13. MUD is prepared by mixing M, U and D (standard prices £1, £2 and £3 per tonne respectively) in the proportions of 1:1:3. A standard loss of 20 per cent is allowed. Last period 1,100 tonnes of M costing £1,000, 1,000 tonnes of U costing £2,200 and 2,900 tonnes of D costing £8,888 were processed to give 3,815 tonnes of MUD. Find the variances.

14. A sales department measures its activity in terms of sales invoices processed. It plans to average 5 articles per invoice. The standard marginal cost of every article carries the following entry: 'Variable sales dept. overheads: 10p.'

In the last period, 11,340 articles were invoiced using 2,504 invoices for a variable overhead cost of £1,521. Compute the relevant variances.

15. The sales budget of the Table & Chairs Co. Ltd. shows budgeted sales of 4,000 chairs at £5 each and 1,000 tables at £30 each. The standard cost of a chair is £2 and of a table £17. Actual sales for the period were 3,100 chairs for £15,215 and 1,200 tables for £35,682. Find the selling price and sales volume margin variances.

16. The actual results of the company referred to in Progress test 14, question 12, for the first period were as follows:

		£	£	£
Sales:	95 15-gallon containers of Z			56,084
Costs:	Purchases: A: 2,500 gal		7,720	
	Containers: 100		794	
			8,514	
	Less Closing stocks:			
	A: 320 gal at £3	960		
	Containers: 1 at £8	8	−968	
			7,546	
Dept. 1: D. labour,	Grade I: 1,470½ hrs		8,888	
	Grade II: 1,050 hrs		3,124	
	Overheads (2,550 process hrs)		18,540	
Dept. 2: D. labour 625 hrs			2,451	
	Overheads (200½ Ind. lab. hrs)		2,101	
Marketing overheads			14,990	
			57,640	
Less Work-in-progress (Dept. 2):				
Z: 140 gal at £24		3,360		
Finished goods stock: Full				
containers: 3 at £414		1,242	−4,602	53,038
Actual profit				£3,046

Production statistics:
    Dept. 1: 1,610 gal of Z
    Dept. 2: 98 15-gallon containers of Z

There were no opening stocks in any of the stores or opening work-in-progress.
Find the total profit variance and prepare a variance analysis.

17. Rework question 16 using a marginal cost form of variance analysis.

18. On the basis of a production/sales level of 10,000 units a month the standard unit cost of a carton of Gimmet which sells for £48 is:

		£
Material:	12 kg at £2	24.00
Labour:	1½ hrs at £6.40	9.60
Fixed overhead		2.40

The operating statement for November 19–7 was as follows:

	£	£	£
Budgeted profit			120,000
Add favourable variances			
Sales volume margin	6,000		
Material price	5,072		
Labour efficiency	960		
Fixed overhead volume	1,200	13,232	
Less adverse variances			
Sales price	4,000		
Material usage	1,600		
Wages rates	3,120		
Fixed overhead expenditure	800	9,520	
Net favourable variance			3,712
Actual profit			£123,712

Prepare the conventional actual profit statement.

(ACCA, modified)

19. A company manufactures a food product, data for which for one week has been analysed as follows:

Standard cost data:

	£
Direct materials: 10 units at £1.50	15
Direct wages: 5 hours at £4.00	20
Production overhead: 5 hours at £5.00	25
	£60

Other overhead may be ignored.
Profit margin is 20% of sales price.
Budgeted sales are £30,000 per week.

Actual data:

Sales	£29,880
Direct materials	£6,435
Direct wages	£8,162

Analysis of variances:

		Adverse	Favourable
Direct materials:	price	585	
	usage		375
Direct labour:	rate		318
	efficiency	180	
Production overhead:	expenditure		200
	volume		375

It can be assumed that the production and sales achieved resulted in no changes of stock.

You are required, from the data given, to calculate: (*i*) the actual output; (*ii*) the actual profit; (*iii*) the actual price per unit of material; (*iv*) the actual rate per labour hour; (*v*) the amount of production overhead incurred; (*vi*) the amount of production overhead absorbed; (*vii*) the production overhead efficiency variance; (*viii*) the selling price variance; (*ix*) the sales volume profit variance.

(*CIMA*)

20. The following standard costs apply in a business that manufactures a single product.

Standard weight to produce one unit	12 kilos
Standard price per kilo	£9
Standard hours to produce one unit	10
Standard rate per hour	£4

Actual production and costs for one accounting period.

Material used	3,770 kilos
Material cost	£35,815
Hours worked	2,755
Wages paid	£11,571

The actual output was 290 units.

Required:

(a) Calculate relevant material and labour cost variances, and present these in a format suitable for presentation to the management of the company.

(b) Explain how standard costs for material and labour might be compiled. (14:**20(a)** and **(b)**)

(AAT June 90 Part question — balance in Progress test 17, question 2)

Aspects of profit control

With the mechanics of variance analysis behind us, we can now turn to look at what the figures are telling us and what they should be telling us.

Causes of variances

Having computed a variance and found it to be of significance, the next step is to determine why it arose.

1. Basis variance causes

Variances can arise for all sorts of reasons. Initially, though, the cause of a variance can be analysed into one of the following categories (and to illustrate each it will be assumed that 10 hours were planned for an operation that in the event actually took 15 hours):

(a) *Operating variance.* This is caused by the failure of actual operations to meet a valid plan. This, of course, is the normal cause of a variance and so, if the operation in our illustration took 15 hours because of the inefficiency of the operative concerned, the variance arising from the 5 excess hours would be an operating variance.

(b) *Planning variance.* This is caused by a planning failure rather than a failure in operations. Such a failure can take one of two forms.

    (i) *Prediction failure.* Where there is a prediction failure the plan wrongly *predicts* some future value. Thus, the 10

hours planned time could have been a predicted time based on the expected future availability of certain material-handling equipment. If the 5 hours excess time arose because in the event this equipment was not available, then the variance arising is a planning variance. The commonest form of predictive failure relates, of course, to price and wage rate standards since these kinds of variance more often result from wrong predictions than from bad buying or poor labour recruitment.

(ii) *Modelling failure.* All plans are based on models or mental conceptions of the circumstances that apply in a situation. Thus, the plan for 10 hours could have been based on the belief that the operation did not involve a setting-up step when, in fact, it did (and required a total of 5 hours to complete). So when there is a modelling failure the plan wrongly *models* the situation. Clerical slips can be considered a form of this type of failure and one common example is where a material standard fails to include a standard loss, even though such a loss is inevitable.

(c) *Measurement error variance.* In practice variances often arise as a result of errors in measurement. Thus, our illustrative operation may well have been completed in 10 hours but inadvertently 15 hours were booked on the job.

(d) *Random variance.* Actuals very rarely exactly equal plan if only because of chance events. Everybody has peaks and troughs in their work cycle and obviously these can lead to adverse and favourable variances of roughly equal frequency. Such variances are random variances.

Each of these kinds of variance calls for a different action. Only the first, the operating variance, calls for action of an operating nature. Planning variances naturally call for improved forecasting and modelling techniques, measurement error variances for improved measuring devices or procedures, while random variances call for no action at all.

For simplicity it will be assumed in the remainder of this book that all variances are operating variances.

2. Causes of operating variances

It was, of course, operating variances that we were analysing in Chapter 15. To control operating variances it is necessary to have some idea as to just how they arose. The commonest causes include the following:

(a) *Materials price variance*: change in purchase price; change in delivery costs; non-standard material purchased; bad buying.

(b) *Materials usage variance*: waste or scrap excessive; defective material (e.g. due to deterioration, poor handling, bad buying); rejection of completed work necessitating additional material withdrawals from store; pilferage; non-standard material used; incorrect booking of material usage.

(c) *Labour rate variance*: general rise in wage rates; individual increase in specific wage rate; non-standard grade of employee.

(d) *Labour efficiency variance*: slow employee; employee delayed by factors outside his/her control (e.g. breakdowns; no materials); poor working conditions; output deliberately restricted by employee; abnormal length of run; employee handicapped by physical disability (e.g. bandaged finger); quality of supervision; non-standard grade of employee; non-standard material used; non-standard job method used; incorrect booking of labour times.

(e) *Overhead expenditure variance*: excessive or under-utilization of a service (i.e. wasteful or economical use of service); price change for service (e.g. rate per kW/hr); change in the nature of service (e.g. using gas for heating in lieu of electricity).

(f) *Overhead efficiency variance*: (variable and productivity). These variances often arise in conjunction with a labour efficiency variance — in which case they will be due to the same causes (*see* **(d)**).

(g) *Capacity variance*: absenteeism; industrial action; injuries; staff shortages; breakdowns; adverse weather; overtime.

(h) *Selling price variance*: sales discounts; quantity discounts; sales in non-planned markets (e.g. non-budgeted export sales).

(i) *Sales volume margin variance*: abnormal economic conditions; ineffective marketing; competitors' activities; changing consumer tastes; deteriorating reputation (e.g. due to poor quality, after-sales service, etc.); production failure due to breakdowns, absenteeism, labour or material shortages, strikes, bad production management, design errors, etc.

3. A variance is not a verdict

   A variance is really only a *signal* that something somewhere is not conforming to plan. It is not a *verdict* on anybody or anything.

Thus, a materials usage variance in department Z does not necessarily mean that there are inefficiencies in department Z's operations. It probably goes without saying that there is no set procedure that automatically identifies sources and causes of variances — there is only the accountant's experience, intelligence and detailed knowledge of the operations of the organization. Sometimes the source may be far removed from the place where the variance arises, e.g. when an after-sales service variance arises on account of the earlier purchase of sub-standard components, or the cause may be subtle, e.g. when an adverse materials usage variance arises because of unsuspected loss of moisture between weighing the materials on issue and weighing the product on completion. Often no clear answers are possible. No matter, for it is better to report an inexplicable variance than to attribute it to the wrong cause as a result of a superficial interpretation.

4. Interdependence of variances

Variances are frequently interdependent. Thus, a favourable labour rate variance that arises from the employment of sub-standard labour will very probably be offset by an adverse labour efficiency variance. In such circumstances it would be absurd to praise the personnel manager while castigating the production manager. Although the ultimate cause of a variance may be revealed by a thorough investigation, it speeds up the accountant's work if he is aware from the beginning of probable linkages between variances. Such an accountant will not be surprised if department A, whose supervisor prides himself on always achieving favourable labour efficiency variances, consistently shows an adverse scrap variance while department B, whose supervisor prides himself on his nil scrap variance, consistently shows an adverse labour efficiency variance.

This interdependence of variances does, as it happens, often have an advantage not usually ascribed to a profit control system for it enables 'trade-offs' to be evaluated. For instance, a sales manager may argue that his new generous discount policy benefits the business by virtue of the extra sales made. By comparing the adverse sales price variance arising from the new discounts with the favourable variances arising from the extra sales, the net gain or loss in adopting this policy can be seen.

General principles of profit control

Next we summarize the general principles of profit control. Note first, however, the following points:

(a) *Profit control is a control technique.* It is not a cost ascertainment technique, a book-keeping technique, a decision-making technique, or a technique for anything else. And this in turn means that all principles and conventions relating to these latter techniques have no automatic relevance to the control technique.

(b) *Profit control is a management technique.* It involves both an appreciation of the significance of a difference between actual and planned performance and the authority to take corrective action.

Both these functions fall to management, the latter by definition and the former by virtue of the fact that appreciating the significance of such a difference is best made by the person who is specifically responsible for the performance analysed. The object of profit control, then, is not to enable the books to be balanced or economic returns to be calculated but to enable managers to achieve the profit that they set out to achieve. And the validity of all control principles and procedures must be tested against this objective.

Since profit control is a management technique, it follows that it must be developed from a management point of view and not from an accounting point of view, though of course the accountant may very well operate the necessary clerical procedures. This requirement has as an important corollary the fact that in operating the technique *the accountant has to fit in with the manager*, not the manager with the accountant.

5. Profit control and flexibility

It is a matter of common observation that all sorts of things can go wrong with a profit plan. This means that all sorts of divergences from plan can arise. A fundamental feature of any system which aims to quantify these divergences in terms of the effect on profit must, therefore, be flexibility. For this reason, if no other, formulae cannot be the basis of such a system — if they were, then almost certainly some situation would arise in practice for which no formula existed (in examinations, of course, the examiners can restrict divergences to those formally recognized).

So our profit control technique calls for a flexible strategy that will enable *any* divergence, foreseen or otherwise, to be measured in terms of *the effect on profit*. It is, of course, for this reason that we adopt the 'allowance' approach to computing variances as this gives us just that flexibility (*see* 14:11). (At a more fundamental level adopting this approach enables us to comply with what cyberneticians call the Law of Requisite Variety — i.e. for control there must be as many potential responses as there are potential divergencies from plan, explicit or implicit.)

6. Control, responsibility and authority

All control ultimately depends upon taking appropriate action. Now, action can only be taken by those who are authorized to take it — in an economic enterprise, the managers. So, as we have seen, a profit control system must be designed around the managers who must ultimately achieve the planned profit. And that means it must be designed in terms of the responsibilities and authority of the individual managers.

In view of this, it is important that the system should accurately reflect the organization structure of the enterprise. If, for instance, in a particular enterprise, the marketing manager were responsible for the finished goods store, the profit control system should recognize that fact by ensuring the store control data is reported to the marketing manager. If conversely the store is under the authority of the works manager then it should be to him that the system directs the data.

7. A management technique implies a behavioural context

Management involves people — both the managers and the managed — and where people are involved then all the behavioural implications have to be considered. Unfortunately, the subject of managerial behaviour considerations lies outside the scope of this book and, apart from the few comments below, will not be further discussed. Students nevertheless should be aware of this important aspect of all budgeting and control work in the real, practical world.

There are, however, two points that can be briefly referred to:

(a) *Goal congruence.* The goals of individuals, centres and the organization as a whole should all support each other — i.e. all goals should be congruent. Such goals include recognition, status, paths of advancement, training, fringe benefits, job satisfaction and, of course, pay and profits. Often one goal is incompatible with another but as far as possible management should aim to make all goals congruent.

(b) *Participation.* People are more motivated and able to work more effectively if they are able to participate in the planning and control of operations. So, again, where possible management should aim at engendering the maximum viable participation. In this connection note that a budget prepared on the basis of participation by the people to be controlled by it is called a *participative budget.*

(c) *Budgetary slack.* When managers are involved in budgeting they will often try and arrange for their own budgets to be more easily achievable than they should be. This gap between the optimum target and a manager's manipulated target is referred to as *budgetary slack.*

8. Profit control is a supportive, not punitive, system

A profit control system should be used to *help* managers to achieve their profit plans, not to blame them for their profit failures. The reasons for using the system in this supportive way are as follows:

(a) Profit arises ultimately as a result of team-work. Although profit divergences can be allocated to individual managers for *analytical* purposes, the elimination of such divergences is very often a matter of combined efforts. Thus, production lost due to slow working may be eliminated by the enterprise adopting a new industrial relations policy.

(b) Profit divergences do not always arise in the centre that causes them. For instance, scrap arising in department Z could well be due to poor workmanship on the product in department A. To blame the manager of Z would not only be unjust — it wouldn't even lead to a reduction in the scrap.

(c) The raw data from which performance figures are computed are very 'adjustable'. Managers afraid of being blamed can easily manipulate such data so as to throw at least part of the blame off themselves, at the expense, of course, of a proper understanding of the profit failure. Moreover, if the problems of the enterprise are great enough a punitive system will be so disliked by all the middle managers that an unconscious (at best) conspiracy to destroy the system can form, in which case the system will be destroyed just at the time when it could well be proving its greatest worth.

9. When does a variance arise?

Classically this problem occurs in the context of the materials price variance. One view is that it arises on the issue of the materials and the other that it arises on the receipt of the invoice. The test is, of course, which method gives the better control. Now, clearly, the *sooner* management are made aware of a divergence then:

(a) the sooner corrective action can be taken;

(b) the easier corrective action usually proves to be, since whatever underlay the divergence will probably have not become established, e.g. an informal but less efficient operating method may become formalized if corrective action is delayed too long;

(c) the clearer will be the memories and understanding of the situation in the minds of the people involved;

(d) the greater will be the sense of immediacy, e.g. it will be less likely that the people concerned will regard the matter as being out of date.

From all this it follows that a variance arises the *moment it is detectable*. Indeed, part of the skill of the accountant lies in being able to devise a procedure that advances the moment of detection. This means that the relevant details should ideally come to him either the moment a decision is made or the moment an event which will give rise to the variance occurs.

Utilizing this principle it can be seen that both views in the classical debate are wrong, since frequently a material price variance actually arises the moment a purchase order is raised. Similarly, on conclusion of a union wages agreement the wage rate variances relating to all the rates affected and covering the whole of the remainder of the year arise immediately.

Needless to say, this approach to the detection of variances is contrary to the traditional accounting concept of matching income and expenditure. However, if there is to be effective control this different accounting approach must be accepted.

10. Profit centre

A *profit centre* is a *budget centre to which income as well as costs can be assigned.* For example, a product sales section could be designated a profit centre since all the sales that it made relating to the product could be assigned to it along with its costs. The advantage of a profit centre is that the control budget can specify a budgeted net contribution in respect of the centre and the manager can be assessed primarily in terms of his net contribution variance. This, then, enables authority to be delegated to him so that as long as he achieves his budgeted net contribution he is allowed to change such aspects of his plan, e.g. sales price, advertising costs, as he may feel is necessary.

11. Non-standard variances

Finally, given the method we have adopted for measuring variances it should be appreciated that any kind of variance in any kind of circumstances should be computable. This is important because in practice there is really no exhaustive list of cost standards and so there is no exhaustive list of cost variances. But, bearing in mind the principle that all variances are based on a comparison of actual with allowance, and with the examples given in Chapter 15, the student should have no difficulty computing any variance, however unusual. For example, if a sheep-breeder planned a fertility standard of 1¼ lambs per ewe, such lambs having a standard value of £40, then if 400 ewes produced 440 lambs during a given period the fertility variance would be computed as follows:

Fertility allowance: 400 x 1¼	500	lambs
Actual fertility	440	lambs
Difference	60 A	lambs
Standard value	£40	
Fertility variance	£2,400A	

Principle of non-apportionment

If there is perhaps one absolute principle in profit control it is the principle of non-apportionment which states in effect that in profit control *a figure must never be apportioned*. This prohibition extends not only to budget centres but also to time periods and cost units.

As this principle is so implacably opposed to the normal accounting principles its validity in each context is argued in **12–14** below. Note that although the principle is not restricted to the fixed costs, in the very nature of things it is these costs which are almost exclusively involved.

12. Non-apportionment: to budget centres

Either the manager of a budget centre can control a given item of expenditure or he cannot. If he cannot, it should not be charged to him. If he can, it should all be charged to him. For instance, although a night watchman may patrol and protect all the departments in a company his manager has the sole responsibility for that man and his entire wages should, therefore, be charged to that manager. Charging a part to some other managers not only achieves nothing (since those other managers can do nothing about it) but it also dilutes the full impact of the variance on the one manager who can, with the result that control suffers.

There are, of course, occasions when two managers share a responsibility. For example, two budget centres may share the same workshop and so jointly control the heating system. In such a case any heating variance should be charged to the two managers *jointly*. Nothing at all is gained by apportioning either the cost or the variance. Indeed, it can be said that a cost apportioned is a control lost.

13. Non-apportionment: to time periods

Since a variance must be taken at the moment it arises, then any cost associated with a variance must be charged to the period in which the variance arises. So if, say, the annual rent were payable in March, March must carry the full year's rent and any variance, and no attempt must be made to apportion the cost over the other eleven months.

It is sometimes argued that if the annual costs are not apportioned over time then a profit and loss account cannot be prepared month by month and so management will not know if they are operating profitably or not. While the initial contention is correct, the conclusion is wrong. Management's budgeted profit for the year will indicate their target and the cumulative total profit variance will show them each month the extent to which they have fallen away from that target. Indeed, a strong case can be put forward to show that profit progress is more accurately measured under a profit control system than a conventional accounting system.

Not only is the apportionment of such costs wrong in a control context but also an attempt to make such an apportionment leads to the accountant facing impossible conundrums. Assume that one of his costs is an insurance premium budgeted at £24,000 for the year and payable mid-year. Apportionment then gives £2,000 per month.

The first conundrum the accountant faces is what to record as 'actual' on the first operating statements of the manager responsible for the premium. To show £2,000 on the basis that no other figure is available is to record a pious hope as a hard fact — and if the hope is unrealized the accountant's credibility will suffer.

Imagine now that when the bill comes in it is for £30,000. What does the accountant do now? Re-write the early statements to show a £2,500 actual and a £500 adverse variance (which will discredit the operating statements)? Write off the £6,000 excess relating to the first half of the year and charge a £500 adverse variance for each of the remaining months (in which case the statements will collectively fail to show the full actual premium and variance)? Charge a £1,000 variance to each of the remaining months (which will imply that a manager previously performing well has suddenly become incompetent)?

Yet even if the £30,000 bill were to come in during the first month of the year, the accountant would still have problems. To show a £500 adverse variance month after month would imply a *continuing* failure instead of a once-and-for-all failure on the part of the manager concerned (who would become contemptuous in turn of operating statements, profit control systems and accountants generally). To show the whole £6,000 variance in the first month and then record a £2,000 actual for all subsequent months would, of course, reduce the word 'actual' to a book-keeping fiction.

All these problems, naturally, are avoided if the cost is not apportioned. The plan will then show a £24,000 premium is expected mid-year. If, when the bill comes, it is £30,000, a £6,000 variance is recorded in that same month so that management can see immediately that this item has reduced the hoped-for profit by £6,000 for the year, and so that they can at once consider what action must be taken to avoid a recurrence in the next year. In the other months this item has no control relevance and must therefore be omitted from the records.

14. Non-apportionment: to cost units
Finally, it must be appreciated that the only apportioned costs in a cost unit standard cost are those charged via the fixed overhead rate, since all the other costs are direct, and that the only variances in respect of these costs are all sub-variances of the volume variance. The test of validity, then, is the value of the volume variance in control.

If it is recollected that this variance measures the profit effect of the actual volume diverging from that planned, it will be seen that such a variance has no real value at all. Consider the situation where Sales meet their volume plan but Production manufactures excess units which cannot be sold. The volume variance in such circumstances would be favourable, but have profits really been increased? Of course not; indeed the only practical result will be to create problems in the finished goods store — with the final result that the production manager receives a commendation for achieving a favourable volume variance at the same time as he receives a reprimand for pointlessly increasing the finished goods stock! And a control system that credits favourable profit variances to people who engage in unprofitable activities will quickly earn for itself the contempt it deserves.

Now take the converse situation — where Production fail to achieve the planned production so that Sales are prevented from achieving the planned sales. In this case there is not only an under-recovery of fixed overheads but also a loss of unit profits, i.e. in total, a loss of contribution. So the effect of the apportionment in practice is to apportion the real lost profit (contribution) between Production and Sales in the ratio of budgeted fixed overheads to budgeted profit! Clearly, such an analysis would be nonsensical, and an accountant who insists on such an exercise must not expect his management colleagues to be particularly impressed with either his technique or himself.

It could be that at this point some thoughtful student,

reflecting on the capacity variance (*see* 15:**22**), feels that by measuring the effect of a strike on the under-recovery of fixed overheads something of value is obtained. There is an element of truth in this but the student should appreciate that not only are the fixed overheads under-recovered in such circumstances but also the profit on the unsold units is lost. The total loss, then, turns out to be not just the fixed overheads but instead the *contribution* on the unproduced, unsold units and, of course, such a lost contribution is easily computed under a standard marginal costing system.

Control reporting

Once the accountant has analysed all the control data he can then take the final step in his control function — reporting that data. This in turn will enable the managers to move to their final step — taking action to correct divergences from plans.

Reporting is not just presenting managers with figures. Care needs to be taken in selecting what has control relevance for any individual manager and in the layout of the material selected for reporting.

15. Basic details to be reported

Accounting control information, as we have seen, involves a comparison of actual profit events with the profit plans. In practice, for effective control, the resulting divergences need to be analysed in terms of:

(a) *who* was responsible for the divergence;

(b) *where* the divergence occurred;

(c) *what* factor diverged from plan, e.g. material usage, selling price etc.;

(d) *how much* the profit was affected by the divergence. This latter information enables the manager to judge the importance of the necessary corrective action.

Note the use of the word 'divergence'. Frequently the figures reported will be variances but additionally the difference between actual and planned resource *quantities* will be needed. It is for this reason that the wider term 'divergence' is used rather than just 'variance'.

16. The principles of divergence reporting

Control not only involves reporting divergences but also taking appropriate action. Such action can only be taken on the basis of appropriately presented divergence reporting. To avoid either wasting one's own time or misleading managers it should always be remembered that a divergence must:

(a) only be computed when such a figure can be usefully used;

(b) be computed and presented in the form most likely to enable the receiving manager to use it to make the best decision needed to regain control, i.e. be tailor-made for the situation and the manager;

(c) in the case of a variance, be part of an overall framework of variance analysis and reporting, i.e. the variance must have an unambiguous, exclusive and logical 'slot' in the full variance analysis, so that both:

   (*i*) the 'width' and 'boundaries' of the variance are defined;

   (*ii*) the relationship of the variance to other variances is clear.

For example, a materials usage variance measures the value at standard price of the divergence of actual usages from planned usages of all standard materials. It in no way reflects the usage of non-standard material nor the effect on profit of the *actual price* of the usage divergence differing from plan, though in combination with the materials price variance it will indicate the total standard materials variance.

To the extent that a tailor-made variance for one manager in a given situation may fall outside the framework of variances, (b) and (c) above are incompatible and it is the mark of good accountants that they can achieve a viable measure of compromise.

17. Controllable and non-controllable factors

Since a manager can only take action in respect of those factors for which he is responsible and over which he has authority — which can be termed *controllable factors* — there is little control value in giving him data relating to other factors. A good profit control system, then, ensures that essentially only data relating to the controllable factors of a given manager is reported to that manager. Note that this does not mean that other kinds of data reported for other reasons should be rigidly excluded. For instance, sales trends could be reported to the works manager so that he can bear such trends in mind when making relatively long-term planning decisions.

From this it follows that any variance relating to an uncontrollable factor can be classified as an *uncontrollable variance*. Similarly a variance relating to a controllable factor can be classified as *a controllable variance* and defined as a *variance that relates to a factor that falls under the authority of the person for whom the variance is computed*. It also follows that no manager should be charged with an uncontrollable variance.

The accountant must be very careful to distinguish between controllable and uncontrollable variances. Although in this context the analysis of variances generally needs to do no more than follow the lines of formal authority, problems sometimes arise. Who, for example, would be responsible for the loss incurred as a result of a non-standard operation by a production employee (who had been improperly trained in a training department) on inappropriate material erroneously issued by the stores?

Note, incidentally, that a system of accounting that is designed to present managers with information relating to their individual fields of responsibility is termed *responsibility accounting*.

18. Variance synthesis
So far only variance analysis has been discussed. But there is a serious disadvantage in making a full analysis and that is that the total profit variance may be subdivided to the point where the end result is no more than a large number of relatively insignificant variances. Yet frequently there are times when a number of such variances have a common cause, and it is more meaningful to report these variances as a combined total rather than separately. For example, a strike by a group of employees can give rise to both a sales volume margin variance and a number of associated efficiency variances (labour and variable overhead particularly). Collecting all these variances together and reporting them as a single 'strike variance' may well prove the most useful way of reporting them to management. Similarly, the variances arising as a result of government action (e.g. complying with a three-day week decree) can be collected together in the same way.

Clearly, then, good control systems will enable variances to be 'synthesized'. In the main this only involves detecting and adding the appropriate variances, though care must be taken that variance synthesis does not lead to variance double-counting.

19. Departmental operating statement

A *departmental operating statement* is a *formal, regular report made at the end of each control period to the budget centre manager outlining that manager's variances and any other control data relating to the control period.* It is the one regular document in control reporting and the one upon which all other control reports centre.

The following points should be noted in connection with a departmental operating statement.

(a) *Layout.* The layout essentially ensures that the following data is appropriately shown.

    (*i*) Name of *budget centre.*

    (*ii*) Name of *person responsible.* Action can only be taken by a person, not by a department or a product, and so every statement must name the controlling person. Indeed, every figure on the statement will relate to his performance specifically.

    (*iii*) The *period reported on* and the *date reported.* These are both vital pieces of information and must be clearly stated.

    (*iv*) *Variances,* shown individually and in total.

    (*v*) *Reasons* for variances.

(b) *Functions.* The statement functions as:

    (*i*) *Profit control feedback to the manager concerned.* This is its basic and most important function. It acts as the crucial link between the accountant and the manager concerned in a profit control exercise.

    (*ii*) *A chronological record of performance.* Performance assessment over a single control period can often be distorted by a non-recurring difficulty or an event that seriously affects operations in the short term but which is of minor consequence in the long term. A chronological record extending over a number of control periods, therefore, enables a more balanced and accurate assessment of the performance of the manager concerned to be made. Moreover, a sounder interpretation of the more subtle causes of variances can sometimes be guided by studying trends over a number of control periods and a file of past departmental operating statements relating to a budget centre can form the basic records for such a trend study.

(*iii*)   *Advice to higher management.* Higher management exercises control through the performance of subordinates and so departmental operating statements form a good practical basis for evaluating the actual performance of subordinates in terms of the profit plan. In addition, an intelligent scrutiny of such a statement can often indicate to higher managers where their intervention can overcome a particularly serious or intractable difficulty that has fallen to one of their subordinates whose authority is more limited than their own, e.g. low labour efficiency may possibly be eliminated by the purchase of new plant, or abnormal material usage reduced by introducing an improved training scheme.

(c)   *Other control data*. There will, of course, be other data that the manager may consider of value. The following are frequently found in a well-designed departmental operating statement:

(*i*)   variance percentages;
(*ii*)   cumulative variances;
(*iii*)   control ratios (*see* **20**);
(*iv*)   non-monetary performance measures, e.g. percentage down-time, percentage defectives, ratio seconds to firsts, absenteeism, overtime hours.

(d)   *Timing of statements*. A departmental operating statement should be presented at the earliest possible moment after the end of the control period.

(e)   *Prior discussion with managers*. Since a profit control system should be supportive rather than punitive (*see* **8**) departmental operating statements must not be used by higher managers to browbeat their subordinates but as tools to help and guide budget centre managers in their attempts to control their profit performance. So it is vitally important that the statement should be discussed with the manager concerned *before completion* — the purpose of such discussion being:

(*i*) to give the manager early notice of any significant variances;

(*ii*) to give the manager the opportunity to correct erroneous factual data, challenge the logic of possible variance charges, and qualify otherwise misleading variances, e.g. part of an adverse materials usage variance may have been due to an unrecorded and unascertained quantity of unused material on the shop floor at the end of the control period;

(*iii*) to give the manager advance notice of the information that his superiors will ultimately have at hand;

(*iv*) to enable any '*Reason*' column on the statement to be completed (since in the first instance only the manager responsible can suggest just why a particular variance arose).

20. Control ratios

These are factor ratios that management often find useful for control purposes. The most important of these, and their methods of calculation, are as follows:

(a) Efficiency ratio $= \dfrac{\text{Allowed hours}}{\text{Actual hours worked}} \times 100$

(b) Capacity ratio $= \dfrac{\text{Actual hours worked}}{\text{Budgeted hours}} \times 100$

(c) Activity ratio $= \dfrac{\text{Allowed hours}}{\text{Budgeted hours}} \times 100$

Example

Using the figures in our earlier illustration we have:

Efficiency ratio (15:15) = 4000/4425 x 100 = 90½%
Capacity ratio (15:15 and 14:24(b)) = 4425/(60,000 ÷ 12) x 100 = 88½%
Activity ratio (15:15 and 14:24(b)) = 4000/(60,000 ÷ 12) x 100 = 80%

21. Cost of variance investigations

Not only must accountants always be aware of the need to investigate variances in order to determine their true cause but they must also bear in mind at all times the need to balance the benefits of the information obtained against the cost of obtaining it. Better to make a reduced profit and be ignorant of the cause of the reduction than to sustain a massive loss that nevertheless can be fully accounted for. And in control work the temptation to spend money on uneconomic analysis is greater than in any other field of accountancy work.

Progress test 16

Principles

1. What are the basic variance causes? **(1)**

2. What are the causes of operating variances? **(2)**

3. Are variances independent of each other? **(4)**

4. What is (*a*) a participative budget; **(7(b))** (*b*) budgetary slack; **(7(c))** (*c*) a profit centre? **(10)**

5. When does a variance arise? **(9)**

6. What is the principle of apportionment in a profit control system? **(12–14)**

7. What are the principles of control reporting? **(15–18)**

8. What are the features of a departmental operating statement? **(19)**

9. Give the formulae for three control ratios. **(20)**

17

Standard cost accounts

We have already indicated that the traditional standard costing and budgetary control technique is essentially an accounting technique. It is, therefore, understandable that the culmination of all the analyses looked at so far should be the incorporation of the resulting figures into the traditional cost book-keeping pattern.

1. Basic principles of standard cost-book-keeping

In traditional standard cost book-keeping the framework of the accounts is the normal cost book-keeping pattern as illustrated in Fig. 5.1. On to this pattern are then grafted variance accounts which record the variances disclosed by the variance analysis. The following are the basic principles underlying the operation of these accounts.

(a) Variances are transferred to individual variance accounts.

(b) As far as possible, transfers between the main accounts are at standard. (You should envisage these accounts as having such a distaste for actual figures that they shed the variances as quickly as possible so that actuals are thereby converted into standard values.)

(c) From (b) it follows that variances should be accounted for as near as is practical to the moment of occurrence.

(d) Variances are written off to profit and loss at the end of the period.

2. Flow chart for standard absorption cost book-keeping

See Fig.17.1. The following points should be noted.

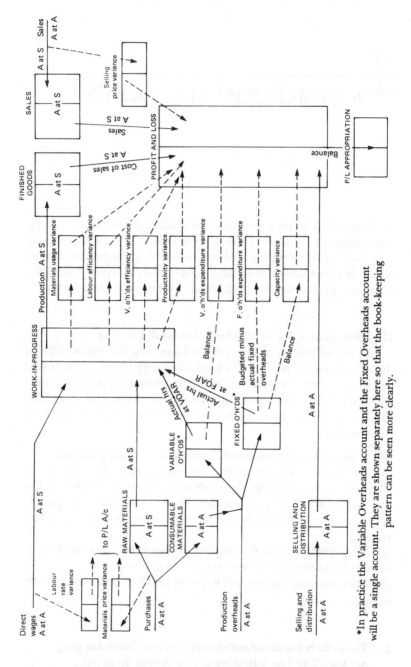

Figure 17.1 *Flow chart for standard absorption cost book-keeping*
The following abbreviations are used: A at A = actual quantity at actual price;
A at S = actual quantity at standard price; VOAR = variable overhead absorption
rate; FOAR = fixed overhead absorption rate. The flow of variances is indicated
by broken lines.

(a) Material standards are usually maintained for production materials only. Consequently, purchases must be segregated into standard materials and non-standard materials, the latter comprising mainly consumable and maintenance stores. Non-standard materials are debited to their stores accounts at actual prices and issued using a non-standard issue price method.

(b) The materials price variance on standard materials can be calculated *immediately on receipt of the invoice* by comparing the actual and allowed invoice purchase cost, i.e.:

Price variance =
Invoice amount − Invoice quantity at standard price.

This enables the price variance to be taken immediately to the Materials Price Variance account, and the materials charged to the Raw Materials account are at standard prices.

(c) On issue, materials are charged to the Work-in-Progress account at standard prices.

(d) The labour rate variance can also be calculated immediately. If desired, the calculation could be made on the payroll itself by inserting alongside the gross wages column two additional columns, thus:

Gross Wages	*Allowed wages:* *Actual hours at* *standard rate*	*Difference* *Labour rate variance*
Totals: Cr. Wages a/c	Dr. Work in Progress a/c	Dr. (or Cr.) Wage Rate Variance a/c

The labour rate variance can be found either in total only or, if desired, for each individual employee.

(e) The Production Overhead accounts are debited with the actual overheads and credited with the fixed and variable overheads absorbed. Expenditure and capacity variances are taken out at the end of the period.

(f) The Selling and Distribution or Marketing Overheads account is traditionally left unchanged in the cost accounts, i.e. the account is debited with the actual overheads as they are incurred and then the total overheads are transferred to the Profit and Loss account at the period end. This means there will be no expenditure or volume variance accounts in respect of these overheads.

(g) The following three points should be noted with regard to the Work-in-Progress account:

(*i*) The account is credited with the *actual units produced at the standard costs* as shown on the standard cost cards.

(*ii*) As soon as the total production is known (and remember that this figure will be modified by the increase or decrease in work-in-progress over the period — though examiners rarely include this factor in their questions), variances relating to efficiency and usage can be computed and transferred from the Work-in-Progress account to the appropriate Variance accounts.

(*iii*) The balance remaining and carried down on the Work-in-Progress account is the end-of-period work-in-progress valued at standard.

(h) All finished goods in the Finished Goods account are carried at standard cost. The standard cost value of the finished goods sold is transferred to the Profit and Loss account.

(i) Selling price variances can be computed at the time of invoicing in the same manner as materials price variances, and can be taken at once to a Selling Price Variance account. This will result in the Sales account showing the actual sales at standard prices.

(j) All variances are transferred to the Profit and Loss account.

(k) The final balance on the Profit and Loss account will be the actual profit for the period and will, of course, be transferred to the Profit and Loss Appropriation account.

(l) The chart, for reasons of clarity, does not show all variances. However, students should have little difficulty with other variances; e.g. materials mixture and yield variances merely require a sub-division of the Materials Usage Variance account.

3. Worked example of standard cost accounts

In Fig. 17.2 the cost accounts and accounting entries relating to the variances computed in Chapter 15 are given. It should be appreciated that these accounts are rather more simple than would occur in practice (e.g. there are no opening stocks), and that not all the ledger accounts have been shown (e.g. there are no fixed assets or capital accounts).

Main accounts

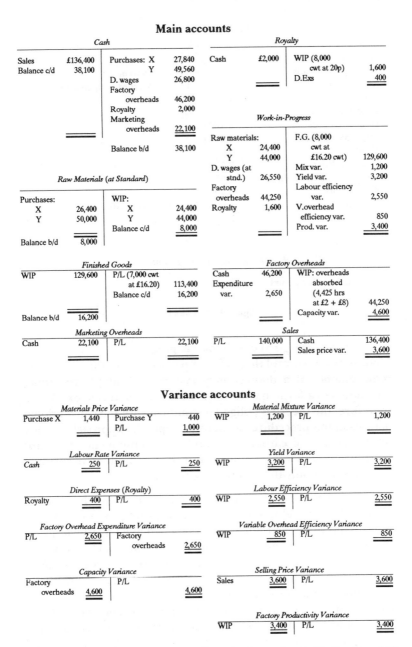

Cash					
Sales	£136,400	Purchases: X	27,840		
Balance c/d	38,100	Y	49,560		
		D. wages	26,800		
		Factory overheads	46,200		
		Royalty	2,000		
		Marketing overheads	22,100		
		Balance b/d	38,100		

Raw Materials (at Standard)

Purchases:		WIP:	
X	26,400	X	24,400
Y	50,000	Y	44,000
		Balance c/d	8,000
Balance b/d	8,000		

Finished Goods

WIP	129,600	P/L (7,000 cwt at £16.20)	113,400
		Balance c/d	16,200
Balance b/d	16,200		

Marketing Overheads

Cash	22,100	P/L	22,100

Royalty

Cash	£2,000	WIP (8,000 cwt at 20p)	1,600
		D.Exs	400

Work-in-Progress

Raw materials:		F.G. (8,000 cwt at £16.20 cwt)	129,600
X	24,400		
Y	44,000		
D. wages (at stnd.)	26,550	Mix var.	1,200
		Yield var.	3,200
Factory overheads	44,250	Labour efficiency var.	2,550
Royalty	1,600	V.overhead efficiency var.	850
		Prod. var.	3,400

Factory Overheads

Cash	46,200	WIP: overheads absorbed (4,425 hrs at £2 + £8)	44,250
Expenditure var.	2,650	Capacity var.	4,600

Sales

P/L	140,000	Cash	136,400
		Sales price var.	3,600

Variance accounts

Materials Price Variance

Purchase X	1,440	Purchase Y	440
		P/L	1,000

Labour Rate Variance

Cash	250	P/L	250

Direct Expenses (Royalty)

Royalty	400	P/L	400

Factory Overhead Expenditure Variance

P/L	2,650	Factory overheads	2,650

Capacity Variance

Factory overheads	4,600	P/L	4,600

Material Mixture Variance

WIP	1,200	P/L	1,200

Yield Variance

WIP	3,200	P/L	3,200

Labour Efficiency Variance

WIP	2,550	P/L	2,550

Variable Overhead Efficiency Variance

WIP	850	P/L	850

Selling Price Variance

Sales	3,600	P/L	3,600

Factory Productivity Variance

WIP	3,400	P/L	3,400

Figure 17.2 *Standard cost accounts for illustrative figures given in Chapters 14 and 15*

Profit and Loss

Finished goods (cost of sales)	113,400	Sales (at standard prices)	140,000
Marketing overheads	22,100	Favourable variances:	
Adverse variances:		Factory overhead expenditure	2,650
Materials price	1,000		
Labour rate	250		
Direct expenses	400		
Materials mixture	1,200		
Yield	3,200		
Labour efficiency	2,550		
Variance overhead efficiency	850		
Productivity	3,400		
Capacity	4,600	Balance – actual loss	
Selling price	3,600	to P/L Appropriation	13,900

Profit and Loss Appropriation

P/L – actual loss for period	13,900	

Figure 17.2 *(continued)*

4. Standard marginal cost book-keeping

Modern profit control theory is not particularly enthralled by the requirements of a double-entry system and adopts recording techniques of a form that lie outside the scope of this book. When, therefore, the theory is obliged to conform with the conventional book-keeping procedures it merely adopts the approach already illustrated in the earlier paragraphs. In consequence standard marginal cost book-keeping differs from standard absorption book-keeping only in the following respects:

(a) *Fixed Overhead account.* There is no transfer of overheads from the Fixed Overhead account to the Work-in-Progress account. The only credits to this account are the budgeted fixed overheads, with the double-entry being taken to the P/L account, and the resulting balance on the account, which, of course, is the fixed overhead expenditure variance, being transferred to the Fixed Overhead Expenditure Variance account.

(b) *Work-in-Progress and Finished Goods accounts.* The units in these accounts are all valued at standard marginal cost. Under marginal costing no productivity variance can arise and so there is no transfer of any amount out of the Work-in-Progress account in respect of this kind of variance.

(c) *Variance accounts.* The Productivity Variance account and the Capacity Variance account are both eliminated from the cost ledger.

(d) *P/L account.* This account is debited with a cost of sales at standard marginal cost and also with the *budgeted* fixed overhead.

5. Implications of transferring variances to profit and loss

When a price variance computed at the time of purchase is transferred to profit and loss it may well contain a favourable variance relating to unissued materials, i.e. an *unrealized profit* is taken. This may also happen with favourable efficiency and usage variances relating to work-in-progress or unsold finished goods stock.

To allow for this some accountants, and particularly auditors, hold back favourable variances in the Variance accounts until the production to which they relate is sold.

This 'holding back' is achieved by prorating the variances between the closing stock values and the Profit and Loss account in proportion to the extent to which the profit has actually been realized. This, of course, can lead to quite complicated calculations when favourable raw material price variances arise since it calls for adjustments to be made not only to the Raw Materials account but also to the Work-in-Progress and the Finished Goods accounts in respect of products incorporating the materials on which the variances arose.

This complication is a good example of the kind of problem encountered when a single set of accounts is used for more than one purpose. Profit control is essentially a technique for reporting performance to management, not for making an assessment of the enterprise profit on the basis of the normal accounting conventions. If the purpose is the measurement of management performance then all favourable variances must be taken to the Profit and Loss account when they occur since the ultimate profit will be improved by this improved performance, albeit some time may need to elapse before the profit is formally realized. If, however, the purpose is to show the profit available for distribution, the normal conservative accounting convention under which unrealized profits must *not* be taken applies.

6. **Profit and loss statement**

The normal book-keeping profit and loss statement is one that simply lists income and expenditure to arrive at a net profit. Managers, however, are more concerned to know *where their efforts are failing* rather than money totals. Therefore a statement that highlights the place and consequences of these failings is much more valuable. Budgets and standard costs enable this to be done, since the profit and loss statement can start with the sales at standard prices and, by incorporating all the variances, end with the actual profit. A Profit and Loss account in the form referred to in Fig 17.2 is, then, much more useful to managers than one in the normal income and expenditure format.

Some managements prefer the statement to start with budgeted sales. This is a doubtful practice, since management's interest should be primarily in profits (sales margins) rather than sales. Moreover, it involves introducing a non-ledger figure and this in turn means that an extra step has to be taken (adding or subtracting the difference between the budgeted and actual sales) to adjust the budgeted sales to the actual sales at standard prices. However, should a manager request his performance to be reported in this form the accountant must comply with his request. In such a case the exact structure of the Profit and Loss account report would need to be tailored to the precise requirements of the manager concerned.

Progress test 17

Practice

1. Last period the Alpha and Beta Company Ltd. budgeted to sell 1,000 Sets for £280,000, but owing to bad trading conditions they only managed to sell 840 for a mere £228,400. Their production, however, was 900 Sets. They had no opening stocks at all, and they had no closing work-in-progress. During

the trading period they suffered breakdowns amounting to 25 hours, during which time normal 'direct' wages were paid. To add to their troubles they found 120 MTs broken in the store, apparently due to bad stacking. Other figures relating to the period were as follows:

Purchases (5,000 MTs)	£59,200
Direct wages (4,450 hours)	£36,560 (this includes breakdown hours and pay)
Variable overheads	£18,320
Fixed overheads	£83,600
Selling and distribution costs	£28,000

4,550 MTs were issued to production.

The company operates standard costs (a Set standard cost is shown below) and you are to prepare all cost and variance accounts for the period, including the profit and loss.

Standard Cost Card: 1 Set

	£
Direct materials (5 MTs at £12 each)	60
Direct labour (5 hours at £8 per hour)	40
Variable overheads (varying with production)	20
Fixed overheads (at £16 per labour hour)	80
Factory standard cost	200
Selling and distribution overheads	32
Total standard cost	232
Standard profit (sales margin)	48
Standard selling price	£280

2. Continuation of Progress test 15, question **20**: Present the accounts for:

(a) Stores.
(b) Wages.
(c) Work in progress.

3. Wegrow Ltd specializes in growing young plants for sale to both commercial and retail outlets. The plants are grown from seed pellets which are sown in a compost mix in boxes of 40 plants in an automatic sowing department. The boxes are then transferred into a germinating room. Any seed which does not germinate is removed before the boxes of germinated seed are transferred into growing houses. Any diseased or damaged plants are removed before the young plants are then transferred to the despatch department for delivery to customers.

Wegrow Ltd keeps accounting records for each process. Each process account is charged with the actual costs directly incurred, but transfers between processes are made at standard cost per box of plants. Any difference between the total costs incurred by the process and the standard cost transferred from each process is simply shown as a variance which is transferred to profit and loss account.

Budgeted/standard data based on the maximum capacity of the premises are as follows:

Automatic sowing department
Monthly production: 125,000 boxes each containing 40 seed pellets (variety A 60,000 boxes; variety B 45,000 boxes; variety C 20,000 boxes).

	Costs	*Losses as a percentage of good output*
Seed pellets	1p each	2%
Compost mix	20p per kilo	2.5%
(3 kilos per output box)		
Boxes	10p each	1%
Operating costs	£30,000 per month	

(There are assumed to be no losses of complete boxes in the automatic sowing department.)

Germinating room
   Operating costs per month: £50,000
   Normal loss: 20% of input

Growing houses
   Operating costs per month: £27,000
   Normal loss: 10% of input

Actual usage, cost and output data for the month of May are as follows:

Automatic sowing department
Seed pellets: 5,200,000 pellets costing £52,000
Compost: 370,000 kilos at 21p per kilo
Boxes: 129,000 boxes costing £14,190
Operating costs: £29,800
125,000 boxes of sown pellets were transferred to the germinating room.

Germinating room
Operating costs: £50,000
Transfers to growing houses: 100,000 boxes of plants

Growing houses
Operating costs: £30,000
Transfers to despatch department: 86,000 boxes of plants

There is no opening or closing work-in-progress in any of the processes.

Required:
(a) Calculate the standard cost per box of plants at the end of each of the three processes.
(b) Prepare the process account for the automatic sowing process showing a detailed analysis of the variances and comment on the usefulness of this information to management.
(c) Additional analysis of the actual output quantities of each of the three varieties during May is as follows:

	Variety A (boxes)	Variety B (boxes)	Variety C (boxes)
Ex-growing houses	46,000	30,000	10,000
Selling price per box of plants	£3.00	£3.30	£3.50

The actual selling price per box is the same as that budgeted for all varieties.

(i) Prepare the growing houses process account using a profit centre approach.
(ii) Prepare a summary which shows the reconciliation of standard profit with the actual profit reported in the growing houses process account in (i) above. The reconciliation should show all variances including the sales quantity and mix variances using standard

weighted average margin as the variance valuation base.

Comment on the arguments which may be given in favour of the weighted average approach for sales variance calculations. (15:26)

(ACCA Dec 88)

Appendix 1
Examination technique

To pass any examination you must:

(a) have the knowledge;
(b) convince the examiner you have the knowledge;
(c) convince him within the time allowed.

In the book so far we have considered the first of these only. Success in the other two respects will be much more assured if you apply the examination hints given below.

1. Answer the question

Apart from ignorance, *failure to answer the question is undoubtedly the greatest bar to success*. No matter how often students are told, they always seem to be guilty of this fault. If you are asked for a control report, *don't* give a product cost statement; if asked to give the advantages of standard costs, *don't* detail the steps for computing them. You can write a hundred pages of brilliant exposition, but if it's not in answer to the set question you will be given no more marks than if it had been a paragraph of utter drivel. To ensure you answer the question:

(a) read the question carefully;
(b) decide what the examiner wants;
(c) underline the nub of the question;
(d) do just what the examiner asks;
(e) keep referring to the question in your mind as you write.

2. Put your ideas in logical order

It's quicker, more accurate and gives a greater impression of competence if you follow a predetermined logical path instead of jumping about from place to place as ideas come to you. This *initially* requires more time before starting to write, but it is time ultimately well spent.

3. Maximize the points you make

Examiners are more impressed by a solid mass of points than an unending development of one solitary idea, no matter how sophisticated and exhaustive. Don't allow yourself to become bogged down with your favourite hobby-horse.

4 Allocate your time

The marks for questions often bear a close relationship to the time needed for an appropriate answer. Consequently the time spent on a question should be in proportion to the marks. Divide the total exam marks into the total exam time (less planning time) to obtain a 'minutes per mark' figure, and allow that many minutes per mark of each individual question.

5. Attempt all required questions

Always remember that the first 50 per cent of the marks for any question is the easier to earn. Unless you are working in complete ignorance, you will always earn more marks per minute while answering a new question than while continuing to answer one that is more than half done. Thus, you can earn many more marks by half-completing two answers than by completing either one individually.

6. Don't show your ignorance

Concentrate on displaying your knowledge, not your ignorance. There is almost always one question you need to attempt and are not happy about. In answer to such a question put down all you *do* know, and then devote the unused time to improving some other answer. Certainly you won't get full marks by doing this, but neither will you if you fill your page with nonsense. By spending the saved time on another answer you will at least be gaining the odd mark or so.

7. If time runs out

(a) If it is a numerical answer, don't bother to work out the figures. Show the examiner by means of your layout that you know what steps need to be taken and which pieces of data are applicable. He is very much more concerned with this than with your ability to calculate.

(b) If it is an essay answer, put down your answer in the form of notes. It is surprising what a large percentage of the question marks can be obtained by a dozen terse, relevant notes.

(c) Make sure that every question and question part has some answer — no matter how short — that summarizes the key elements.

(d) Don't worry. Shortage of time is more often a sign of knowing too much than too little.

8. Avoid panic, but welcome 'nerves'

Being nervous (that is having the adrenalin flow) enables one to work at a much more concentrated pitch for a longer time without fatigue. Panic, on the other hand, destroys one's judgement. To avoid panic:

(a) know your subject (this is your best 'panic-killer');

(b) give yourself a generous time allowance to read the paper — quick starters are usually poor performers;

(c) take two or three deep breaths (there are good physiological reasons why this helps);

(d) concentrate simply on maximizing your marks — leave considerations of passing or failing until after;

(e) answer the easiest question first — it helps to build confidence;

(f) don't let first impressions of the paper upset you — given a few minutes, it is amazing what one's subconscious will throw up. This , too, is a good reason for answering the easiest question first; it gives your subconscious more time to 'crack' the difficult ones.

Report-writing in examinations

9. Purpose of report-writing: in practice

In practice, reports are written so that the person reported to receives in a permanent form information which has been selected and presented *with a specific object in mind.*

Good report-writing involves *clear, logical and attractive presentation of information that is pertinent to the basic objective.* Usually action is taken on the basis of a report, and in order that appropriate action is taken the report must embody these qualities. The extent to which a report aids the achievement of the objective that initially gave rise to its commission is the ultimate measure of the quality of a report.

10. Purpose of report-writing: in examinations

Examiners ask for reports in examinations to see if:

(a) candidates appreciate the qualities needed to write a good report and can embody these qualities in their own writing, i.e. it is a test of lucid, logical and attractive presentation and the ability to select the relevant from the irrelevant;

(b) candidates know their subject — clearly knowledge (or the converse) of subject matter shows itself in the candidate's report;

(c) candidates know how to lay out a report properly.

11. Report layout

(a) *Heading.* A simple heading for an examination report is as follows:

TO: ....(Person's title)   REPORT REFERENCE: ....
FROM:.................(Person's title)   DATE:....................................
COPIES TO:....... (Persons' titles)   ....
TITLE

The 'Copies to' space enables candidates to indicate that they appreciate which people in the organization are likely to be affected by the contents of the report.

Titles are sometimes difficult to compose on the spur of the moment, but the attempt shows the examiner that the candidate is aware of the need of a title for a report.

(b) *Reason for report.* If possible the first paragraph should outline the reason for the report. The time available for the question will indicate whether this outline should be given or whether a higher priority should be put on getting down to the subject matter.

(c) *Main body.* This will usually be the major part of the examination report and will state the findings and arguments in a lucid and logical manner.

(d) *Conclusions and/or recommendations.* Candidates should *never* forget this part of the report. It is absolutely essential that some conclusions and/or recommendations are given. This will indicate the extent to which the candidate is able to appreciate the significance of the information he has reported. Often candidates leave the examiners to dig out the conclusions. To be blunt, the examiners won't do this — they prefer to regard the omission as indicating the candidate's lack of ability to do this himself.

(e) *Signature.* A report must be signed. In addition it is usual to add the title of the person signing, e.g. Management accountant. Beware of using 'Yours faithfully' (or 'Dear Sir' at the beginning). This only applies to reports to *clients,* and even then can be omitted if it is assumed that a covering letter (not given in the answer, of course) is sent with the report.

(f) *Appendices.* These give all the details upon which the main body of the report was built (in practice they often form the bulk of the report). Time in the examination does not usually allow appendices to be given, though use of an appendix to give specimen figures or suggested form design should be borne in mind.

Finally, note that a good report layout requires *all paragraphs to be numbered.*

12. Report-writing technique

(a) *Length.* The shorter a report the better, provided all relevant information is given, Brevity not only saves time, it also improves clarity. If an idea can be given in a sentence it is better understood than if two pages are used to express it. This may be paradoxical but it's a psychological fact. Length only keeps a person thinking about it *longer* (which has been the sole purpose of the last three sentences).

(b) *Paragraphs.* Decide before you start writing what each paragraph will contain. This will aid logical writing.

(c) *Style.* Keep sentences short. Good reports state facts and opinions tersely.

(d) *Technical jargon.* The reader of the report must always be borne in mind, and jargon that would not be clearly understood by him should not be used. Candidates should check the question carefully to see what level of sophistication the reader may be assumed to have — some examiners make this a major factor in their questions.

(e) *Assumptions.* Some reports require assumptions to be made.

Others do not as there is enough 'meat' in the question without conjuring up more (though whether the candidate will appreciate this is another matter). As a general rule do *not* make assumptions in your answer unless it is absolutely necessary.

(f) *Specimen figures.* If the subject matter allows it, try and give specimen figures. A few simple but well-chosen figures will often make a point much more effectively than a paragraph of writing.

(g) *Presentation of data.* When presenting data consider the possible use of tables and graphs. Figures should be presented wherever possible in a comparative form, i.e. in adjacent columns, headed, for example *This year/Last year, Current/Proposed*.

13. Reporting is a form of communication

A report is not an end-product — it is a device for communicating information to somebody who wants to *use* such information. If this person cannot understand it, is misled by it, or is repelled by its appearance so that he cannot get to grips with it, then no matter how accurate and painstaking the collection and analysis of detail, no matter how comprehensive the arguments, no matter how brilliant the conclusions and recommendations, the writer has failed and *all* his work (not just the writing of the report) is to no avail. After all, the writer alone has the choice of matter to be included, its order, and the words used to express it — the onus is on him for the comprehension of the report. Always remember that:

If the reader hasn't understood, the writer hasn't reported.

14. Practise

You should now look at other people's reports, e.g. model answers, and criticize them. Make a start by criticizing this part of the appendix as a *report*. Criticizing others will teach you to look at your own reports with a more critical eye.

Appendix 2

Examination questions

Below are reproduced questions from past examination papers. The following abbreviations are used:

AAT — Association of Accounting Technicians.
ACCA — Chartered Association of Certified Accountants.
CIMA —Chartered Institute of Management Accountants.
ICA —Institute of Chartered Accountants in England and Wales.

1. The following information is provided concerning a particular raw material:

Average usage	1,000 kilos per day
Minimum usage	800 kilos per day
Maximum usage	1,350 kilos per day
Order quantity	9,000 kilos

The stock level is reviewed at the end of each day and an order is placed the following day if the normal re-order level has been reached. Delivery is reliably expected at the beginning of the fourth day following order.

Required:
(a) From the above information calculate three normal control levels used for stock control purposes.
(b) Draw a graph demonstrating the changing level of stock of the material based on the following actual usage over a 14-day period:

First five days	1,020 kilos per day
Next four days	1,200 kilos per day
Final five days	900 kilos per day

The stock at the beginning of day 1 was 6,000 kilos.

Show clearly on the graph the three control levels calculated in (a).

(c) Contrast the actual minimum stock level over the period with the normal control level established, and comment on the difference and any action required.

(ACCA Dec 91)

2. The following details relate to the payroll of XYZ Limited for the week ended 27 October 1990:

	£
Net wages paid	34,000
PAYE deducted	16,500
National Insurance:	
Employees	2,900
Employers	3,300

The company pays its employees £5.00 per hour plus an overtime premium of £2.50 per hour in excess of the normal working week.

A summary of the employees' time sheets for the same week shows:

Hours worked on customers' jobs	8,260
Hours worked on company capital expenditure	1,300
Non-productive hours	940
	10,500

The figure for hours worked on customers' jobs includes 80 hours' overtime which was worked at the specific request of a customer who has agreed to pay for the overtime premium.

You are required:
(a) to show the journal entry for the wages of the company for week ended 27 October 1990 including an appropriate narrative;
(b) to explain the treatment of costs incurred on the company's capital expenditure and the implications for profit measurement.

(CIMA Nov 90)

3. X Ltd has an average of 42 workers employed in one of its factories in a period during which seven workers left and were replaced.

The company pays a basic rate of £4.60 per hour to all its direct personnel. This is used as the standard rate. In addition, a factory wide bonus scheme is in operation. A bonus of half of the efficiency ratio in excess of 100% is added as a percentage to the basic hourly rate e.g. if the efficiency ratio is 110% then the hourly rate is £4.83 (i.e. £4.60 + (£4.60 x 5%)).

During the period 114,268 units of the company's single product were manufactured in 4,900 hours. The standard hour is 22 units.

Required:
(a) Calculate the labour turnover percentage for the period.
(b) Identify the reasons for, and costs of, labour turnover, and discuss how it may be reduced.
(c) Calculate the hourly wage rate paid for the period, and the total labour variance.

(ACCA Dec 90)

4. XYZ Limited is a small engineering company which specializes in the manufacture of machinery parts for the construction industry. The parts made require a mixture of specialized components which are bought and delivered to XYZ Limited as required, and the use of sheet steel which is purchased in bulk and held in stock by XYZ Limited to be used as required.

The company has three manufacturing departments — Machining, Assembly and Finishing — together with its own Stores and Purchasing department. There is also an administration department which is regarded as a central overhead cost.

During March 1991 the following purchases of sheet steel were made:

2 March	500 sheets at £20.00 each
9 March	300 sheets at £21.00 each
16 March	400 sheets at £20.00 each
23 March	600 sheets at £22.00 each
30 March	300 sheets at £21.00 each

All of the purchases were made from the same supplier, the

variation in prices paid being due to price fluctuations in the sheet steel commodity market.

Issues of the steel sheets were made to production as follows:

4 March	400 sheets
11 March	300 sheets
18 March	500 sheets
25 March	600 sheets

The company had a nil stock of steel sheets on 1 March 1991. The company did not have any unused steel sheets in its workshop on 31 March.

During the month the following costs were incurred:

		£
Direct wages —	Machining	10,200
.	Assembly	3,600
	Finishing	2,200
	Stores	2,400
Indirect wages —	Machining	4,400
	Assembly	1,300
	Finishing	900
Salaries —	Administration	4,300

Direct materials (other than the purchases of the sheet steel) amounted to £43,250. These items were all used in the manufacture of 16,000 units of part A.

Factory overhead expenses:

	£
Rent and business rates	12,600
Power	6,500
Heating and lighting	1,350
Telephone, postages, etc.	850

These factory overheads are apportioned to each department using a suitable basis of apportionment.

The factory is divided into individual units which are occupied by each of the departments. The floor space occupied by each department is:

square feet

Machining	12,000
Assembly	6,500
Finishing	4,150
Stores	8,000
Administration	850

Machines are used in all of the production departments and the stores and have the following horse powers:

Machining	14,000
Assembly	2,000
Finishing	3,000
Stores	500

Telephone and postage costs are incurred according to the following percentages:

Machining	10%
Assembly	15%
Finishing	5%
Stores	25%
Administration	45%

The Stores department spends 70% of its time providing a service to the Machining department, and the remainder of its time is divided equally between the Assembly and Finishing departments.

XYZ Limited did not manufacture any products other than part A during the month of March 1991. It had an opening stock of 200 components on 1 March 1991 which were valued at £1,950.

During the month 15,500 components were sold for £224,867.

The company uses the weighted average method of valuing its stock of steel sheets and average production cost of the month for valuing its closing stock of finished components.

There was no opening or closing work-in-progress.

You are required:
(a) to draft
    (i) the stores ledger card for March 1991 in respect of the sheet steel,

(*ii*) the overhead analysis sheet of the company for March 1991,

(*iii*) the profit and loss account for March 1991 and a balance sheet extract showing the valuation of closing stock;

(b) to comment on the company's buying policy for steel sheets, assuming that every time an order is placed there is an administrative cost of £150 and the cost of holding stock is equal to 10% of its purchase cost. The annual demand is estimated to be 20,000 sheets;

(c) to comment on the company's stock valuation policy for finished units of part A.

(CIMA May 91)

5. To attract more tourists to a beautiful part of a country, a contract has been awarded to Y p.l.c. to build an expressway road at an estimated price of £102 million which includes a budgeted profit of £27 million. The contract includes the building of slip roads and also a tunnel under a river in order to preserve the appearance of the nearby ancient town which is dominated by a castle. The time scale for the contract from start to finish is five years unless unforeseen difficulties arise.

Work commenced on 1 April 1986 and for the three-year period to 31 March 1989, the following data are available.

	£000
Invoice value of work certified to date	50,000
Progress payments received from customer	40,000
Costs:	
Planning, estimating and surveyors' fees	2,000
Materials delivered to sites	15,000
Materials returned from sites	500
Direct wages paid	8,000
Wage-related costs	1,000
Plant — hired	3,500
Site office costs: rent and rates	156
salaries and related costs	1,200
Apportioned head office costs	750
Direct expenses incurred (insurance, bank interest etc)	1,804

The invoiced value of work certified to date includes all work to 31 March 1989 so cost of work not certified is nil.

Plant owned by the contractors bought specifically for this

contract originally cost £8 million and has been in use almost continuously since the beginning of the contract and is expected to have a residual value of £500,000 at the end of the five-year contract. The straight-line method of depreciation is in use.

Cost of materials on sites at 31 March 1989 is estimated at £400,000.

Direct wages owed at 31 March 1989 were £55,000.

The contract is regarded by management to be approximately half complete and is expected to be completed on schedule. In the previous two financial years no profits were included in the company's accounts in respect of this particular contract but the directors would now like to show a profit which is appropriate to their estimate of the degree of completion of the contract as at 31 March 1989.

You are required to:

(a) (i) show the contract account for the three-year period to 31 March 1989,

  (ii) evaluate the work-in-progress including some profit, showing the basis and the reason(s) for your profit figure at 31 March 1989,

  (iii) calculate *one* alternative profit figure to that given in your answer to (a)(ii) above which ought to be acceptable to the directors;

(b) explain why it is regarded as desirable for contracting companies to include some profit on uncompleted contracts — your explanation should contain some reference to prudence.

(*CIMA May 89*)

6. Hensau Ltd has a single production process for which the following costs have been estimated for the period ending 31 December 1991:

	£
Material receipt and inspection cost	15,600
Power cost	19,500
Material handling cost	13,650

Three products — X, Y and Z are produced by workers who perform a number of operations on material blanks using hand-held electrically powered drills. The workers have a wage rate of £4 per hour.

The following budgeted information has been obtained for the period ending 31 December 1991:

	Product X	Product Y	Product Z
Production quantity (units)	2,000	1,500	800
Batches of material	10	5	16
Data per product unit:			
Direct material (sq. metres)	4	6	3
Direct material (£)	5	3	6
Direct labour (minutes)	24	40	60
Number of power drill operations	6	3	2

Overhead costs for material receipt and inspection, process power and material handling are presently each absorbed by product units using rates per direct labour hour.

An activity based costing investigation has revealed that the cost-drivers for the overhead costs are as follows:

Material receipt and inspection: number of batches of material.
Process power: number of power drill operations.
Material handling: quantity of material (sq. metres) handled.

Required:
(a) Prepare a summary which shows the budgeted product cost per unit for each of products X, Y and Z for the period ending 31 December 1991 detailing the unit costs for each cost element:
  (i) using the existing method for the absorption of overhead costs and
  (ii) using an approach which recognizes the cost-drivers revealed in the activity based costing investigation.
(b) Explain the relevance of cost-drivers in activity based costing. Make use of figures from the summary statement prepared in (a) to illustrate your answer.

(*ACCA June 91*)

7. Kaminsky Ltd. manufactures belts and braces. The firm is organized into five departments. These are belt-making, braces-making, and three services departments (maintenance, warehousing, and administration).

Direct costs are accumulated for each department. Factory-wide indirect costs (which are fixed for all production levels within the present capacity limits) are apportioned to departments on the basis of the percentage of floor-space occupied. Service department costs are apportioned on the basis of estimated usage, measured as the percentage of the labour-hours operated in the service department utilized by the user department.

Each service department also services at least one other service department.

Budgeted data for 1981 are as follows:

		Belts	Braces	Admin-istration	Main-tenance	Ware-housing	Company Total
				Departments			
1.	Output and sales (units						
	Output capacity	150,000	60,000				
	Output budgeted	100,000	50,000				
	Sales budgeted	100,000	50,000				
2.	Direct variable costs (£000)						
	Materials	120	130	—	20	30	300
	Labour	80	70	50	80	20	300
	Total	200	200	50	100	50	600
3.	Factory-wide fixed indirect costs (£000)						1,000
4.	Floor-space (%)	40	40	5	10	5	100
5.	Usage of service department labour-hours (%)						
	Administration	40	40	—	10	10	100
	Warehousing	50	25	—	25	—	100
	Maintenance	30	30	—	—	40	100

(a) You are required to calculate the total cost per unit of belts and braces respectively, in accordance with the system operated by Kaminsky Ltd.

(b) In addition to the above data, it has been decided that the selling prices of the products are to be determined on a cost-plus basis, as the unit total cost plus 20%.

Two special orders have been received, outside the normal run of business, and not provided for in the budget.

They are as follows:

(i) an order for 1,000 belts from Camfam, an

international relief organization, offering to pay
£5,000 for them;

(*ii*) a contract to supply 2,000 belts a week for 50 weeks to
Mixon Spenders, a chain-store, at a price per belt of
'unit total cost plus 10%'.

You are required to set out the considerations which the
management of Kaminsky Ltd. should take into account in
deciding whether to accept each of these orders, and to advise
them as far as you are able on the basis of the information given.

(c) 'Normalized overhead rates largely eliminate from
inventories, from cost of goods sold, and from gross
margin any unfavourable impact of having production
out of balance with the long-run demand for a
company's products.'·

You are required to explain and comment upon the above
statement.

(*CA*)

8. Using the information given below for the month of October,
in respect of A Limited, you are required to:

(a) write up the integrated accounts;
(b) prepare a trading and profit and loss account for
October;
(c) compile a trial balance as at 31st October;
(d) comment on the difference in the level of stocks and
state which administration cost will be increased
following the changed levels of stocks.

1. List of balances at 1st October, 1983:

	£000
Fixed assets — production	1,000
Provision for depreciation of fixed assets	400
Material stores control	100
Work-in-progress stock	50
Finished goods stock	20
Debtors	600
Creditors	290

Creditor for PAYE and national insurance	85
Wages control — credit balance (accrued direct wages)	20
Cash	5
Bank — overdrawn	300
Share capital	600
Profit and loss appropriation: credit balance	80

2. Transactions for the month of October:

	£000
Received from debtors	380
Paid to creditors	170
Expenses paid by cheque: production	60
administration	40
selling	30
Bank interest on overdraft	10
Paid to creditor for PAYE and national insurance	60
Depreciation of fixed assets (for production)	25
Materials received and invoiced	110
Materials price variance, favourable, extracted as	
materials are received	10
Materials issued to production, at standard prices	80
Materials issued to production maintenance	20
Transfers from work-in-progress to finished goods	230
Sales on credit	310
Sales for cash	10
Production cost of goods sold	200

	Gross	PAYE/ Nat. Ins.	
	£000	£000	£000
Direct wages paid	86	20	66
Direct wages accrued	22	—	22
Indirect wages paid			
(production)	24	4	20
Administrative staff salaries			
paid	12	4	8
Selling staff salaries paid	20	4	16
Employer's contribution, national insurance:			
production			9
administration			3
selling			2
Cash paid into bank			13

Production overhead is absorbed on the basis of 150% on direct wages; any under or over absorption is transferred to profit and loss account.

Administration and selling costs are not absorbed into product costs.

(CIMA)

9. A company manufactures a single product from one basic raw material. The standard purchase price of the raw material is £3.50 per kilo, and standard usage is five kilos per unit of finished product. Material price variance is identified on purchase of raw material. Actual direct labour costs and production overhead absorbed are charged to units of finished product based upon weighted average costs. The production overhead absorption rate is 200% of direct labour cost.

Balances in the company's integrated accounts at the beginning of a period included:

Raw materials:
  Direct material, 5,240 kilos
  Indirect materials, £1,484

Production overhead:
  Accrued at the end of the previous period, £3,840

Work in progress:
  Direct material, £4,550
  Direct labour and production overhead, £1,950

  260 units, complete as to direct material, 50% complete as to direct labour and production overhead.

Finished goods:
  1,470 units, £47,775.

Costs incurred during the period were:

Raw materials purchased:
  Direct material, 7600 kilos, £26,904
  Indirect materials, £2,107.

Raw materials issued:
  Direct material, 7,460 kilos
  Indirect materials, £1,963

Production wages paid:

	Direct workers £	*Indirect workers* £
Gross	8,670	2,235
Employees' deductions	2,688	693
Net	5,982	1,542

The cost of the productive time of direct workers was £7,950. The balance of the wages paid to direct workers is charged to production overhead.

Other production overhead incurred: £9,252

Period sales: 1,520 units

Production output of the single product during the period was:

Completed and transferred to finished goods stock, 1,450 units.

Closing work in progress 310 units, complete as to direct material, 60% complete as to direct labour and production overhead.

A physical stock check of the basic raw material at the end of the period revealed that 5,310 kilos remained in stock. Production overhead to be accrued totalled £4,170.

Required:

Prepare accounting entries for the period in the following accounts:

(*i*) raw material stock,
(*ii*) production wages,
(*iii*) production overhead,
(*iv*) work in progress,
(*v*) finished goods stock.

(*ACCA Dec 90*)

10. The manufacture of one of the products of A Ltd requires three separate processes. In the last of the three processes, costs, production and stock for the month just ended were:

1. Transfers from Process 2: 180,000 units at a cost of £394,200.

2. Process 3 costs: materials £110,520, conversion costs £76,506.

3. Work in process at the beginning of the month: 20,000 units at a cost of £55,160 (based on FIFO pricing method). Units were 70% complete for materials, and 40 % complete for conversion costs.

4. Work in process at the end of the month: 18,000 units which were 90% complete for materials, and 70% complete for conversion costs.

5. Product is inspected when it is complete. Normally no losses are expected but during the month 60 units were rejected and sold for £1.50 per unit.

Required:

(a) Prepare the Process 3 account for the month just ended.

(b) Explain how, and why, your calculations would be affected if the 60 units lost were treated as normal losses.

(c) Explain how your calculations would be affected by the use of weighted average pricing instead of FIFO.

(ACCA June 91)

11. (a) Explain the features that distinguish each of the following forms of accounting.

   (*i*) Integrated accounts
   (*ii*) Inter-locking accounts.

(b) The following information relates to the PM Company that uses a continuous process to produce its product.

   Process 1

   April — input of material 10,000 kilos at £2.80 per kilo
        conversion costs £31,200
        normal loss 10% of input
        closing work in progress 3,000 kilos 60% complete for
        conversion costs.
        Scrap value £1 per kilo
        Output 6,000 kilos

The output from Process 1 is transferred to Process 2 where there was no opening work in progress at the beginning of April. The following information relates to Process 2.

Conversion costs £27,000
Normal loss 5% of input
Closing work in progress 1,000 kilos 70% complete for conversion costs.
Scrap value £2.25 per kilo
Output 4,900 kilos

Required:
Prepare accounts for Process 1 and Process 2 and for any losses or gains.

(c) Describe the features of 'contract costing' and bring out the problems of:
   (i) The calculation of profit on each contract
   (ii) The valuation of work in progress.

(*AAT June 90*)

12. (a) 'Whilst the ascertainment of product costs could be said to be one of the objectives of cost accounting, where joint products are produced and joint costs incurred, the total cost computed for the product may depend upon the method selected for the apportionment of joint costs, thus making it difficult for management to make decisions about the future of products.'

You are required to discuss the above statement and to state *two* different methods of apportioning joint costs to joint products.

(b) A company using process costing manufactures a single product which passes through two processes, the output of process 1 becoming the input to process 2. Normal losses and abnormal losses are defective units having a scrap value and cash is received at the end of the period for all such units.

The following information relates to the four-week period of accounting period number 7.

Raw material issued to process 1 was 3,000 units at a cost of £5 per unit.

There was no opening or closing work-in-progress but opening and closing stocks of finished goods were £20,000 and £23,000 respectively.

	Process 1	Process 2
Normal loss as a percentage of input	10%	5%
Output in units	2,800	2,600
Scrap value per unit	£2	£5
Additional components	£1,000	£780
Direct wages incurred	£4,000	£6,000
Direct expenses incurred	£10,000	£14,000
Production overhead as a percentage of direct wages	75%	125%

You are required to present the accounts for
   Process 1
   Process 2
   Finished goods
   Normal loss
   Abnormal loss
   Abnormal gain
   Profit and loss (so far as it relates to any of the accounts
      listed above).

(*CIMA Nov 89*)

13. C Ltd operates a process which produces three joint products. In the period just ended costs of production totalled £509,640. Output from the process during the period was:

   Product W   276,000 kilos
   Product X   334,000 kilos
   Product Y   134,000 kilos

   There were no opening stocks of the three products. Products W and X are sold in this state. Product Y is subjected to further processing. Sales of Products W and X during the period were:

   Product W   255,000 kilos at £0.945 per kilo
   Product X   312,000 kilos at £0.890 per kilo

   128,000 kilos of Product Y were further processed during the period. The balance of the period production of the three products W, X and Y remained in stock at the end of the period. The value of closing stock of individual products is calculated by apportioning costs according to weight of output.

The additional costs in the period of further processing Product Y, which is converted into Product Z, were:

Direct labour	£10,850
Production overhead	£7,070

96,000 kilos of Product Z were produced from the 128,000 kilos of Product Y. A by-product BP is also produced which can be sold for £0.12 per kilo. 8,000 kilos of BP were produced and sold in the period.

Sales of Product Z during the period were 94,000 kilos, with a total revenue of £100,110. Opening stock of Product Z was 8,000 kilos, valued at £8,640. The FIFO method is used for pricing transfers of Product Z to cost of sales.

Selling and administration costs are charged to all main products when sold, at 10% of revenue.

Required:
(a) Prepare a profit and loss account for the period, identifying separately the profitability of each of the three main products.
(b) C Ltd has now received an offer from another company to purchase the total output of Product Y (i.e. before further processing), for £0.62 per kilo. Calculate the viability of this alternative.
(c) Discuss briefly the methods of, and rationale for, joint cost apportionment.

(ACCA June 90)

14. A company has decided to diversify its activities and a new product has been developed which will be included in the master budget preparation for the coming year.

(a) Explain ways in which the learning curve effect may create problems in the preparation of the master budget and in its use as a base against which to measure actual results in each four week accounting period.
(b) Comment on potential problems where short-term profit maximization is seen as the main objective when setting the budget for the new product.

(ACCA Dec 90)

15. Limitation plc commenced the manufacture and sale of a new product in the fourth quarter of 1991. In order to facilitate the budgeting process for quarters 1 and 2 of 1992, the following information has been collected:

(*i*)   Forecast production/sales (batches of product):

quarter 4, 1991	30 batches
quarter 1, 1992	45 batches
quarter 2, 1992	45 batches

(*ii*)   It is estimated that direct labour is subject to a learning curve effect of 90%. The labour cost of batch 1 of quarter 4, 1991 was £600 (at £5 per hour). The labour output rates from the commencement of production of the product, after adjusting for learning effects, are as follows:

Total batches produced (batches)	Overall average time per batch (hours)
15	79.51
30	71.56
45	67.28
60	64.40
75	62.25
90	60.55
105	59.15
120	57.96

Labour hours worked and paid for will be adjusted to eliminate spare capacity during each quarter. All time will be paid for at £5 per hour.

(*iii*) Direct material is used at the rate of 200 units per batch of product for the first 20 batches of quarter 4, 1991. Units of material used per batch will fall by 2% of the original level for each 20 batches thereafter as the learning curve effect improves the efficiency with which the material is used. All material will be bought at £1.80 per unit during 1992. Delivery of the total material requirement for a quarter will be made on day one of the quarter. Stock will be held in storage capacity hired at a cost of 30p per quarter per unit held in stock. Material will be used at an even rate throughout each quarter.

(iv) Variable overhead is estimated at 150% of direct labour cost during 1992.

(v) All units produced will be sold in the quarter of production at £1,200 per batch.

Required:

(a) Calculate the labour hours requirement for the second batch and the sum of the labour hours for the third and fourth batches produced in quarter 4, 1991.

(b) Prepare a budget for each of quarters 1 and 2, 1992 showing the contribution earned from the product. Show all relevant workings.

(c) The supplier of the raw material has offered to deliver on a 'just-in-time' basis in return for a price increase to £1.90 per unit in quarter 1, 1992 and £2 per unit thereafter.

(i) Use information for quarters 1 and 2, 1992 to determine whether the offer should be accepted on financial grounds.

(ii) Comment on other factors which should be considered before a final decision is reached.

(d) Limitation plc wish to prepare a quotation for 12 batches of the product to be produced at the start of quarter 3, 1992.

Explain how the learning curve formula $y = ax^b$ may be used in the calculation of the labour cost of the quotation. Your answer should identify each of the variables y, a, x and b. No calculations are required.

(*ACCA Dec 91*)

16. The manager of a small business has received enquiries about printing three different types of advertising leaflet. Information concerning these three leaflets is shown below:

Leaflet type	A	B	C
	£	£	£
Selling price, per 1,000 leaflets	100	220	450
Estimated printing costs:			
Variable, per 1,000 leaflets	40	70	130
Specific fixed costs, per month	2,400	4,000	9,500

In addition to the specific fixed costs a further £4,000 per month would be incurred in renting special premises if any or all of the above three leaflets were printed.

The minimum printing order would be for 30,000 of each type of leaflet per month and the maximum possible order is estimated to be 60,000 of each leaflet per month.

Required:

(a) (i) Examine and comment upon the potential profitability of leaflet printing. Make whatever calculations you consider appropriate.

(ii) Assuming that orders have been received to print each month 50,000 of both Leaflet *A* and Leaflet *B* calculate the quantity of Leaflet *C* which would need to be ordered to produce an overall profit, for all three leaflets, of £1,800 per month.

(b) It is possible that a special type of paper used in printing the leaflets will be difficult to obtain during the first few months. The estimated consumption of this special paper for each type of leaflet is:

Leaflet *A*   2 packs per 1,000 leaflets
Leaflet *B*   6 packs per 1,000 leaflets
Leaflet *C*   16 packs per 1,000 leaflets

Advise the manager on the quantity of each leaflet which should be printed in order to maximize profit in the first month, if 50,000 of each type of leaflet have been printed, there remains unfulfilled orders of 10,000 for each type of leaflet and there are 170 packs of special paper available for the rest of the month.

(c) 'If the manager of the above business wastes ten packs of special paper then the cost to the business of that waste is simply the original cost of that paper.'

Critically examine the validity of the above statement.

(*ACCA*)

17. Woodwind Ltd manufactures and sells three products, Baubles, Bangles and Beads, holding respectively 10%, 6% and 8% of the national market for them. It has no plans to produce any other product. It is generally believed in the industry that demand for each of the products is little affected by demand for the other two. Like the other smaller firms in the industry, Woodwind Ltd has always followed the prices set by the market leader, Goodman Ltd. Woodwind Ltd is operating at well below full capacity and faces no foreseeable production constraints.

For the year to 30th June 1980 the following historic cost management accounts were produced for Woodwind Ltd. (All the data are in £000.)

	Baubles	Bangles	Beads	Total	Nature of cost (V = variable; F = fixed)
Rent, rates & insurance	602	494	562	1,658	F — allocated by floor area
Direct labour	2,752	1,306	1,465	5,523	V
Indirect labour	882	424	460	1,766	F — allocated by direct labour
Energy	194	192	194	580	F — allocated by cubic space
Materials & supplies	1,568	968	960	3,496	V
Depreciation	1,130	854	730	2,714	F — allocated by plant value
Total manufacturing cost	7,128	4,238	4,371	15,737	
Selling expenses	1,820	916	940	3,676	F — allocated by sales value
Administration	690	260	356	1,306	F — allocated by time spent
Interest	104	80	106	290	F — allocated by asset value
Total cost	9,742	5,494	5,773	21,009	
Sales (less cash discounts)	10,354	5,208	5,344	20,906	
Profit (Loss)	612	(286)	(429)	(103)	
Unit sales (in thousand dozens):					
Actual	2,160	1,034	970	4,164	
Budget	2,000	1,000	1,000	4,000	
Unit selling price per dozen: (before discounts)	£5.00	£5.20	£5.40	£5.15	(average)

Beads have shown a loss in the management accounts for four of the last five years (including the year to 30th June 1980).

Bangles showed a small loss in the year to 30th June 1979. Sales in the industry have declined slowly for the past three years. Goodman Ltd has just announced a reduction in the price of its brand of Baubles to £4.50 per dozen, effective immediately.

Woodwind Ltd's marketing director has estimated that, if Woodwind makes a similar price reduction immediately, then its unit sales of Baubles in the year to 30th June 1981 will be 2,000,000 dozen; that if it maintains its price at £5.00 per dozen sales will be 1,400,000 dozen units; and that if the price is dropped to £4.25 per dozen unit sales will be 2,200,000 dozen units. He estimates also that, barring price changes relative to competitors, sales of Bangles and Beads will be 1,000,000 dozen units each in the year to 30th June 1981.

You are required to set out the various issues which the directors of Woodwind Ltd should consider in relation to their production and pricing policies at their meeting to be held on 20th July 1980, and to write a short report to the Board summarizing the advice which you would offer to them.

(CA)

18. Bruno Ltd is considering proposals for design changes in one of a range of soft toys. The proposals are as follows:

A. Eliminate some of the decorative stitching from the toy.
B. Use plastic eyes instead of glass eyes in the toys (two eyes per toy).
C. Change the filling material used. It is proposed that scrap fabric left over from the body manufacture be used instead of the synthetic material which is currently used.

The design change proposals have been considered by the management team and the following information has been gathered:

(i) Plastic eyes will cost £15 per hundred whereas the existing glass eyes cost £20 per hundred. The plastic eyes will be more liable to damage on insertion into the toy. It is estimated that scrap plastic eyes will be

10% of the quantity issued from stores as compared to 5% of issues of glass eyes at present.

(*ii*) The synthetic filling material costs £80 per tonne. One tonne of filling is sufficient for 2,000 soft toys.

(*iii*) Scrap fabric to be used as filling material will need to be cut into smaller pieces before use and this will cost 5p per soft toy. There is sufficient scrap fabric for the purpose.

(*iv*) The elimination of the decorative stitching is expected to reduce the appeal of the product, with an estimated fall in sales by 10% from the current level. It is not felt that the change in eyes or filling material will adversely affect sales volume. The elimination of the stitching will reduce production costs by 60p per soft toy.

(*v*) The current sales level of the soft toy is 300,000 units per annum. Apportioned fixed costs per annum are £450,000. The net profit per soft toy at the current sales level is £3.

Required:

(a) Using the information given in the question, prepare an analysis which shows the estimated effect on annual profit if all three proposals are implemented, and which enables management to check whether each proposal will achieve an annual target profit increase of £25,000. The proposals for plastic eyes and the use of scrap fabric should be evaluated after the stitching elimination proposal has been evaluated.

(b) Calculate the percentage reduction in sales due to the stitching elimination at which the implementation of all three design change proposals would result in the same total profit from the toy as that earned before the implementation of the changes in design.

(c) Prepare a report which indicates additional information which should be obtained before a final decision is taken with regard to the implementation of the proposals.

(*ACCA Dec 91*)

19. A company manufactures and sells a wide range of products. The products are manufactured in various locations and sold in a number of quite separate markets. The company's operations are organized into five divisions which may supply each other as well as selling on the open market.

The following financial information is available concerning the company for the year just ended:

	£000
Sales	8,600
Production cost of sales	5,332
Gross profit	3,268
Other expenses	2,532
Net profit	736

An offer to purchase Division 5, which has been performing poorly, has been received by the company.

The gross profit percentage of sales, earned by Division 5 in the year, was half that earned by the company as a whole. Division 5 sales were 10% of total company sales. Of the production expenses incurred by Division 5, fixed costs were £316,000. Other expenses (i.e. other than production expenses) incurred by the division totalled £156,000, all of which can be regarded as fixed. These include £38,000 apportionment of general company expenses which would not be affected by the decision concerning the possible sale of Division 5.

In the year ahead, if Division 5 is not sold, fixed costs of the division would be expected to increase by 5% and variable costs to remain at the same percentage of sales. Sales would be expected to increase by 10%.

If the division is sold, it is expected that some sales of other divisions would be lost. These would provide a contribution to profits of £20,000 in the year ahead. Also, if the division is sold, the capital sum received could be invested so as to yield a return of £75,000 in the year ahead.

Required:
(a) Calculate whether it would be in the best interests of the company, based upon the expected situation in the year ahead, to sell Division 5.

(b) Discuss other factors that you feel should influence the decision.

(c) Calculate the percentage increase in Division 5 sales required in the year ahead (compared with the current year) for the financial viability of the two alternatives to be the same. (You are to assume that all other factors in the above situation will remain as forecast for the year ahead.)

(ACCA Dec 88)

20. DEF Limited, a company having a year end of 31 December, makes a single product which it sells to consumers for £34. The current costs of the product are as follows:

	£
Direct labour (2 hours @ £4.50)	9
Direct materials	10
Direct expenses	2
Overhead (fixed)	9
	£29

Overhead is absorbed into product costs on the basis of direct labour hours used to produce each unit, and this year's overhead is based on an annual production of £80,000 units.

For many years the company has produced its budgets and forecasts using absorption (total) costing but the Managing Director has recently returned from a conference on cost control where he has heard that marginal (variable) costing is better.

The following information relates to next year.

(1) Costs are expected to increase as follows:

	%
Direct labour rates	4
Direct materials	5
Direct expenses	7
Fixed overhead	12.5

(2) Opening stocks are expected to be 4,500 units valued at current costs, with annual production remaining at 80,000 units arising evenly during the year.

(3) Sales are expected to be:

6 months to 30 June	39,000 units @ £34 each
6 months to 31 December	42,000 units @ £36 each

(a) You are required to prepare forecasts for next year for each half-year separately and the annual total, based on the information given above showing sales, costs, and profit, using:

    (*i*) absorption costing,

    (*ii*) marginal costing.

Explain the difference between the total profit given by each method.

(b) Explain:

    (*i*) the term 'Under/Over absorption of fixed overhead cost';

    (*ii*) the conditions which cause either an under or over absorption of fixed overhead cost to occur;

    (*iii*) why most organisations have no choice but to accept these conditions.

(c) Cost accounting classifies costs in a different way to financial accounting. Why is this and how does this difference affect the use of an integrated accounting system?

(*CIMA May 89*)

21. (a) The following information relates to two hospitals for the year ended 31.12.1985.

	St. Mathew's	St. Mark's
Number of in-patients	15,400	710
Average stay per in-patient	10 days	156 days
Total number of out-patient attendances	130,000	3,500
Number of available beds	510	320
Average number of beds occupied	402	307

Cost Analysis	In-patients £	Out-patients £	In-patients £	Out-patients £
A. *Patient Care Services*				
1. Direct treatment services and supplies (e.g. nursing staff)	6,213,900	1,076,400	1,793,204	70,490
2. Medical supporting services:				
2.1 Diagnostic (e.g. pathology)	480,480	312,000	22,152	20,650
2.2 Other services (e.g. occupational therapy)	237,160	288,600	77,532	27,790
B. *General Services*				
1. Patient related (e.g. catering)	634,480	15,600	399,843	7,700
2. General (e.g. administration)	2,196,760	947,700	1,412,900	56,700

NOTE: In-patients are those who receive treatment whilst remaining in hospital. Out-patients visit hospital during the day to receive treatment.

Required:
   (*i*) Prepare separate statements for each hospital for each cost heading:
       (a) cost per in-patient day, £ to two decimal places.
       (b) cost per out-patient attendance, £ to two decimal places.
   (*ii*) Calculate for each hospital the bed-occupation percentage.
   (*iii*) Comment briefly on your findings.

(b) A transport company operates with one vehicle only, and has produced the following forecast for next year:

Estimated operating kilometres	30,000
	£
Revenue	30,000
Total wages cost	10,000
Total standing costs	6,000
Total vehicle running costs	12,000

Revenue and vehicle running costs are directly variable with operating kilometres.

Required:
  (*i*) Calculate the break-even point and margin of safety in kilometres for the forecast period.
  (*ii*) Prepare a table showing the profit and loss at the following levels of activity:
      (a) 20,000 kilometres
      (b) 30,000 kilometres
      (c) 40,000 kilometres
  (*iii*) Calculate the break-even point in kilometres if the operating kilometres were forecast to be only 28,500 kilometres and the annual wage costs were cut to £8,000.

(*AAT*)

22. Z Ltd manufactures and sells three products with the following selling prices and variable costs:

	Product A £/unit	Product B £/unit	Product C £/unit
Selling price	3.00	2.45	4.00
Variable cost	1.20	1.67	2.60

The company is considering expenditure on advertising and promotion of Product A. It is hoped that such expenditure, together with a reduction in the selling price of the product, would increase sales. Existing annual sales volume of the three products is:

Product A	460,000 units
Product B	1,000,000 units
Product C	380,000 units

If £60,000 per annum was to be invested in advertising and sales promotion, sales of Product A at reduced selling prices would be expected to be:
      590,000 units at £2.75 per unit
  or 650,000 units at £2.55 per unit
Annual fixed costs are currently £1,710,000 per annum.

  Required:
  (a) Calculate the current break-even sales revenue of the business.
  (b) Advise the management of Z Ltd as to whether the

expenditure on advertising and promotion, together with selling price reduction, should be introduced on Product A.

(c) Calculate the required unit sales of Product A, at a selling price of £2.75 per unit, in order to justify the expenditure on advertising and promotion.

(d) Explain the term 'margin of safety', with particular reference to the circumstances of Z Ltd.

(ACCA June 89)

23. (a) Describe three methods of cost classification and explain the utility of each method.

(b) A company is establishing a new factory operation in order to manufacture a new product. It expects to sell 330,000 units of the product in the first year following launch, divided 40%:60% between the first and second six-month periods.

Production is planned at an even rate, totalling 365,000 units in the same 12-month period. Prior to this, a stock of 50,000 units will be established. This will be valued, at the beginning of the period, at the forecast manufacturing cost per unit.

Direct materials and labour are expected to total £1.30 per unit. Manufacturing overheads, which will be at the same level for each six-month period, will total £325,500 in the year. They will be absorbed into the cost of the product at a rate based on normal activity, which has been estimated at 350,000 units. Sales commissions will be £0.20 per unit and other variable selling and administration expenses are estimated at 4% of selling price. Fixed selling and administration expenses will be incurred evenly and will total £112,860 in the 12-month period. They will be absorbed into the cost of units sold at a percentage of selling price sufficient to absorb them fully on sales in the period. The selling price of the product will be £3.80 per unit.

Required:
Prepare a forecast profit and loss account for the first year of sales, also split into the two six-month periods. (Any over/under

absorbed overhead balances should be shown separately as an adjustment to the profit in each six-month period.)

(ACCA June 89)

24. The VX Company has produced the following information from which a cash budget for the first six months of the next year is required.

The company makes a single product which sells for £50 and the variable cost of each unit is:

Material £26

Labour £8

Overhead £2

Fixed costs excluding depreciation are budgeted at £5,500 per month payable on the 23rd of each month.

Other details:

(*i*) Sales for the last two months of this year

November	December
1,000	1,200

(*ii*) Budgeted sales for next year

January	February	March	April	May	June
1,400	1,600	1,800	2,000	2,200	2,600

(*iii*) Production quantities for the last two months of this year

November	December
1,200	1,400

(*iv*) Budgeted production units for next year

January	February	March	April	May	June
1,600	2,000	2,400	2,600	2,400	2,200

(*v*) Wages are paid in the month when output is produced.

(*vi*) Variable overhead is paid 50% in the month when the cost is incurred and 50% the following month.

(*vii*) Suppliers of material are paid 2 months after the material is used in production.

(*viii*) Customers are expected to pay at the end of the second month following sale.

(*ix*) A new machine is scheduled for January costing £34,000, this is to be paid for in February.

(*x*) An old machine is to be sold for cash in January for £1,200.

(*xi*) The company expects to have a cash balance of £35,000 on 1st January.

Required:

(a) A month by month cash budget for the first six months of next year.

(b) Comment on the action management might take in the light of the cash budget you have prepared.

(c) Explain how depreciation would affect:
  (*i*) A cash budget and
  (*ii*) The calculation of profit in a business.

(d) Explain the term 'Flexible Budget' and describe the uses and benefits that can be derived from a system that uses flexible budgets.

(*AAT June 90*)

25. Snecas Ltd manufacture a range of products using a series of machine operations. One product type is made from steel bar. At present the factory layout is somewhat haphazard and machines are used for a particular job as they become available. Company management have decided to create a 'dedicated cell' of machines which will specialize in the manufacture of the steel bar products with specialist machine minders and a foreman in charge. The machines in the 'cell' will be grouped by machine type to facilitate a smooth flow of steel bar products. There are three steel bar products which are manufactured as follows:

Product A: Saw the steel bar to size; turn the bar on a turning machine; harden in a hardening process; grind the bar on a grinding machine.

Product B: Saw the steel bar to size; turn on a turning machine; grind on a grinding machine.

Product C: Saw the steel bar to size; turn on a turning machine; drill on a drilling machine; harden in a hardening process; grind on a grinding machine.

Snecas Ltd currently operate a system whereby labour and

overhead costs for all products are absorbed into product units at 225% of direct material costs. The direct material cost per metre of each steel bar product is £70.

This system results in the net profit or loss per metre of steel bar product being reported as £12.50 profit, £27.50 loss and £12.50 profit for products A, B and C respectively.

A study by the management accountant has resulted in the following budget data for the coming year for the steel bar product 'cell':

(i)	Machine operation	Fixed labour and overhead (total)	Variable labour and overhead per metre
		£000	£
	Saw	88	36
	Turn	110	14
	Drill	108	40
	Harden	320	26
	Grind	154	25

(ii) Production/sales quantity

Product A	8,000 metres	
Product B	2,000 metres	
Product C	12,000 metres	

(iii) Direct material prices will rise by 6% from the current year level.

(iv) Selling prices will be increased by 5% from the current year level.

(v) Variable labour and overhead costs will be absorbed at the budgeted rate per metre for each machine type listed in (i) above.

(vi) Fixed costs for each machine type will be absorbed at a rate per metre based on the aggregate quantity of products A, B and C budgeted to pass through each machine type.

Required:

(a) Prepare a diagram which illustrates the layout of the new steel bar product machine group and shows the aggregate quantity (metres) of products passing through each machine type.

(b) Prepare a budget summary for the coming year which details for each product:

    (*i*)   costs and revenues per metre and in total,
    (*ii*) fixed and variable costs by machine operation,
    (*iii*) contribution earned per metre and in total,
    (*iv*) net profit or loss per metre and in total.
(c) Identify and briefly comment on FOUR distinct ways in which the proposed system for steel bar product manufacture and the accounting control thereof may lead to increased profitability for Snecas Ltd.

(ACCA Dec 89)

26. ABC Limited, a manufacturing and trading company, operates a standard costing system. The standard costs which are used to calculate the variances are taken from the company's standard cost card for the year. The appropriate data for the year to 30 September 1989 were:

	£/unit
Direct materials (5 litres)	10.00
Direct labour (4 hours)	16.00
Direct expenses	4.00
	30.00
Production overhead	20.00
Production cost	50.00
Profit	30.00
Selling price	80.00

During the year the company operated at standard efficiency but actual production costs differed from standard costs due to differences in prices paid.

The following total cost variances arose during the year:

	£
Direct materials	4,900 Favourable
Direct labour	7,840 Adverse
Direct expenses	490 Favourable
Production overhead	4,150 Adverse

Budget production was 10,000 units but actual production was 9,800 units and sales were 9,750 units. All sales were made at the standard selling price of £80 per unit.

At 30 September 1989, there were 700 units of the finished product in stock valued at £34.00 each (stocks are valued at standard variable production cost based on the average expected cost for the year).

The company is considering its plans for the year to 30 September 1990. The following data have emerged from discussions:

(1) Sales are expected as follows:

October–December 1989	2,100 units
January–March 1990	4,800 units
April–June 1990	1,500 units
July–September 1990	3,000 units

(2) Stocks of finished units held at the end of December, March and June are to be equal to one-third of the following quarter's sales. At the end of September 1990 such stocks are to be 960 units.

(3) Direct material prices are expected to be greater than the average actual price paid in the year to 30 September 1989 by the following percentages:

October 1989–March 1990	3%
April 1990–September 1990	4%

Direct materials are received in the month of production and paid for one month later. Consequently, no raw material stocks are held.

(4) Direct wage rates from 1 January 1990 are expected to be 8% above the average actual rate paid during the year ended 30 September 1989. No change is expected until that date. Direct wages are paid in the month in which they are incurred.

(5) Direct expenses are not expected to change for the year to 30 September 1990. They will continue to be incurred at the same rate per unit of output as they were in the year to 30 September 1989. They are paid in the quarter following the quarter in which they are incurred.

(6) An analysis of the production overhead incurred in the year to 30 September 1989 confirmed that 80% was fixed, the

remaining 20% varying in proportion to output. This was as expected in the standard costs shown above. The variable overhead per unit is expected to be 5% higher than the average variable overhead cost incurred in the year to 30 September 1989. This increase is to be effective from 1 October 1989. All production overhead costs are paid in the month following that in which they are incurred except for 10% of the fixed overhead cost which relates to depreciation.

(7) Selling prices are to remain at £80.00 per unit of output until 1 April 1990 when they are to increase to £90.00 per unit for the remainder of the year. All sales are on credit; 50% are settled in the same quarter as the sale, 45% in the following quarter, and the remainder are bad debts.

You are required to

(a) (i) prepare a production budget in terms of units to be produced for the quarter ending 31 March 1990.

(ii) prepare columnar profit and loss accounts for each of the six-month periods ending 31 March 1990 and 30 September 1990 and for the year in total (all figures to the nearest £1);

(iii) show the cash budget for the quarter January to March 1990, assuming an opening balance at the beginning of January 1990 of £124,678 overdrawn;

(b) explain how a microcomputer spreadsheet package might be used to produce the budgets of a company such as ABC Limited. What are the advantages of using a spreadsheet for this type of work?

(CIMA Nov 89)

27. A company mixes two materials X and Y in the production process. A system of standard costing and variance analysis is in operation. The standard material requirement per tonne of mixed output is 60% material X at £30 per tonne and 40% material Y at £45 per tonne, with a standard yield of 90%.

The following information has been gathered for the three months January to March:

	January	*February*	*March*
Output achieved (tonnes)	810	765	900
Actual material input:			
X (tonnes)	540	480	700
Y (tonnes)	360	360	360
Actual material cost (£)	32,400	31,560	38,600
(X plus Y)			

The actual price per tonne of material Y throughout the January to March period was £45.

Required:
   (a) Prepare material variance summaries for each of January, February and March which include yield and mix variances in total plus usage and price variances for each material and in total.
   (b) Prepare comments for management on each variance including variance trend.
   (c) Discuss the relevance of the variances calculated above in the light of the following additional information: the company has an agreement to purchase 360 tonnes of material Y each month and the perishable nature of the material means that it must be used in the month of purchase and additional supplies in excess of 360 tonnes per month are not available.

   (ACCA June 91)

28. Tungach Ltd make and sell a single product. Demand for the product exceeds the expected production capacity of Tungach Ltd. The holding of stocks of the finished product is avoided if possible because the physical nature of the product is such that it deteriorates quickly and stocks may become unsaleable.

   A standard marginal cost system is in operation. Feedback reporting takes planning and operational variances into consideration.

   The management accountant has produced the following operating statement for period 9:

Tungach Ltd
Operating Statement — Period 9

	£		£
Original budgeted contribution			36,000
Revision variances:			
Material usage	9,600	(A)	
Material price	3,600	(F)	
Wage rate	1,600	(F)	4,400(A)
Revised budgeted contribution			31,600
Sales volume variance:			
Causal factor			
Extra capacity	4,740	(F)	
Productivity drop	987.5	(A)	
Idle time	592.5	(A)	
Stock increase	2,370	(A)	790 (F)
Revised standard contribution for sales achieved			32,390
Other variances:			
Material usage	900	(F)	
Material price	3,120	(A)	
Labour efficiency	1,075	(A)	
Labour idle time	645	(A)	
Wage rate	2,760	(A)	6,700(A)
Actual contribution			25,690

(F) = favourable   (A) = adverse

Other data are available as follows:

(*i*) The original standard contribution per product unit as determined at period 1 was:

	£	£
Selling price		30
Less: Direct material 1.5 kilos at £8	12	
Direct labour 2 hours at £4.50	9	21
Contribution		9

(*ii*) A permanent change in the product specification was implemented from period 7 onwards. It was estimated that this change would require 20% additional material per product unit. The current efficient price of the material has settled at £7.50 per kilo.

(*iii*) Actual direct material used during period 9 was 7,800 kilos at £7.90 per kilo. Any residual variances are due to operational problems.

(iv) The original standard wage rate overestimated the degree of trade union pressure during negotiations and was 20p higher than the rate subsequently agreed. Tungach Ltd made a short-term operational decision to pay the workforce at £4.60 per hour during periods 7 to 9 in an attempt to minimize the drop in efficiency likely because of the product specification change. Management succeeded in extending the production capacity during period 9 and the total labour hours paid for were 9,200 hours. These included 150 hours of idle time.

(v) Budgeted production and
sales quantity (period 9)	4,000 units
Actual sales quantity (period 9)	4,100 units
Actual production quantity (period 9)	4,400 units

(vi) Stocks of finished goods are valued at the current efficient standard cost.

Required:

(a) Prepare detailed figures showing how the material and labour variances in the operating statement have been calculated.

(b) Prepare detailed figures showing how the sales volume variance has been calculated for each causal factor shown in the operating statement.

(c) Prepare a report to the management of Tungach Ltd explaining the meaning and relevance of the figures given in the operating statement for period 9. The report should contain specific comments for any two of the sales volume variance causal factors and any two of the 'other variances'. The comments should suggest possible reasons for each variance, the management member likely to be answerable for each variance and possible corrective action.

(ACCA Dec 89)

29. (a) Q Limited operates a system of standard costing and in respect of one of its products which is manufactured within a single cost centre, the following information is given.

For one unit of product the standard material input is 16 litres at a standard price of £2.50 per litre.

The standard wage rate is £5 per hour and 6 hours are allowed in which to produce one unit. Fixed production overhead is absorbed at the rate of 120% of direct wages cost.

During the last four-week accounting period:
The material price variance was extracted on purchase and the actual price paid was £2.45 per litre.
Total direct wages cost was £121,500.
Fixed production overhead incurred was £150,000

Variances	Favourable	Adverse
	£	£
Direct material price	8,000	
Direct material usage		6,000
Direct labour rate		4,500
Direct labour efficiency	3,600	
Fixed production overhead expenditure		6,000

You are required to calculate for the four-week period:
    (*i*) budgeted output in units,
   (*ii*) number of litres purchased,
  (*iii*) number of litres used above standard allowed,
  (*iv*) actual units produced,
    (*v*) actual hours worked,
   (*vi*) average actual wage rate per hour.

(b) 'Physical measures of output and technical measures of production efficiency are often more useful than financial measures, particularly at the lower levels of an organization.'

You are required, in the context of variance analysis, to discuss and expand on the above statement.

(*CIMA Nov 89*)

30. Perchance Products Ltd manufacture and sell cassette recorders. Their budgets, standard costs and actual figures for Period 4 were as follows:

	Budget	*Standard*	*Actual*	
Sales	15,000 units	£28 each	14,600 units totalling	
				£401,500
Materials		£10 unit	Total	£147,460
Wages		£5 unit	Total	£72,730
Factory overhead		£6 unit	Total	£85,980
Administration (fixed)	£30,000		Total	£29,000
Selling (fixed)	£20,000		Total	£21,000
Selling (variable)		2% sales	Total	£7,960

Required
(a) The budgeted results for period 4.
(b) The variances between actual and standard results for the period in which the manufacturing operations achieved standard efficiency.
(c) A Costing Trading and Profit & Loss Account for Period 4 reconciling the budgeted profit with actual profit achieved. (Note — assume no stocks exist at the beginning or end of period 4).

(*AAT*)

31. A company uses Material Z in several of its manufacturing processes. On 1 November, 9,000 kilos of the material were in stock. These materials cost £9,630 when purchased.
Receipts and issues of Material Z during November were:

Receipts
    4 November, 10,000 kilos costing £10,530
   23 November, 8,000 kilos costing £8,480
Issues
    2 November, 2,000 kilos to Process 1
    7 November, 4,500 kilos to Process 2
   20 November, 4,000 kilos to Process 1
   27 November, 6,000 kilos to Process 3

The company operates a standard costing system. The standard cost of Material Z during November was £1.04 per kilo.
Process 1 is exclusively concerned with the production of Product X. Production information for November is as follows:

Opening work-in-process, 6,000 units
— complete as to materials; 50% complete for direct labour and overheads.
Completed units, 9,970.
Closing work-in-process, 8,000 units
— complete as to materials; 75% complete for direct labour and overheads.

The standard cost per unit of Product X comprises the following:

Material Z, 0.5 kilos at £1.04 per kilo
Direct labour, 0.1 hours at £4.80 per hour
Overhead, absorbed on direct labour hours at £5.00 per hour.

Costs (other than Material Z) incurred in Process 1 during November were:

Direct labour, 1,340 hours at £4.80 per hour
Overheads, £6,680.

Required:
(a) Prepare the stock account and material price variance account for Material Z for the month of November on the assumption that:
 (i) The material price variance is identified on purchase of material.
 (ii) The material price variance is identified at the time of issue of material to production (assume that the weighted average pricing method is used).
(b) State which of the above two methods, (a) (i) or (a) (ii), you would prefer. State briefly the reasons for your preference.
(c) Prepare the account for Process 1 for the month of November. (Assume that Material Z is charged to the process at standard price.)

(ACCA Dec 88)

32. Claylock Ltd make and sell a single product. The company operates a standard cost system and the following information is available for period 5, 1990:

(i) Standard product cost per unit: £
    Direct material 8 kilos at £5.40 per kilo 43.20
    Direct labour 2.5 hours at £4.50 per hour 11.25
    Fixed production overhead 17.00

(ii) The standard selling price per unit is £90.

(iii) Direct labour hours worked total 12,000 hours. Labour productivity in comparison to standard was 90%.

(iv) 42,000 kilos of direct material were purchased at £5.60 per kilo. Issues from stores to production totalled 36,000 kilos during the period.

(v) Stocks of finished goods rose from nil to 300 units during the period. It was budgeted that all units produced would be sold during the period.

(vi) Stocks of raw materials and finished goods are valued at standard cost.

(vii) Summary operating statement for period 5, 1990:

			£	
Budgeted sales revenue			450,000	
Sales volume variance			88,200	(A)
Standard sales revenue			361,800	
Less: Standard cost of sales			287,229	
Standard production margin			74,571	
	(F)	(A)		
Variance analysis:	£	£		
Sales price	30,150			
Direct material cost		16,176		
Fixed overhead volume		11,560		
Fixed overhead expenditure	1,500			
	31,650	27,736	3,914	(F)
Actual production margin			78,485	

Note: (F) = favourable (A) = adverse.

Required:

(a) Determine the values of the sales volume variance when it is expressed alternatively in terms of: standard revenue; standard production margin; and standard contribution. Discuss which valuation, when combined with the sales price variance, provides a measure of whether the sales variances have resulted in a net cash benefit to the company.

(b) Analyse the direct material cost variance into relevant sub-variances and comment on the method by which material usage is valued by Claylock Ltd.

(c) Analyse the fixed overhead volume variance into two sub-variances and comment on the relevance of each sub-variance as perceived by adherents of absorption costing.

(d) Prepare an operating statement for period 5, 1990 which amends the statement given in the question into standard marginal cost format. Explain the reason for any difference in the actual production margin from that reported under the present system. Comment also on any changes in the variances reported in the amended statement.

(ACCA Dec 90)

33. (a) Planning is expressed by the budgets which are prepared, but, prior to this, it is necessary to go through a forecasting exercise.

You are required to discuss briefly *five* problems which are likely to arise when forecasting for a business.

(b) C Limited employs 300 people and has sales of £9 million. It has five producing departments, two service departments and manufactures one product.

No effective planning or financial control system has been established but after one of the directors had attended a CIMA course on 'Finance for Non-Financial Managers' he decided to introduce a budget system and performance reports related to responsibilities. Other directors and management had some reservations about the introduction of this system but they were persuaded to allow its introduction.

After the end of April, which was the first month of the current financial year, departmental performance reports were issued to all departmental supervisors. These took the form of that illustrated below for Production Department 'D' which was produced by the office manager — the senior person on the administrative staff. (A separate report was issued relating to direct material and direct labour.)

Monthly report: Department 'D' —April 1990

	Actual	Planning budget	Variance
Units produced	1,100	1,000	100
	£	£	£
Salaries and wages	10,000	10,500	500
Indirect labour	8,000	7,000	1,000*
Maintenance	3,500	2,750	750*
Overhead allocated	3,000	2,750	250*
Consumable stores	1,600	1,500	100*
Depreciation	2,500	2,500	0
Insurance	1,100	1,000	100*
Sundries	1,000	500	500*
	30,700	28,500	2,200

*Note — considerable inefficiency; action should be taken to improve cost control in this department.

J, the supervisor for department 'D', was not pleased on receiving her report and declared she did not have time to bother with such paperwork and, in any case, the report was inaccurate and unfair. Her comment was typical of others who had received similar reports.

You are required
(i) to state what changes ought to be made to the report and why;
(ii) to assess the situation as it now stands in May and indicate what should be done in respect of the budget system and the departmental performance reports.

(*CIMA May 90*)

34. (a) State, and define, Cost Accounting ratios which may be used in the measurement of:
(1) Production, and
(2) Productivity

(b) Illustrate your answer to (a) above by calculating the appropriate ratios from the following data for each department.

(i) Department P	Model A	Model B
Output in units	17,600	16,800
Standard time per unit	9 minutes	16.5 minutes
Time taken in department	6,400 hours	
Budget/output, in standard hours	2,500	4,700

(ii) *Department Q*

Output in units	10,500
Standard time per unit	0.9 hours
Time taken in department	12,400 hours
Budget output, in standard hours	12,600 hours

(c) What is the significance of the answers to (b) above? (*AAT*)

35. A company manufactures four different products in one of the departments in its factory. Activity of the department is measured in machine hours.

Activity budgeted for the department in a period was as follows:

		Machine
	Units	hours
Product 1	48,000	12,000
Product 2	26,000	15,600
Product 3	7,000	3,500
Product 4	48,500	9,700

During the period actual machine hours worked were 40,120. Production of the four products was:

	Units
Product 1	45,500
Product 2	26,300
Product 3	7,900
Product 4	54,150

Required:
(a) Calculate the efficiency variance of the department during the period, expressing the variance both in machine hours and also as a ratio.
(b) Calculate the capacity usage and production volume (activity) ratios of the department for the period.
(c) Provide an explanation of the department's performance as demonstrated by the three ratios in (a) and (b).
(d) Explain what is meant by the term 'standard hour', and how the concept may be useful.

(*ACCA* Dec 88)

36. Exe operates an integrated accounting system and prepares its final accounts monthly.

Balances as at 1st October

	£000
Issued share capital	1,500
Profit and loss balance	460
Freehold buildings	1,000
Plant and machinery, at cost	500
Plant and machinery: depreciation provision	300
Motor vehicles, at cost	240
Motor vehicles, depreciation provision	80
10% Debentures	240
Creditors (materials)	144
Creditors (expenses)	36
Stock — raw materials	520
Wages payable	40
Debtors	246
Bank	162
Stock — finished goods	132

Data for the month of October

Materials purchased — 400,000 units at £4.90 per unit
Issued to production — 328,000 units
Paid to creditors — £1,800,000
Direct wages incurred — 225,000 hours at £4.20 per hour
Direct wages paid — £920,000
Production overhead incurred on credit — £1,490,000
Expense creditors paid — £1,900,000
Cash received from debtors — £4,800,000
Sales — £4,875,000
Plant and machinery purchased for cash on 1st October — £100,000
Administration and selling overhead incurred on credit — £895,000
Production and sales — 39,000 units

Additional data

Debenture interest — payable monthly
Depreciation provision — plant and machinery, 20% p.a. on cost
— motor vehicles, 25% p.a. on cost
Stocks of raw materials and finished goods are maintained at standard
There are four working weeks in the month of October
The operation of motor vehicles is regarded as a cost of selling

Standard data

Direct material price — £5.00 per unit
Direct material usage — 8 units per product
Direct wages — £4.00 per hour
Direct labour — 6 hours per product
Production overhead — absorbed at 150% of direct wages

Gross profit — calculated at 16⅔% of selling price
Budgeted output — 10,000 units per week.

You are required to:
(a) calculate the appropriate variances for October;
(b) show the accounts for October as they would be expected to appear in the ledger;
(c) prepare a profit and loss statement for October, together with a balance sheet as at the end of that month.

(*CIMA*)

37. A company manufactures a range of products by passing materials through a number of processes. A number of service departments provide support to the production processes.

(a) Define responsibility accounting and comment on the application of responsibility accounting in the context of the above situation.
(b) Explain how responsibility may be shared in respect of the cost of the maintenance department and suggest ways in which the management accounting system may assist in recognizing such shared responsibility.
(c) Explain ways in which the provision of more information need not lead to more effective management of a cost centre.

(*ACCA Dec 1990*)

Appendix 3
Suggested answers

Progress test 2

19. The three control levels are the minimum level, the re-order level and the maximum level.

Minimum level. To be on the safe side when setting this, one should assume that after making an immediate order the maximum usage is experienced at the same time as the maximum wait for new supplies. The level, then, is:

Maximum usage x maximum lead time =
800 kilos x 14 days = 11,200 kilos.

Re-order level. To compromise between panic on reaching the minimum level and the extra costs arising from carrying unnecessarily high stocks, it may be assumed that after placing the order average usage will be experienced for the average lead time, i.e. 600 x 12 = 7,200 kilos. By setting a re-order level this much above the minimum level the compromise is met — i.e. the re-order level = 7,200 + 11,200 = 18,400 kilos.

Maximum level. Stocks will be at a maximum (or, to speak more in control terms, will only exceed such a maximum if something is wrong) if, after placing an order at the re-order level, there is minimum usage during a minimum lead time before the re-order quantity is received. So the maximum level is 18,400 − (400 x 10) + 12,000 = 26,400 kilos.

20. (a) FIFO: (40 at £25 + 40 at £30) − (30 at £25 + 10 at £20 +20 at £30) = £600. Alternatively 20 at £30.
(b) LIFO: (40 at £25 + 40 at £30) − (30 at £25 + 30 at £30) = £550. Alternatively 10 at £25 + 10 at £30.

(c) Weighted average:

Receipts 1/6/	= 40 x £25 =	£1,000
Issues 2/6/	= 30 x £25 =	750
Balance		
in stock:	10 units for	250
Receipts 8/6/	= 40 units for	1,200
	50	£1,450

$\therefore$ New average price $= \dfrac{£1,450}{50} = £29$

$\therefore$ Value of 20 units closing stock $= 20$ at £29 $= \underline{\underline{£580}}$

21. In this situation there are in effect two prices: £10 and £10 less 2 per cent = £9.80. In the EOQ formula, therefore, S will be either 25 per cent of £10 = £2.50 or 25 per cent of £9.80 = £2.45. And the first step is to compute the EOQ associated with each price and see what quantities are involved. We have, then:

$$\text{EOQ at £10} = \sqrt{\frac{2 \times 105 \times 60,000}{2.5}} = 2,245 \text{ units}$$

$$\text{EOQ at £9.80} = \sqrt{\frac{2 \times 105 \times 60,000}{2.45}} = 2,268 \text{ units}$$

Now the EOQ for the £9.80 price is way below the quantity discount level and so cannot be realized. And since the total cost curve rises continuously beyond this point (*see* Fig 2.1), the attainable EOQ for this price is at the discount level of 14,000 units.

Given that we now have two EOQs, 2,245 and 14,000 units, the next step is to compute the total costs involved for a year at both levels. And these are:

Year's costs with EOQ of 2,245 units = Purchasing costs of £105 x 60,000/2,245 + holding costs of £2.5 x 2,245/2 = 2,806.50 + 2,806.50
$\qquad\qquad$ =£5,612.50
Year's costs with EOQ of 14,000 units = Purchasing costs of £105 x 60,000/14,000 + holding costs of £2.45 x 14,000/2 – discount of 2 per cent on 60,000 at £10 = £450 + £17,150 – 12,000 = £5,600.00

In theory, then, a re-order level of 14,000 rather than 2,245 units saves £12.50 a year. Clearly, however, when the difference in costs is as trivial as this the decision will be made on the basis of some factor other than cost.

22. (a)

	X	Y
Total time allowance	189 x ⅓ = 63 hrs	204 x ¼ = 51 hrs
Less time taken	45 hrs	39 hrs
Time saved	18 hrs	12 hrs
∴ Bonus payable	18 x ½ x £4 = £36	12 x ½ x £4 = £24

(b)

	X	Y
Basic week's pay	42 x £4 = £168	42 x £4 = £168
Overtime	3 x 1½ x £4 = £18	Nil
∴ Gross wage payable	36 + 168 +18 = £222	24 + 168 = 192

(c)

	X	Y
Good units made	189 – 6 = 183	204 – 4 = 200
∴ Wage cost per good unit	$\dfrac{£222}{183}$ = £1.213	$\dfrac{£(192-12)^*}{200}$ = 90p

*Assume 3 hours at £4 per hour booked to dayrate work.

Progress test 3

Answer to Question **10** appears on p.423.

11. (Costs to nearest £)
Overhead rates:

Filling: £110,040/13,100 = £8.40 per direct labour hour.
Sealing: £53,300/10,250 = £5.20 per direct labour hour.

Apportionment of actual service department overheads:

	Maintenance	Canteen
Original costs	£25,050	£24,375
Cross apportionment	3%	8%
1st apportionment	1,950	752
2nd apportionment	60	58
3rd apportionment	5	2
4th apportionment	<1	<1
Total cost	£27,065	£25,187

10.

Overhead Analysis and Overhead Absorption Rates

Overhead	Basis of apportionment	Total £	Rate Units	Rate £/unit	Maintenance Units	Maintenance £	Stores Units	Stores £	General Units	General £	Machine X Units	Machine X £	Machine Y Units	Machine Y £	Assembly Units	Assembly £	Packing Units	Packing £
Indirect wages and supervision	Allocation	204,000				22,500		11,500		24,250		38,000		43,500		41,250		23,000
Maintenance wages	Allocation	52,000				5,000		2,500		4,500		10,000		20,000		5,000		5,000
Indirect materials	Allocation	127,750				9,000		6,750		4,000		27,000		36,000		18,000		27,000
Power	Effective HP	60,000	100	£ 600	10	6,000	–	–	–	–	40	24,000	40	24,000	–	–	10	6,000
Rent and rates	Area (000 sq ft)	80,000	50	£1600	3	4,800	5	8,000	2	3,200	10	16,000	7.5	12,000	15	24,000	7.5	12,000
Lighting and heating	Area (000 sq ft)	20,000	50	£ 400	3	1,200	5	2,000	2	800	10	4,000	7.5	3,000	15	6,000	7.5	3,000
Insurance	Book values (£000s)	10,000	400	£ 25	60	1,500	10	250	10	250	120	3,000	160	4,000	20	500	20	500
Depreciation	Book values (£000s)	200,000	400	£ 500	60	30,000	10	5,000	10	5,000	120	60,000	160	80,000	20	10,000	20	10,000
Total		753,750				80,000		36,000		42,000		182,000		222,500		104,750		86,500
Services: Maintenance	Maintenance wages	40,000*	£2†			–80,000					10,000	20,000	20,000	40,000	5,000	10,000	5,000	10,000
Stores	Direct labour hours (000s)	Nil	300	£120				36,000			100	12,000	75	9,000	75	9,000	50	6,000
General	Direct labour hours (000s)	Nil	300	£140				–36,000		42,000 –42,000	100	14,000	75	10,500	75	10,500	50	7,000
Total		£753,750				Nil		Nil		Nil		228,000		282,000		134,250		109,500
Hours (machine/labour)												50,000		60,000		75,000		50,000
Overhead absorption rate (per machine/direct labour hour)												£4.560		£4.700		£1.790		£2.190

*Wages allocated in second line to non-service departments sharing apportionment (see question)

† i.e. £2 maintenance overhead per £1 maintenance wages.

Total production department costs:

	Filling	Sealing
Apportionments:		
Maintenance (£27,065)	70%	27%
	£18,946	£7,308
Canteen (£25,187)	60%	32%
	£15,112	£8,060
Original costs	£74,260	£38,115
Total actual costs	£108,318	£53,483

Overheads u/o absorbed:

	Filling	Sealing
Direct labour hrs	12,820	10,075
Overhead rate	£8.40	£5.20
∴ overheads absorbed	£107,688	£52,390
Total actual costs	£108,318	£53,483
∴ u/o absorption	£630 under	£1,093 under

(Note: £1 rounding error)

Progress test 4

8.

(*i*) Radley Contract Account

[*Costs incurred section*]

	£000s		£000s
Materials issued to site	600	Materials returned to store	50
Wages paid	250	Materials on site c/d	20
Sub-contractors' charges	25	Plant at site c/d	60
Plant	100	Bal: Total cost incurred c/d	900
Overheads allocated	25		
Wages accrued c/d	30		
	1030		1030

[*Cost matching section*]			
	£000s		£000s
Total cost b/d	900	WIP — work not certified c/d	120
		Matched costs to Contract P/L a/c	780
(Cost deemed incurred)	900		900

[*Future section*]			
	£000s		£000s
Materials on site c/d	20	Wages accrued b/d	30
Plant at site c/d	60		
WIP b/d	120		

(*ii*)   Radley Contractee Account

	£000s		£000s
Contract P/L a/c	900	Cash payment on account	1000

(*iii*)   Contract P/L Account

	£000s		£000s
Contract a/c: matched costs	780	Value work certified	900
Bal: Contract profit to P/L	120		
	900		900

9. *Balance sheet items*

Following the procedure shown in Fig 4.3, the resulting computations are as follows (£000s):

> IS = Incurred costs – matched cost = 900 – 780 = 120
> Since there are no foreseeable losses then IS remains at 120
> X = Cumulative turnover – cumulative payments on account
>   = 900 – 1000 = –100
> Since this is negative IS = 120 – 100 = 20
> Since this is positive the balance sheet will show:

> 'Stock, at net cost less payments on account: £20,000'

Progress test 5

6. *Accounts and trial balance for Tiny Ltd.*

FINANCIAL LEDGER

Creditors Control

Cash	1,500	Balance	2,000
Discounts	100	Purchases (cost	
Balance c/d	2,400	control)	2,000
	4,000		4,000
		Balance b/d	2,400

Debtors Control

Balance	1,000	Cash	2,000
Sales		Discounts	150
(cost control)	2,500	Balance c/d	1,350
	3,500		3,500
Balance b/d	1,350		

Bank

Balance	1,000	Creditors	1,500
Debtors	2,000	Wages (cost	
		control)	1,000
Balance c/d	500	Gen. operating	
		expenses (cost	
		control)	1,000
	3,500		3,500
		Balance b/d	500

Fixed Assets

Balance	3,000	Depreciation	30
Additions (cost		Balance c/d	3,470
control)	500		
	3,500		3,500
Balance b/d	3,470		

Capital

		Balance	10,000

Discounts Allowed

Debtors	150	P/L	150

Discounts Received

P/L	100	Creditors	100

Cost Control

Balance	7,000	Debtors	2,500
Creditors	2,000		
Wages	1,000	Fixed assets	500
Gen. operating			
expenses	1,000	Balance c/d	8,630
Depreciation	30		
Notional			
rent (P/L)	100		
Profit (P/L)	500		
	11,630		11,630
Balance b/d			
RM	1,000		
WIP	2,630		
FG	5,000		
	8,630		

Financial P/L

Discounts		Notional	
allowed	150	rent written	
Net profit to		back	100
appro-			
priation	550	Cost profit	
		(cost control)	500
		Discounts	
		received	100
	700		700

P/L Appropriation

		P/L	550

COST LEDGER

Stores				Overhead Control			
Balance	2,000	WIP	3,000	Gen. operating		WIP	1,130
Purchases	2,000	Balance c/d	1,000	expenses	1,000		
				Notional			
				rent	100		
	4,000		4,000	Depreciation	30		
Balance b/d	1,000				1,130		1,130

Capital Expenditure				Notional Rent			
WIP	500	Fixed assets	500	Financial P/L	100	Overheads	100

Sales				Finished Goods			
P/L	2,500	Debtors	2,500	Balance	3,000	Cost of sales	
				WIP	4,000	(P/L)	2,000
						Balance c/d	5,000
Cost P/L					7,000		7,000
Finished		Sales	2,500				
goods	2,000			Balance b/d	5,000		
Cost profit							
c/d	500						
	2,500		2,500				

Trial Balance – Tiny Ltd.
as at 31/1/. . . . . . .

Financial P/L	500	Cost profit b/d	500			

					£	£
Work-in-Progress				Capital		10,000
Balance	2,000	Finished		Creditors		2,400
Wages	1,000	goods	4,000	Debtors	1,350	
Raw		Capital		Bank		500
materials	3,000	expenditure	500	Cost control:		
Overheads	1,130	Balance c/d	2,630	RM	1,000	
	7,130		7,130	WIP	2,630	
Balance b/d	2,630			FG	5,000	8,630
				Fixed assets		3,470
				P/L appropriation		550
				£	13,450	13,450

7. *Reconciliation Statement*

	£	£
Profit as per cost accounts:		19,770
Add:		
Selling expenses difference £(7,500 – 7,100)	400	
Discounts received (not in cost accounts)	260	
Profit on sale of land (not in cost accounts)	2,340	3,000
		22,770

Subtract:

Closing stock difference £(4,280 – 4,080)	200	
Works expenses difference £(12,130 – 10,500)	1,630	
Administration expenses difference £(5,340 – 5,000)	340	
Depreciation difference £(1,100 – 800)	300	2,470
Profit as per financial accounts		£20,300

Progress test 6

9.

Cost element	Opening WIP	Period cost	Total cost	Complete units	Work-in-progress			Total equivalent units	CPU	WIP value
					Units	%	Equivalent			
	£	£	£						£	£
Material	29,600	112,400	142,000	28,000	12,000	100	12,000	40,000	3.550	42,600
Wages	6,600	33,400	40,000	28,000	12,000	$33\frac{1}{3}$	4,000	32,000	1.250	5,000
Overhead	5,800	30,200	36,000	28,000	12,000	$33\frac{1}{3}$	4,000	32,000	1.125	4,500
Total	42,000	176,000	218,000						5.925	52,100

Total value completed output = 28,000 at £5.925 = £165,900

(Input/output cross-check: £165,900 + £52,100 = £218,000.)

10. From the information in the answer to Question 9 above, the 8,000 units lost can only affect the completed units.

Now value of 8,000 units = 8,000 x £5.925 = £47,400

∴ Extra cost per unit to be charged to remaining completed good units = $\frac{£47,400}{20,000}$ = £2.370

∴ Complete cost per unit = £5.925 + £2.370 = £8.295.

The work-in-progress value remains the same, as such work has not reached the rejection point and cannot, therefore, carry any of the costs of such losses.

11.

Cost element	Cost	Complete units	WIP Units	WIP % complete	WIP Equiv units	Normal loss Units	Normal loss % complete	Normal loss Equiv units	Abnormal loss Units	Abnormal loss % complete	Abnormal loss Equiv units	Total equiv units	CPU	Normal loss	Abnormal loss	WIP
	£												£	£	£	£
Input	14,700	3,930	800	100	800	150*	100	150	120	100	120	5,000	2.940	441	353	2,352
Materials	13,830	3,930	800	75	600	150	66⅔	100	120	66⅔	80	4,710	2.936	294	235	1,762
Labour	6,555	3,930	800	50	400	150	33⅓	50	120	33⅓	40	4,420	1.483	74	59	593
Overheads	7,470	3,930	800	25	200	150	16⅔	25	120	16⅔	20	4,175	1.789	45	36	358
	42,555												9.148	854	683	5,065
Scrap: 270 @ £1	−270													−150	−120	
Total	42,285												9.148	704	563	5,065
															17	116
															580	5,181

Normal loss of £704 shared out equally between all units that passed the loss point, i.e. all units except the normal loss units.

$$\text{CPU loss} = \frac{704}{5,000 - 150} = 0.145$$

Final CPU £ 9.293

Charge for normal lost units:
120 units abnormal loss and 800 units WIP @ £0.145

Value check

	£
Completed units = 3,930 x £9,293	= 36,522
Abnormal units transferred	= 580
Work-in-process	= 5,181
Total (as per Total cost bar £2)	= 42,283

*Since all the WIP units have passed the point of rejection; then 5,000 units reached this point and the 3% normal loss must be based on this number.

12. Total joint cost = £31,200 + £13,800 = £45,000.

	Product A	*Product B*
Sales	£38,000	£42,000
Selling costs	5,000	20,000
Net realizable value	33,000	22,000
Join cost apportionment (ratio of 3:2)	27,000	18,000
Profit	£6,000	£4,000

Progress test 7

10. In this question the variable from which an estimate is to be made is the dependent, y, variable and so y must be substituted for z in the general regression formula given in **4**. Hence the appropriate formulae are:

$$d = \frac{n\Sigma xy - \Sigma x\Sigma y}{n\Sigma y^2 - (\Sigma y)^2}$$

$$c = \frac{\Sigma x - d\Sigma y}{n}$$

The layout in **5** gives all the necessary figures except Σy^2 which is $54^2 + 45^2 + 64^2 + 55^2 + 59^2 + 50^2 + 63^2 + 62^2 = 25,856$. So:

$$d = \frac{8 \times 2,107.6 - 36.7 \times 452}{8 \times 25,856 - 452^2} = 0.1071$$

$$c = \frac{36.7 - 0.1071 \times 452 \cdot}{8} = -1.464$$

$$\therefore \quad x = -1.464 + 0.1071y$$

So when $y = 63$ then $x = -1.464 + 0.1071 \times 63 = 5.283$, i.e. 5,283 hours.

11. In this situation the learning index (where 'time' is measured in minutes) is:

$$\begin{aligned} i &= (\log y - \log a)/\log x = (\log (5 \times 60/30) - \log 20) / \log 30 \\ &= (\log 10 - \log 20)/\log 30 = (1 - 1.301)/1.477 \\ &= 0.204 \end{aligned}$$

So learning curve is $y = 20x^{-0.204}$, or $y = 20/x^{0.204}$.

(a) The learning curve can be drawn from the following computations:

x	$x^{0.204}$	$y = 20/x^{0.204}$
1	1.00	20.0
5	1.39	14.4
10	1.60	12.5
20	1.84	10.9
30	2.00	10.0
40	2.12	9.4
60	2.31	8.7
80	2.44	8.2
90	2.50	8.0
100	2.56	7.8

For curve, *see* Fig. **A3.1**.

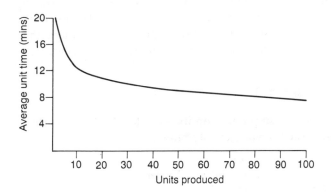

Figure A3.1 *Progress test 7, question 11(a) — learning curve*

(b) If the average time per unit for 100 units is 7.8 minutes then the total time is 7.8 x 100 = 780 minutes.

∴ Total cost = £10 x 780/60 = £130

(c) From the table in (a) it can be seen that the average unit time for 90 units is 8 minutes. So the total time is 8 x 90 = 720 minutes. Since it takes 780 minutes to produce all 100 units (*see* (b)), then the time to complete

> the last 10 units must be $780 - 720 = 60$ minutes $= 1$ hour. So average unit time $= 6$ minutes.

12. A scattergraph analysis indicates that C and D are the least likely cost-drivers and while the A and B figures provide some grounds for their consideration the best driver would appear to be D. The fact that there is a *negative* link between potential driver and cost does not mean the factor cannot 'win' — all it means is that it drives the cost in a negative direction so that as it increases the cost reduces. And such a situation can arise where the cost is the cost of an after-sales service and the cost-driver is hours of inspection on the final product. This certainly can be the case here if the D figures are, in fact, the average monthly hours spent on such inspection.

(Note that a more sophisticated analysis, outside the scope of this book, will show that the best driver is actually E, for if the symbol for the E figures is designated as y then applying the formula $100 \times (100y)^{0.25} + 10,000$ will predict the x cost figure for the period *following*. This less obvious application of the technique of estimation indicates that it is a technique that must be employed with a great deal of thoughtful analysis.)

Progress test 8

7. The first step is to identify those levels of activity that lie outside the relevant activity range.

Period	Interview conducted (No.)	Analyses prepared (pages)
1	6,290 *	310
2	4,550	200 *
3	6,200	600 *
4	4,630	480
5	6,200	400
6	3,800	440
7	3,560 *	440
8	4,770	330
Total	40,000	3,200

Mean	5,000	400
Mean +25%	6,250	500
Mean −25%	3,750	300

*Levels found to lie outside the relevant activity range and so ignored in the analysis.

The second step is to sketch roughly the two scattergraphs resulting from using each of the possible activity measures and to see which measure is the more closely associated with the cost. Such sketches at once show that number of interviews conducted is the better activity measure of the two.

The third step is to prepare more carefully the scattergraph showing cost plotted against number of interviews conducted. The line of best fit is then drawn on the graph. From this (or by computing the regression line) it can be seen that there is a fixed cost element of about £10,300 (computed, £10,350) and a variable cost per interview element of about £2 (computed, £2.09).

The final step is to compute the required predicted cost for period 9 as follows (using computed figures):

Predicted cost = 10,350 + 2.09 × 4,000 = £18,710

NOTE: If the interviews conducted are added to the pages of analysis prepared to give an artificial activity unit then an even better activity measure results since analysing the cost in this situation (again after excluding levels outside the relevant range) gives a scattergraph with a perfect straight line fit of the points. From this graph it will be seen that there is a fixed cost element of £10,000 and a variable cost element of £2 per activity unit. Applying these new costs to the period 9 expectations gives a predicted cost of 10,000 + 2 × (4,000 + 480) = £18,960.

Though in the normal way interviews conducted and pages prepared cannot be added, if it so happens that together they provide a variable that is highly correlated with cost then they can legitimately be added together for the purpose of creating an activity unit.

Progress test 10

7.

	Existing machine*	New machine*
Alternative		
Cash in:†		
Receipts from production	£50,000	£60,000
Residual value	4,000	2,000
From sale of existing machine	—	10,000
	+£54,000	+£72,000
Cash out:		
Cash running costs	45,000	30,000
Purchase of new machine	—	30,000
	−£45,000	−£60,000
Net cash flow	+£9,000	+£12,000

*Take one alternative at a time and consider what cash would actually flow in and out if that alternative were the one selected.
†Take all figures over the full life of the project, i.e. five years.

Since the net cash flow from the new machine is higher than that from the existing, the correct decision is *to replace the existing machine*.

It should be noted that the book value of £24,000 for the existing machine does not enter the computation anywhere. It is important to appreciate that book values relate to book-keeping only and *have no relevance whatsoever in decision-making*. Only actual current and future economic values should be used in this type of work.

8. In the situation in question the following figures will remain unchanged whether the new machine is purchased or not: the total contract income; the cost price of the existing machine (£22,000); the fixed production and selling overheads (£40,000 and £80,000); the variable selling overheads. The decision, therefore, can be made by ascertaining which is the lower of the remaining two sets of costs, i.e.:

	Existing machine £	New machine £
Direct material, per unit	1.50	1.57½ [(a)]
Direct labour, per unit	1.00	0.80 [(b)]
Variable production overheads (60% direct labour)	0.60	0.48
Total variable cost per unit	3.10	2.85½
∴ Total variable cost for 200,000 units	620,000	571,000
Additional machine purchase costs	0 [(c)]	31,000 [(d)]
Residual machine value	–2,000	0
Total differential cost	£618,000	£602,000

∴   Since new machine has the lowest differential cost it should be purchased.

NOTES:
(a) £1.50 + 5 per cent
(b) If 25 per cent more units can be produced per hour, then cost drops by 20 per cent (not 25 per cent).
(c) No *additional* cost for keeping existing machine.
(d) £36,000 – £5,000 trade-in allowance.

9.

Alternative:	Old Product	New Product
Volume of production and sales p.a. (units):	5,000	20,000[*]
Income per year	£200,000	£320,000
Direct material cost per year	£20,000	£120,000

[*]Since the labour time per unit of the new product is only a quarter that of the old, four times as many units can be made in a year.

Additional fixed cost per year	—		12,000	
	20,000	20,000	132,000	132,000
Net differential income*		£180,000		£188,000

*No other figures are needed to determine the net differential income as all other amounts (labour and normal fixed costs) remain unchanged. The unrecovered tooling cost is quite irrelevant (though if the tools had any scrap value this would have been a credit to the *new* product).

Since new product shows highest net differential income it should be manufactured in lieu of the old product.

10. Limit of own production – 200 tonnes material = 100 halves.

Alternative: Sales		Both halves made 100 units		R.h. halves bought 200 units
Sales at £200 per unit		£20,000		£40,000
Assembly costs at £20 per unit	£2,000		£4,000	
Transport costs	—		400	
	2,000	2,000	4,400	4,400
Net differential income* (excluding cost of bought halves)		£18,000		£35,600

*Casting costs do not enter the analysis for whichever alternative is selected they will be the same, i.e. 200 halves will be cast in either event.

Since the relative differential income when the halves are bought (excluding purchase price) is 35,600 – 18,000 = £17,600, then the foundry could afford to pay up to £17,600 for these halves.

∴ since 200 right-hand halves will be required, maximum price will be 17,600/200 = £88 per r.h. half.

11. (*a*) If the machine were sold to VW Ltd then AB would sacrifice the following opportunity costs relating to disposals:

Sale of P to scrap merchant		£6,000
Sale of Q to scrap merchant	£4,000	
Less Preparation costs — 120 x £3	360	3,640
Scrapping of R		−1,200 [i]
Sale of design and specifications		3,000
		£11,440

Also by converting rather than scrapping AB will incur the following additional opportunity costs:

Conversion materials used ex stock — cash sacrifice to be made on replacement	£7,600
Contribution from work that would otherwise be done in Department L — 3 x 4 x 300 x £2.50	9,000
Direct labour and variable overheads in Department M	0 [ii]
	£16,600

Finally, AB will incur the following normal future costs on conversion:

Marginal costs:	
Department L Direct labour – 3 x 4 x £300	£3,600 [b][iii]
Identifiable fixed costs:	
Temporary supervision	1,800
	£5,400

Summary:

Opportunity costs:	
Arising from scrapping machine	£11,440
Arising from converting machine	16,600
Future costs to be incurred	5,400
Total cost of converting machine for sale to VW Ltd	£33,440
∴ Minimum price that AB should accept for the machine	= £33,440

NOTES:

(i) Since selling the machine to VW Ltd will result in this disposal cost being avoided, then the £1,200 is a negative opportunity cost.

(ii) Since the direct labour in this department has spare time during which nothing else can be done but must nevertheless be paid for, the opportunity cost of using this labour is zero (*see* also (*b*)(*ii*)).

(*b*) The following assumptions have been made.
   (*i*) The only disposal cost of the machine is the cost of scrapping the type R material, e.g. there would be no costs of scrapping the machine.
   (*ii*) Variable overheads continue to be incurred even when the direct labour is idle.
   (*iii*) The £2.50 per £1 of labour figure given in (*c*) of the question is a contribution towards the variable as well as the fixed overheads.

Although the style of the question indicates that the examiner is probably looking for an opportunity-costs form of solution, it should be noted that a differential cash flow format could possibly be a simpler approach. Certainly such an approach avoids mixing different kinds of costs which the student may well find confusing. Below, then, the answer is re-presented using this format.

Machine Scrapped

Differential Cash Flow In [i]		*Differential Cash Flow Out*	
Sale of P	£6,000	Preparation costs of Q	£360
Sale of Q	4,000	Scrapping of R	1,200
Sale of design and specifications	3,000		
Added value from Dept L	12,600 [ii]		
	£25,600		£1,560

Net cash flow   £+24,040

Machine Converted

Differential cash flow out:	
Future cash to be spent replacing materials	£7,600
Temporary supervision	1,800
Net cash flow	£–9,400

Differential Net Cash Flow

Machine scrapped	£+24,040
Machine converted	−9,400
Differential NCF	£33,440

∴ If the cash flow in from sale to VW Ltd does not reach £33,440, it is more profitable to scrap the machine than to sell it.

NOTES:

(*i*) *Differential cash flow*, i.e. any cash flow that remains unchanged whether machine is scrapped or converted is ignored. Since all direct labour and variable overheads fall into this category they are excluded along with the fixed overheads.

(*ii*) Perhaps the only figure that really calls for careful thought. It is made up of the direct labour (3 X 4 X £300 = £3,600) and the contribution loading (3,600 X £2.50 = £9,000) that would be charged to other customers in respect of the work that would be displaced by the conversion alternative, i.e. if the conversion were to be carried out this cash flow in would not arise.

Progress test 11

13. (*a*) If 16,000 chairs represent 80 per cent capacity then full capacity is 20,000. The order for 3,000 chairs, then, can be met within the existing capacity and is equal to 15 per cent of capacity. So the *additional* variable costs of the order can be calculated as follows (all figures £000s):

Cost element	Total cost	Fixed element	Variable element at 80%	at 15%
Materials	192	0	192	36
Labour	196	20	176	33
Overheads	200	40	160	30
TOTAL	588	60	528	99

∴ 3,000 extra chairs will have a marginal cost of £99,000/3000 = £33 per chair — i.e. each *additional* chair manufactured will give rise to an additional £33 costs.

(*i*) At a selling price of £30 the organization will, therefore, make a loss.

(*ii*) At a selling price of £36 the organization will make a contribution from the 3000 chairs of 3000 x (36 – 33) = £9,000 — and will, therefore, make an additional £9,000 profit by accepting the order.

(*b*) By accepting this order the total production will reach 19,000 chairs — i.e. there will only be spare capacity for another 1,000 chairs. So the most important factor to be taken into consideration before the order is accepted is whether or not an even better order may become available — an order which, given the near-full capacity working, would have to be passed over.

Other factors involve consideration of delivery costs (it is, after all, an overseas order), the reliability of the customer re payment and the possibility of exchange rate movements.

14. (*a*) In view of the scarcity of labour, labour hours are obviously a key factor. Since any new work undertaken by the company will entail diverting labour from the standard product (for which there is a heavy demand) the first thing that must be done is find the contribution per hour sacrificed by such a diversion:

Standard product

Selling price of product		£120
Marginal cost: Materials	£48	
Labour: 2 hrs at £6	12	60
Contribution		60
Contribution per labour hour		£30

(*b*) The next step is to determine whether to make or buy the special component in the event of accepting the contract:

Make cost for component:

Materials	£240
Labour: 12 hrs at £6	72
Opportunity cost: 12 hrs at £30	360
Total	£672

Since this component can be purchased for only £600, the company should buy it rather than make it.

(c) Knowing the component will cost £600, the cost of the contract can now be computed:

Contract cost:

Materials	£2,280
Special component	600
Labour: 200 hrs ar £6	1,200
Opportunity cost: 200 hrs at £30	6,000
Total	£10,080

Since the total cost, including lost contribution from the 100 standard units to be displaced, is less than the contract price of £10,800, the contract should be accepted.

(d) *Conclusion.* Management, therefore, will be advised to accept the contract and buy the component from an outside supplier. Company profit as a result will be £10,800 – 10,080 = £720 higher.

NOTE: The fixed costs given in the question are, in fact, irrelevant to the solution. Indeed, since labour is a key factor and will always be used to its maximum, the total company wage bill will be the same whatever production is undertaken, i.e. the wages and fixed overheads can both be regarded as a committed cost to be covered by the sales less the materials. Using this approach, the opportunity cost per labour hour in respect of the standard product is (£120 – 48)/2 = £36. Hence the opportunity cost of the special component is £240 + 12 x £36 = £672 and the contract cost is £2,280 + £600 + 200 x £36 = £10,080 — as before, though more simply calculated.

15.

	Staked tomatoes	Ground tomatoes	Cucumbers	Green beans
Boxes per acre	700	200	150	300
Income per acre:	($)	($)	($)	($)
Price per box	3.86	3.86	4.56	5.68
Income per acre	2,702	772	684	1,704
Marginal cost per box:				
Harvesting and packing labour	0.80	0.72	1.00	1.20
Transport and export	1.30	1.30	1.00	2.40
Marginal cost per box	2.10	2.02	2.00	3.60
Marginal cost per acre:				
Marginal cost per acre for boxes	1,470	404	300	1,080
Materials	189	74	63	108
Growing labour	224	152	93	132
Marginal cost per acre	1,883	630	456	1,320
∴ Contribution per acre	819	142	228	384

These figures show that staked tomatoes are the most profitable. However, on 70 acres only cucumbers and ground tomatoes can be grown. The figures show that cucumbers are the more profitable of these two latter products.

Ideally, then, the farmer should concentrate on staked tomatoes and, where these cannot be grown, cucumbers. Market policy, though, requires him to produce a minimum of 5,000 boxes of each product. His profit, then, is maximized by growing up to 5,000 boxes of ground tomatoes on part of the 70 poor acres and cucumbers on the remaining balance, and similarly growing up to 5,000 boxes of green beans on the $240 - 70 = 170$ other acres and staked tomatoes on the balance of these acres. His production, then, will be scheduled as follows:

	Total acres available	Boxes per acre	Low contribution production Acres required for 5,000 boxes	High contribution production Acres available	Boxes per acre	Boxes
Green beans/ staked tomatoes	170	300	17 *	153	700	107,100
Ground tomatoes/ cucumbers	70	200	25	45	150	6,750

*Rounded up to complete acre.

It is now possible to complete the workings and answers; (*i*) and (*ii*) are given in the table below:

	(*i*) Area to be cultivated (acres)	Contribution per acre ($)	(*ii*) Profit Total contribution ($)
Staked tomatoes	153	819	125,307
Ground tomatoes	25	142	3,550
Cucumbers	45	228	10,260
Green beans	17	384	6,528
Total	240		145,645

Less Fixed costs:	$	
Growing	36,000	
Harvesting	12,000	
Transport and export	12,000	
General administration	40,000	
Notional rent	12,000	112,000
Profit		**$33,645**

16. Table of contributions per module:

		1 Module		2 Modules		
					Contribution	
Range	*Cont. Ratio*	*Sales £*	*Cont. £*	*Sales £*	*Total £*	*2nd module* £*
A	20%	6,750	1,350	12,500	2,500	1,150
B	40%	3,500	1,400	6,300	2,520	1,120
C	25%	4,800	1,200	9,200	2,300	1,100
D	25%	6,400	1,600	10,400	2,600	1,000
E	30%	3,333	1,000	7,334	2,200	N/a[†]

*Contribution from 2 modules — contribution from 1st module =
Additional contribution from 2nd module.
[†]Since in the case of E 2 modules make a *higher* contribution than
double 1, and since it is impossible to have the second without the 1st,
2 modules of E will be selected in preference to 1 (on the basis of the
average contribution from both — i.e. £1,100) unless there is only
space for one more module in which case the 2nd module contribution
is irrelevant and the decision will be based on the £1,000 contribution
arising from selecting the single E module.

Contributions ranked in descending order up to 7 modules
(ascertained by inspecting the contributions shown in the above
table):

			Modules	
Rank	*Contribution*	*Range*	*Number*	*Cumulative no.*
1	£1,600	D	1	1
2	1,400	B	1	2
3	1,350	A	1	3
4	1,200	C	1	4
5	1,150	A	1	5
6	1,120	B	1	6
7	1,100	C	1	7*

*Note that although 2 E modules also have an average of £1,100
contribution, the fact that there is here only space for a single module
means that the single E module must be considered. Since this only has
a contribution of £1,000 it must give way to the 2nd C module as this has
a contribution of £1,100.

(*a*) Range allocation:

Range	Modules	Sales Average £	Sales Total £	Contribution £	Apportionment Operating cost* £	(*b*) Profit £
A	2	6,250	12,500	2,500	1,600	900
B	2	3,150	6,300	2,520	1,600	920
C	2	4,600	9,200	2,300	1,600	700
D	1	6,400	6,400	1,600	800	800
TOTAL	7		34,400	8,920	5,600	3,320

*£5,600/7 = £800 per module.

17. (*a*) Contribution = £5 – £3 = £2 unit.

∴ No. of units to give contribution equal to fixed costs

$$= \frac{10,000}{2} = 5,000 \text{ units} = \text{B/E point.}$$

£40,000 sales must come from $\frac{40,000}{5} = 8,000$ units.

∴ Contribution, 8,000 x £2 = £16,000
Less fixed costs = £10,000

Profit £6,000

(*b*) Contribution = £80,000 – 60,000 = £20,000.

∴ P/V ratio $= \frac{20,000}{80,000} = 25\%.$

∴ Contribution from B/E sales = 25% x 60,000
= £15,000.

∴ Fixed cost = £15,000.

∴ Profit = contribution – fixed costs
= £20,000 – £15,000 = £5,000.

(*c*) Since profit = contribution – fixed costs, then
contribution = profit + fixed costs, i.e. in this case
contribution = £5,000 + £15,000 = £20,000. At the
break-even point contribution from sales equals fixed
costs. As the £20,000 contribution came from £60,000

sales, then £15,000 contribution will come from sales of $\frac{£15,000}{£20,000}$ x £60,000 = £45,000.

Therefore, break-even point = £45,000.

(d) At break-even point the contribution equals the fixed costs. Therefore £80,000 sales would bring in a contribution of £20,000 and so the P/V ratio is 25 per cent. With a P/V ratio of 25 per cent, sales of £100,000 will bring in a total of £25,000 contribution; and after deducting fixed costs of £20,000 the profit remaining is £5,000.

(e) Again, sales of £20,000 brings a contribution equal to the fixed costs, i.e. £10,000. Therefore the P/V ratio is 50 per cent. Since profit is all the contribution earned above the break-even point, the £5,000 profit equals the contribution from sales above break-even. With a P/V ratio of 50 per cent, a contribution of £5,000 is earned from £10,000 sales. Therefore total sales are £10,000 + sales at break-even = £10,000 + £20,000 = £30,000.

18. (a) (i) The total costs for the two periods can be plotted at 10,000 and 12,000 units respectively. By joining these points and extending the line to the *y* axis, the fixed cost is found to be £28,000. Alternatively, the fixed cost can be found as follows:

	Period 1	Period 2	Difference
Total material, labour and overheads	£93,000	£106,000	£13,000
Production (units)	10,000	12,000	2,000

∴ 2,000 extra units incurred additional (i.e. variable) cost of £13,000.

∴ 10,000 units have a variable cost of $\frac{13,000}{2,000}$ x 10,000 = £65,000.

But the *total* cost of 10,000 units = £93,000 (*see* above).

∴ The fixed cost must be 93,000 – 65,000 = £28,000.

(ii) See chart below which shows that the B/E point is 8,000 units.

(*b*) See chart below where:
   (*i*) new break-even = 8,800 units;
   (*ii*) The plan will obviously not be worth operating as long
   as the new total cost exceeds the old. This situation
   holds until the indifference point is reached, i.e. where
   the two cost curves cross. The graph shows that this
   does not occur until the activity reaches 11,600 units.
   Therefore, unless a minimum sales of 11,600 units can
   be achieved the new plan should not be adopted.

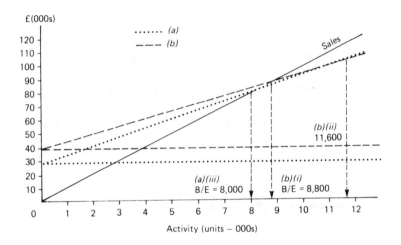

Figure A3.2

NOTE: In examinations the examiners almost invariably want
mathematical-type questions answered on a basis of pure break-even
theory.

19. The answer here depends upon the number of units
involved. It is therefore necessary to find the points of
indifference, noting that at the very lowest numbers A's quote is
the best and that it always pays to take a lower variable cost
quote *providing* that the actual quantity will exceed the point of
indifference.

Supplier	Extra fixed cost (£)	Variable cost savings per unit (£)	Point of indifference (units)
Start with A and consider switch to: B	1,000	5	200
C	3,000	10	300
D	5,000	15	333⅓

∴ Over 200 units, switch to B.

Then consider

switch to:			
C	2,000	5	400
D	4,000	10	400

∴ Over 400 units, switch to D.

So if the actual number is under 200, the supplier should be A; between 200 and 400, the supplier should be B; and over 400, the supplier should be D. Regrettably for C his quote is never better than his competitors.

This problem could also have been solved by plotting all four total cost curves and then selecting at the actual level of activity the supplier whose cost curve was lowest at that point.

NOTE: In this case the points of indifference will be marked by the crossing of the curves.

20. Cost of a set of tyres: our vehicle 4 x £90 = £360;
his vehicle 6 x £80 = £480.

(*a*) Cost of tyres per 1,000 miles:
our vehicle   £360 ÷ 6 = £60;
his vehicle   £480 ÷ 10 = £48.

∴   His customer saves £60 – 48 = £12 per 1,000 miles on tyres but pays £9990 – 9000 = £990 more for the vehicle.

∴   No. of miles customer must travel at a saving of £12 per 1,000 miles to recoup the £990 extra vehicle

$$\text{cost} = \frac{990}{12} \text{ x } 1,000 = 82,500 \text{ miles.}$$

At this distance, then, customer is indifferent as to which vehicle he buys.

(*b*) If the vehicle life is 120,000 miles and his customer

changes his tyres every 10,000 miles then he will have a total cost for 120,000 miles of

$$£9,990 + \frac{120,000}{10,000} \times £480 = £15,750.$$

∴ Total cost to our customer must not exceed £15,750. Now since £9,000 is spent on the vehicle 15,750 − 9000 = £6,750 is available for tyres, which, at £360 a set, allow for $\frac{6750}{360}$ = 18.75 sets*

And since these must cover 120,000 miles the life of a set must be $\frac{120,000}{18.75}$ = 6,400 miles.

If the sales manager were to include a free set of tyres in the price of £9,000, then our customer would still have £6,750 available for tyres which would again buy 18.75 sets. However, since the vehicle starts with a complete set of tyres there will be a total cf 19.75 sets to cover the 120,000 miles — meaning each set requires a life of 120,000/19.75 = 6,076 miles.

*It is assumed that the last set of tyres, still having a quarter of their life left, can be transferred to another vehicle.

21. Since in this question hours are a key factor it suggests that the appropriate solution would involve maximizing the contribution per hour. However, a quicker way is to adopt a more sophisticated differential costing technique.

First it must be noted that it always pays the company to manufacture a component rather than to sub-contract it and have idle time since the marginal costs of all the components are less than the sub-contract prices. Therefore, whichever components are sub-contracted, profit is only maximized when the factory is working at its capacity of 50,000 hours. This in turn means that whatever sub-contracting is done, the combined labour and variable overheads will *always* be 50,000 × (£4.40 + £1.60) = £300,000. If this figure is added to the fixed cost of £140,000 we see that whatever alternative is selected we will always have constant costs of £440,000 in respect of labour and overheads, and therefore these factors can be ignored in our analysis.

All this means that we need only take into consideration material costs and sub-contract prices. Note next that if the company makes a component as against sub-contracting it, the only additional cost will be the material cost and so the only saving will be the difference between the material cost and the sub-contract price. Such a saving, however, is only obtained at the expense of using valuable key factor hours. This shows that profit will be maximized *by maximizing the savings per hour*. This approach will underlie our solution to this question.

(a) Note that currently the sub-contracted price of a complete suite [(1 x 200) + (2 x 80) + (4 x 60) = £600] exactly equals the selling price. If, then, we sub-contract all the components the sales income will exactly cover our sub-contract costs no matter how many suites are sold. Let us assume we adopt this approach and at the same time have the factory *working at capacity producing nothing*. Our factory costs will clearly be our constant cost of £440,000 (no material costs will be incurred in such a situation) and our loss, therefore, also £440,000.

Next let us compute the saving we can make by manufacturing components instead of sub-contracting them and find the saving per hour (remember material costs only are the additional factory costs incurred):

	Settee	Armchair	Armless chair
Sub-contract price saved	£200	£80	£60
Direct material cost incurred	£80	£40	£44
Saving per component	£120	£40	£16
Hours required per component	10	5	1
Saving per hour	£12	£8	£16

Making armless chairs maximizes our saving. However, only 8,000 x 4 = 32,000 chairs are required to meet current sales. These chairs will use only 32,000 of our 50,000 hours and so 18,000 hours can be allocated to the next most profitable alternative, namely manufacturing settees. In 18,000 hours 1,800 settees will be made, leaving 6,200 to be sub-contracted.

The company therefore should manufacture 32,000 armless chairs and 1,800 settees, and should sub-contract 6,200 settees and 16,000 armchairs.

(b) (i) Profit = Saving from manufacture *less* constant costs. Now, savings while manufacturing armless chairs and settees are at £16 and £120 per component respectively. Therefore profit at current level of sales:

$$(32,000 \times £16) + (1,800 \times £120) - £440,000 = \underline{\underline{£288,000}}$$

(ii) If sales are unlimited then profit is maximized by manufacturing armless chairs only. Since the saving per hour is £16, the 50,000 hours available will give a total saving of £800,000 which, after deduction of constant costs of £440,000, leaves a profit of £360,000.

(c) If the selling price drops to £560 then it is no longer true that the selling price of a suite exactly equals its sub-contract cost, and indeed, since we make £40 less contribution per suite, selling 8,000 units would lead to £320,000 less contribution — i.e. it would wipe out all the profit. Now, in this situation we need to see what would happen if we gave up selling one suite. First, note that this would release 4 hours of labour (4 chairs at 1 hour each). These hours we could then devote to reducing the sub-contracted work — for a settee not sub-contracted we would save

$$\frac{4}{10} \times (200 - 80) = £48$$

and for an armchair

$$\frac{4}{5} \times (80 - 40) = £32.$$

In this case, then, we would elect to make 0.4 of a settee and save £48.

Next, we need to compute the loss of contribution from the sale we have given up. Since this particular sale would have involved a sub-contracted settee the contribution lost is $560 - (200 + 2 \times 80 + 4 \times 44) = £24$. This loss is only half the saving so the sacrifice is profitable. And if it is profitable for one sale it is profitable for all sales involving sub-contracted settees. So we can improve the profit by making all our own settees as well as armless chairs.

The analysis continues at the next level, i.e. where we are sub-contracting armchairs only. Now the contribution per suite is $560 - (80 + 2 \times 80 + 4 \times 44) = £144$. If here we give up selling a suite we gain 10 settee hours $+ 4 \times 1$ armless chair hours $= 14$ hours, which allows us to make 14/5 armchairs and so save

$$\frac{14}{5} \times (80 - 40) = £112.$$

In this case, though, the savings do not match the lost contribution of £144 and so we will continue to sub-contract armchairs.

Finally, if we are making settees and armless chairs which together require 14 hours per suite we can only manufacture $50,000/14 = 3,571$ suites (with 6 hours spare). So the profit earned will be:

$$3,571 \times (560 - (80 + 2 \times 80 + 4 \times 44)) - 440,000 = \underline{\underline{£74,224}}$$

(actually, £74,260 since the labour and variable overheads for the six saved hours won't need to be paid for).

NOTE: The solution indicates that in the new situation the most profitable course of action is to reduce sales from 8,000 to 3,571 — i.e., unusually, profit is maximized by cutting sales by over 50 per cent!

Progress test 13

8. Work sheet (*i*)

	Month				
	1	*2*	*3*	*4*	*Total*
Sales: Barrels					
silcpercys (*ii*)	10,000	15,000	20,000	25,000	70,000
Value (£50 + 20%)	£600,000	900,000	1,200,000	1,500,000	4,200,000
FG month end:					
(*iii*) Barrels	10,000	15,000	20,000	0	
FG stock change:					
Barrels	−5,000	+5,000	+5,000	−20,000	

Production (sales + stock change)	5,000	20,000	25,000	5,000	55,000
Purchases: (*iv*)					
Barrels sowzeers	100,000	20,000	120,000(*v*)	0	240,000
Value (£5 +20%)	£600,000	120,000	720,000	0	1,440,000
Marketing costs (£5,000 + 1% sales)	£11,000	14,000	17,000	20,000	62,000
Sales at 5% discount (70%)	£420,000	630,000	840,000	1,050,000	2,940,000
Other sales (30%)	£180,000	270,000	360,000	450,000	1,260,000

Profit budget for first four months

		£	£
Sales: 70,000 barrels* silcpercys at £60			4,200,000
Less discount, 5% of 70% of £4.2m			−147,000
			4,053,000
Costs: Purchases: 240,000 barrels* sowzeers at £6		1,440,000	
Plus 100,000 barrels opening stock (old B/S)		500,000	
340,000		1,940,000	
Less 120,000* barrels closing stock at £6		−720,000	
220,000		1,220,000	
Direct wages: 55,000 barrels silcpercys* at £12 (*vi*)		660,000	
Variable overheads: 50% direct wages (*vii*)		330,000	
Fixed overheads: 66⅔ direct wages (*viii*)		440,000	
Total production cost:	55,000 barrels silcpercys	2,650,000	
Plus Opening stock:	15,000 barrels silcpercys	675,000	
Manufacturing costs of sales:	70,000 barrels silcpercys	3,325,000	
Marketing contract costs*		62,000	
Total costs of sales			3,387,000
Budgeted profit			£666,000

*See work-sheet.

Cash budget.

	Month			
	1	*2*	*3*	*4*
	£	£	£	£
Receipts				
Debtors taking 5% discount,				
70% previous month's sales*	140,000 *(ix)*	420,000	630,000	840,000
Less 5% discount	−7,000	−21,000	−31,500	−42,000
	133,000	399,000	598,500	798,000
Debtors not taking discount, 30%				
of sales 2 months previous*	30,000*(ix)*	60,000 *(ix)*	180,000	270,000
Total	163,000	459,000	778,500	1,068,000
Payments				
RM creditors, previous				
month's purchases*	400,000*(x)*	600,000	120,000	720,000
Direct wages, £12 per				
barrel produced*	60,000	240,000	300,000	60,000
Variable overheads, 50%				
previous month's wages	20,000 *(x)*	30,000	120,000	150,000
Fixed overheads (excl. rent and				
deprec.), previous month	41,667*(x)*	50,000	50,000	50,000
Rent	—	—	110,000	—
Marketing cost, 1 month				
in advance*	14,000	17,000	20,000	8,000*(xi)*
Plant and equipment	—	—	—	100,000
Total	535,667	937,000	720,000	1,088,000
Excess receipts over payments	(372,667)	(478,000)	58,500	(20,000)
Opening cash balance	500,000*(x)*	127,333	(350,667)	(292,167)
Closing cash balance	127,333	(350,667)	(292,167)	(312,167)

*See work sheet.

Budgeted balance sheet.

Assets	£	£
Plant and equipment (900,000 + 100,000)		1,000,000
Less depreciation (⅓ x 10% of £900,000 + £360,000)		−390,000
		610,000
Stocks: RM, 120,000 barrels* sowzeers at £6	720,000	
FG, nil (*iii*)	0	720,000
Debtors: Entitled to 5% discount (month 4 sales)	1,500,000	
Not entitled to discount (30% month 3 sales)	360,000	
	1,860,000	
Less provision for discount (5% of 70% of £1.5m)	−52,500	1,807,500
Prepayments: Marketing costs (*xi*)		8,000
Cash (*xii*)		(312,167)
		£2,833,333
Financed by:		
Head office: Opening balance (*x*)		2,014,833
Plus profit (*xiii*)	666,000	
Plus overhead suspense (*xiv*)	122,500	788,500
Accruals: Variable overheads (50% of £60,000 D. wages, month 4)		30,000
		£2,833,333

*See work sheet.

NOTES (lower case letters refer to question):

(*i*) In any extensive budget exercise it usually proves useful to prepare a work-sheet which lays out the basic operating data.

(*ii*) The planned annual sales must be the old 80,000 + 25 per cent = 100,000 barrels of silcpercys (*a*). These will divide up over the months as follows (*b*):

Month			
1	10%	10,000 barrels
2	15%	15,000
3	20%	20,000
4	25%	25,000
5	5%	5,000
6–12	25%	25,000

(*iii*) (*g*).

(*iv*) Production two months hence (*d*) x 4 (since 4 barrels of sowzeers are needed to make 1 barrel of silcpercys, see *Profit and Loss* in question).

(*v*) Purchases equivalent to sales in months 5–12 (*f*) = (5,000 + 25,000) (*ii*) x 4 = 120,000 barrels.

(*vi*) £10 per barrel (*Profit and Loss* in question) + 20 per cent (*c*).

(*vii*) The *Profit and Loss* in question shows that the variable overheads were 50 per cent of the direct wages. Since both are to increase as a result of inflation by the same percentage this proportion will remain unchanged.

(*viii*) The old fixed overheads were £500,000 excluding £200,000 for depreciation and rent. Inflation will increase these by 20 per cent to £600,000, and adding back the unaffected £200,000 gives a total overhead of £800,000. At the same time the approximate direct wages for the year will be 100,000 (*ii*) x £12 (*vi*) = £1,200,000 ('approximate' since the 100,000 is the budgeted sales and not the budgeted production which will be slightly different if any change in the year-end finished goods stock is planned).

(*ix*) The old balance sheet debtors divide as follows: Paying in month 1 — 70% of £200,000 + £30,000; Paying in month 2 — 30% of £200,000.

(*x*) See old balance sheet.

(*xi*) Sales for month 5 will be 5,000 (*ii*) x £60 = £300,000. Therefore £5,000 + 1 per cent sales = 5,000 + 3,000 = £8,000. This, of course, is a prepayment.

(*xii*) From cash budget.

(*xiii*) From profit budget.

(*xiv*) Probably the most difficult figure in the exercise. The point here is that the profit budget was charged with fixed overheads absorbed on a basis of production whereas for the balance sheet they have to reflect the time periods in which the overheads are incurred, i.e. the prepayments and accruals. Probably the best way to do this is to prepare the Fixed Overhead account. Bearing in mind that the fixed overheads consist of the regular monthly cash overheads, rent and depreciation this account will look as follows:

Fixed Overheads Account

Opening B/S: Rent	27,500	Opening B/S: Accrual	41,667
Cash payments:		P/L (Profit budget)	440,000
Month 1	41,667		
Months 2,3,4,	150,000		
Rent	110,000		
Depreciation (4 months)	30,000		
Balance: Suspense c/d	122,500		
	481,667		481,667
		Suspense b/d	122,500

At the *year* end the balance on this account will be one month's accrued fixed overheads and 3 months' prepaid rent (in a budgeting exercise there is no under- or over-absorption of overheads, of course).

9. (*a*) (Note: It is assumed that the charges relating to employee benefits apply to hourly paid labour only (i.e. that it covers such items as sick and holiday pay, etc.)

Annual costs

Material Handling Department	£	*Maintenance Department*	£
Level 1		*Level 1*	
Labourers: 30 x 40 x 48 x £4	230,400	Engineers: 2 x £18,000	36,000
O/T premium: 30 x 5 x 48 x £2	14,400	Outside contractors	250,000
	244,800		
Employee benefits:			
20% £244,800	48,960		
V. overheads: 30 x 40 x 48 x 12p	6,912		
Incremental cost — Level 1	300,672	*Incremental cost — Level 1*	286,000
Level 2		*Level 2*	
Fork-lift trucks: 10 x £2,000	20,000	Fitters: 10 x £11,000	110,000
Truck labour: 10 x 48 x £155	74,400	Materials	48,000
Employee benefits: 20% £74,400	14,880	Procurement costs	1,200
V. overheads: 10 x 48 x £150	72,000	Overheads	50,000
		Contractor:	
		£160,000 − 250,000	−90,000
Incremental cost — Level 2	181,280	*Incremental cost — Level 2*	119,200

contd

Level 3
Computer lease:

20,000 + 18,000 + 16,200 + 14,580	68,780
Labour saved: 30 x 4 x 48 x £4	-23,040
O/T premium: 30 x 2 x 48 x £2	-5,760
Incremental cost — Level 3	**39,980**

Level 3

Extra fitters: 6 x £11,000	66,000
Extra material	48,000
Procurement costs* : -253 - 1,200	-1,453
Extra overheads	20,000
Contractor: 90,000 - 160,000	-70,000
Incremental costs — Level 3	**62,547**

*Procurement (purchasing and stock-holding) costs:

Purchase order	No. of orders Level		Purchasing cost Level		Average stock	Holding cost Level		Discount Level 3	TOTAL Level	
	2	3	2	3		2 15%	3 13⅓%	2%	2	3
			£	£	£	£	£	£	£	£
4,000	12	24	1,200	N/A	2,000	300	N/A	N/A	1,500	N/A
8,000	6	12	600	1,200	4,000	600	533	N/A	1,200	1,733	←—Minimum Level 2
12,000	4	8	400	800	6,000	900	800	N/A	1,300	1,600
16,000	3	6	300	600	8,000	1,200	1,067	-1,920	1,500	-253	←—Minimum Level 3

(b) *Costs and desirability factor:*

MATERIAL HANDLING					MAINTENANCE			
LEVEL	Cost – £	Factor	Score	Ranking	Cost – £	Factor	Score	Ranking
1	300,672	1.00	300,672	1	286,000	1.00	286,000	2
2	181,280	0.60	108,768	3	119,200	0.80	95,360	4
3	39,980	0.50	19,990	5	62,547	0.20	12,509	6

Cumulative incremental costs in order of rankings:

Ranking:	1	2	3	4	5	6
Incremental cost (£)	300,672	286,000	181,280	119,200	39,980	62,547
Cumulative cost (£)	300,672	586,672	767,952	887,152	927,132	989,679
					Cut-off	

So to remain within budget total of £925,000, both the Material Handling Department and the Maintenance Department budgets can be implemented up to and including Level 2.

Progress test 14

12. (*a*) Control plans:
Flexible budget: Dept 1:

Overhead	Budget	Fixed	Variable	Variable per process hour
	Budgeted activity — 25,000 process hours			
	£	£	£	£
Fixed	55,000	55,000	—	—
Variable	125,000	—	125,000	5
	180,000	55,000	125,000	5

Standard fixed overhead rate:
£55,000/25,000 = £2.20 per process hour.

Flexible budget: Dept. 2:

Overhead	Budget	Fixed	Variable	Variable per ind. lab. hr.
	Budgeted activity — 2,000 indirect labour hours			
	£	£	£	£
Fixed	14,000	14,000	—	—
Variable	8,000	—	8,000	4
	22,000	14,000	8,000	4

Standard fixed overhead rate:
£14,000/2,000 = £7 per indirect labour hour.

Flexible budget: Marketing:

	Budgeted activity — 1,000 containers			
Overhead	Budget	Fixed	Variable	Variable per container sold
	£	£	£	£
Fixed	60,000	60,000	—	—
Variable	50,000	—	50,000	50
	110,000	60,000	50,000	50

Standard fixed overhead rate: £60,000/1,000 = £60 per container.

Standard cost — 1 15-gal container of Z.

	£
Dept. 1: D. mats: 20 gal of A at £3 per gal	60
D. lab.: Grade I 15 hrs at £6 per hr	90
Grade II 10 hrs at £3 per hr	30
V. overheads: 25 process hrs at £5 per hr	125
F. overheads: 25 process hrs at £2.20 per hr	55
Standard cost: 15 gal Z*	360
Dept. 2: D. mats: 1 container at £8	8
D. lab.: 6 hrs at £4 per hr	24
V. overheads: 2 hrs at £4 per hr	8
F. overheads: 2 hrs at £7 per hr	14
Standard factory cost: 1 15-gal container Z	414
Marketing: V. Overheads	50
F. Overheads	60
Standard total cost	524
Standard profit	76
Standard selling price	£600

*Standard yield 75 per cent. Note that the standard cost of output is £360/15 = £24 per gal Z.

Control profit budget for year	£
Budgeted profit 1,000 15-gal containers Z	
at £76 profit each	76,000

(*b*) *Control profit budget for first period*

£

Budgeted profit ($1\frac{1}{10}$ of year): 100 15-gal
    containers Z at £76 profit each   <u>7,600</u>

Progress test 15

10 and 11.
All units: Question 10 — gallons at a standard price of £2.5 per gallon.
            Question 11 — hours at a standard rate of £4 per hour.

Quest	Variance Name	Allowance Units	Actual Units	Divergence Units	Allowance £	Actual £	Variance £
10(*a*)	Material price	*	24	*	60	60	0
	Material usage	20	24	4	*	*	10A
(*b*)	Material price	*	20	*	50	70	20A
	Material usage	20	20	0	*	*	0
(*c*)	Material price	*	24	*	60	84	24A
	Material usage	20	24	4	*	*	10A
(*d*)	Material price	*	18	*	45	50	5A
	Material usage	20	18	2	*	*	5F
11(*a*)	Labour rate	*	110	*	440	385	55F
	Labour efficiency	100	110	10	*	*	40A
(*b*)	Labour rate	*	95	*	380	368	12F
	Labour efficiency	100	95	5	*	*	20F

* = Column not applicable

12. Standard cost 6 cu ft HO₅:

	£
1 cu ft H at £0.50	0.50
5 cu ft O at £0.05	0.25
$\underline{6}$	<u>£0.75</u>

Actual input at standard price:

	£
10,200 cu ft H at £0.50	5,100
57,600 cu ft O at £0.05	2,880
67,800	£7,980

Allowed cost of 67,800 cu ft input =

$$\frac{67,800}{6} \times 0.75 = \underline{£8,475}$$

Materials mix variance   £495 F

> NOTE: Favourable mixture variances should not really be allowed to occur; they do not so much indicate a saving as an adulterated product (since an excessive quantity of the cheaper component has been allowed into the final product).

13.

Standard cost card for MUD:	£
1 tonne M at £1	1
1 tonne U at £2	2
3 tonnes D at £3	9
5 tonnes input	12
− 1 tonne 20% loss	—
4 tonnes (80% yield) MUD	£ 12

∴   1 tonne MUD has standard cost of £12/4 = £3.

		Allowed cost	Actual cost	Price variance
Actual mix at standard prices:		£	£	£
M	1,100 tonnes at £1	1,100	1,000	100F
U	1,000 tonnes at £2	2,000	2,200	200A
D	2,900 tonnes at £3	8,700	8,888	188A
	5,000 tonnes	£11,800	£12,088	£288A

Allowed cost of 5,000 tonnes of input   =

$$\frac{5,000}{5} \times £12 \qquad = \qquad £12,000$$

∴   *Materials mix variance*   =   £200F

Allowed yield from 5,000 tonnes input

= 5,000 x 80% =	4,000 tonnes
Actual yield =	3,815
Difference	185A
∴ Yield variance = 185 tonnes at £3 =	£555A

∴   *Total materials variance* = £288A + £200F +£555A =   £643A

NOTE: Cross-check: Total actual cost =   £12,088
Allowed cost of actual output = 3,815 x £3 =   £11,445

Total variance   £643A

14.

Variable overhead allowance for 11,340 articles

= 11,340 x 10p =	£1,134
Actual overhead cost	1,521
Total overhead variance	£387A

Analysis of variance:
No. of invoices allowed for 11,340 articles

= 11,340 ÷ 5 =	2,268
Actual no. of invoices	2,504
Difference (excess invoices)	236
Standard variable cost per invoice	50p*
∴ *Variable overhead efficiency variance* = 236 x 50p =	£118A

Expenditure allowance for 2,504 invoices

= 2,504 x 50p* =	£1,252
Actual expenditure	1,521
∴ *Overhead expenditure variance*	£269A

*If each article has standard variable overhead of 10p and if 5 articles are planned per invoice, then the standard cost per invoice (i.e. unit of activity) is 50p.

15.

	Chairs	Tables	Total (£)
Allowed sales value	3,100 x £5	1,200 x £30	
	= £15,500	=£36,000	51,500
Actual sales value	£15,215	£35,682	50,897
∴ *Selling price variance*	£285 A	£318 A	£603A
Allowed (budgeted) sales quantities	4,000	1,000	
Actual sales quantities	3,100	1,200	
Differences	900 A	200 F	
Standard profit	£3	£13	
∴ *Sales volume margin variance*	£2,700 A	£2,600 F	£100A

16. (The student should refer to the control plans detailed in the answer to question 12 of Progress test 14.)

Profit variance	£
Budgeted profit	7,600
Actual profit	3,046
Total profit variance	£4,554A

Variance analysis
Materials price variance:

	A		Containers	
		£		£
Allowed cost of actual purchases	2,500 gals		100 conts.	
	A x £3 = 7,500		x 8 = 800	
Actual cost		7,720		794
Materials price variance		£220A		£6F

Materials usage variance:

A: Allowed usage for 1,610 gal Z = $\dfrac{1,610}{15}$ x 20 = 2,146 ⅔ gal

Actual usage = 2,500 − 320 = 2,180 gal

Excess usage 33⅓ gal

Standard price £3

∴ *Materials usage variance* (A) = 33⅓ x £3 = £100A

Containers: Allowed usage for 98 15-gal
           containers   = 98 containers
           Actual usage   = 100 − 1   = 99

           Excess usage   1

           Standard price   £8
∴   *Materials usage variance (containers)*   £8 A

Z: Allowed usage for 98 15-gal
        containers = 98 x 15   = 1,470 gal
        Actual usage = 1,610 — 140   = 1,470 gal

        Difference   *Nil*

∴   No material usage variance in respect of Z arises.

Labour rate variance:

| | Dept. 1 | | Dept. 2 |
	Grade I	Grade II	
Allowed wages	1,470½ hrs x £6 = £8,823	1,050 hrs x £3 = £3,150	625 hrs x £4 = £2,500
Actual wages	£8,888	£3,124	£2,451
∴ *Labour rate variance*	£65A	£26F	£49F

Labour efficiency variance:

	Grade I	Grade II
Dept 1:		
Allowed hrs for 1,610 gal Z	$\frac{1,610}{15}$ x 15 =	$\frac{1,610}{15}$ x 10 =
	1,610	1,073⅓
Actual hrs	1,470½	1,050
Difference (saving)	139 ½	23 ⅓
Standard wage rate	£6	£3
∴ *Labour efficiency variance*	£837F	£70 F

Dept 2:
  Allowed hrs for 98 15-gal containers
    Z = 98 × 6 =   588
  Actual hrs   625
  Excess hrs $\overline{37}$
  Standard wage rate   £4
  ∴   *Labour efficiency variance*   £148 A

Overhead expenditure variance:

	Dept. 1	Dept. 2	Marketing
Activity measure	Process hrs	Ind. lab. hrs	Containers
Actual units of activity	2,550	200½	95
Standard variable overhead per unit(a)	£5	£4	£50
Variable overhead allowance	£12,750	£802	£4,750
Fixed overhead allowance(b): ($\frac{1}{10}$ budgeted for year)	£5,500	£1,400	£6,000
Total overhead allowance	£18,250	£2,202	£10,750
Actual overhead	£18,540	£2,101	£14,990
∴ *Overhead expenditure variance*	£290 A	£101F	£4,240 A

Variable overhead efficiency variance:
Dept. 1:   Allowed activity for 1,610 gal Z =

$$\frac{1,610}{15} \times 25 \ = \ 2,683\tfrac{1}{3} \text{ process hrs}$$

          Actual activity   ·   2,550 process hrs
          Saving $\overline{133\tfrac{1}{3}}$ process hrs
          Standard variable cost per process
            hour   £5

          ∴   *Variable overhead efficiency*
               variance (Dept. 1)   £666⅔F

Dept. 2:   Allowed activity for 98 15-gal
              containers = 98 × 2   = 196   ind. lab. hrs
           Actual activity   200½ ind. lab. hrs
           Excess activity $\overline{4\tfrac{1}{2}}$ ind. lab. hrs
           Standard variable cost per ind.
             lab. hr   £4

∴   *Variable overhead efficiency*
    variance (Dept. 2)   £18A

NOTE: No variable overhead efficiency variance can arise in the case of the Marketing Department since activity is there measured in cost units.

Fixed overhead variances:

	Dept. 1	*Dept. 2*	*Marketing*
Activity measure	Process hours	Ind. lab. hours	Containers
Budgeted activity	2,500	200	100
Actual activity	2,550	200½	95
Difference	50F	½F	5 A
Stnd. overhead rate	£2.20	£7	£60
Capacity variance	£110F	£3½F	£300 A
Actual production	1,610 gals	98 containers	Not applicable — activity measure same
Allowed hours	$\frac{1,610}{15}$ x 25	98 x 2	as cost unit (*see* note to **18**)
	= 2,683⅓	=196	
Actual hours	2,550	200½	
Difference	133⅓F	4½A	
Stnd. overhead rate	£2.20	£7	
Productivity variance	£293⅓F	£31½A	

Sales profit variances: £

Price: Allowed sales value for 95 15-gal
         containers = 95 x £600   = 57,000
         Actual sales value   56,084
     ∴   *Selling price variance*   £916A

Quantity: Allowed sales quantity(c)   100 15-gal containers
          Actual sales quantity   95
          Deficit   5
          Standard profit   £76
     ∴   *Sales volume profit variance*   £380 A

NOTES:
(*a*) *See* flexible budgets in answer to **12**(*a*), Progress test 14.
(*b*) On basis of ten control periods for the year.
(*c*) *See* control profit budget for first period in answer to **12**(*b*), Progress test 14.

SUMMARY:

Variance		£	£
Materials price:	A	220 A	
	Containers	6 F	214 A
Materials usage:	A	100 A	
	Containers	8 A	108 A
Labour rate:	Dept. 1, Grade I	65 A	
	Dept. 1, Grade II	26 F	
	Dept. 2	49 F	10 F
Labour efficiency:	Dept. 1, Grade I	837 F	
	Dept. 1, Grade II	70 F	
	Dept. 2	148 A	759 F
Overhead expenditure:	Dept. 1	290 A	
	Dept. 2	101 F	
	Marketing	4,240 A	4,429 A
Variable overhead efficiency:	Dept. 1	666⅔ F	
	Dept. 2	18 A	648⅔ F
Total variable cost variances			3,333⅓ A
Capacity: Dept. 1		110 F	
Dept. 2		3½ A	
Marketing		300 A	186½ A
Productivity:	Dept. 1	293⅓ F	
	Dept. 2	31½ A	261⅚ F
Selling price		916 A	
Sales volume profit		380 A	1,296 A
Total profit variance			£4,554ADV

17. (*a*) Standard variable cost of 1 15-gal container of Z (*see* answer to question **12**(*a*), Progress test 14):

Dept. 1: Variable cost of 15 gallons Z: 60 + 90 + 30 + 125   £305*
Dept. 2: Variable costs: 8 + 24 + 8   40
Marketing: Variable costs   50
               Total variable costs   395
Standard contribution   205
Standard selling price   £600

*Standard yield 75%. Note that the variable standard cost of output is

$$305/15 = £20\tfrac{1}{3} \text{ per gal Z.}$$

(b) Amendment to actual profit and loss statement in question **16**:

WIP variable cost Dept. 2: 140 gallons Z at £20⅓ = £2,846⅔
FG variable cost: 3 full containers at £(305 + 40) = £1,035

So actual profit = 3,046 − (3,360 − 2,846⅔) − (1,242 − 1,035) = £2,325⅔

(c) The variances are all the same as those in question 16 save for the following:

Total profit variance = 7,600 − 2,325⅔ = £5,274⅓A

Sales volume contribution variance = 5 containers at a standard contribution of £205 = £1,025A

(d) Variance summary:

Total variable cost variances as in
  answer 16, up to and including Variable
  Overhead Efficiency variance   3,333⅓A
Selling price variance (as before)   916A
Sales volume contribution variance — 5 containers
               at £205 contribution   1,025A
                                                                          1,941A

               Total profit variance   £5,274⅓A

18. NOTE: This question and the next involve what can be termed 'reverse' analyses, i.e. the end result of a conventional analysis is given and the question calls for information that in practice would be available before the analysis began. This type of problem, testing as it does the student's grasp of the principles involved, is popular with examiners. Finding the answers, though, essentially calls for no more than finding the missing figures in either of the following equations:

Variance = £(Allowance – actual)

Variance = (Allowance – actual) units × standard cost.

In the working sheet that follows the 'actual' figure is the last to be computed. Note that the non-monetary actuals are needed in order to compute the monetary actuals at later points on the sheet.

Note	Cost element	Variance	Stnd. cost	Difference	Allowance	Actual
(a)	Fixed overhead volume	£1,200	£2.40	500 units	Budgeted quantity = 10,000	10,500 units
	Fixed overhead expenditure	£(800)			10,000 x £2.40 = £24,000	£24,800
(b)	Material usage	£(1,600)	£2	(800)kg	10,500* x 12 kg = 126,000 kg	126,800 kg
(c)	Material price	£5,072			126,800* x £2 = £253,600	£248,528
(b)	Labour efficiency	£960	£6.40	150 hrs	10,500* x 1½ = 15,750 hrs	15,600 hrs
	Wages rates	£(3,120)			15,600* x £6.40 = £99,840	£102,960
(d)	Sales volume margin	£6,000	£12†	500 units	Budgeted quantity = 10,000	10,500 units
	Sales price margin	£(4,000)			10,500* x £48 = £504,000	£500,000

*From 'Actual' column.
†£48 – (24 + 9.6 + 2.4) = £12

NOTES:

(a) Since the material usage and labour efficiency variances depend upon the actual volume of production, this variance needs to be computed first.

(b) To find out the material price and wages rates allowances it is necessary to know the actual material usage and labour hours, so these variances must be computed first.

(c) It is assumed that there is no change in the raw material stocks.

(d) Again, to find the sales price allowance it is necessary to know the actual sales quantity, so this variance must be computed first. Note, too, that since the actual sales quantity equals the actual production there has been no change in the finished goods stocks.

Actual profit statement:

		£	£
Sales			500,000
Cost:	Purchases	248,528	
	Wages	102,960	
	Fixed overheads	24,800	376,288
Actual profit (as per question)			£123,712

19. (*See* note at introduction to question 18.)
Unit selling price = £60 + 20% of selling price = £75.
So budgeted sales and production = 30,000/75 = 400 units.

Working sheet:

Line	Cost element	Variance	Stnd. cost	Difference	Allowance	Actual
(a)	Overhead volume	£375F	£25	15 units	Budgeted prod. = 400	415 units
(b)	Overhead expend	£200F			Budgeted overhead 400 x 25 = £10,000	£9,800
(c)	Materials usage	£375F	£1.5	250 units	415 x 10 = 4,150	3,900 units
(d)	Labour efficiency	£180A	£4	45 hrs	415 x 5 = 2,075	2,120 hrs

In answers below italicized numbers are taken from the question and letters refer to lines in the working sheet.

(i) $\underline{\underline{415 \text{ units}}}$ (a)

(ii) Actual profit = Sales – (materials + wages + overheads)
= *29,880* – (*6,435* + *8,162* + 9,800(b)) = $\underline{\underline{\text{£5,483}}}$

(iii) *6,435*/3,900(c) = $\underline{\underline{\text{£1.65}}}$

(iv) *8,162*/2,120(d) = $\underline{\underline{\text{£3.85}}}$

(v) £9,800(b)

(vi) Overhead absorbed = 2,120(d) x £5 = $\underline{\underline{\text{£10,600}}}$

(vii) Standard hours produced = 415(a) x *5 hours* = 2,075 hrs
Actual hours worked = 2,120(d)
∴ production overhead efficiency variance = (2,120 – 2,075)
x £5 = $\underline{\underline{\text{£225A}}}$

(viii) Allowed sales value = 415(a) x *£75* = £31,125
∴ selling price variance = 31,125 – *29,880* = $\underline{\underline{\text{£1,245A}}}$

(ix) Allowance = *400 units*. Actual = 415(a) units.
∴ sales volume profit variance = (415 – 400) x (*£75* – *£60*)
= $\underline{\underline{\text{£225F}}}$

20. (*a*)

Material and labour variances for period

Cost element	Stnd price	Allowance	Actual	Divergence	Variance £
Material					
Price	£9 kilo	3,770 kilos x £9 = £33,930	£35,815	n/a	1,885 A
Usage	£9 kilo	290 x 12 kilos = 3,480	3,770	290A	2,610 A
Labour					
Rate	£4 hour	2,755 x £4 = £11,020	£11,571	n/a	551 A
Efficiency	£4 hour	290 x 10 hours = 2,900	2,755	145F	580 F
Total					£4,466 A

Cross-check: Standard cost of 1 unit = £9 x 12 + £4 x 10 = £148

$\therefore$ standard cost of 290 units = 290 x £148 =   £42,920
Actual cost of 290 units = £35,815 + £11,571 =   47,386
Total material and labour variances =   £4,466A

These figures should now be re-presented in a format suitable for management as directed in the question.

Progress test 17

1. The cost and variance accounts in answer to this question are given on the following pages. The letters in brackets refer to the explanatory notes given below. (It should, perhaps, be appreciated that providing the basic principles are not violated there are valid alternative ways of making some of the minor book-keeping entries.)

MAIN ACCOUNTS

Raw Material Stores

Purchases(a)	59,200	WIP(b)	54,600
Price var.	800	Breakages	1,440
		Balance c/d	3,960
	60,000		60,000
Balance b/d	3,960		

Work-in-Progress

Materials	54,600	Finished	
Direct wages	35,400	goods(g)	180,000
V. ohds.	18,000	Materials	
F. ohds.	70,800	usage var.(h)	600
Labour effic.			
var.(i)	600		
Productivity			
var.(i)	1,200		

Direct Wages

Cash	36,560	Labour rate	
		var.(c)	960
		Breakdowns(d)	200
		WIP(e)	35,400

Finished Goods

WIP	180,000	P/L(j)	168,000
		Balance c/d	12,000
	180,000		180,000
Balance b/d	12,000		

Variable Overheads

Cash	18,320	WIP(f)	18,000
		Expenditure var.	320

Selling and Distribution Overheads

Cash	28,000	P/L(n)	28,000

Fixed Overheads

Cash	83,600	WIP(k)	70,800
		Expenditure	
		var.(l)	3,600
		Capacity	
		var.(m)	9,200

Cash

Sales	228,400	Mat. purchases	59,200
		Wages	36,560
		V. ohds	18,320
		F. ohds	83,600
		Sell. and	
		Dist. ohds	28,000
		Balance c/d	2,720
	228,400		228,400
Balance b/d	2,720		

Sales

P/L	235,200	Cash	228,400
		Selling	
		price var.(o)	6,800

VARIANCE ACCOUNTS

Direct Materials Price

P/L	800	RM stores	800

Variable Overhead Expenditure

V. ohds	320	P/L	320

Breakages(q)

RM stores	1,440	P/L	1,440

Direct Labour Efficiency

P/L	600	WIP	600

Labour Rate

Direct wages	960	P/L	960

Productivity

P/L	1,200	WIP	1,200

Capacity

F. ohds	9,200	Breakdowns(p)	400
		P/L	8,800

Breakdown(q)

Direct wages	200	P/L	600
Capacity var.	400		

Direct Materials Usage

WIP	600	P/L	600

Fixed Overhead Expenditure

F. ohds	3,600	P/L	3,600

Selling Price

Sales	6,800	P/L	6,800

FINAL ACCOUNTS

Profit and Loss Account

FG: Cost of Sales	168,000	Sales	235,200
Selling and Distribution	28,000		
Adverse variances:		*Favourable variances:*	
Breakages	1,440	Direct materials price	800
Labour rate	960	Direct labour efficiency	600
Capacity	8,800	Productivity	1,200
V. ohds expenditure	320		
Breakdowns (*q*)	600		
Direct material usage	600		
F. ohds expenditure	3,600		
Selling price	6,800		
Net profit to			
Appropriation	18,680		
	237,800		237,800

Appropriation Account

P/L	18,680

(a) 'Actual purchases' figure shown in this account for simplicity.
(b) 4,550 at £12.
(c) £36,560 – 4,450 at £8.
(d) 25 hours at £8.
(e) 4,425 hours at £8.
(f) 900 at £20. (The allowance here is not based on hours but on production as indicated by the note on the standard cost card.)
(g) 900 at £200.
(h) Allowed usage (900 x 5) – 4,550 = 50 at £12.
(i) (900 x 5) – 4,425 = 75 hours at the appropriate rate.
(j) Allowed cost of sales, i.e. 840 at £200.
(k) Since there were 25 hours breakdowns, only 4,450 – 25 = 4,425 hours were production hours. So the WIP charge is 4,425 at £16.
(l) Budgeted fixed overheads clearly must have been 1,000 x £80 = £80,000 (i.e. budgeted set production x standard fixed overheads per set). Therefore the expenditure variance = £80,000 – £83,600.
(m) 5,000 budgeted hours – 4,425 production hours, at £16.
(n) By tradition no variance extracted, although if the question had indicated the degree of variability of this cost it would have been advisable to see if a variance could be calculated and extracted.
(o) £228,400 – (840 at £280).

(p) Fixed overheads chargeable to breakdowns = 25 hours at £16. (This step is optional.)

(q) Since no breakages or breakdowns were 'planned' these costs are, in effect, variances and so have been included among the variances.

Note that this traditional form of standard cost accounting does not show the Sales margin volume variance (which here is (1,000 − 840) x £48 = £7,680A — no insignificant amount).

2. For data, *see* Progress test **15**, question and answer **20**.

(a) Stores account

Purchases	35,815	Issues — WIP	33,930
		Variances(A):	
		Price	1,885
	35,815		35,815

(b) Wages account

Cash	11,571	WIP	11,020
		Variances(A):	
		Wage Rate	551
	11,571		11,571

(c) Work in Progress account

Materials	33,930	*Variances(A):*	
Labour	11,020	Mat. Usage	2,610
Variances(F):			
Efficiency	580	Bal c/d	42,920
	45,530		45,530
Bal b/d	42,920 *		

*Total standard materials and labour cost of 290 units produced at £148 each (overheads to be added).

3. (a) *Standard cost per box of plants*

Boxes	Cost element	Total cost £	Standard cost p
	Automatic Sowing Department		
125,000	Seed pellets: (40+2½%*) x 125,000 x 1p	51,000	40.80
	Compost mix:		
	(3 + 2½%*) kilos x 125,000 x 20p	76,875	61.50
	Boxes: (1 + 1%*) x 125,000 x 10p	12,625	10.10
	Operating costs	30,000	24.00
		170,500	136.40
	Germinating room		
−25,000	Normal loss — 20%	—	
100,000		170,500	170.50
	Operating costs	50,000	50.00
		220,500	220.50

	Growing houses		
−10,000	Normal loss — 10%	—	
90,000		220,500	245.00
	Operating costs	27,000	30.00
	Total standard cost	£247,500	275.00

*There is an ambiguity about these losses. Do they occur before or after sowing (the ambiguity is not helped by the statement that there are no losses of *complete* boxes in the sowing department — implying that there are losses of less than complete boxes!)? Since the difference in interpretation involves trivial figures and any other form of calculation leads to awkward decimals, a simple addition of the given percentages to the input is made in this answer. After all, the principles of variance analysis are unaffected by such minor details.

(b)

AUTOMATIC SOWING DEPARTMENT PROCESS ACCOUNT*

Purchases:		Transfer to Germinating room		170,500
Seed pellets	52,000	*Adverse variances:*		
Compost mix	77,700			
Boxes	14,190	Pellets — Usage		1,000
Operating costs	29,800	Compost mix — Price		3,700
Favourable variances:		Boxes — Price		1,290
Compost mix — usage	2,875	Usage		275
Operating costs — Expenditure	200			
	176,765			176,765

*Working figures

Transfer to Germinating room: 125,000 x 136.40p = £170,500

Pellets: Price = 5,200,00 x 1p − £52,000 = 0; Usage = (125,000 x 40.8 − 5,200,000) x 1p = £1,000A

Compost mix: Price = 370,000 x (20 − 21)p = £3,700A; Usage = (125,000 x 3.075 − 370,000) x 20p = £2,875F

Boxes: Price = 129,000 x 10p − £14,190 = £1,290A; Usage = (125,000 x 1.01 − 129,000) x 10p = £275A

Operating costs: Expenditure = £30,000 − £29,800 = £200F

Comments should indicate that the usefulness of this analysis relates to enabling management to see just where their plans are failing to be achieved and the financial effect of such failures.

(c) (i)

GROWING HOUSES DEPARTMENT PROCESS ACCOUNT

Transfer from Germinating room*	220,500	Sales:		
Operating costs	30,000	Variety: A 46,000 X £3.00		138,000
		B 30,000 X £3.30		99,000
Balance — Profit to P/L	21,500	C 10,000 X £3.50		35,000
	272,000		86,000	272,000

*Transfers from Germinating room = 100,000 x 220.50p = £220,500

(ii)

Variety	Stnd cost £	Stnd SP £	Stnd profit £	Budgeted sales* units	Budgeted profit £	Actual sales units	Divergence units	Sales volume variance £
A	2.75	3.00	0.25	43,200	10,800	46,000	2,800F	700F
B	2.75	3.30	0.55	32,400	17,820	30,000	2,400A	1,320A
C	2.75	3.50	0.75	14,400	10,800	10,000	4,400A	3,300A
Total	-			90,000	39,420	86,000	4,000A	3,920A

*Total sales of 90,000 units (*see* standard cost) in the initial input ratios of 60,000:45,000:20,000 = 12:9:4

∴   Standard weighted average margin = £39,420/90,000 = 43.8p per box.

Reconciliation:

Budgeted profit as per above table	£39,420
Actual profit as per process account	21,500
Difference to be reconciled	£17,920

Box abnormal loss:
   Standard yield 90,000 — actual yield 86,000 = 4,000 boxes.

So abnormal loss variance = 4,000 @ £2.75 =	£11,000A
Overhead expenditure variance = £27,000 – £30,000	3,000A
Sales quantity profit variance[†] =	1,752A
Sales mix profit variance[†] =	2,168A
Total Growing Houses profit variance	£17,920A

[†]Apparent sales volume variance = volume divergence x standard weighted average margin
                      = 4,000 x 43.8p = £1,752A = sales quantity profit variance.
   But the true sales volume profit variance is (*see* above) £3,920A
   ∴   sales mix profit variance = 3,920A – 1,752A = £2,168A.

Index